STORY OF A FRIENDSHIP

Also available from Faber
SHOSTAKOVICH: A LIFE REMEMBERED
Elizabeth Wilson

STORY OF A FRIENDSHIP

The Letters of
Dmitry Shostakovich
to Isaak Glikman
1941–1975

WITH A COMMENTARY BY
ISAAK GLIKMAN

TRANSLATED BY
ANTHONY PHILLIPS

faber and faber

First published in 1993 as *Letters to a Friend* by DSCH Publishers, Moscow
and Kompozitor Publishers, St Petersburg

This translation first published in 2001
by Faber and Faber Limited
3 Queen Square London WC1N 3AU

Typeset by Refinecatch Ltd, Bungay, Suffolk
Printed in England by Clays Ltd, St Ives plc

A CIP record for this book
is available from the British Library

ISBN 0–571–20982–3

2 4 6 8 10 9 7 5 3 1

Contents

[v]

A NOTE ON TRANSLITERATION,
AND OTHER CONVENTIONS

The transliteration system adopted for this book is a modified version of the system used by the *New Grove Dictionary of Music and Musicians* (London, 1980). The aim has been to be as consistent as possible within the sometimes conflicting demands of scholarship and familiarity to the English-speaking reader. How names sound has been considered more important than how they are spelt, hence Kovalyov rather than Kovalyev. Forms of well-known names that already have wide currency in English have been retained: Richter, Tchaikovsky, Stiedry; and the common '-ский' ending appears as '-sky'. Hard and soft signs have been ignored and the Russian letter ы is represented by ï. First names have generally not been anglicized, so Maksim and Aleksandr rather than Maxim and Alexander. Russianized foreign names have been transliterated, not translated, so Viliams not Williams and Moris not Maurice.

The nuances of the different names and titles used by Russians when addressing or referring to one another have a range and effect analogous to English conventions, but they are not necessarily familiar to English ears. The widespread Russian, especially Soviet, convention of using the initial letters of the first name and patronymic, even when the person is well known to both correspondents, roughly corresponds to English use of the first name and surname, so the latter convention has usually been adopted in the interests of stylistic familiarity; the full three-name style appears in the Index. A notable exception to this is the letter of 29 December 1957, where the author's repetition of the initials is used for deliberatively ironic effect, and has accordingly been retained. The use of the full first name and patronymic without the surname would usually correspond in English to the polite formality of 'Mr Glikman'. However, Shostakovich had very idiosyncratic attitudes to this aspect of his relationships, and often addressed even his most intimate friends in the formal manner, as he invariably does Isaak Glikman.

Most of the farewell courtesies with which the letters end, while more affectionate than would be required by convention, have no English equivalent, and have therefore been translated literally.

Isaak Glikman's annotations to the Letters, indispensable for an understanding of the context, are unusually copious. Occasionally I have felt it necessary to add notes on matters that would not normally be familiar to readers who had not lived in Soviet Russia, or on which later research has shed more light. The result is a quantity of footnotes that would seriously disrupt the flow of correspondence if they were to be accommodated on the pages to which they refer, so the reader's indulgence is asked for the decision to place all the notes at the end of the book.

For the sake of clarity, it should be noted that the decision to divide the letters into chapters, each prefaced by a brief sketch of the chronological background, is mine and not the author's; this arrangement has not been reproduced from the original Russian.

Anthony Phillips

Dmitry Shostakovich and Isaak Glikman, Leningrad, 1958

Preface

After considerable hesitation and soul-searching, I have decided to publish the letters Dmitry Dmitriyevich Shostakovich wrote to me.

One question I have been unable to answer to my own satisfaction is: how would he have reacted to their publication? Because these letters, while they contain little of a particularly private or confidential nature, were nevertheless addressed to me alone; none of them was intended for public scrutiny. It is true – and as far as it goes it reassures me – that Shostakovich had no objection to the inclusion in a commemorative volume for the late Ivan Sollertinsky (Moscow 1974) of one of his letters to me, but the subject of that letter was after all one of his dearest friends.

In the last years of his life, Shostakovich was often asked to write his reminiscences of departed artistic colleagues, but he did not generally take kindly to these requests. He used to say: 'Why ask me? After all, I'm not a writer. Anyhow, who needs these so-called reminiscences? I certainly hope that when I'm dead, Irina [Antonovna, Shostakovich's third wife] isn't going to go round knocking on people's doors asking them to write their "reminiscences" of me!'

I have put inverted commas round 'reminiscences', because on Shostakovich's lips the word always carried an overtone of irony and disdain, although he did once agree to write 'a little something', as he put it, about the writer Mikhail Zoshchenko: 'Well, I suppose I could have a go at writing something about him, always supposing I can summon up enough wit to do so.' But in the end even this idea remained unrealized.

Although uncomfortably aware of Shostakovich's hostility to the genre, I do recall one occasion when I risked approaching him with a request to write a few lines about Leonid Nikolayev, who had been Shostakovich's much loved and admired piano teacher. I found myself in the unenviable role of intermediary between Shostakovich and some energetic, not to say pushy, editors planning a Festschrift of articles and memoirs about Nikolayev. The locus I chose for my attempt was the première of Moysey Vainberg's opera *Madonna and the Soldier*, which took place on 17 March 1975 in the Maly

Opera in Leningrad. I sat next to Shostakovich, and during the interval embarked with some diffidence on the suggestion that . . . it would . . . so to say . . . not to put too fine a point upon it . . . would he mind? . . . I could rough out . . . perhaps a sort of sketch of a little article . . .

Shostakovich exploded. His habitual restraint deserted him completely and, rounding furiously on me, he hissed: 'Why don't you just tell these people I don't write words? I can write music, more or less, but I certainly can't write memoirs about other people or about myself!' Of course, I was mortified that I had so upset him. If only I had known that this was the final spring of his life.

In a strange way, this outburst of memoirophobia brings to mind Pushkin's response to learning that Thomas Moore had burnt Byron's memoirs. Byron was a poet whom Pushkin revered, but far from lamenting or condemning the loss of the precious manuscript, Pushkin approved wholeheartedly. He thought the poet had revealed himself fully in his work and posterity had no need of his memoirs. In a letter written in late November 1825 from his estate at Mikhailovskoye to his friend Vyazemsky, Pushkin expressed these views with some heat.[1] He adopts an unexpectedly oblique attitude to the general question of memoirs: his main thesis is that genius must be protected from the vulgar curiosity of the crowd, whose prurient desire to uncover the private weaknesses in every man seeks to bring the genius down to their level. For Pushkin, 'the crowd' is sluggish and stupid, an inert force ranged against the poet. This idea, as is well known, lies at the heart of much of Pushkin's verse.

Here are some key passages from the letter:

> Why bemoan the loss of these scribblings by Byron? Devil take them! Thank God they *are* lost. It is in his verse, when he is transported by the rapture of his poetry, that he reveals himself . . . We must distance ourselves from the curiosity of the crowd, and be at one with Genius . . . We know everything of Byron that we need to. We have seen him enthroned in glory, seen him in the torments of his magnificent soul, seen him in his tomb amid the resurrected Greece. But you want to see him on his chamber-pot. The crowd always longs to read confessions, private notes and so on, because in the baseness of its nature it enjoys seeing the mighty brought low, the strong made weak. Revelations of all manner of abominations thrill them: 'Look, he is small, like us; he is vile, like us.' You lie, you scoundrels! Yes, he may be small, and vile, but not like you, quite otherwise![2]

Taking Pushkin's line, it could be argued that Shostakovich revealed himself in music of such towering intrinsic worth that it is there that the biography of the inner man should be sought. I can confirm from my own observations that Shostakovich had no interest at all in external accounts of his life. He himself did not keep letters that were sent to him, and urged others to follow his example. I often heard him say: 'You keep letters? Why? What on earth's the point?' In saying this, Shostakovich plainly had in mind letters from himself, because he attached no importance whatsoever to them.

Very occasionally he kept letters he had received that for some reason or other had given him pleasure, so that he would be able to read them again. One such rare exception was a letter I wrote to him on 16 June 1975, seven weeks before his death. I trust that Irina Antonovna Shostakovich will not be offended if I here reproduce (verbatim) what she said to me on 12 August 1975 at Zhukovka, three days after the composer's death, as we stood in his now tragically empty studio. While recounting the details of the last days of Shostakovich's life, with tears in her eyes, she took my letter out of the desk and said: 'Mitya loved your letter; he read it several times and it made him laugh. When he was in hospital, he kept saying to me "Where is Isaak Davydovich's letter? Please bring it to me." So I took it to him in the hospital.' Holding my letter in her hands, Irina Antonovna went on: 'Take it now, if you would like to. You know, Mitya never kept letters. But he did enjoy reading yours.' And I took the letter away with me as a keepsake, thinking with a heavy heart that I should never again be able to write to my friend. Readers may think it immodest of me to repeat here what Irina Antonovna said to me; I do so, not in order to boast of my literary powers (to which I make no claim), but to shed light on Shostakovich's attitude to correspondence. Even when a letter did particularly arouse his interest, he did not usually keep it for long, although there were exceptions. (One was a letter from Vsevolod Meyerhold dated 13 November 1936, a dark time indeed for Shostakovich. This letter survived, and was published twenty-two years later in the two-volume *Reminiscences of Meyerhold*.)

To read long-forgotten letters is to bring back for a brief moment the buried past. Whether carefully composed or dashed off in haste, these lines from Shostakovich's letters bring to life once again the uniquely personal intonations of the writer, his face, his gestures, his powers of mimicry, his mannerisms. And there in the background, now clearly, now muted, is the voice of times past.

It is a matter of great sadness to me that all the letters Shostakovich wrote to me during the 1930s disappeared without trace during the blockade of Leningrad. For this was the decade of the composition of such great works as *Lady Macbeth of Mtsensk*, the Fourth, Fifth and Sixth Symphonies, the Cello Sonata, the Piano Quintet. Shostakovich wrote to me about all of them, sometimes *en passant*, sometimes in great detail, on his frequent forays away from Leningrad. But when I bemoaned the loss of these letters, his reaction was one of complete indifference and equanimity.

This leads me back to Pushkin, this time to his essay on Voltaire, written and published in 1831, eleven years after the philippic against the genre of memoirs I quoted earlier. In this later essay, he sets out an entirely different view of the legacy left to us by great figures: now he has become persuaded that interest and value for posterity do lie not only in letters and memoirs but indeed in every scrap of paper left by a great writer. Pushkin develops his thought with marvellous clarity:

> Every line a great writer has written is valuable to posterity. We long to read all original manuscripts, though they be nothing more than a page from an accounts book or a note to a tailor putting off paying his bill. We cannot escape the thought that the hand that wrote these humble figures or these insignificant words, in this very handwriting and perhaps with this very pen, also wrote the immortal words which demand our study and command our admiration.[3]

I have to admit that, living as I did for many years in close contact with Shostakovich, I did not completely share Pushkin's view, and there were many routine and in my view unimportant notes that I failed to preserve for posterity. But I was as careful as I could be to keep all actual letters, however brief, that he wrote to me, although it is possible that one or two may have gone astray after the war.

Every letter Shostakovich wrote to me contained to a greater or a lesser extent essential elements of the man himself. This is why I hold them precious. I hope that those readers who love Shostakovich as a composer and as a man of genius may now share something of my experience.

At this point, willy nilly, I must tell the reader something about myself. Bearing in mind David Hume's aphorism: 'It is hard for a man to speak long of himself without vanity',[4] I shall to try to be as brief as possible.

From my earliest years, I was in thrall to Shostakovich's music. I loved the First Symphony, and my first hearing of *The Nose* had a seismic effect on me. I felt absolutely that it was what Gogol himself would have written had he ever thought to set his incomparable text to music. Shostakovich became my idol. I admired not only his talent but also the way he looked. I was captivated by the refinement, the originality, the nobility of his features; the way his fine grey eyes, by turns penetrating and reflective, sparkled with intelligence and laughter behind the spectacles.

Some accounts portray the young Shostakovich as a puny, sickly weakling. This was far from the case. He was well-proportioned, slim, supple and strong; he wore clothes well, and in tails or a dinner jacket cut a most attractive figure. He had a splendid head of light-brown hair, usually neatly brushed but sometimes 'poetically' dishevelled with a mischievous, unruly lock falling over his forehead. When he smiled, he displayed his excellent teeth. In his thirties, Shostakovich looked much younger than his years.

At the time, it seemed no more than an impossible dream that I might get to meet Shostakovich personally. But the dream came true through a mutual acquaintance, Ivan Sollertinsky, in the autumn of 1931 at the Philharmonia.[5] Then, it was a great event for me merely to shake the genius's hand, but a year later I was appointed Head of the Philharmonia's Mass Education Unit and I got the chance to meet Shostakovich more often.

In the Leningrad of the 1930s, composers often came to concerts at the Philharmonia and Shostakovich was, needless to say, no exception. There was another custom as well, now lapsed, in accordance with which musicians of all sorts and conditions used to congregate of an afternoon in the huge drawing-room next to the office of the Director of the Philharmonia. It was a bit like a club at which one would frequently catch sight of such musical figures as Vladimir Shcherbachov, Yury Shaporin, Vladimir Deshevov, Boris Arapov, Aleksey Zhivotov, Andrey Pashchenko, Valery Zhelobinsky, Leonid Nikolayev, Vladimir Sofronitsky, Aleksandr Gauk, Yevgeny Mravinsky, Nikolai Rabinovich, Mikhail Druskin and, of course, Sollertinsky.[6] Shostakovich, too, liked to drop in on this informal club. There would be relaxed conversation about music, theatre or simply shop talk, sometimes interspersed with a private play-through of a new orchestral piece. Gauk and Rabinovich would sit down at two pianos and read it through, brilliantly, at sight.

I never took my eyes off Shostakovich. I drank in every word he said. Every now and then I would butt in with the recklessness of youth, or crack a joke witty enough to draw a laugh from my idol. One way or another, I succeeded in attracting his notice and this became a source of great pride to me. But all the time the bond between Sollertinsky and me was growing closer, and it was he who eventually engineered my closer acquaintance with Shostakovich. By the time the year 1932 drew to a close, it would not be an exaggeration to say that we had become friends. We used the intimate second-person-singular form of address and, to begin with, called each other simply by our first names, although later on, at Shostakovich's initiative, patronymics were added. Perhaps he was following an older tradition, but it was his custom in any case to mark subtle distinctions in his manner of addressing acquaintances or close friends according to the nuances of some private code understood only by himself. Thus, for example, the composer Vissarion Shebalin and the pianist Lev Oborin were always addressed both by the intimate form and by their given or pet names, while Sollertinsky and I were addressed in the second person singular but with full names and patronymics. Once established, these forms never varied, either verbally or in writing.

Meanwhile, an evening devoted to Shostakovich's music in the Great Hall of the Philharmonia was approaching. I had arranged a small exhibition about the composer to go with the concert and was on tenterhooks of anticipation and excitement. The concert took place on 17 January 1933, with a programme including the Organ Passacaglia from *Lady Macbeth of Mtsensk*, which had not yet been staged at the Maly Opera or anywhere else. This wonderful work drew warm applause from the audience, but the two ballet suites from *The Golden Age* and *Bolt*, several numbers from which had to be encored, were even more thunderously received. I was very happy.

Shostakovich, pleased by the success of the concert, included me in an invitation to supper at his home on Marat Street (or Nikolayevskaya Street as we usually called it). It was a great honour for me, and I was beside myself with excitement as I walked through the freezing night to the house which had until such a short time ago been closed to me. I was the youngest and most insignificant of the guests, yet Shostakovich, man of true breeding that he was, accorded the same welcome to everyone irrespective of rank. In that (for me) unforgettable night, he was irresistibly gay, graceful, alert, ardent. Pleasantly merry after a couple of drinks, he was happy to sit at the piano and play his own and anyone else's music for those who wanted to dance – which they did with the best will in the world, notably Lev Knipper, the composer of the famous song *Polyushko-Pole* and his radiantly beautiful wife, who had come from Moscow especially for the concert. I have a vivid memory of the large, old-fashioned frame of

Yury Shaporin lumbering around the floor, contrasting comically with the delicate grace of our host.

I felt strongly that there was considerably more that was fuelling Shostakovich's high spirits that January night than just the triumph of the concert we had heard earlier on – an irrepressible wellspring of creative energy seemed to be seething and bubbling away in him. That evening in the Philharmonia, we had heard no more than a fragment of the magnificent new opera; soon we should be able to see and hear it in its entirety in the theatre. Something to gladden the heart, indeed!

During that evening, with its supper and its dancing, I felt instinctively that invisible threads of friendship were drawing Shostakovich and me together. Bidding me goodnight, he asked me to keep in touch – 'Don't forget now' was a favourite phrase of his – and to drop in any time, especially as we now had a reason for meeting, to talk over details of the forthcoming Maly Opera production of *Lady Macbeth*. From that evening on, I became a regular visitor to Marat Street and subsequently all the apartments in Leningrad in which Shostakovich lived: Dmitrovsky Pereulok, Kirov Prospect, Bolshaya Pushkarskaya. And my correspondence with Dmitry Shostakovich dates from that time too; two years later, I became his private secretary and took responsibility for the steadily growing correspondence of a famous composer.

Somewhere in the course of his analytical observations, that great poet and wise man Heinrich Heine comes to the disconcerting conclusion that the personality of an artist of genius may be no match for the works he creates: the two concepts are discrete and alien to one another. Heine wrote: 'The pen of the genius is always greater than he is himself.'[7]

I have often asked myself: was this also true of Shostakovich? I think it was not. I am convinced that Shostakovich's character was in complete accord with his music. Both were pure in spirit, sincere, noble, humane, majestic in their suffering, sparkling with wit in moments of joy, sarcastic in the face of injustice. He liked to repeat the words Pushkin puts into Mozart's mouth on the subject of genius and evil: it is a phrase that was Holy Writ for Shostakovich, admitting of no sophistry whatsoever in its interpretation.[8]

A telling example of this was his attitude to Wagner. For Shostakovich, racism was evil made manifest and therefore, however boundless his appreciation of Wagner's music, he could not regard him as a genius. The composer of *The Ring of the Nibelungen* was a racist and thus was by definition not a genius, since 'genius and evil are two things incompatible'. To some people, this maximalist approach to Wagner may seem extreme, but it was very characteristic of Shostakovich, who was inspired by a burning hatred of evil in whatever form it might present itself to him – feelings, as everybody knows, which are incarnate in his music. In Shostakovich, character and art made up an indivisible unity.

During the 1930s, Shostakovich went through appalling experiences, but I never had cause to lose my admiration for his behaviour. Whatever he did seemed to me to be in some intangible way part and parcel of the heroes, ghostly yet throbbing with life, who permeate the pages of his symphonies and chamber music, their sorrowing meditations mixed with invincible spiritual strength. I found veiled support for my ideas in some of the letters Shostakovich wrote at the time.

The full story of the dramatic *Lady Macbeth* saga has not by any means yet been told and it is outside the scope of the present book since I no longer have the letters of this period; as I have already explained, they were lost. *Lady Macbeth* brought Shostakovich a level of celebrity unparalleled in my experience. Productions of the opera, both at home and abroad, provoked storms of acclamation. Yet the moment when its triumph was at its apogee was the very moment when disaster was unleashed upon it. The *Pravda* article 'Muddle Instead of Music', published at the end of January 1936, toppled Shostakovich from the dizzy heights to which his magnificent opera had taken him.

The cataclysm overtook Shostakovich in the city of Arkhangelsk, where he was in the middle of a concert tour, and drew from the twenty-nine-year-old composer a wisdom which would not have been out of place in a lifelong student of psychology and human nature. The first thing he did was to send me an amazing telegram asking me to take out a subscription at the post office to get all the relevant press cuttings. It was the first time that he had ever, to my knowledge, shown the slightest interest in press notices of any kind, even when, as they generally were, they were eulogistic. What on earth could he want them for now? I was at a loss, but of course did as he asked. It emerged that he wanted to find out what statements well-known musicians were going to come out with now about *Lady Macbeth*. Alas, his gloomy forebodings were fulfilled, and there had indeed been some point in subscribing to the press-cutting service. In newspaper after newspaper, former devotees of the opera were loud in their condemnation of its defects. Shostakovich read the daily avalanche of cuttings with extraordinary self-control and restraint. I went to see him almost every day, and we read them together. But our reactions could hardly have been more different: I emphatically giving voice to my indignation; he reading without comment, in silence.

The iron had gone deep into his soul, but he bore himself with extraordinary dignity and a proud nobility of purpose, not looking to any quarter for support or sympathy. There were plenty of false friends to shake their heads dolefully and bleat about the 'decline and fall' of the composer of *Lady Macbeth*, but he himself, the least self-important or complacent person imaginable, held fast to his belief in his own creative powers – powers, I would add, that were boundless and inexhaustible: the Fourth Symphony was already nearing completion and someone with a crystal ball might already even have been able to glimpse the outlines of the Fifth.

It was about this time that Shostakovich said to me one day: 'Even if they cut off both my hands and I have to hold the pen in my teeth, I shall still go on writing music.' This terrible remark shook me to the core, but it was uttered matter-of-factly and with a simplicity quite devoid of affectation. The image made my flesh creep, and for an instant I imagined the horrible, Dantesque phantasmagoria actually taking place. Lost for words, I lapsed into a bewildered silence. But I do not believe that it had been Shostakovich's purpose to astonish or upset me with his remark. He looked at me calmly, straight in the eye and immediately changed the subject. For some reason, that morning we were talking standing face to face. The sun was shining through the window of Shostakovich's study, and he stood there bathed in its light, not yet thirty, in all the radiant flower of his youth and fearless determination to pursue his art, come what may.

When the *Pravda* article came out, Shostakovich deliberately kept away from the debating sessions which went on for days in the Leningrad Union of Composers. There were some in authority who took this as a mark of arrogance. The discussions were difficult, tedious and painful – depending, of course, on who you were: some of the speakers clearly revelled in the oratory with which they poured scorn on the derided opera. (For more details on these sessions, see Appendix 2.)

Being out of the way in Moscow, Shostakovich asked me to write to him after each session, relaying what was said in as much detail as possible and as a detached, emotionally uninvolved rapporteur. I obeyed to the letter. Many years later, Shostakovich expressed regret that my letters, bearing as they did the stamp of a contemporary record, had vanished without trace – but truth to tell, his regret was somewhat rhetorical since for his part he never kept letters anyway. But what was extraordinary was the truly phenomenal memory which allowed him to recall both form and content of these letters, received when he was little more than a youth.

It is not my purpose to write a biography of Dmitry Shostakovich. Some fragmentary and disconnected episodes from his life have nonetheless found their way, as if by instinct, into this preface; I hope I may be forgiven for this. I have dwelt at some length on *Lady Macbeth* not simply because this work occupies a vitally important place in Shostakovich's creative history, but because I later received several letters from him dealing with the proposed revivals of the opera in the 1950s and 1960s, about which more will be said later.

Looking back on it, the time I am describing did not pass quickly, flashing past like the landscape seen from the window of an express train. Days stretched out, time moved slowly, for it was filled with a multitude of impressions, each one of which would bring its measure of foreboding or of joy. Shostakovich is the focus of these impressions, which I present not in strict chronological order but with the aim of bringing to light details probably unknown to anybody but myself.

At the end of May 1936, the world-famous conductor Otto Klemperer came to Leningrad to give two concerts. Klemperer was an ardent admirer of Shostakovich's First Symphony and had been one of the first foreign conductors to programme it. Among other things, one purpose of his visit was to get to know Shostakovich's new Fourth Symphony, about which he had already heard reports. On 29 May, I went to the Great Hall of the Philharmonia to listen to Klemperer rehearsing Beethoven's Third and Fifth Symphonies. On to the platform stepped an extremely tall, powerfully built and handsome figure, with strong, severe features. The orchestra greeted him with an ovation; they well remembered from his visits in the 1920s the outstanding musician they were welcoming.

Here I should mention in parenthesis that orchestral musicians of this time were apt to behave in a very independent fashion: they could be highly critical of conductors and had an extensive repertoire of ways to express their dissatisfaction. But that was not all. Veterans of the orchestra, like principal cellist Ilya Brik, who had in his time served as the Artistic Director of the Philharmonia, or the outstanding principal bassoon Aleksandr Vasilyyev and several others, would not scruple to hide their sceptical feelings about a new work by a contemporary composer from Moscow or Leningrad. This should be borne in mind when considering the atmosphere surrounding the rehearsals for Shostakovich's Fourth Symphony.

Klemperer's rehearsals went splendidly, without a hitch.

On the evening of that same spring day, I was telling Shostakovich how I had been at the Philharmonia, and he in turn told me that the following day, at noon, he was due to demonstrate his Fourth Symphony to the visiting celebrity. He asked me to be present and to be sure to be on time; I accepted with alacrity. Shostakovich said, a touch anxiously, that it was going to be no easy matter to give a good account of such an enormous and complex symphony, moreover one on which he placed such hopes. Hot from his hands as it still was, he loved this work deeply. Later there would be times when Shostakovich's attitude to it would be much more ambivalent: sometimes he spoke of it with great warmth but at other times less so, sometimes even slightingly. But all that lay in the future.

On the evening in question, he and his wife Nina and I were discussing what sort of hospitality it would be appropriate to offer Klemperer after the play-through of the symphony. Just as we were deep in menu possibilities, the doorbell suddenly sounded, and in the hall appeared the tall figure of Otto Klemperer, accompanied by Ivan Sollertinsky. Shouting with laughter, they explained how they had contrived to slip away from the Maly Opera, where Fritz Stiedry had been conducting *The Marriage of Figaro*. Klemperer and Sollertinsky had gone to the performance at Stiedry's pressing invitation, but at the end of the first act the distinguished and impatient guest had had, as he put it, the brilliant notion that they should come to see Shostakovich right away, and not wait until the following day.

Shostakovich was not a great lover of unbidden guests and usually reacted to them with ill-concealed irritation, but the sudden appearance in his home of Klemperer, who, after rushing from the other end of the world, wanted to meet him as soon as possible, quite won him over. The guest was welcomed warmly, but without fuss. Klemperer proved to be a highly cultivated man, an excellent conversationalist and raconteur. He told me in an aside that one of the favourite programmes in his extensive repertoire, one which he had performed throughout North and South America, was an all-Shostakovich programme. It consisted of the First Symphony, the Piano Concerto and the Suites from *The Golden Age* and *Bolt*. The public responded to this programme *'toujours avec un succès formidable'* – I particularly remember this phrase. The conversation proceeded mainly in French, out of deference to Nina, who spoke the language.

The party broke up at one o'clock, and early the next morning Shostakovich telephoned me with the glad tidings that during the night he had become a father.[9] Without pause for thought, I rushed over to the happy father with a bottle of champagne under one arm, and at noon Klemperer, Fritz Stiedry, Ivan Sollertinsky, Aleksandr Gauk, Lev Oborin and Emil Nelius (Secretary of the Philharmonia) all arrived. Hearing the news, they too rushed out for champagne, and thereupon it was decided to send a letter of congratulation to Nina Vasilyyevna in hospital. For some reason it was Klemperer who took it upon himself to write the letter in French, and we all signed our names at the bottom.

Shostakovich had had a night entirely without sleep and was hardly in top form, but he was a past master at taking control of himself and played through the symphony with tremendous brilliance and élan. The conductors – Klemperer, Stiedry and Gauk – all crowded round to pore over the score lying open on the table, Klemperer, I remember, having the advantage because of his great height. The symphony produced a huge impression on them (Sollertinsky and I had heard it before.) The enthusiasm of Klemperer and Stiedry was manifest: they both planned to perform it that autumn, the one in South America, the other in Leningrad in his capacity as Chief Conductor of the Philharmonia.

But it was all to turn out quite differently.

At the dinner table, an impassioned Klemperer announced that he regarded so magnificent a work as a gift from heaven, and he could hardly wait to conduct it. He had, however, a humble request to make of the composer: would it be possible to reduce the number of flutes? Because, you see, one might find oneself touring to all kinds of places where one could not rely on finding six first-class flautists. Shostakovich, unimpressed, replied with a smile: 'What the pen has written, even the axe may not cut out.' Sollertinsky had some trouble translating this proverb into German or French or Spanish or English, all of which languages Klemperer spoke.

That evening, Klemperer conducted a hugely successful Beethoven programme in a Philharmonia Great Hall filled to bursting point. Tired and overstressed to the point of exhaustion, Shostakovich did not go to the concert, but Sollertinsky and I did. At the end of the performance we went round to congratulate the conductor, who repeated to us with great emphasis that on that day it was not he who should be receiving the plaudits but the composer of the new Fourth Symphony.

Rehearsals for the symphony began that autumn. Stiedry was a musician and conductor of great stature who had emigrated from Fascist Germany, settled in Leningrad and was now in command of the Leningrad Philharmonic Orchestra. Shostakovich regarded him highly; their first artistic encounter had been a happy one at the opening of the autumn 1933 Philharmonia season, when Stiedry had conducted a brilliant première of the First Piano Concerto in which the composer had given a superlative account of the solo part.

The new symphony had been allocated an impressive number of rehearsals, and I attended all of them at Shostakovich's request. Stiedry had bent the full force of his gifts and experience to an intensive study of this gigantic new composition. I cannot speak for Shostakovich, but personally I detected a strong sense of wariness in the hall; rumours had been circulating in musical circles – and even more significantly, on their fringes – that Shostakovich had not heeded the criticism to which he had lately been subjected, but had persisted in writing a symphony of diabolical complexity and crammed full of formalist tendencies.

And so, one fine day, who should turn up at rehearsal but Composers' Union Secretary Vladimir Iokhelson, with another authority figure from Smolny, Yakov Smirnov, in tow. The next thing that happened was that the Director of the Philharmonia, the pianist I. M. Renzin, asked Shostakovich to attend him in his office. The two of them went up by the internal spiral staircase while I waited behind in the Hall. A quarter of an hour or so later, Shostakovich came to find me and we left to walk back to No. 14, Kirovsky Prospekt.

My companion seemed thoroughly downcast, and his long silence only added to my sense of anxiety. At last he told me in flat, expressionless tones that there would be no performance of the symphony. It had been removed from the programme at the insistent recommendation of Renzin who, reluctant to be forced to take administrative measures himself, had urged the composer to take the step of withdrawing it.

Many years have gone by since that time, and a mythology has grown up around the withdrawal of the Fourth Symphony, a mythology to which writings about Shostakovich have unfortunately lent quasi-scriptural status. The essence of the legend is that the composer, persuaded that Fritz Stiedry was inadequate to meet the demands of the symphony, had made the decision to cancel the performance.

It would be hard to imagine anything more absurd.

It is true that in 1956 Shostakovich wrote of what he described as the shortcomings of the Fourth Symphony. He said then that it suffered from 'delusions of grandeur'.[10] Yet five years after writing that, on 30 December 1961, in the Great Hall of the Moscow Conservatoire, the Fourth Symphony finally received its first performance under the baton of Kirill

Kondrashin, and I sat next to Shostakovich. As the music launched into the earth-shattering introduction, I was sure I could hear his heart beating faster. His agitation lasted right up to the magnificent coda.

Back at home, after the tremendous success of the concert, and still under the spell of what he had been listening to, Shostakovich said: 'I think that in many respects the Fourth is superior to my later symphonies.'[11] Quite an admission! It may indeed have contained a hint of exaggeration, but if so, it was plainly conditioned by the impulse to defend a work that had been so unjustly neglected. For a quarter of a century, the author had himself looked askance on the symphony with the cold eye of objectivity, but now that it could actually be heard in all its overwhelming power, he immersed himself in its emotional world, identified with it and felt again his blood kinship with the paragraphs and images now brought so vividly to life.[12]

The Fifth Symphony, written a year later, had a much happier fate than the Fourth.[13]

Needless to say, Shostakovich had his share of individual detractors and those who were envious of his success – of what genius can this not be said? But I dare say that by and large musical Leningrad was proud of its brilliant young Shostakovich and loved him dearly. The audiences who heard the Fifth Symphony paid their own tribute with their unstinting admiration for the work; I found it deeply moving to see large numbers of people, men as well as women, weeping openly during the Largo third movement.

Among those who attended the concert was the celebrated philologist and member of the Academy, Vladimir Shishmaryov, an excellent musician and fine man whom I knew well. Vladimir Fyodorovich told me that the only other time in his life that he had experienced such a triumph for a composer, or such powerful emotion among the audience, was the occasion when, shortly before his death, Tchaikovsky conducted his Sixth Symphony. I was thrilled by this analogy from a source such as Shishmaryov, a man noted for the cool objectivity of his judgements, but naturally allowed myself to hope that Shostakovich would enjoy a rather longer subsequent life span than his great colleague.

At one later performance of the Fifth Symphony, an unexpected event took place. As the final sounds of the Finale died away, a group of people active in the fields of culture, the arts and science mounted the stage to propose sending on behalf of all present a congratulatory telegram to

Shostakovich, who was in Moscow attending the première there of the Fifth Symphony. The text was read out to the audience by the famous actor Yury Yurev, star of the Alexandrinsky Theatre. I was not myself a witness of this remarkable event since I was with Shostakovich in Moscow; I heard the details from Ivan Sollertinsky, who drew an analogy with the famous telegrams sent to Chekhov in the Crimea by the Moscow Arts Theatre.

In Moscow, the reception accorded the symphony's performance by Aleksandr Gauk was every bit as rapturous as in Leningrad. Looking round the Great Hall of the Conservatoire before the performance, I saw a bevy of the capital's notables, recognizable from their photographs in newspapers and magazines of the time, all of them swept up in the general fever of enthusiasm.

Here may be a good time to point out that the ovations that now cascaded over Shostakovich did not turn his head in the slightest degree. He steadfastly maintained his customary reserve, his dignified poise; the only outward sign of satisfaction was the smile that was more often to be seen playing about his features. The days were filled with the heady wine of success, but Shostakovich observed with philosophical detachment that in music, as everywhere else in the world, everything is relative, everything is transitory. One should never, he said, allow circumstances to drive one either to careless rapture or to despair.

We recalled how, while the Fifth Symphony was in rehearsal, there had been some who had expressed doubts about it. There was nothing particularly unusual in that; it was par for the course. But not until after the first performance did I tell Shostakovich of the warnings I had had from some of the orchestral musicians: that the critics would be bound to take the work to task, especially the first movement, which according to my informants was incoherent, unnecessarily raucous and inaccessible.

These opinions were not intended to be malicious, indeed they were quite sympathetic to the composer. I tried, fruitlessly, to convince the musicians that they were in error, but later, when I was crowing over those whom events had proved so wrong, Shostakovich did not find it at all amusing. In this, he was of course quite right. Indeed, how can one blame ordinary orchestral players when even professional critics at first failed to understand the Fifth Symphony? Interpretations of the Largo for example, that lyrical jewel of passionate symphonic writing, varied wildly. One day Shostakovich, without comment, passed me a page in a magazine he had come across, in which I read that the Largo's problem was that it was saturated with 'echoes of the grave and of despair'. Shostakovich made no remark on this revelation by a well-known critic, but the look on his face was graphic enough expression of his puzzled disbelief.

Shostakovich had a unique ability to read all sorts of idiotic statements and theories about himself, and even to listen to abuse, without descending to argument with his opponents. I often thought that Cato the Younger – the ancient Roman moralist and Republican who said that 'those that stay silent, being in the right, are like to the gods' – would probably have been moved to place Shostakovich among his gods. But Shostakovich's silence could also be an extremely effective technique for boxing incautiously garrulous critics into a corner.

Shostakovich had three spells of teaching in his life, and his pedagogic activities have been well documented by different generations of his former students. Nevertheless, I should like to add a few details culled from my personal observations of the young professor.

In the spring of 1937, I was surprised to hear Shostakovich announce that he was now an enlisted man: whereas previously he had been free as a bird, henceforward he was to serve a prestigious institution and would be obliged to carry out the grave responsibilities placed upon him, etc., etc. I might laugh, but he was referring to the high calling of pedagogy. As usual, Shostakovich was leavening his mock-solemn speech with a mask of humour, but I knew full well that he would fulfil his obligations in this new field with dedication and serious purpose, and moreover that his huge talent and irresistible charm would be bound to win the hearts of his students.

And so it proved, yet as time went by Shostakovich grew more and more dissatisfied with himself as a teacher, and I heard him complain several times that he felt himself to be fundamentally inadequate in this role. He always compared himself unfavourably with Vissarion Shebalin, who had the magic quality in abundance. Ordinarily the last person in the world to disparage himself, Shostakovich continually harked back to this refrain throughout his teaching career. What he obviously failed to take into account was the fact that, purely by virtue of being in contact with him, hearing what he had to say, absorbing his insights into and advice on musical techniques and aesthetics, his young student composers were enriching themselves immeasurably. Goethe was right to say that 'one best learns from those one loves'; Shostakovich's students loved their teacher very much, and learned incalculably much from him.

This love was by no means unrequited. Shostakovich was passionately interested in his students' compositions and was thrilled, sometimes even transported, by those he thought successful. I remember him one day emerging from the Conservatoire and insisting that I immediately come and listen to some songs by Yury Sviridov. Radiant with pleasure, he sat down at the piano without a score and played them through from memory several times, insisting that they were not merely splendid compositions in themselves and evidence of real talent, but works of genius – this was the term he used. It was always the same with him: indifference to art was anathema to him, and there was something magnificent in his passions. The music of Venyamin Fleishman, the composer of the opera *Rothschild's Violin*, moved and astonished him by the delicacy with which the fledgling composer had penetrated the spirit and essence of Chekhov's many-layered story.

Breaking with Conservatoire convention, Shostakovich customarily addressed his students by the polite second person plural and by name and patronymic, treating them as colleagues and equals without a hint of condescension. To this day I marvel at the natural, unforced, winning simplicity of his manners. It seemed to me then that in every aspect of his demeanour, Shostakovich was the true heir to Pushkin's Mozart.

The names of Leningrad footballers crop up in quite a number of the letters Shostakovich wrote to me, so it seems appropriate to say something about his football mania, as it has been called. The subject has perhaps been rather done to death: you would think from the accounts of some people that Shostakovich was some kind of crazed fanatic, but in fact this was far from being the case.

In the 1930s, compared with today, the world of football fans was not a large one. Women, for example, were not as a rule much interested in the game, and even if some of them did come to the Lenin stadium, it was mainly to breathe some fresh air and to enjoy a spectacle the point of which to all intents and purposes escaped them.

The ranks of musicians, artists and writers did include some football aficionados, but not many of them, so the appearance of a new recruit from among them in the stands was bound to arouse comment. This is what happened in Shostakovich's case. As I recall, it was Vladimir Lebedev – the well-known artist, sportsman and professional boxing referee – who first got Shostakovich interested in football, and I at his earnest insistence became his constant companion on the stands. (Ivan Sollertinsky stood firm against all such blandishments.) Despite what seemed to me his mature years, Lebedev carried on in an extraordinarily uninhibited fashion at football matches, shrieking encouragement at his favourite players like a ten-year-old, loudly complaining about bungled passes and fumbled balls, hurling imprecations at the referee, and so on. As for Shostakovich, his excitement was no less intense, but he never lost his phenomenal reserve and never raised his voice. He watched in silence, betraying his emotions only by the expressions that now and again flitted across his face. In those days, the actual process of play was very important, characterized by elegant and intricate movements and a special kind of football choreography: not for nothing was one of the Dynamo stars, Pyotr Dementiyev, affectionately known locally as 'The Ballerina'. When Dementiyev was injured by one of the Moscow Locomotive players, the entire stadium erupted in protest. Lebedev and I were screaming at the tops of our voices like everyone else, but Shostakovich, although equally outraged, typically contented himself with indignant, sotto-voce mutterings of: 'Hooligan! Hooligan!'

Shostakovich disliked bad temper, aggressive or foul play on the pitch. He loved it best when the game was open, honourable and chivalrous. He found intensely moving the selfless absorption and even ecstasy with which the great players strove to achieve the apparently impossible task of putting the ball between the posts. What attracted Shostakovich to football, I believe, was an idealized vision of the game.

Whenever we visited Lebedev in his studio on Belinsky Street, the last thing he would want to talk about would be his paintings. It was usually a hard job to persuade him to show us any of his marvellous pictures, but every aspect of sport excited him, particularly boxing, in which he enjoyed a reputation as a great expert. To convince us of its charms, he invited us to a match in the Velikan cinema between a team from France and a team from Leningrad. There were no vacant seats, but Lebedev as referee was able to find a place for us in an area that we in our theatre-derived inexperience thought of as the wings, while he in snow-white uniform and with a whistle between his lips disported himself in the ring. The scrupulous fairness coupled with passionate enthusiasm with which he carried out his task impressed Shostakovich, and as a result he developed an even greater partiality for his artist–sportsman friend. Lebedev's gallant refereeing was marked by a celebratory dinner at the Shostakoviches' afterwards.

I have read many fanciful stories about Shostakovich wandering from city to city, even as far as Tbilisi, in search of epic football matches. Nothing like that ever happened in my experience of him. But I do remember one particular football odyssey that may be of some interest, in which I myself played a part. In July 1937, Shostakovich invited me to spend some time with him at the dacha he had rented in a small village called Daimish-che, not far from the town of Luga. To get there, we had to board a stuffy, overcrowded train, and then after a leisurely journey of about four hours, transfer to a horse and cart. Eventually we arrived at our destination. For me, it had been a wretched and uncomfortable journey, but Shostakovich endured it with philosophical composure and had no sympathy with my complaints.

Once we were there, Daimishche was wonderful: fields, meadows, woods, a gently murmuring stream, everything peaceful and serene. But after a few days had gone by, Shostakovich suggested with a guilty smile that we interrupt our holiday and go back to Leningrad, where there was a football match that promised to be interesting. I tried everything to dissuade him, but to no avail, and eventually we set off on the long journey back. At the appointed hour, after an apocalyptic storm with thunder and lightning, we found ourselves in the stadium. This (for me) involuntary trip was probably the acme of Shostakovich's passion for football. Even he would sometimes joke about his weakness for the game, but one could tell that he had no intention of ever doing anything about it.

The writer Kuprin loved circus people, Hemingway felt the same about bullfighters. Whatever some biographers may say, Shostakovich's circle of friends and acquaintances did not extend to the footballing community. However, he did take an interest in finding out what sort of people they might be away from the football pitch, beyond the particular and highly charged circumstances of the game; what they would be like to meet in ordinary, everyday life. Some players knew of the interest taken in them by the famous composer; they appreciated it and were flattered by it. To satisfy his desire to know a little more about them, one day (when Nina Vasilyyevna was away), Shostakovich invited the members of the Zenith team to a meal. I was also invited. It went off very well; the worries Shostakovich had had beforehand proved groundless. He was the soul of hospitality, thoughtful and attentive without lapsing into the over-effusiveness from which his innate good manners would in any case have insulated him. Initially the players were rather subdued and polite in the unfamiliar home. The search for conversational topics of mutual interest proved as problematic as it always does, but little by little the difficulties were overcome and the atmosphere round the dinner table grew relaxed and easy.

After the meal, we repaired to Shostakovich's study, and one of the players, producing a guitar, asked his host to play some of his music on the piano, a request with which he was glad to comply. When the last guest had departed, Shostakovich stretched out on the sofa with the air of a man who knows he has done a good day's work, and said: 'Well, now we've actually got to know some of our heroes. Up till now we've only been able to see them from far off at the top of the stands.'

In one of my letters from Shostakovich the reader will notice the name of Mikhail Svetlov. Shostakovich much admired this poet and playwright, and not long before the war he expressed a desire to write an opera in collaboration with him, a project probably no one besides myself knows about. This is how it happened.

In 1938 the Kirov Theatre launched an associate opera company under the direction of the outstanding singer and actor Nikolai Pechkovsky and the conductor Sergey Yeltsin, in the People's House – a building in which in his time Fyodor Chalyapin had sung. It operated under the aegis of the parent Kirov Theatre, and I was its literary director. Our objective was to establish a mixed repertoire of classical and contemporary operas, and we accepted for production an opera by one of Shostakovich's students, Yury Levitin, entitled *Monna-Marianne*, based on Gorky's *Italian Tales*, with marvellous lyrics by the poet Natalya Krandiyevskaya. *Monna-Marianne* was to be produced by Emanuil Kaplan and designed by Valentina Khoda-sevich. Work started and the production got under way.

But we were cherishing a secret dream of our own: that Levitin's teacher would also write an opera for the new theatre. Our ambitions would prob-ably never have left the ground at all, had it not been for an unexpected event: Shostakovich had come across a half-factual, half-fictional account of an incident in the Civil War in an anthology, and something in it struck a chord with him as being piquant, colourful and full of dramatic tension. The plot had something in common with a short story, 'The Forty-First' by B. A. Lavrenev, but instead of a young girl guarding a captured lieutenant, the protagonists in our story were a Red Army soldier and the daughter of the local priest. A tragically irreconcilable conflict of love and duty unfolds on railway platforms and in the carriage of a long-distance train. Shosta-kovich felt drawn to the subject and agreed to write an opera based on it. I was beside myself with excitement. Shostakovich was about to return to the opera stage!

An initial approach was made to Vladimir Bragin – the librettist of Dmitry Kabalevsky's *Colas Breugnon* – to provide the libretto. It was not, however, a relationship that progressed well,[14] and Shostakovich suggested approaching Mikhail Svetlov instead. I was deputed to go to Moscow to start discussions with the celebrated author of 'Grenada'.

I did not know Mikhail Arkadyevich personally, but he received me with great cordiality and invited me to dine with him. However, I soon began to feel uneasy: Svetlov was full of compliments about Shostakovich, whom, he kept telling me, he admired deeply, but he resolutely avoided any concrete discussion of the subject I had come to see him about. He said he knew little about opera and was rather afraid of it, and told an admirably witty story to this effect. It gradually dawned on me that my mission was not going to be crowned with success.

Svetlov did not reject what he called this flattering proposal out of hand, but he did not accept it either: he asked for time to think about it. And in the event, the hoped-for creative encounter between Shostakovich and Svetlov never took place. No doubt the war was partly responsible, as it was for turning so many of Shostakovich's plans upside-down.

The Moscow première of the Sixth Symphony was accompanied by an exchange of letters between Shostakovich and me that sadly have not survived. The symphony was completed in the summer of 1939 and was put in to the schedule for the opening of the Leningrad Philharmonia's autumn season. The first performance was awaited with keen anticipation.

Long before the first performance, Shostakovich showed the new work to Ivan Sollertinsky and to me. He played through the Finale twice and, contrary to his usual practice, praised it. 'For the first time I think I've written a successful Finale. I don't think even the severest critics will find anything to carp at in it.' He said nothing about the first and second movements, but we were both captivated not only by the ravishing Finale, which was indeed irresistible, but also by the majestic Largo and the dazzling Scherzo, and we said so. Utterly bowled over and not caring if I embarrassed the modest composer, I launched into a panegyric over the Finale along the lines of: 'If Mozart and Rossini had been alive in the twentieth century and if they had been planning a finale to a symphony, they would have come up with something like what we have just heard.' Sollertinsky, while not disagreeing, could not resist taking me down a peg: 'Do stop pontificating like an ancient Roman orator: if the Muses had spoken in Latin, they would have used language like Plautus!' Needless to say, I was not offended but impressed by Sollertinsky's erudition.

'What's this about "orators"? What have they got to do with anything?'

Shostakovich put in, frowning. He did not like his friends crossing swords with one another in even the most innocent way. It was an axiom for him that friends saw eye to eye in everything – that was the definition of real friendship. He could never understand the furious arguments that sometimes broke out in even the most friendly of gatherings. 'What are the ties of friendship that bind people together?' was a question he would sometimes pose, and he would give his own answer: 'A correspondence of opinions; complete understanding with no need for words. Where there is not that understanding, there is no friendship. And by the way, a true friendship is not hierarchical.' Shostakovich held true to this idea throughout his life, and if ever that complete understanding showed signs of weakening or eroding, an estrangement would grow up between him and the friend concerned, henceforward to be designated as 'former friend'.

The première of the Sixth Symphony, which took place under Yevgeny Mravinsky on 5 November 1939, was a tremendous success.[15] The Finale was encored, a rare event in first performances of symphonies. But the electric fervour that had gripped the hall at the first performance of the Fifth Symphony was not repeated; that occasion had been *sui generis*. It seemed then as though it could never be repeated; however, in the Seventh, Eighth and Fourteenth Symphonies, Shostakovich wrote works of comparable inspirational power.

Shostakovich was not able to attend the Moscow première of the Sixth Symphony personally. He asked me to go to Moscow to hear the rehearsals and keep an eye on the general course of events, and to write to him with my impressions. This I did, as a result staying in Moscow for quite some time. I wrote to him each evening, and found a way of sending the letters by messenger so that he would have them in his hands the following morning. Needless to say, I refrained from passing on to him the gist of many conversations I could not avoid having with musicians of varying positions and influence. Most of these conversations plunged me into despair. One view was that the arrogant young composer had deliberately flouted the traditions of the symphony by writing a three-movement piece devoid of any discernible form. Others were spitefully putting it about that Shostakovich must have walled himself up in an ivory tower where he was oblivious to all that was going on around him, and in consequence had written a Largo that from start to finish would put the listener to sleep as surely as if he had taken a dose of deadly nightshade. Others, smiling indulgently, said the Finale was just a musical representation of a football match, with fortunes swinging from one side to the other. As a matter of fact, this vulgarly insensitive interpretation of the Sixth Symphony's Finale has gained a regrettably wide currency in musical circles and on their fringes.

Conversations like these were of course swept into oblivion by the great new work when it was eventually heard, triumphantly, in the Great Hall of the Moscow Conservatoire. But the strange thing was that afterwards, when I returned to Leningrad, I found I could not slough off the memory of these unwanted exchanges. I tried and tried to enter into the feelings of my interlocutors, to grasp their thought processes, but the attempt proved beyond my powers.

In the spring of 1940, following the Sixth Symphony and all the criticism it provoked, Shostakovich composed the Quintet for two violins, viola, cello and piano, a work acclaimed by the public and critics everywhere. Each performance by the composer with the excellent Glazunov Quartet or the equally excellent Beethoven Quartet was an important and joyful event in the musical life of Leningrad or Moscow. Shostakovich himself played the piano part with inimitable mastery, displaying an expressiveness and imaginative power unique to him. It is no exaggeration to say that in performances of this work, no less than in the Second Piano Trio, even Lev Oborin and Sviatoslav Richter could not rival him. To this day, I can hear his playing in my head.

Shostakovich himself told me that his original intention had been to write a second string quartet (the first had been written in 1938). What had led him to change the original conception? His explanation of the change was idiosyncratic, to say the least. According to him, his change of heart had not been dominated by artistic considerations at all, but purely practical concerns. 'Do you want to know why I wrote a piano part into the quartet? I did it so that I could play it myself and have a reason to go on tour to different towns and places. So now the Glazunovs and the Beethovens, who get to go everywhere, will have to take me with them, and I will get my chance to see the world as well!' We both laughed. 'You're not serious?' I said. Shostakovich replied: 'Absolutely! You're a dyed-in-the-wool stay-at-home, but I'm a dyed-in-the-wool wanderer!' It was hard to tell from the expression on his face if he were serious or not. This exchange took place in the summer of the year before war was declared.

On Saturday, 21 June 1941 Shostakovich announced that the following day there were two football matches that we must without fail attend, followed by supper in a restaurant. That Sunday morning was bright and sunny, but on the way to the stadium I heard a voice on the radio announcing that war had been declared. From that tragic morning on, my meetings with Shostakovich became infrequent and spasmodic. We spoke on the telephone, but I was occupied with defence work in the militia while he was keeping watch for incendiary bombs on the roof of the Conservatoire and composing popular songs for concert troupes performing at the front. The reports that came in of the general military situation became more and more alarming.

For some time I remained in ignorance of the projected Seventh Symphony. But then, at the beginning of August, Shostakovich telephoned me and asked me to come to his apartment on Bolshaya Pushkarskaya Street, which of course I did. It was a steel-grey, depressing sort of day. Famine had not yet gripped Leningrad in its deadly embrace; even so, Shostakovich looked as if he had lost weight. Hunger, I was surprised to see, had made him seem taller; it had stretched out his form and given him an air of fragility. His face was unsmiling, frowning, thoughtful. He told me the reason he had wanted to see me was to show me the first pages of a new work he was planning; one, however, that might be of no use to anybody now that this war of unprecedented savagery was raging.

After a moment's hesitation, he sat down at the piano and played the magnificent, noble exposition of the Seventh Symphony and the variation theme depicting the Fascist invasion. We were both extremely agitated; it was a rare event for Shostakovich to play a new work with such manifest emotion. We sat on, plunged in silence, broken at last by Shostakovich with these words (I have them written down): 'I don't know what the fate of this piece will be.' After a further pause, he added: 'I suppose that critics with nothing better to do will damn me for copying Ravel's *Bolero*. Well, let them. That is how I hear war.' I believe that on that memorable August day Shostakovich was still unaware of the titanic scale of his symphony, for which a fate unique in the history of music was already in preparation. Parting, we embraced and kissed, not suspecting that before us lay a prolonged separation.

As I have already said, Shostakovich's letters to me were not intended for publication. They were written with no pretensions to literary style, with none of the careful drafting famous people might think it incumbent on them to labour over; the letters have no crossings-out or corrections but are written straight through in one breath. They deal with specific matters in a businesslike, informative way, sometimes discussing ideas for new works, more rarely subjects of general concern. For the most part, they employ a colloquial language sprinkled with allusions and are often embellished with humour. Shostakovich spoke very good Russian; his speech, richly inflected and marked by a lively simplicity, clarity and an elegant elasticity of phrasing, was free from elaborate circumlocutions or figures of speech. His pronunciation was impeccable, but his conversation abounded in little turns of phrase or verbal mannerisms like 'so to say' – this particular one, incidentally, could encompass a whole dictionary full of meanings. This habit has led some ill-informed biographers to characterize Shostakovich, wrongly, as incoherent, mumbling and otherwise verbally defective.

The letters which I now propose to publish are a one-sided discourse, since the voice of the respondent cannot be heard. It is moreover a fragmentary one, sometimes interrupted by long gaps. Nevertheless, in sum the letters seem to me to offer a slice of the raw material of Shostakovich's life, and it has always been the case that myriad visible and invisible threads from the life of any great artist are woven inextricably into his art.

The war brought me separation from Shostakovich. In September 1941, I found myself in the far-off, unfamiliar and (to me) mysterious city of Tashkent, to which the Leningrad Conservatoire, of which I was now on the teaching staff, had been evacuated. Shostakovich had stayed behind in besieged Leningrad. I was naturally fearful both for him and for his family, not to mention the fate of the new Seventh Symphony, the opening of which I could still not get out of my head. And then, in February 1942, I received a summons out of the blue to go to the post office in Tashkent, where, after an exhausting three-hour wait in a musty, dimly lit room, there occurred what seemed to me a small miracle: I heard in my ear the dear, familiar voice of Dmitry Dmitriyevich speaking on the telephone from Kuybïshev. In those wartime days, private long-distance phone calls entailed almost insuperable difficulties. Conversation was practically impossible, owing to the terrible background noise, and consisted mainly of innumerable exclamations and questions, the answers to which lost themselves in the hissing and crackling of the wires. But though the words themselves were mostly incomprehensible, the familiar, lively and inimitable intonations of his voice were enough to arouse the strongest feelings in me. Somehow we had found one another again; it was as though there was a sort of magic power hidden in the telephone equipment that instantly connected us, long parted by the cruel circumstances of war. The agitation was not only on my side: as he told me later, Shostakovich experienced similar feelings.

[xxxv]

Coming out of the post office, I could not help looking back at it in gratitude. The unprepossessing building was transformed before my eyes into a shrine housing a previously unsuspected power, thanks to which I had been able to reach out across the thousands of kilometres separating me from my friend and speak to him. Returning home, if 'home' is the right word for the cramped corridor in which I was living, I felt myself strong and happy again, ready for anything that might come my way. The music of the Seventh Symphony inspired in me bright hopes for the future. Such was my state of mind on that foul February evening after my conversation with the great composer who was, I dare to say, my dearest friend.

On 13 February 1942, *Pravda* published an article by A. N. Tolstoy under the headline: 'At a Rehearsal of Shostakovich's Seventh Symphony'. Not a performance, note – a rehearsal: presumably the author felt he could not wait to transmit to his millions of readers how overwhelmingly significant, not only to the music-loving public but to the whole life of a country in the grip of war, was the forthcoming performance. The article was reprinted in a number of newspapers, including the Tashkent paper. I read and reread it, consumed with interest. Tolstoy was not a musician but he was a superb writer, endowed with a rich and powerful imagination. In the middle section of the article, devoted to a commentary on the magnificent opening movement, the writer had found vivid and expressive imagery with which to clothe the penetrating truth of what he had experienced while hearing the music. It was a splendid article, and justly merited its widespread popularity.

The rehearsal that Aleksei Tolstoy had heard took place in Kuybïshev under the direction of Samuil Samosud, Chief Conductor of the Bolshoy Theatre, which had been temporarily evacuated to that city on the banks of the River Volga. I was in no doubt whatsoever that the outstanding conductor of an outstanding orchestra would have lavished the greatest care and inspiration on this stupendous work. Shostakovich had a high opinion of Samosud, regarding him, for example, as the supreme interpreter of *Lady Macbeth of the Mtsensk District* (as *Katerina Izmailova* had been known in Leningrad).

I have mentioned before that I already knew the opening of the symphony from the composer's piano version. Reading Tolstoy's article, I could imagine the splendour of the introduction's orchestral colours, the invasion theme and indeed everything that followed. In my mind's eye I saw the figure of Shostakovich, unobtrusively sitting in his usual place in the fifth or sixth row of the stalls, listening intently to the rehearsal but not interfering in the work of the conductor and generally behaving for all the world as though not he but somebody else had created this wonderful music. I seemed to see his face standing out in sharp relief from all around him, deep in reflection at the music he was hearing. Such were the visions that my reading of A. N. Tolstoy's article brought involuntarily to my mind.

I was consumed with impatience to find some way to get to Kuybïshev to hear for myself the symphony, which we knew was due to receive its first performance there on 5 March. But in wartime there was not the smallest hope of realizing the dream. However, before long it became known that the première was to be broadcast over all radio stations in the Soviet Union, which meant that we would be able to listen to it in Tashkent.

The director of the Conservatoire, Pavel Serebryakov, had managed to get hold of a radio from somewhere, so that evening a small group of us professors found ourselves expectantly huddled round the decrepit, tinny little set. Despite the continual interference, we could hear the fateful, tragic music of the first movement, the searing lyricism of the scherzo, the savagely triumphant beauty of the Adagio and the heroic spirit of the finale. Even though many precious details were lost in the awful reception, we were all overwhelmed by the power of the music.

Serebryakov, with my enthusiastic support, determined that come what may, the symphony must be performed by the orchestral forces of the Leningrad Conservatoire – after all, the composer of this great work had been an illustrious student and later professor there. It later turned out that Shostakovich also was anxious for this to happen, as he himself felt the closest ties with his alma mater. On that memorable evening, however, I had no idea that I was to be entrusted with the vital mission of going to Kuybïshev to obtain a copy of the score. The first plan was for the Deputy Director of the Conservatoire, Aron Ostrovsky, to undertake the hazardous trip. Ostrovsky was an imposing figure of great competence and energy. But events took an unexpected turn: Shostakovich sent a telegram requesting that I should come to Kuybïshev.

Serebryakov and I were on perfectly good terms, but he was undoubtedly somewhat put out by this request, which seemed to him to smack of the peremptory. He had no reason to know just how close my relationship was with Shostakovich, while Ostrovsky had no inkling of it at all and was most surprised by the telegram. I could well understand the senior management of the Conservatoire having serious doubts that I, an inexperienced nonentity, would be able to cope with the complex problems of getting hold of manuscript paper, making a copy of the score and getting safely it back to Tashkent. But a second telegram from Shostakovich merely confirmed his wish that I should be the courier. I, of course, realized that he was desperately anxious to see me and was using the business of the score as a pretext for our long-awaited meeting.

In the ordinary way I dislike travelling, but this time I was thrilled by the prospect of the trip. Poor Serebryakov and his assistants had no option but to buckle down and go in search of a rail ticket, in itself a task of daunting complexity. I also needed a sleeping-car reservation, a bonus necessitated by enlightened self-interest, since in a general open carriage I could easily have contracted the typhus which was then raging and the precious score of the Seventh Symphony would not be obtained.

After seemingly endless delays and setbacks, the ticket was finally in my hands and on 5 April 1942, my heart beating fit to burst out of my chest with excitement, I set off on my journey. On the eve of my departure, the Local Committee of the Conservatoire decided after an animated debate to furnish me with provisions for the journey in the shape of twenty rock-hard pies – after all, this was a time of great hunger across the land. Differences of opinion surfaced during the meeting, one camp insisting that ten pies would be quite sufficient, since it was a ten-day journey to Kuybïshev and life could be sustained quite adequately on a pie a day. The other side, championed by Ostrovsky, held out for twenty on the grounds that the train might be delayed for all sorts of reasons, in which case I would be reduced to gnawing the wood of my sleeping berth. I am glad to say that the humanitarian wing won the day. But there was more to come. My own students also showed a touching concern for the traveller and turned up at the station bearing extra hunks of bread and a bottle of red wine. They claimed that the latter was to ward off any gastric attacks to which I might be subjected.

The train left at night. The stars shone brightly in the blackness of the sky and a spring wind wafted over the crowds swarming on the platform. Morning came, and the conductress proffered something vaguely resembling tea – without sugar, to be sure. Considerable physical strength was needed to break open the first of my twenty precious pies – but horror of horrors! It was alive with little Tashkent ants, like poppy-seeds. God alone knows how they could have got into it in such incredible numbers. My companion (it was a two-berth sleeper), a gentleman of great respectability with the Order of Lenin in his lapel, observed my distress. Without a word, he broke off a piece of the pie, liberally seasoned with ants, and with what seemed to me a courage worthy of Pasteur risking his life in the service of humanity, put it in his mouth. Then this excellent man clicked his tongue and announced triumphantly: 'Speaking as a doctor, I can assure you this pie is perfectly edible.' It turned out that he was an eminent medical man, travelling to Moscow via Kuybïshev. Somewhat timidly, I followed his example, and then, as I gradually gained courage, the two of us dined together for the ten days of the journey, demolishing all twenty of the pies and becoming connoisseurs, for the first and I hope the last time, of the singular taste of the Central Asian ant.

I have related the incident with the pies not simply for its entertainment value, but because it serves to illustrate a little slice of life in those far-off wartime days, the memory of which is already dimmed by the passing of the decades. But the real point is a more important one: no material hardship could stifle the voice of the muses, nor could the guns. The fire of the spirit burned as fiercely as ever, there was no lessening of passion for music in general and for Shostakovich's new symphony in particular. Everywhere there was a burning desire to hear this work performed. During the long journey my imagination ranged freely, trying to picture the daily life of the composer, to reconstruct in my mind the story of the Seventh Symphony's completion, the preparations for its première, and finally the triumphant Kuybïshev and Moscow performances on 5 and 29 March 1942. I knew something about these things from Shostakovich's letters to me, but of course nothing could replace the face-to-face conversations that I hoped awaited me in the very near future.

Meanwhile, the train continued on its meandering journey, stopping interminably at every station. After the harsh brilliance of the Tashkent sky, it was a shock to look out of the window and see clouds, snow-covered fields, the noble sight of cranes on the wing, frozen wells, and once again to smell on the breeze, as they say, the well-remembered aspen trees of home. At long last, the ten days of the journey were over and on the evening of 15 April I finally arrived at the unfamiliar city of Kuybïshev, where I bade a cordial farewell to my travelling companion who had rescued me from starvation by his forthright rehabilitation of Ant Pies *à la mode de Tashkent*.

Dmitry Dmitriyevich was on the platform to meet me, having come to the station with a small entourage in which I recognized, to my great delight, the smiling eyes and gleaming smile of the famous pianist Lev Oborin. While I was taking off my rucksack, a visibly excited Shostakovich, slimmer than I remembered him, came rushing up and we warmly embraced, exchanging the usual words of greeting. To cover his agitation, he snatched a pack of cigarettes from his pocket and lit up, forgetting in his confusion to offer one to me – an incorrigible smoker.

Noticing that he was dressed from head to toe in smart new clothes – new hat, new overcoat, new shoes – I learned that he had recently been issued with a complete range of clothing coupons because, as he had told me in one of his letters, his luggage and possessions had been lost *en route* from Moscow to Kuybïshev. Excited and in the sunniest of moods, Dmitry Dmitriyevich announced that although it was quite a long way, we should walk to his quarters because there was an epidemic in the town that made it unsafe to go by tram. Naturally, there were many official organizations that would have been only too happy to provide Shostakovich with a car, but to get one he would have had to apply to the powers that be; in other words, do precisely what he could never bear to do: ask a favour.

This would always cause him agonies of embarrassment, no matter how trifling the request, and so when the time came for me to leave Kuybïshev at the end of my stay, we had to repeat the route-march back to the station. Shostakovich could not bear the thought of placing himself under any obligation to an official by requesting a car, so in consequence of his principled stand, he and I set out in darkness on foot with my heavy rucksack[16] to the railway station, whence we took a suburban train out to the airfield. I remember what a state Shostakovich was in at having to apply to the local Executive Director of the USSR Council of Ministers (in those days it was called the Council of People's Commissars) for permission for me to eat with him and his family in the Kuybïshev National Hotel. When he returned bearing the precious bit of paper, his face was aglow with pleasure, a reaction I found strangely touching. Until that moment he had been very dubious about his appeal to the mandarin being crowned with success: even after the world-shaking first performance of the Seventh Symphony, Shostakovich had no conception of the power and influence which was in reality his to command. Times without number, he found himself solving problems for other people; for himself, never. This he neither could nor would do.

For this reason, we now went on foot to No. 2a Vilonovsky Street, where Shostakovich and his family occupied four rooms and a bathroom. For Kuybïshev in those days, this constituted the height of luxury, but needless to say it was not the result of any steps Shostakovich had taken. In the reasonably spacious room he used as a study, Shostakovich had installed a grand piano, a desk, several armchairs and hand chairs, and a decent-sized divan on which I slept very comfortably for a month. Everything was arranged with the same order and neatness that characterized Shostakovich's rooms in all the apartments that he ever occupied in Leningrad and Moscow.

Nina Vasilyyevna, as mistress of the household, welcomed me with great cordiality. She had gone to a lot of trouble to arrange a supper party for my arrival to which all the guests had, by mutual agreement, brought along whatever God had seen fit to bestow upon them to eat and drink. This was common practice during the war. I had become accustomed to real hunger in Tashkent, not to mention the train journey, and the modest supper seemed to me like a Lucullan orgy.

That evening, Shostakovich was elated. I was happy just to be sitting near him and to be able to steal covert glances at his handsome, animated face. I use the world 'covert' deliberately: had I openly regarded him, he would immediately have turned his face away in irritation. Any overt attention paid to him he used half-jokingly to call 'unhealthy curiosity'.

After I had been in Kuybïshev a few days, Shostakovich acceded to my request that he play through the whole of the Seventh Symphony on the piano. He played wonderfully, bringing out many of the subtlest nuances in the second and third movements. At the end of the Finale, he heaved a little sigh, got up from the piano stool and said: 'On the whole, I think I'm happy with the symphony. But you know, when I was writing the Finale, the place was full of rumours and I got a great deal of advice from people here, some of which I had asked for and some I hadn't.' And he proceeded to tell me many details on this subject that he had omitted from his letters.

Then we began to discuss the problem of how to make a copy of the score. This was not an easy task; indeed, it proved to be extremely difficult. 'It seems to have become a very fashionable piece just now. Couriers arrive from all over the place, asking me to help them get hold of a copy of the score. Of course, there is nothing I can do, and I just have to get rid of them. Couriers, couriers, couriers. Nothing but couriers, thirty-five thousand of them!' Quoting Khlestakov, Shostakovich burst out laughing.[17] Serious again, he went on: 'But don't worry. You won't go back to Tashkent without a copy of the score. I'll see to that.' And so it turned out. In the middle of May, I flew back to Tashkent with the precious score of the Seventh Symphony, and five weeks later it was performed by the Leningrad

Conservatoire orchestra conducted by Ilya Musin. After the March premières in Kuybïshev and Moscow, this was the very next performance to take place anywhere, at home or abroad.

On several occasions during my stay in Kuybïshev, Shostakovich played me excerpts from Verdi's *Otello*: Iago's 'Credo', the Willow Song, Desdemona's Prayer, Otello's final scene and much else besides. Before the war in Leningrad, at the end of the 1930s, I remember Shostakovich telling me of his lasting and unshakeable love for *Otello*; it was one of the operas he loved best in the world. Around that time, the Kirov Theatre was mounting a new production of *Otello* and Shostakovich invited me to accompany him to one of the performances. The production had been directed by Nikolai Pechkovsky, who also sang the title role. Shostakovich liked the singer, but was upset by the conductor's interpretation. It annoyed him so much that he immediately fired off a review to the *Sovetskoye Iskusstvo* newspaper, in which he sharply criticized the conductor in question, Sergey Yeltsin. Shostakovich showed me a rough copy of his notice before it was printed and I was taken aback by its uncompromising tone. Shostakovich respected Yeltsin as a musician, but on this occasion the truth as he saw it overrode any feelings of friendship. The same thing happened after he saw the film *Rimsky-Korsakov*, a disastrous affair which elicited from him a searingly caustic article. (Nevertheless, it was rare for Shostakovich to publish a bad review.)

And so, listening to these excerpts from *Otello*, I wondered aloud whether Shostakovich was planning to write something on a Shakespearean theme? The reply was unexpected: he was indeed thinking about an opera, but the subject would not be from Shakespeare,[18] it would be from Gogol. He was thinking of *The Gamblers*.

Developing the idea with enthusiasm, he went on: 'Yes, after a break of fourteen years, now I have decided to go back to Gogol. But *The Gamblers* won't be anything like *The Nose*. The starting-point will be completely different. In *The Nose* I treated Gogol's text with great freedom, but in *The Gamblers* I plan to be absolutely faithful to the author. I shall keep in every word of every line, as Dargomïzhsky did in *The Stone Guest*. My librettist will be none other than Gogol himself!

'It seems that no one has ever written an opera entirely without parts for women, so you might argue that it's a problem that *The Gamblers* has no female characters. Well, we'll just have to put up with this odd state of affairs. Anyhow, what an extraordinary comedy Gogol wrote! Do you remember that marvellous play within the play written by the hero, Stepan Ivanovich Uteshitelny? Incredible originality!'

Fascinated by what Shostakovich had had to say in what was for him quite a long speech, I hazarded what seemed to me an original thought of my own. 'Do you think', I asked, 'the new opera could form the third leg of a trilogy of operas about cards: Tchaikovsky's *The Queen of Spades*, Prokofiev's *The Gambler*, Shostakovich's *The Gamblers*? After all, strange as it may seem, cards are an eternal theme!' Shostakovich considered for a moment, and then said: 'I loved to play cards when I was young – but I always lost. Maybe my own modest experience will come to my aid and I will participate in this recently conceived trilogy of yours.' Both of us burst out laughing at that.

There were several aspects to the notion of *The Gamblers* that amazed and delighted me: first, the return to opera, which Shostakovich had apparently abandoned for ever after the unhappy fate of *Lady Macbeth of the Mtsensk District*; second, the return to his beloved Gogol despite the fact that *The Nose* had had a far from successful history on the stage; and third, the ambition to write something in a comic vein immediately after the epic tragedy of the Seventh Symphony – not to mention the Eighth Symphony, that most tragic of all Shostakovich's works, the composition of which was imminent. *The Gamblers* would thus take on the character of a comic interlude, something like the satire embedded in Greek tragedies.

The eventual fate of *The Gamblers* is well known. Shostakovich reluctantly came to the conclusion that if the text of Gogol's one-act play were to be uncut it would far exceed the limits of contemporary operatic convention. He abandoned work on it after composing forty minutes of magnificent, coruscatingly witty music, which we were eventually able to hear at the Leningrad Philharmonia in a performance conducted by Gennady Rozhdestvensky.

Another happy event in Kuybïshev was the chance to talk on the telephone to Ivan Sollertinsky, my dear friend and mentor. He had called Shostako-vich from Novosibirsk, where the Leningrad Philharmonia had been evacuated, so of course I also took advantage of the call. The main reason for it was that Yevgeny Mravinsky was preparing to perform the Seventh Symphony and very much wanted the composer to be at the rehearsals and the first performance, just as he had been not long before for the Fifth and the Sixth Symphonies in Leningrad. Ivan Ivanovich, in his dual capacity as Artistic Director of the Philharmonia and Shostakovich's intimate friend, found it an easy matter to persuade him to come to Novosibirsk. Not much persuasion was needed: in any case, the composer was longing to see his old friend and to hear the Seventh Symphony in Mravinsky's performance following that by Samosud. He gave me a full account of it in a letter that summer, after he had been to Novosibirsk and attended the local première, which took place at the beginning of July 1942.

My own conversation with Sollertinsky was brief though deeply affecting. It was the last time I was to hear his voice; less than two years later, this great man was no more.

Returning to Tashkent, I was distressed to discover that several of Shostakovich's letters to me had inexplicably been lost. I had been looking forward to rereading everything he had written and comparing it with what I had seen for myself in Kuybïshev. However, all the remaining letters which I now present in this book are alive with the inflections of Shostakovich's conversation, laden with the ironic allusions and subtexts so characteristic of him and meaningful to the recipient alone.

In virtually all instances, the letters and the writer's syntax are reproduced in full, with no excisions or alterations.

All envelopes and postcards carry the stamp: 'Passed by the military censor'.

I
War and Separation
1941–1945

Poster advertising the Seventh Symphony conducted by Mravinsky in Novosibirsk,
July 1942

When the correspondence begins, the main musical institutions of Leningrad have been evacuated from the besieged city: the Philharmonia with its musicians and ensembles to Novosibirsk; the Conservatoire to Tashkent, the capital city of Uzbekistan in Central Asia; the Kirov Theatre to Perm in Siberia. Isaak Glikman is with his Conservatoire colleagues in Tashkent, while Shostakovich has just arrived with his wife and children in Kuybïshev (now Samara), a provincial city on the banks of the Volga in Central Russia: the Bolshoy Theatre and many other Moscow musicians are there. The first three movements of Shostakovich's Seventh Symphony, the 'Leningrad', were completed in the besieged city; the fourth has not yet been begun. As the war proceeds towards its appalling climax, with the protracted destruction and suffering endured by both sides in the battle for Stalingrad, Shostakovich completes the cycle of war symphonies, Nos 7, 8 and 9, and the Second Piano Trio, dedicated to the memory of his friend Ivan Sollertinsky, who died in Novosibirsk in February 1944.

30 November 1941 Kuybïshev

Dear Isaak Davïdovich,

I received your letter of 18 November today; I don't need to tell you what tremendous pleasure it gave me. I am glad to know that you are alive and well, and your living arrangements more or less fixed up.

I stayed in Leningrad until 1 October. On 3 September I completed the first movement of my Seventh Symphony. I finished the second movement on 17 September, and the third on 29 September. I might have managed to finish the fourth movement as well, but as things have turned out it is not ready yet – worse than that, in fact – I have not yet even begun it. There are of course several reasons for this, but the main one is that the strain of concentrating all my efforts on the first three movements has completely exhausted me. As you have already observed, everything to do with composition puts me in a state of great nervous excitement, and that is why I began my letter with this subject.

On 30 September I had a telephone call at 11 o'clock at night from Comrade Kalinnikova of the Leningrad Party Committee. She told me that

I was to go by air to Moscow the following day, 1 October, and so that very day I left our beloved home town with my wife and two children.

When we first arrived in Moscow, we put up at the Moskva Hotel. On the evening of 14 October we moved to an apartment that had been prepared for us, but the following morning, 15 October, we went to the railway station and at 10 o'clock that evening we left on the train to Sverdlovsk. The journey was not a comfortable one.

En route we lost two suitcases with clothes and linen, as well as finishing up all our food supplies. On 22 October we arrived at Kuybïshev. We found space in the Bolshoy Theatre hostel, and early in November, thanks to the efforts of Mikhail Khrapchenko,[1] we were allocated a room of our own. It's quite a decent room (twenty-two square metres), and it's warm and comfortable. We're living there now. Conditions are not very conducive to creative work, but a short while ago I was called in to see Comrade Rozaliya Zemlyachka,[2] who promised to arrange a two-room billet for us. Everybody is very kind to me here, and as soon as I am able to do something about getting some proper clothes and shoes I shall be quite content. And if we really do get two rooms where I can get away from the children from time to time, then probably I shall be able to finish the Seventh Symphony.

For the time being I can't leave Kuybïshev; they want me to stay here. Materially (that is to say, financially), I am quite well off, and I fear that the money situation would probably be less good in Tashkent.[3] Nevertheless I do intend to go there if I can have a few sessions with a hypnotherapist to help get over my fear of such a long journey. But in any case they want me to stay here because of the possibility of my visiting the USA. If they leave it up to me to decide I shall decline, because I have no inclination whatever for the trip. I would rather finish my symphony and stay in my homeland than go to foreign soil.

Well, that's about all I have to say about myself. My mother[4] and sister[5] and her son are in Leningrad. Although we were promised they would get away, this has still not happened. Vladimir Lebedev[6] and Nikolai Rabinovich[7] are still in Leningrad. I miss you very much and long for your company. However, I am still hoping to get to Tashkent, and then we shall be able to spend some time together. Do you have any news at all of Ivan Sollertinsky?[8] I sent him a telegram and wrote to him from here, but have not received any reply. Just in case, here is his address: Apartment 50, 35 Romanova Street, Novosibirsk. Vissarion Shebalin, who is now in Sverdlovsk, gave me his address when I was in Moscow. My friend Lev Oborin is living here, and among other friends are Samuil Samosud, Barsova, Ivan Kozlovsky and Ilya Erenburg.[9]

Do please write to me more often. I am sure you will be interested to learn what has happened to V. V. Fyodorov (Leningrad Dynamo left half). He, Alov, Sazonov and Sïchev were all working in the 27 Police Division, where they took turns doing duty at the Kazan Cathedral. I don't know what became of Bobrov, Nabutov, Peki Dementiyev and the other football stars. As for Arkady Klyachkin,[10] he was as cheerful and full of beans as ever.

My dear friend, I hope we shall soon see one another and go to football matches again. My best wishes to Tatyana Ivanovna.[11] Nina, Galina and Maksim[12] send their greetings to you both.

I kiss you warmly,

D. Shostakovich

PS Please try to get in touch with Abel Startsev[13] through the Union of Soviet Writers, and let him know our address.[14]

22 December 1941 Kuybïshev

Dear Isaak Davïdovich,

I am seizing the chance to write a few lines to you. First of all, please don't forget me, and write to me more often. Secondly, I have a new address: Apartment 9, 146 Frunze Street, Kuybïshev District. I now have my own separate two-roomed flat. It has made life easier, and I am finishing the Finale of the Symphony. It was Comrade Zemlyachka who arranged the flat, and she has also helped us a lot in a number of other ways. We are hopeful that my mother will soon be able to join us here.

A branch of the Union of Soviet Composers has been set up here in Kuybïshev, and we meet on Wednesdays to listen to our compositions. I expect you will be interested to know who is on the Committee of the Kuybïshev USC. Here is the membership: myself (Chairman); David Rabinovich[15] (Vice-Chairman); Aleksei Ogolovets[16] (Executive Secretary); Semyon Chernetsky[17] and Semyon Shlifshteyn[18] (members). The Union has eighteen members all told; among them are Comrades Szabo,[19] Tsfasman,[20] Zhak,[21] Antyufeyev,[22] Solodukho,[23] Zdenek Nejedly[24] and others.

Today there should have been a concert of my works, but since Comrade Moris Gurvich (the viola player of the quartet) has been taken ill with pneumonia, the concert has been postponed until 29 December. I am doing some four-hand playing with Lev Oborin. We are all well, and have enough to eat. I miss not only hearing orchestral music, but also just being in Moscow and in Leningrad. I long to go home as soon as possible. Once again: please write more, and more often. Greetings to Tatyana Ivanovna. Nina sends best respects.

Your

D. Shostakovich

4 January 1942 Kuybïshev

Dear Isaak Davïdovich,

I am writing to you a lot these days, as much in fact as my supply of envelopes will allow – this particular product of the papermaking industry is extraordinarily hard to come by in Kuybïshev. The same is true of postcards. I was very glad to get your letter, dated 21 December last year. I send you my best wishes for the New Year and wish you health and happiness. I wish the same to Tatyana Ivanovna, plus the opportunity to perfect her skills in the culinary department without the need to restrict her experiments exclusively to rice. Levitin[25] was obviously right.

We have moved to a new apartment and as far as space is concerned are living very well. For this I am indebted to Comrade Zemlyachka, who asked me to come in and see her one day and has helped me in many ways. The only circumstance which could be improved is my financial situation, which is not so much bad as just rather unstable. But I suppose it has never really been anything other than that.

My apartment consists of two rooms, and its chief advantage is that we are the only family living in it. I finished my Seventh Symphony here. Apart from this landmark distinction,[26] the apartment boasts a bathroom, a kitchen and a lavatory. A few words about the Symphony: the first movement lasts twenty-five minutes and was finished on 3 September 1941. The second movement lasts eight minutes and was finished on 17 September 1941. The third movement lasts seventeen minutes; finished 29 September 1941. The fourth movement lasts twenty minutes; finished 27 December 1941.

Those who have heard the Symphony find the first three movements very good. So far I have shown the fourth movement to only a few people. Those few generally like it, but there were some reservations among the chorus of approval. For instance, my friend Soso Begiashvili thinks it (the fourth movement) not optimistic enough. Samuil Samosud[27] thinks it is all very fine but not, in his opinion, a proper finale. For it to be so, he thinks I ought to bring in a choir and soloists. There were many more similarly

[6]

valuable observations on the fourth movement, which I accept for purposes of information rather than for guidance, since I don't believe the movement needs either chorus or soloists and it has quite enough optimism as it is. My friend Soso Begiashvili is a splendid fellow, but not particularly well endowed in the intellectual department, and therefore one should not take his opinions too seriously.[28] Lev Oborin, David Rabinovich and Semyon Shlifshteyn liked the whole work and rated it all very highly.[29]

Tomorrow there is to be a concert of my works. This is the programme: Preludes, Pushkin Songs (performed by Aleksandr Baturin),[30] Cello Sonata (performed by V. Ostrovsky) and the Quintet (performed by the Bolshoy Theatre Quartet and myself). This concert was supposed to have been on 22 December, but had to be postponed until tomorrow because of the illness of Comrade Gurvich (the quartet's viola player).

Nina, the children and I are all well. But my nervous system is playing up. I miss you very much but cling to the hope that we shall soon see one another. The All-Union Higher Education Committee has appointed me Chairman of the State Examination Board for the Piano Faculty of the Leningrad Conservatoire, and so if I get the opportunity and feel strong enough I will come to Tashkent; then we shall be able to meet and talk.[31]

I didn't tell you that my Seventh Symphony has been nominated for a possible Stalin Prize. There is a proposal to perform it here with the Bolshoy Theatre Orchestra and Samosud. I worry that there are not enough orchestral forces here to cope, because the symphony does call for a very large orchestra. I should really like to hear Mravinsky perform this work, but at the moment this is difficult. I don't have great faith in Samosud as a symphonic conductor.[32] I am letting all this worry me more than I should in view of the shaky state of my nervous system.

Our life here carries on without too many problems, in peace and quiet. Sometimes at nights I don't sleep, and I weep. The tears flow thick and fast, and bitter. Nina and the children sleep in the other room, so there is nothing to prevent me from giving way to my tears. Then I calm myself. My nerves are really playing up.[33]

Judging by your last letter there are no football matches in Tashkent. I went to an ice-hockey match here one day, but didn't enjoy it much. They weren't bad players, but the teams had no strips and the only way the players were able to overcome this minor handicap was by knowing one another personally. Most of the time I had no idea which side a player was on, and the referee didn't help to make things much clearer either. You could tell who he was though, because he had a fur coat and felt boots, but no skates. Anyhow, I watched the match and then went home thinking of K. Sazonov, that whole tribe of Fyodorovs, Peki Dementiyev, Levin-Kogan and the others.[34]

I press your hand, my dear friend. My greetings to Tatyana Ivanovna. Nina and the children send their respects.

D. Shostakovich

6 February 1942 Kuybïshev

To: Isaak Davïdovich Glikman, 18 Ulyanovskaya Street, Tashkent

Dear Isaak Davïdovich,

I am taking advantage of the kindness of some friends of mine from Tashkent to send you this letter.

Things are not good with me.[35] Day and night I think of my family and loved ones, whom I had to leave behind in Leningrad. I seldom get news of them. There are no more cats and dogs left. Not only that but my mother is short of money, because she cannot rely on what I regularly send her; it often gets delayed or misrouted on the way. Vasily Varzar[36] is ill with malnutrition and Nina's niece Allochka[37] has the same problem. I wrote to your mother and told her that you were alive and well.[38] Every day I try to do something about getting my loved ones away from Leningrad, and until I manage to do this I am not going to leave Kuybïshev, because from here I can sometimes manage to get things sent to them from Moscow, even occasionally directly from here. Tashkent is so far away I am afraid that communications from there would be practically impossible.[39] To tell you the truth, I haven't much else to write to you about, since the foregoing preoccupations are the main tenor of my life.

The saga continues.[40] The Bolshoy Theatre Orchestra is rehearsing my rather long Seventh Symphony outstandingly well. Yesterday was the first full orchestral play-through of the first and second movements. It made a great impression on me and for half a day I rejoiced over my baby.[41]

Quite a few of the people who came to Kuybïshev are going back to Moscow now. The Bolshoy Theatre is still here, but probably when they go it will be time for me to leave Kuybïshev as well.[42] If I manage to get my family here from Leningrad, then I will come to Tashkent. Materially we are not badly off here. I have enough money and we have enough to eat, although the situation is not as good as it was a month ago. Because of the exodus to Moscow[43] all sorts of canteens, shops and so on are winding down their activities. A. N. Tolstoy came here for a meeting to review candidates for Stalin Prize awards; he was telling me about Tashkent and telling me I ought to go there. Kuybïshev has a distinctly continental climate; we had forty-five degrees of frost here the other day. Our apartment is cold, and we are frozen all the time. Do write to me more often. You cannot imagine what joy it is to have news of friends and know what they are up to. I have one more event to relate: we have acquired a gingery-coloured dog who sort of wandered in off the street. He's a real 'courtier'.[44] We hadn't the heart to shoo him away, so now he lives with us. The children call him Ginger. He seems to like his name.

Greetings to Tatyana Ivanovna. All my family sends their best to you.

D. Shostakovich

14 February 1942 Kuybïshev

Dear Isaak Davïdovich,

I hardly need to tell you how excited I was by our telephone conversation. As you must have observed (after all, we have known one another for a long time) I am not much of a talker, especially on the telephone.[45] So far as I remember, the longest telephone conversation you and I ever had was on 19 June, after the Zenith (L[eningrad]) – Spartak (M[oscow]) match, the one which was decided by a single goal scored by the Zenith right winger Comrade Levin-Kogan in the final minutes of the first half. You weren't there, so in my best colourful and descriptive language I relayed the entire course of the game to you on the telephone.

Yesterday's was the second long conversation we have had (10 minutes), but this time you were in Tashkent and I in Kuybïshev. Although we may not actually have said very much,[46] I was still extremely excited by our talk. Assuming I am alive and well, I should be in Tashkent from 5 to 15 April, as Chairman of the State Committee of Piano Studies.[47] I very much want to come, but if I cannot make the journey by air then I am nervous of coming by train.[48] My tip is to wear an amulet of garlic round the neck and wrists. Girls don't like the smell much, of course, but neither do all kinds of bugs. So it is probably sensible to sacrifice the girls, for the time being. Actually, I am not very interested in them (girls) at the moment. Wretched nerves playing up ... All the same, there is a certain Yelena Pavlovna, and the possibility of finding her here was one of the reasons I settled on Kuybïshev to come to. But my quest has been unsuccessful, a circumstance which strikes me as mysterious in the highest degree.[49]

[9]

Yesterday Ya. L. Leontyev, the local Bolshoy Theatre chief, dragged me out from rehearsal to tell me that he had just been speaking on the phone to Solodovnikov (Khrapchenko's deputy) in Moscow. He asked Leontyev to pass on the news from Zemlyachka that my family is to be evacuated from Leningrad without having to wait in the queue. This news gave me the greatest joy, and I spent the next two or three hours in the best of spirits.

Dear Isaak Davïdovich, I kiss you warmly. Greetings to you and Tatyana Ivanovna from all of us. Also, Lyova Oborin sends you his greetings.

D. Shostakovich

Please write more often. I will ring you again soon.

11 March 1942 Kuybïshev

Dear Isaak Davïdovich,

There has been yet another event in my life: we have moved to a new apartment. Please note the address and telephone number: Kuybïshev, 2 Vilonovskaya Street, Apartment 2, telephone 22–73. Thank you very much for your telegram about the symphony,[50] which I presume you heard on the radio. What a pity it could not be in the flesh; you lose such a lot in a broadcast.

Yesterday a telegram arrived sent from Cherepovets; here is what it said: 'Got away safely from Leningrad longing to see you soon love to all Babka.' I was absolutely overjoyed by this telegram. If only they can get here to us safely. We are expecting eight people altogether: Mama, Marusya,[51] Mitya,[52] Sof. Mikh.,[53] Vas. Vas.,[54] Irina,[55] G. G. Efros[56] and Allochka.[57] Somehow or other we'll all manage to squash in; I now have a bigger apartment with four rooms.

I received your letter yesterday, in which you tell me that Serebryakov[58] is thinking of sending you to Kuybïshev to collect my symphony. I don't need to tell you how happy I should be to see you here. Please come, we'll arrange everything for you here. I'm in good spirits, except for worrying about my travellers. In a few days I shall fly to Moscow[59]; Samosud has already left to fix up an orchestra there for my symphony.[60] Well, that's all. Write to me. I kiss you warmly.

D. Shostakovich

PS Did you receive the money?[61]

This letter is written on a rectangular piece of white cardboard to which a 20-kopeck stamp has been affixed, instead of a postcard. Presumably because of the shortage of envelopes in Kuybïshev, for the next few months Shostakovich wrote postcards.

31 March 1942 Moscow

Dear Isaak Davïdovich,

I've been in Moscow for ten days now. I flew here for the performances of my Seventh Symphony which took place yesterday and the day before. It will be played twice more on 4 and 6 March. On top of that, on 5 March[62] I have to give a speech to the Second Pan-Slavic Radio Congress. My dear friend, how greatly I am in need of your company in these days, so difficult but so important for me.[63]

The day before I flew to Moscow, my mother, sister and nephew arrived in Kuybïshev. My mother is nothing but skin and bone but Marusya and Mitya seem all right. I met up with my father- and mother-in-law in Moscow and saw them off on their journey to Kuybïshev. Vasily Vasilyyevich looked absolutely terrible and his wits seemed to be wandering.[64] Sofya Mikhailovna was in better shape. They have no news of your mother. I asked my own mother about her, but they were living too far apart to visit one another. Nobody knows anything about what has become of Pasha or Fenya.[65] Valerian Bogdanov-Berezovsky's[66] mother brought me a letter from him. He told me that Golts,[67] Kalafati,[68] Fradkin,[69] Budyakovsky[70] and several other composers have all died.

It's possible that I shall fly from here to Tashkent, but more likely back to Kuybïshev. I think I have already told you that I have moved to a new apartment in Kuybïshev. Here is the address: 2 Vilonovskaya Street, Apartment 2, telephone 22–73. I now face a big problem which is seriously worrying me: how to feed and care for all the members of my family who have come to be with me. I kiss you warmly. Greetings to Tatyana Ivanovna. Let us hope we shall see one another some time.

D. Shostakovich

PS I sent you some coffee with my friend Yevgeny Boltin.[71] Did you get it all right?

29 June 1942 Novosibirsk

Dear Isaak Davïdovich,

The day I arrived in Novosibirsk[72] I was handed the letter that I am enclosing herewith. As far as I can see, it concerns Lyalya Konstantinovskaya.[73] Please be so kind as to pass it on to her. I don't know her address, that's why I am bothering you with this.

I have been in Novosibirsk for three days now. I can't tell you what a joy it was to see Ivan Ivanovich[74] and Yury Sviridov.[75] I get the impression that Sviridov has matured and developed intellectually to an extraordinary degree, although from the start I always rated his intellectual powers highly. I am very busy here and have not yet had time to present my compliments[76] to a whole series of friends (Blanter,[77] Shcherbachov[78] and others). I am going be here for another two weeks.

Mravinsky starts rehearsals for my Seventh Symphony today. I shall return to Kuybïshev after the concert on 8 July.

Please write, don't forget me.

My respects to Tatyana Ivanovna.

I kiss you warmly.

D. Shostakovich.

Please give my greetings to Lyalya Konstantinovskaya.

I'm sending you the programme of a football match in Kazan, which Dynamo won four–nil. The Dynamo team contains many of our old friends.[79] A friend of mine brought me the programme from Kazan.

This letter is written on a small scrap of paper, which Shostakovich had no doubt had great difficulty in procuring.

26 July 1942 Kuybïshev

Dear Isaak Davïdovich,

First of all, please give my very best greetings to your mother. I am so happy that she has managed to get to Tashkent and that she is in reasonably good health.[80] I do hope that now you will have less to worry you and that you will be in better spirits. I spent a whole month in Novosibirsk.[81] You can imagine how happy I was to see Ivan Sollertinsky. On my return I found a letter from Oleg Oshentsov,[82] which I thought you would be interested to read, so I'm sending it on to you by registered post. I also sent you earlier a letter from Novosibirsk with an enclosure from a friend of Yelena Konstantinovskaya – did you get this and did you manage to pass it on to her?[83]

We are all well. Pasha has turned up in Moscow and is coming to Kuybïshev. I had a telegram from Fenya[84], and she will also be coming. So I shall not be short of company.[85]

Thank you for your letters. I kiss you warmly. Greetings to all of yours.

D. Shostakovich

17 September 1942 Moscow

Dear Isaak Davïdovich,

I haven't had any news of you for a long time and I am concerned. How are you? How are all your people? Do please write and tell me everything that is happening, and send it to Kuybïshev, as I shall soon be there. I've been in Moscow for two weeks, and I have played my Quintet three times with the Beethoven Quartet.[86] Now I must finish a piece for the NKVD ensemble,[87] and as soon as I have delivered it I shall return to Kuybïshev. We are all well, and everything is more or less all right. I recently received an invitation from the New York Philharmonic to conduct eight concerts in October.[88] I turned it down, as I am no conductor.[89] All the same, when I heard my Seventh Symphony conducted by Konstantin Ivanov[90] three days later, I was regretting my decision having come to the conclusion that the art of conducting can't be as difficult as all that.[91]

So that's what's going on. I had a telegram from Sollertinsky inviting me to move to Novosibirsk, and perhaps I will go. You were asking after Vasily Vasilyyevich and Sofya Mikhailovna, and I hasten to gratify your urge to know: the answer is that they are well and flourishing.[92] I kiss you warmly.

D. Shostakovich

14 October 1942 Moscow

Dear Isaak Davïdovich,

I'm taking advantage of the kindness of my friend Iosif Utkin,[93] who is flying to Tashkent and so will be able to get this postcard to you quickly. I don't have much news to speak of, except that my room number has changed from 430 to 506.[94]

I was immensely saddened to hear of Leonid Nikolayev's death. I loved him greatly and it grieves me to think that I shall never see him again. I have thought much about his life and shall miss him sorely.[95] Today I received news that Pyotr Ryazanov[96] had died in Tbilisi. Please pass this on to your colleagues in the conservatory.

I am staying on here to finish the piece for the NKVD Song and Dance Ensemble. It has taken longer than I expected, and I have already had to spend an extra month in Moscow because of it. The moment I finish the piece I shall go to Kuybïshev. I miss very much not having any news of you, and hope that when I get there I shall find a letter from you.

I long to see you. Some time or other we shall manage it, I expect. I saw Aleksandr Solodovnikov[97] today, and he told me something of life at the Conservatoire and about Pavel Serebryakov. Unfortunately he could not tell me anything about you. If Iosif Utkin does give you my letter, please tell him from me how grateful I am.[98] He is a splendid person and quickly became a friend. Give my greetings to all your people. I kiss you warmly.

D. Shostakovich

4 November 1942 Kuybïshev

Dear Isaak Davïdovich,

I cannot yet tell you anything definite about my move to Novosibirsk.[99] I have my doubts that it is going to come off, since it involves so many complications – just think for example how many people my family consists of. I am extremely worried about my sister Zoya,[100] who is living in Samarkand. Her husband Grigory Khrushchov[101] has been seriously ill for two months with tropical fever, and life has generally become extremely hard for her. When I think about all the hardships she has to endure I am overwhelmed by feelings of sadness about many things. I grieve for Leonid Nikolayev; he was a fine man. The same applies to Pyotr Ryazanov, an outstanding musician.

Krasny Sport [*Red Sport*] of 27 October carried a report of our Leningrad football clubs' successes in Alma-Ata: Zenith won two–nil against Alma-Ata Dynamo, and Leningrad Dynamo won seven–two against their fellow Leningraders. P. Dementiyev and Levin-Kogan were outstanding for Zenith, and from our Dynamo team Arkhangelsky, A. Fyodorov, Alov and some of the others had a brilliant game. I am so happy for them. I saw Dynamo play in Moscow, and thought back to our times together at the Lenin Stadium. Happy days. I kiss you warmly.

D. Shostakovich

[14]

I have just received a letter from A. M. Klyachkin in Leningrad. He is alive and well, and brimming with optimism.[102]

On the back of Shostakovich's postcard, no doubt used because of the shortage of paper, I found a note scribbled by my wife which throws into sharp relief the privations of our life in Tashkent: 'Isaak! Don't go there [i.e. to my wife's sister]. It's cold and dark and there's no light except a smoky oil lamp. There's some cold food in the little bowl, but no way of heating it. Must dash. Talya.' This note must have been written on 18 or 19 November 1942.

6 November 1942 Kuybïshev

Dear Isaak Davïdovich,

My warmest congratulations and best wishes to you on the 25th anniversary of the Great October Socialist Revolution.

I have just listened to the radio broadcast of the speech by Comrade Stalin. My dear friend! How sad it is that circumstances have forced us to hear this speech so far apart from one another.[103]

I kiss you warmly,

D. Shostakovich

22 November 1942 Kuybïshev

Dear Isaak Davïdovich,

I am missing you very much. Why haven't you written?[104] Are you in good health?

How are things with you? Generally speaking, everything is all right here. The children have been a bit under the weather, which has been a worry. However the grown-ups, thanks be to God, have not been under the weather, are not currently under the weather and, one must suppose, do not propose in the future to be under the weather.[105] I am very worried about my sister Zoya in Samarkand. It is getting very hard for her to carry on. On 24 November my mother is making the journey to Samarkand to see her, and she has to change trains at Tashkent,[106] while I have to go to Moscow on the 23rd. I should so much like to hear something from you. Please write. I kiss you warmly.

D. Shostakovich

6 December 1942 Kuybïshev

Dear Isaak Davïdovich,

I found your letter when I returned from Moscow. I was very glad to get it, but upset at what it contained. I am distressed that my opus in the *Uchitelskaya Gazeta* [*Education Gazette*] so upset your Director.[107] I cannot think how mention of the performance in Tashkent of my symphony got left out.[108] It was probably an editorial mistake, but it might have been mine. Whatever the facts, I very much regret what happened.

I went to Moscow to take part in an anti-Fascist rally of workers in the arts.[109] Now I am back in Kuybïshev. Mama has gone to Samarkand. All of us are well, except for the children who get the odd sniffle. Life goes on as usual. We eat in the restaurant, but – and this is the biggest development in our daily life – it has moved to a new location. This is a great improvement, because the restaurant is now much nearer than where it used to be in the National Hotel.[110]

I hope you and yours are all in good health.

I kiss you warmly,

D. Shostakovich

PS That great musician and my dear friend, Boleslav Yavorsky, has died.[111]

23 December 1942

Dear Isaak Davïdovich,

Your latest letters made such sad reading I'm in complete despair.[112]

I don't know how it could have happened that you and N. N. Kostromitin missed meeting my mother,[113] as she left on schedule and arrived in Samarkand on 2 December. It is true that I was not there when she left, because I was still in Moscow. You were absolutely right, your songs have not dated, they are as topical as ever.[114] It is much to be regretted that you pay so little heed to this side of your multifarious talents. You have the instincts of a true folk-song writer, and I believe your place would be, if not the first, certainly not the last in the glorious Pléiade of Dunayevsky,[115] Pokrass, Kruchinin, Kheif, Zinovy Dunayevsky, Kats and many others.[116]

All is well with us, everyone is fit and well.[117] A week ago I left Kuybïshev for a concert tour to Ufa and Belebey; it was quite a quite a hard trip. I got very tired, and on top of everything else caught a cold. I gave two concerts in Ufa, collaborating with Comrades Zhuk, Veltman, Gurvich and Buravsky who all work in the Bolshoy Theatre and have formed a good string quartet. In Belebey there is a wind orchestra which had learned the first movement of my Seventh Symphony[118] and they played it through for me. That's about all my news for now. I kiss you warmly and press your hand. Think of me. My greetings to all your people.

D. Shostakovich

Write to me in Kuybïshev. If I am away, it won't be for long. D.S.

1 March 1943 Kuybïshev

Dear Isaak Davïdovich,

Thank you for your telegram, in which you tell me that you had received my songs and thank me for the dedication,[119] but there's nothing to thank me for; I love you dearly and that is the reason for the dedication. I miss you very much. Like the sun, you are not entirely free from spots, but you have far fewer than I do, and many other people too.

Anyhow, enough of this lyrical effusion; in my view letters ought to be businesslike.[120] Briefly about matters in hand then. My health is better, although I get very tired from walking.[121] The Cultural Affairs Committee has treated me with great sensitivity[122] and has arranged for me to get a travel pass and a stay in a sanatorium near Moscow. I leave tomorrow. It would be nice if I were to find a line from you when get to Moscow after leaving the sanatorium. Please write to the following address: c/o V. Shebalin, Moscow Conservatoire, 13 Herzen Street, Moscow.[123] I plan to be in Moscow for quite some time.

Everybody in my family is well, and spends the whole time talking in a loud voice about things to eat. As a result of these conversations I have forgotten a large part of my vocabulary, but I have excellent retention of the following: bread, butter, half a kilo, vodka, two hundred grams, ration card, confectionery department, and several other words.[124] I cling fast to the belief that we shall soon be back in our own homes and able to visit one another.[125]

I am hard at work. As well as the songs which you know about, I have composed the first movement of a piano sonata.[126] I was making good progress with the opera *The Gamblers*, but am not advertising the fact[127] since I have already abandoned work on it.[128] Best respects to all your people. Ivan Ivanovich's[129] wife and elder son are ill with pneumonia, and the younger one has mumps. He is having a bad time of it. I kiss you warmly.

D. Shostakovich

28 March 1943 Arkhangelskoye Sanatorium

Dear Isaak Davïdovich,

I've been in this sanatorium nursing myself back to health for three weeks now; getting better and gathering strength. I miss you though. You were much in my thoughts as I was reading Comrade Yegolin's[130] article in *Pravda* of 27 March about Maksim Gorky. I have vivid memories of my plan to set Gorky's *Death and the Maiden* to music, and of your wise counsel about the chorus with which it was planned to end the work. I trust that we shall soon be able to meet in our native city of Leningrad, when we shall return to the theme of *Death and the Maiden* and I shall be able to act on your advice.[131]

My future plans are as follows: I am going to stay in Moscow as a Professor at the Conservatoire. I start work there on 10 April. I don't yet have an apartment and nothing is organized in terms of living arrangements, so I am not exactly thrilled at this change in my circumstances.[132] But still less am I attracted by the thought of going back to Kuybïshev. Nina has already arrived in Moscow and is busying herself with all manner of things. And here I am in the Arkhangelskoye. Well, that's all for now. I'm off to the cinema to see *The Circus*.

I kiss you warmly. Greetings to all your family.

D. Shostakovich

Write to this address: The Conservatoire, 13 Herzen Street, Moscow, for my attention.

The Arkhangelskoye sanatorium was located in Krasnogorsk, near Moscow, and Shostakovich gave this as the return address on his postcard.

17 April 1943 Moscow

Dear Isaak Davïdovich,

First of all, please forgive me for not writing for such a long time. Tatyana Ivanovna's death[133] caused me such grief that I could not bring myself to write.[134] It is terribly sad. I can but wish you all the strength and courage you will need to endure this grievous loss.

Secondly, forgive me for not sending the money straight away.[135] I did not have it at the time, and when I did manage to get hold of a little, a long time had elapsed.

As soon as I get the apartment fixed up (I have already got all the paperwork for it) I hope you will come to me in Moscow. If all goes well, within about two or three weeks it will be more or less habitable and then I should be so happy if you could come to stay with us. I shall try to get a posting for you, and persuade Comrade Serebryakov to give you leave for a spell so that you can come to Moscow.[136]

I am so very sorry that this tragedy has befallen you. Bear up, be strong, do not weaken. Nina sends her greetings and sympathy.

I kiss you warmly. My greetings to your mother.

D. Shostakovich

21 April 1943 Moscow

Dear Isaak Davïdovich,

Emil Gilels[137] came to see me today, and brought me your sad letter.

My dear friend, be strong and bear your heavy loss with courage. I know that sooner or later time will ease your pain, and you will take up the threads of your life again. I have a plan to organize a visit to Moscow for you, hoping that perhaps it might help a little to take your mind off your troubles. About five days ago I sent you some money, and I hope to be able to send more in a little while.[138]

I am in the midst of moving into the new apartment. Please make a note of the address: Apartment 48, 21 Kirov Street, Central Moscow. There is no telephone as yet, nor anything else come to that: just bare walls.[139] Nevertheless, I am determined to stay on in Moscow, and hope that before long I shall be able to offer you hospitality. Yevgeny Boltin telephoned me today. I am glad he has come here; he is an attractive person and good company.[140] It would be so good if you could contrive to tear yourself away from Tashkent and come to Moscow. If the idea appeals to you, let's make a start on attacking the problem.[141] I am having quite a difficult time myself, but my problems are trivial compared to yours. I recently composed a piano sonata, which I dedicated to the memory of Leonid Nikolayev.

I kiss you warmly. Nina sends her greetings. My best respects to your mother.

Your D. Shostakovich

[19]

Please write to me at the Conservatoire.

10 May 1943 Moscow

Dear Isaak Davïdovich,

I am sad not to have news of you.[142] Please get on and write. We were invited to the Boltins' recently, and talked of you.[143] I have moved to Moscow, and my address is Apartment 48, 21 Kirov Street, Central Moscow, telephone K 5–98–72. The family is still in Kuybïshev, but I shall soon get them up here. Life is more interesting here than in Kuybïshev: there is the world of music to think about and take one beyond the sheer business of getting enough to eat.[144]

I am meeting lots of people, among whom I would single out a high-up cleric from the Ukraine, Metropolitan Nikolai of Kiev and Galicia.[145] And Boris Klyuzner[146] arrived in Moscow recently – do you remember him? He had been based near Sverdlovsk for some time. Some other mutual friends now in Moscow include Valerian Bogdanov-Berezovsky, Aleksandr Kamensky[147] and his wife, Nikolai Timofeyev,[148] Valery Zhelobinsky,[149] and there are many others. All send their greetings to you.

I am anxious to see you and acquaint you with the piano sonata I composed recently.[150] I very much want to organize a visit to Moscow for you. I think you might enjoy it, and it might help to dispel your depression.[151]

Please give my greetings to Nonya Perelman.[152] My spirits are a bit subdued at the moment. I long to see you. Be sure and write to me. It is Maksim's birthday today; he is five years old. Guests are arriving for the party, and I must close.

D. Shostakovich

26 May 1943 Moscow

Dear Isaak Davïdovich,

At long last, after a long hiatus, I've had a letter from you. I was very sad, and also a little hurt, when I read it.[153] You are of course quite right to draw attention to my distaste for any kind of fuss and bother. Thinking back to the time you were with us in Kuybïshev,[154] I am afraid there may have been some reason to make you feel that way. If that is the case, it would nevertheless only have been from an external point of view. Inside it is not like that at all, and I hope that the moment I manage to get my life here into a more or less civilized state I can organize your visit to Moscow and show you how wrong you are.[155]

My family is still in Kuybïshev. Nina is there now, and will return on 5 or 6 June with Galina, Maksim and Pasha. The others will stay in Kuybïshev. My life continues to have many bothersome twists and turns. I cannot extricate myself from a whole lot of various activities – meetings, conferences and so on – which tire me out. Although I haven't yet managed to sort out a proper way of life, I am feeling quite buoyant. Please write to me at the apartment, because I have now fixed a letter box on the door, and so correspondence won't get lost. I kiss you warmly. Greetings to your Mama.

D. Shostakovich

8 October 1943 Moscow

Dear Isaak Davïdovich,

Regarding your coming to Moscow, there seems to be nothing doing for the time being. I have made many requests and entreaties, but it simply does not seem to be possible at present.[156] Ivan Sollertinsky left Moscow a few days ago; it was such a joy to see him while he was here.

You may already know that I have finished my Eighth Symphony.[157] It consists of five movements.[158] The first performance is scheduled for 3 November, to be conducted by Mravinsky.[159] I am very worried about it; I suppose I am always worried, for reasons we composers know only too well.[160] I passed on to Tatyana Maksimovna your greetings and your admiration for her realistic portrayal of a character in a realistic film.[161] I have fallen in love with the cinema, and have been to quite a few art films and documentaries, some of which I've seen more than once.

I kiss you warmly.

D. Shostakovich

8 December 1943 Moscow

Dear Isaak Davïdovich,

My dear friend, I have recently been having a lot of problems. Maksim has not been at all well for some time; he lost weight, became very pale and so thin that it was painful to look at the poor boy. I felt dreadfully sorry for him. Then I became ill myself. It lasted a week, and I only got out of bed today. Then yesterday Nina went down with a high temperature. There seems no end to the sickness 'in my house'.[162] My other relations are, however, all in excellent health.

I am very sad that you have not yet been able to hear my Eighth Symphony, but I was happy with the way it went. Mravinsky has done it here four times, and there will be a fifth performance on 10 December. There was supposed to have been a discussion of it at the Union of Soviet Composers, but it was postponed on account of my illness. However this discussion is going to take place soon. I am sure that it will give rise to valuable critical observations which will both inspire me to future creative work and provide insights enabling me to review that which I have created in the past. Rather than take a step backward I shall thus succeed in taking one forward.[163]

At the moment I am writing a trio for piano, violin and cello.[164] Please write to me. I miss hearing from you, although I miss you yourself even more. Forgive me for not writing more. My pen seems somehow to lack epistolary style.

With all my best wishes,

D. Shostakovich

While the triumphant progress of the Seventh Symphony was still reverberating around the whole world, Shostakovich was already at work on the Eighth. Despite being one of his greatest creations, it was not immediately understood and appreciated. While it was still in rehearsal, and again after its initial performances, some of Shostakovich's most entrenched critics began their *sotto voce* chorus of bewildered scepticism.

Some musicologists and critics so completely misunderstood the epic scale and tragic spirit of the symphony that they interpreted the sombre opening as signifying the triumph of darkness over light. Experts on the proper proportion of positive and negative elements in works of art voiced their dissatisfaction with the respective weights allotted in the new work to these elements, while the exceptionally complex and abstract idiom in which the symphony is cast similarly came in for muttered criticism. The net result was that the work could not be seen as a step forward from the Seventh Symphony. If not a step forward, then it must be a step back – or at least sideways, so the reasoning went.

Comments like these reached Shostakovich's ears, and he was hurt by them. The most rigorously self-critical of composers, no one knew better than he in which direction he was heading. Nevertheless, it was many years before the Eighth Symphony achieved its true recognition as a work of genius.

It is entirely typical that the first person to recognize and write about the unprecedented originality and greatness of the symphony was not a professional musician, but the writer Leonid Leonov. Three days after the Eighth Symphony's première, Leonov published an absorbing article entitled 'First Impressions', in which he described in masterly fashion his impressions on hearing it. A similar response to the Seventh Symphony had come from another writer, A. N. Tolstoy, who wrote a widely publicized account of a rehearsal he had attended.

31 December 1943 Moscow

My dear friend,

This is to send you greetings for a Happy New Year and to wish you health, happiness and success. Pavel Serebryakov brought me your greetings; thank you for not forgetting me. Now it is 4 o'clock in the afternoon of the last day of 1943. A blizzard is raging outside the windows as 1944 approaches. It will be a year of happiness, of joy, of victory, a year that will bring us all much joy.

The freedom-loving peoples will at last throw off the yoke of Hitlerism, peace will reign over the whole world, and we shall live once more in peace under the sun of Stalin's Constitution.[165] Of this I am convinced, and consequently experience feelings of unalloyed joy. At present you and I are far away from one another; if only I could be with you so that we might celebrate together the glorious victories of our Red Army under the supreme generalship of Comrade Stalin.

Meanwhile, however, I embrace you. May we meet soon. Please write.

D. Shostakovich

3 January 1944 Moscow

Dear Isaak Davïdovich,

Your last postcard upset me deeply: I see that I have offended you, and with your characteristic clarity and precision you have set out the cause. It is true that I have not written much lately, because I have not been well and I have also had many other troubles. And I did not want to cry on your shoulder. But now all these afflictions are in the past, and I feel able to take up my pen once more.

Not long ago I sent you New Year greetings; I hope you received them. At present I am in good health and I am composing a Trio for piano, violin and cello. I am also completing the opera *Rothschild's Violin* by Fleishman,[166] my former student at the Leningrad Conservatoire.

I received a letter from Tamara Bryanskaya in Alma-Ata recently.[167] She informed me that Yury Bryansky – I am sure you knew him well – had died heroically in the fight for our Soviet Motherland.[168] It is sad and painful to think that this young life has been cut short. But he carried out his duty honourably, and we shall ever revere his memory. Don't be angry with me, my dear friend, for my silence. I kiss you warmly. Give my warmest greetings to your mother.

    D. Shostakovich

Please write to me and stay in touch. I hope we shall soon see one another.

13 February 1944 Moscow

Dear Isaak Davïdovich,

    I must share with you bitter and most heartfelt condolences on the death of our closest and most beloved friend Ivan Ivanovich Sollertinsky.[169] He died on 11 February 1944. We shall not see him again. I have no words with which to express the pain that racks my entire being. May his memorial be our abiding love for him, and our faith in the inspired talent and phenomenal love for the art of music to which he devoted his match-less life. Ivan Ivanovich is no more. It is very hard to bear. My dear friend, do not forget me, and write to me. This I ask you to do: beg, borrow or steal from wherever you can some vodka, so that at precisely 7 o'clock in the evening Moscow time on 11 March you, in Tashkent and I in Moscow may together raise a glass to mark one month since Ivan Ivanovich's passing.[170]

    D. Shostakovich

19 April 1944 Moscow

Dear Isaak Davïdovich,

    If it is not too much trouble, please give the enclosed document to Nikolai Rabinovich,[171] along with my greetings. He asked me to give it to Pavel Serebryakov, but I could not do this because I did not manage to get hold of him before he left for Leningrad. To avoid any further delay, I thought it would be better if I sent it to you so that you can give it back to Rabinovich.

    Regarding Gavriil Davïdovich, I spoke to Grabar.[172] He could not offer any direct reassurance, but he did promise to come back with an answer soon. For the time being I can't track Grabar down in Moscow; he has gone away but as soon as he returns I will ask him again.

[24]

Ten days ago I came down with flu; it has left me with an infected spot on my left lung and now I have a terrible cough. Every now and again they give me an X-ray and tell me the little spot is still there. This little spot has prevented me from leaving my own little domestic spot (forgive the pun),[173] so I'm at home bored and coughing. The doctor came today and told me it will soon clear up. A nurse comes every other day to apply cupping glasses. This is the sum total of my life at present. In addition I am exceedingly short of money and see little prospect of getting any, at least by honest means.

I can't work, and am not composing anything. This is upsetting me greatly and I feel as though I shall never be able to compose another note.[174] I may come to Tashkent at the end of May for the Congress of the Uzbek Union of Soviet Composers. I saw my dear teacher Maksimilian Shteynberg in Moscow, and heard his symphony, which had such a success in Tashkent.[175] If I do manage to get there you can imagine how glad I shall be to see you.[176]

Well, that's all my news. I find I have no words to tell you my impressions of the festival of Soviet musical culture that took place yesterday, including the first performance of Shaporin's patriotic folk-oratorio *The Story of the Fight for Russia*. Illness most unfortunately compelled me to go home, so I was prevented from hearing and appreciating what I am sure must be an outstanding work.

I kiss you warmly.

D. Shostakovich

2 June 1944 Moscow

Dear Isaak Davïdovich,

I haven't written for some time because I have not been well again, and neither have Nina and the children. It has all been rather depressing. But now I am much more cheerful, and your brother Gavriil's visit made a great contribution to this upturn in my spirits.[177] I was delighted to see him. First of all, he is very like you. Secondly, it was a great joy to see such an impressive, well-turned-out officer full of the joys of life and imbued with positive belief in the splendid future of our country and our people. Among many other things we talked a great deal about you and about Grabar, who unfortunately has not been able to help over getting Gavriil released to go back to the Academy. When your brother left I felt for a long time a warm glow of pride and satisfaction that our own Red Army can produce such fine officer material.[178]

Gavriil has now left Moscow, ablaze with the excitement of a visit to the capital where he will be able to converse with Manizer[179] and other celebrated figures of Soviet art. Gavriil told me before he left that he had matured greatly as an artist: in his leisure moments from military duties he sculpts soldiers and officers and takes pleasure in having completed a quantity of busts. My dear friend, I kiss you warmly.

Your

D. Shostakovich

I shall not now be coming to Tashkent.

23 July 1944 Moscow

Dear Isaak Davïdovich,

At last a letter from you; I had become very worried at the lack of news. I hope this postcard will get to Tashkent in time to catch you.[180] In any case, there will soon be no more need for us to rely on these postcards as a means of communication, since we shall both be residing in our wonderful city of Leningrad,[181] symbol of the might of the Soviet system and of Stalin's strategic genius.

Tomorrow I come to the end of a stint of State examinations. I am chairman of the State Examination Board for Pianoforte at the Moscow Conservatoire, and tomorrow the candidates sit their test on Foundations of Marxism–Leninism, source of all scientific knowledge. Tomorrow evening I am going away to spend five or six days in Ivanovo; the family is already there. After that I come back to Moscow.

Although I feel physically dreadful – I seem to have some sort of stomach upset – my psychological state has never been better. And how could it be otherwise, when we are surrounded by the crash of victory salutes, and the scent of victory permeates every fibre of one's being?

D. Shostakovich

2 January 1945 Moscow

Dear Isaak Davïdovich,

I send you my greetings and best wishes for a Happy New Year with all health, success and happiness.

I wish with all my heart that you were with me just now. On 30 December my son Maksim fell ill with pneumonia. He is getting better now, but I was terribly worried about him and became ill myself with a gastric upset from which I am still suffering. That was not much fun. Clearly old age and sickness are creeping up on me.[182] All the same we did celebrate the New Year, at home in the apartment. By that time it was too awkward to cancel it; because we had all clubbed together and pooled our resources. It was 'jolly', and extremely noisy. The worst time of all came after 3 a.m.; some guests, whom I did not know and in whom I was not much interested, live a long way away and decided to wait until the first tramcar, which was not until 6 o'clock in the morning (!)[183]

I pray that during 1945 we shall plant the flag of victory in Berlin. My plans for the coming year are not clear. I am not composing at all at the moment,[184] because the circumstances in which I am living are too awful. From six in the morning until six in the evening I am deprived of two essentials: water and light. It is particularly difficult between 3 o'clock and 6 o'clock in the afternoon, because it is already dark by then, the kerosene lamps hardly give any light, and my eyesight is not good enough for me to write by them. The lack of light brings on a state of nervous exhaustion, but there seems little hope of any improvement. I say this because I recently put my name to a petition to the local branch of the Industry Ministry humbly requesting that laureates of the Stalin Prize, People's Artists, Honoured Artists, etc. – in a word the country's leading com-posers – should receive an issue of kerosene, lamps, primus stoves etc., on the grounds that interruption in the supply of electrical energy might be deemed to have a deleterious effect on their creative productivity. This letter was crowned with brilliant success, because on 31 December I received coupons entitling me to six litres of kerosene. I have a car but can't use it; there is no petrol for it. I don't have a driver either, because I can't afford to pay one. So the car just sits in the Musical Fund's filthy garage, and good luck to it.

Life is not much fun, generally speaking. The lights come on at 6 o'clock, although by the time that joyful moment comes around my nerves are strung up to such a pitch that I am absolutely incapable of pulling myself together.[185] I go to bed about midnight, but I sleep badly and wake up while it is still dark. I get up and wash, then I read Blok. I find him a great, and wise, poet, and some of his poems move me to the core of my being.[186]

If you have time and inclination, please write to me. I recently heard that Aron Ostrovsky[187] has given up the position of Vice-Rector at his own request, and that doughty old boy Aleksandr Ossovsky now occupies his chair.[188] What is Ostrovsky doing now? Write and tell me, please. My greetings to your mother and your niece.[189] I kiss you warmly.

D. Shostakovich

I am sending this to the Conservatoire as I have forgotten the number of your apartment. Do send it to me, please.

17 February 1945 Moscow

Dear Isaak Davïdovich,

Thank you for the money and the postcard. It was excessively scrupulous of you to worry about returning the money so quickly.[190] Comrade Soluyanov telephoned me yesterday. He has passed on our request to Marshal Voronov,[191] who in turn passed it to his aide with a note of approval. Soluyanov is in touch with the aide and hopes that the matter will soon be resolved.[192] The Marshal, via Comrade Soluyanov, asked me to compose a 'Battle Song of the Soviet Artillery'. It would be good if you could provide me with a text for this song. I know you are not professionally speaking a poet, but I always remember your 'Railway Travel Song'. It would be wonderful if you could do something similar, but relevant to gunners.[193] I may be coming to Leningrad soon, in which case we can work together on the 'Battle Song of the Soviet Artillery'.[194] Give my greetings to your mother and your niece. I send you my very best wishes.

D. Shostakovich

II
Zhdanovshchina and After
1946–1953

Shostakovich passing a portrait of Stalin, late 1940s

August 1946 saw a vicious press attack on Mikhail Zoshchenko, one of Shostako-
vich's literary heroes. It was an early warning sign of Andrey Zhdanov's campaign
to confine the Soviet artistic intelligentsia within a straitjacket of strict ideological
orthodoxy. Zhdanov's influence gradually spread into every corner of intellectual
and artistic life, until on 10 February 1948 the notorious 'Historic Decree' of the
Party Central Committee branded Shostakovich, Prokofiev, Khachaturian, Sheba-
lin, Myaskovsky and Popov as Formalists and Cosmopolitans. Many of their great-
est works were banned. From a position of celebrity, public honour and high
official standing – Deputy to the Supreme Soviet and People's Artist of the Russian
Federation, Order of Lenin, Chairman of the Leningrad Composers' Union, Pro-
fessor at both Moscow and Leningrad Conservatoires – Shostakovich was trans-
formed overnight into a virtual enemy of the people. Against a background of
increasing terror and persecution, particularly of the Jews, Shostakovich con-
formed in public, producing works like Song of the Forests *and* The Sun Shines
Over the Motherland *which would be acceptable to officialdom. Privately he con-*
tinued with compositions of deeper significance like the First Violin Concerto and
From Jewish Folk Poetry, *which would lie unperformed in the drawer until much*
later. Prokofiev and Stalin died on the same day, 5 March 1953, and after a period
of uncertainty a new era could begin.

12 January 1946 Moscow

Dear Isaak Davïdovich,

Belated best wishes for the New Year. May 1946 be an even happier one
for us than 1945. I am sorry that you are not feeling well. I hope it is not
the onset of something serious but simply some temporary hiccup in your
mighty organism. As you surmise, I am in excellent form, healthy in body
and soul.[1] I met Yury Sviridov a couple of times when he was in Moscow; I
like both him and his new quartet very much.[2] I am working hard, but not
composing anything.[3] With luck this is but a temporary hiccup in my own
modest and insignificant talents. Modesty adorns the man. With fervent
greetings,[4]

D. Shostakovich

[31]

My respects to your mother, Lina, and Gavriil. Give Gavriil my best wishes for his speedy recovery.

11 February 1946 Moscow

Dear Isaak Davïdovich,

Please don't be angry with me. I am distressed that my letter upset you, as this was far from my intention. I love and esteem you very much indeed, and am deeply grateful for the friendship you show me. It helps me to live. But my character is hateful and bad, and my friends just have to understand and forgive this.[5]

Well, that is just about all I wanted to say. In general all's well with my world and I am in a fabulous mood.[6] I trust the same applies to you. I have recently been reading the *Imperial Theatres Yearbook* for 1894/95, from a somewhat one-sided perspective – I just read the obituaries of deceased artists and officials of the Imperial Theatres. What is so striking is the precision and plainness of the language with which these brief accounts encapsulate the life and death of the seventh Mr Ivanov or the eighth Mrs Ivanova. Ten lines, and the whole of a life there in the palm of your hand. Amazing.[7]

D. Shostakovich

24 September 1946 Moscow

Dear Isaak Davïdovich,

In the interests of practicality, I am knocking out this card on the typewriter. How are you? I am all right, and in good health. Tomorrow is my fortieth birthday, and in ten years' time I shall be fifty.[8]

I await with interest the plenum of the Executive Committee of the Union of Soviet Composers, which is due to begin on 30 September. Aram Khachaturian[9] has gone off to Ivanovo, where he is preparing his address. Aleksey Ogolevets is also actively preparing for the plenum. I expect you have already read his sharply polemical article in *Sovetskoye Isskustvo* [*Soviet Art*].[10] My best respects to all your family.

Please don't forget to write, and stay in touch.

Your

D. Shostakovich

12 October 1946 Moscow

Dear Isaak Davïdovich,

Since I began to use a typewriter, I have become enamoured of typing. As you see, I not only type official documents, but also letters to friends. I received your letter, thank you.

I'm not feeling very well at the moment; I have had a tedious and lingering flu. My head aches, as do my legs and my back. I have a cough and a head cold, and it just won't go away. I lie in bed and receive a succession of visitors. They are all very busy people, and in any case I find it hard to entertain visitors with my conversation.

The plenum of the Executive Committee of the Composers' Union has come and gone. I did not attend the closing sessions because I was not well enough, but the early ones were interesting.[11] Nina is still away in Armenia, where she is taking part in a scientific expedition. I expect her back on the 20th.

I observe that illness and certain kinds of experiences are becoming harder to deal with: the years are passing. Write to me. Give my greetings to all your people, and also Aglaya[12] and Yury Sviridov.

Your

D. Shostakovich

20 January 1947 Moscow

Dear Isaak Davïdovich,

Thank you for your letter. As always, I read it with joy and delight. If the doctors will permit it, I shall come soon to Leningrad, and then I shall see you. I am actually better now, although still rather weak.[13] I read the piece on *The Duenna* in *Sovetskoye Isskustvo* and was very upset to see no mention of Solomyak. I looked up the original but I didn't find him mentioned there either. I was distressed by this and have a bad conscience about this gifted artist.[14]

We have moved to a new apartment, Apartment 87, 37–45 Mozhaiskoye Shosse. In a way this is good news, but on the other hand it has meant a lot of disagreeable fuss and bother of one kind and another. My greetings to your family.

Your

D. Shostakovich

12 December 1948 Moscow

Dear Isaak Davïdovich,

Many thanks for your letter. I feel that you are right about some things, but you exaggerate somewhat the virtues of the work in question.[15]

I have been very tired of late. Drawing on my last reserves of strength, I have been making a tremendous effort to get to grips with the score for the film *Meeting on the Elbe*. I don't see the end in sight yet.[16] I shan't manage to get to Leningrad this month. I am also feeling rather poorly physically, and that doesn't help the creative process. I suffer a lot from headaches and feel sick all the time; to put it crudely I keep wanting to throw up.

I must say, it is not at all pleasant. When I look in the shaving mirror and see my face, it is swollen, there are huge bags under the eyes, and the cheeks are purple and puffy. I seem to have got much older in the last week, or maybe a bit longer than that, and the ageing process is accelerating at an unheard-of rate.[17] Unfortunately the ageing of the body seems to be matched by the decay of the mind. But perhaps it's all just the consequence of over-exhaustion. After all, I did write a lot of film music last year.[18] It got me something to live on, but it has utterly worn me out.

Be well, my dear friend. I press your hand.

D. Shostakovich

I have just received some sad news – Ilya Trauberg[19] has died. He was a man of many excellent qualities, and the rare courage he displayed something you and I always admired. He died of a heart attack, with no warning signs whatsoever, never having had a day's illness. He was born in 1906, the same year as I was.

D. S.

24 January 1949 Moscow

Dear Isaak Davïdovich,

Thank you for your greetings, which Matvey Blanter brought to me. I have been meaning to write to you for ages,[20] but the pen kept slipping from my grasp. Besides, this, I keep planning to come to Leningrad, but have not managed to do so yet. I may come in the first few days of February. I have been working extremely hard, and am feeling rather tired. I miss you and other friends very much. Maksim is constantly unwell, which is very upsetting for us. I press your hand warmly.

D. Shostakovich

Please give my greetings to your family, and to Yury Sviridov.

25 February 1949 Moscow

Dear Isaak Davïdovich,

It is a long time since I heard from you, and I miss your news. I have a great favour to ask of you. Could you please telephone my mother and find out how she is? Or better still, go to see her. I have a presentiment that she is seriously ill but in her desire to spare me anxiety, is keeping it from me.[21] I have telephoned several times to ask her and Marusya[22] if I should come, but I am always told no. So please, if you can, go to see Mama and write and tell me how you think she really is. If necessary, I shall come at once.

I warmly press your hand.

D. Shostakovich

29 April 1949 Moscow

Dear Isaak Davïdovich,

Your letter was most upsetting. I hope you will soon be better and that things will go well for you. All is well with me. I hope to be going to Barvikha[23] early in May.

I press your hand warmly.

D. Shostakovich

Give my greetings to your family. D.S.

Between this letter and the preceding one, dated 25 February, an event of no small importance had taken place in Shostakovich's life. I learned of it from him not in a letter but in person. In March 1949 he had been summoned to join a delegation of Soviet scientists and cultural figures travelling to the United States, an invitation that was not merely a total surprise, but a most unwelcome one.

He had recently been the victim of several vicious and merciless attacks: in the Communist Party Central Committee Resolution of 10 February 1948, in the press, and at the first All-Union Congress of Composers in April the same year. His public humiliation had received wide currency internationally, and Shostakovich was afraid that he would inevitably be subjected to an unceremonious onslaught by sensation-seeking American journalists and by ignorant critics who would be neither tactful enough nor knowledgeable enough to appreciate the delicate position of an artist precluded from speaking the truth.

At the beginning of March, shortly before leaving for the United States, Shosta-kovich came to Leningrad in a state of high anxiety and confusion. He told me of his fears, which events proved to have been fully justified. He also made me party to the insistent representations he had received from extremely highly placed individuals that, come what may, he absolutely must join the delegation. And so he departed, resigning himself to the caprices of fate.

After his return from America, Shostakovich came again to Leningrad and recounted in detail his experiences in that hitherto unknown country. He had found much there that was interesting, and much that was good, but also much that was not at all to his taste. He had enjoyed New York not only for its overwhelming scale, but also for the way the ultra-modern was paradoxically juxtaposed with an old-fashioned, attractively patriarchal quality. In this way, in the spring of 1949, Shostakovich came to see with his own clear-sighted eyes the so-called 'city of the Yellow Devil'.

10 June 1949 Moscow

Dear Isaak Davïdovich,

On the 19th I shall come to Leningrad, and go straight to Komarovo where I shall stay until 1 September and where, I hope, you will come to visit me. As soon as I get to Leningrad I shall telephone you. If I don't manage to catch you then, I shall telephone from Komarovo, or you could call me there. On the 20th I shall be in Leningrad, seeing Nina off on her way to Moscow.[24] Also, I should like to see the Zenith–Dynamo game. Perhaps we can recapture our youth and go to see it together?[25]

I am so glad you are feeling better and hope that you are fully recovered. Looking forward to seeing you soon,

I warmly press your hand,

D. Shostakovich

29 July 1949 Komarovo

Dear Isaak Davïdovich,

Thank you for your letter, which brought vividly to life your days on the sheep farm.[26] Yury Sviridov came to call on me today; we talked of you and missed not having you there with us.[27] He brought me a letter from Lyova Atovmyan in Moscow, with terribly distressing news. I shall probably go to Moscow in the next few days, as simply to have a friend around offering support might be some help to him in his present great difficulties.[28]

Alas, what a gloomy letter, please forgive me. I miss you very much, and I hope we shall all see you before long. I am now composing an oratorio about forests, to words by the talented poet Dolmatovsky.[29] I will find out from Trauberg[30] how he managed to cure himself and let you know.

Your

D. Shostakovich

25 September 1949 Sochi

Dear Isaak Davïdovich,

Thank you for your telegram.[31]

I am leaving for Moscow on 30 September, and hope soon to be in Leningrad as well. I should very much like to see you. It has been good here; the weather has been wonderful, warm enough for me to go swimming. I shall have a party for my birthday this evening, but there will not be many guests.[32] I hope all is well with you.

I press your hand warmly.

D. Shostakovich

26 September 1949 Sochi

Dear Isaak Davïdovich,

I forgot to say, when I wrote yesterday, that I should be happy to get from you the same present as you gave me in the summer. If you feel like repeating it, I should be very grateful.

That's all.

D. Shostakovich

9 December 1949 Moscow

Dear Isaak Davïdovich,

I have been hearing rumours that Yury Sviridov is drinking too much. This is terribly bad for him. Please try all you can to persuade him not to do it. He is very fond of you, and you of him.

Do please do what you can to influence him. It would be very sad if he became ill again.[33] I expect to be coming to Leningrad in a week's time, and I hope to see you then.

I warmly press your hand.

D. Shostakovich

[37]

21 December 1949 Moscow

Dear Isaak Davïdovich,

Thank you for your letter. It was a long wait, but at last it came. What a pity it is that one of the greatest composers of the twentieth century, Yury Sviridov, prefers the champagne bottle to *The Marriage of Figaro*.[34] I am worried about him both now and for the future. It seems to me that if only he would think a bit more about immortality he would cherish his huge talent and not sacrifice it on the altar of Bacchus.

I am still ill, having been knocked sideways by angina and flu. I am over them now, but the aftermath is very unpleasant, and I am physically very weak. Excuse the coarsely naturalistic phraseology, but I sweat all the time. I have to change my shirt two or three times a day, and not only my shirt but other articles of male underwear which should not be mentioned in polite conversation, or in writing for that matter. The sweating is a result of the weakness and, I expect, the onset of old age. After all, I am forty-three.[35] Our home is one big sick-bed: Nina is not well and neither is Maksim. Clearly, health is the gift of God. My children lack for nothing: nourishing food, vitamins, medical attention and so on, but they always seem to be ill. Galya had flu recently, and now Maksim is sick. It is very upsetting. God in His wisdom evidently prefers to see V. V. and S. M. Varzar bursting with health and beauty, while G. D. and M. D. Shostakovich just have to put up with feeling rotten.[36]

During my bout of illness, or rather illnesses, I picked up the score of one of my compositions and read it through from beginning to end. I was astounded by its qualities, and thought that I should be proud and happy that I had created such a work. I could hardly believe that it was I who had written it.[37]

And so, my dear friend, until we soon meet again.

I press your hand warmly.

D. Shostakovich

2 February 1950 Moscow

Dear Isaak Davïdovich,

Thank you for your letter. Don't be angry with me that I write so few letters myself. I am not alone in my habit of writing letters only when something or other disagreeable has come up.[38] But there is nothing at all of that kind. Everything is so fine, so perfectly excellent, that I can find almost nothing to write about.[39] The absence of letters from you only reinforces the aforementioned conviction of mine (and not only of mine) that everything is all right with the world. I hope to come to Leningrad soon.

I warmly press your hand.

D. Shostakovich

20 February 1950 Moscow

Dear Isaak Davïdovich,

I hope you have not forgotten that you are planning to pay me a visit. At the end of February I shall be coming to Leningrad, and if nothing prevents you then we could go to Moscow together. Take three or four days out of your working life so that without undue damage to scholarship[40] you could be with me for those three or four days in Moscow. I dare say I shall come up with something to amuse you there. I miss you very much. I trust that my plan evokes a favourable response in your heart.[41]

D. Shostakovich

11 March 1950 Moscow

Dear Isaak Davïdovich,

Thank you for your letter, and for the high praise you accord my achievements in music and gastronomy.[42] I may be coming to Leningrad for two or three days on 16 March, however this is not certain. If you are not going to be in Leningrad at that time, please come to Moscow at the beginning of April.[43] This is because from 21 March until 1 April I shall be away on holiday with the children.

I press your hand warmly.

Your

D. Shostakovich

3 April 1950 Moscow

Dear Isaak Davïdovich,

I hope you reached home safely, that you found everything well there and that you are feeling fit and well,[44] because I have a favour to ask of you.

If you have time, please find out whether it would be possible to get hold of two football season tickets. I shall be living at Komarovo from June onwards, and so I want to get hold of two tickets. Please find out whether this can be done, and what the cost would be. Get good seats if possible.[45] I will send you the appropriate sum, and if it is not too much trouble, perhaps you would get the tickets.

I send you my best wishes.

Your

D. Shostakovich

6 April 1950 Moscow

Dear Isaak Davïdovich,

Thank you for your letter. I should be most grateful if you could arrange for Yury Sviridov and Leonid Trauberg to meet so that they can work out the question of the musical comedy between themselves.[46] Please ask Sviridov to get together with Trauberg and talk it over with him. It would be a great relief to me.[47]

Stay in touch. Write to me.

D. Shostakovich

27 April 1950 Moscow

Dear Isaak Davïdovich,

Thank you very much for going to all that trouble about the season tickets. I think I shall be coming to the dacha between 10 and 15 June. Therefore we should arrange the season tickets from the second half of June. If necessary we can manage without season tickets at all.[48] I sent you the sum you asked for today by post, in the interests of economy; I hope it won't take too long to reach you. I very much want to come to Leningrad, but can't find a pretext at the moment. Give my greetings to Yury Sviridov. I am still in thrall to his marvellous composition.[49]

I press your hand warmly.

D. Shostakovich

9 October 1950 Moscow

Dear Isaak Davïdovich,

Thank you for your letter. I have been meaning to come to Leningrad for some days now to thank you personally,[50] but we have had some problems here. A short while ago Galya was suspected of having developed diphtheria, and now my liver is playing up. I have to stay in bed and fast for three days. But I have confidence in my mighty organism, and hope to get to Leningrad before long.

Your

D. Shostakovich

31 October 1950 Moscow

Dear Isaak Davïdovich,

I had a conversation today with Aleksandr Anisimov.[51] We spoke of Isai Sherman, and Anisimov told me that he had 'given instructions to the personnel department immediately to organize work for I. E. Sherman'.[52] These were his exact words. He told me he considered it essential that proper arrangements be made for I. E., so I hope that he will keep his word and that Sherman's life will be better as a result. I am trying to treat my stomach problems, and am on a diet. I have forgotten what alcohol is, but sometimes I think I should very much like to remember.

I am composing preludes and fugues for piano, and have already written five preludes and five fugues.[53] And so life goes on. I press your hand warmly.

Your

D. Shostakovich

25 December 1950 Moscow

Dear Isaak Davïdovich,

I have not heard from you for a long time. If you have time, please write to me at this address: Composers' House, Staraya Ruza, Moscow District, for my attention. I shall be here until 14 January. It is a very good place to be; I go for long walks and I am composing a lot.[54] I send you my best wishes for the coming New Year.

I press your hand warmly.

D. Shostakovich

17 March 1951 Moscow

Dear Isaak Davïdovich,

Thank you for your letter. Maksim is in hospital, and today he had his tonsils out. The doctors believe that this will have a beneficial effect on his heart. I am so sorry for the poor boy, but of course I am hoping that it will make him better. I hope to be in Leningrad soon.

I press your hand warmly.

D. Shostakovich

5 April 1951 Moscow

Dear Isaak Davïdovich,

Warmest congratulations on your marriage. May God give you a good and happy life. Nina joins my felicitations and sends her best wishes. Please also congratulate Vera Vasiliyevna and tell her I approve her choice.[55]

Maksim was discharged from the hospital a few days ago; he is now at Ruza, which Nina and I have just left. He does feel better, although he gets very tired from any kind of activity. He is supposed to be going back to school from 15 April, which I am nervous about since they make them do such a lot of work there. Somehow he must avoid straining his little heart.

My musical affairs are as follows. On 25 February I finished my 24 Preludes and Fugues. On the whole I am happy with this opus. The main thing is, I am glad I had the strength to complete it.[56] I have also composed ten *a cappella* choral settings. Of these, one is to words by Leonid Radin, two by Yevgeny Tarasov, one by an anonymous writer, three by Aleksei Gmïrev, two by Arkady Kots and one by Vladimir Tan-Bogoraz.[57] I'll tell you my thoughts on these poets when we meet and I hope I can play through this opus to you.[58]

On 31 March I played twelve of the Preludes and Fugues to a big gathering at the Composers' Union, and tomorrow, 5 April,[59] I shall perform the remaining twelve. I played through the choral settings there a little while earlier, and they were warmly received by the musical fraternity. How they will take to the Preludes and Fugues I shall presumably discover tomorrow, as there was no discussion after the first twelve.[60]

From 7 to 13 April I shall be away on tour playing in Minsk, Vilnius and Riga.[61] On 13 April there is a session of the Supreme Soviet of the Russian Federation.[62] Then from 20 to 23 April I shall be in Leningrad, and shall hope to see you and make the acquaintance of Vera Vasiliyevna.

I press your hand warmly.
D. Shostakovich

4 July 1951 Moscow

Dear Isaak Davïdovich,

I have been delayed a little in Moscow for the following reason: I have to have an operation to remove my tonsils. I only came into hospital two days ago. The doctors think that taking out my tonsils will stop me getting angina and colds, and my life will become even better than before. I am not frightened by the following tonsils story which goes like this:

A   Have you heard, N. has had his tonsils removed!
B   Oh, poor chap! And he so wanted to have children.[63]

Having already produced two children, I don't in fact find the prospect of not having any more particularly alarming.[64] So, all will be well. The only disagreeable thing is that I have been told that for two or three days I shall have an excruciatingly sore throat. If you cough your eyes pop out of their sockets with the pain, and sometimes you can faint. God grant that I shall be able to bear it. There has been a bit of delay, because the availability of a bed for me in the hospital kept being put off from day to day.

Warm congratulations to you and Vera Vasiliyevna on moving house.[65] I long to be with you to celebrate belatedly this important happening.[66]

Please don't mention my pre-operation fears to anybody. I do not want my mother to be alarmed. I shall stay in hospital for about ten days after the operation, and then go to Komarovo. I shall be in Moscow until the 20th. Please write to me; if I am still in hospital they will forward it to me. And then after the 20th I shall be in Komarovo.[67] Here is the full address: 24 Bolshoy Prospect, Komarovo Resort, Leningrad. I hope this letter reaches you in Leningrad.

I press your hand warmly. My greetings to Vera Vasiliyevna.
D. Shostakovich

Just now I am in a state of terror at the forthcoming operation (which is shameful, because I know it is minor) and I am supremely bored.[68] After all, here I am in perfect health, lying in hospital. D. S.

21 July 1951 Moscow

Dear Isaak Davïdovich,

I leave for Komarovo today. I'm feeling fine; my throat is still a little sore, but it will soon heal completely. I should be so glad to get a letter from you telling me how you are getting on.[69]

Please call in on the way back. Either Fenya or Pasha will be here, and they will have all instructions to look after you.[70] Lev Atovmyan will give you a form already filled out for tickets from Moscow to Leningrad.[71] His telephone number is K 4–41–55. My greetings to Vera Vasiliyevna.

D. Shostakovich

18 August 1951 Komarovo

Dear Isaak Davïdovich,

By my reckoning you should already be in Leningrad.[72] Please telephone me or let me know by some means or other how you are.

I should very much like to see you.[73]

Please give my greetings to Vera Vasiliyevna.

I press your hand warmly.

D. Shostakovich

24 September 1951 Moscow

Dear Isaak Davïdovich,

Thank you for your letter. I hope very much that life will soon get easier for Gavriil.[74] Everything is fine with me. Tomorrow is my 45th birthday, and we shall have a very modest celebration.[75] My heart is heavy. Give my greetings to Vera Vasiliyevna.

Your

D. Shostakovich

Svyeshnikov[76] is rehearsing my choral pieces. They are turning out not badly. The first performance will be on 10 October. On the 11th I am off on a concert tour to Baku, Yerevan and Tbilisi. I shall be back for the holidays.[77] I may get to Leningrad for a few days at the beginning of October.

D. S.

9 October 1951 Moscow

Dear Isaak Davïdovich,

Please convey my warmest thanks to Gavriil for his present. I like both the sculptures very much.[78] Tomorrow they are going to play, or rather sing, my poems for chorus – this is what I have called the work. It doesn't seem very convincing to me to call them choruses. One might just as well call orchestral pieces 'orchestras'.[79]

I am so sorry you are not well. Get better soon. My greetings to Vera Vasiliyevna.

D. Shostakovich

5 December 1951 Moscow

Dear Isaak Davïdovich,

I received both your letters. I will do whatever I can for Gavriil. It would be a good idea if one of his sculptor colleagues also raised the issue. I am most grateful to you for writing to Nina. She is feeling all right now, but terribly bored.

I warmly press your hand.

D. Shostakovich

Give my greetings to Vera Vasiliyevna.

16 September 1952 Moscow

Dear Isaak Davïdovich,

If you are able to, please come to Moscow on the 25th. Although I am not in the best of spirits, I have decided to celebrate my 46th birthday. If you can come, please bring two sigi[80] and two eels – smoked, of course.[81] Get them an hour or two before your departure. Send me a telegram telling me the date and number of your train, and I will meet you. I'm arranging dinner on the 25th at 7 o'clock.[82] I don't need to tell you how happy I shall be if you come. Give my greetings to Vera Vasiliyevna.

Your

D. Shostakovich

[45]

14 October 1952 Moscow

Dear Isaak Davïdovich,

Here are the summaries, which I am returning to you with my deepest gratitude.[83] Reading your digests has helped me enormously in my study of the Marxist–Leninist classics. Please let me know how you are. Things are going very well for me.[84] Nina is back at home for the present, but after the holidays she will be off again.[85] I may go with her this time, maybe I shall discover some new music in Baku, Yerevan and Tbilisi.[86] But perhaps I shan't go after all.[87] It all depends. Give my greetings to Vera Vasiliyevna and all your family.

Your

D. Shostakovich

16 October 1952 Moscow

Dear Isaak Davïdovich,

Yesterday I was summoned to the Union of Composers, where I was asked to go to Leningrad to listen to works by Leningrad composers, and I agreed to do so. I shall arrive on 26 October. Perhaps you will be able to fulfil my request then; that would be wonderful. I have sent your summaries back to you. They were extremely helpful. So, in the hope of soon seeing you, please give my warmest greetings to all your family.

Your

D. Shostakovich

11 April 1953 Moscow

Dear Isaak Davïdovich,

I am sending on to you a letter I have received from the Leningrad City Department of Health, as it concerns a matter that interests you.[88]

I very much miss seeing you. On 18 April I am going to Kislovodsk for a month.

Give my greetings to Vera Vasiliyevna.

Your

D. Shostakovich

Several letters which I received between the preceding letter and this one have been lost. In the intervening six months several distressing and tragic events had taken place, among them the arrest of the composer Moysey Vainberg. Vainberg was the son-in-law of the famous Jewish actor Solomon Mikhoels, who perished in 1948 and whose name was infamously blackened after his death.

Shostakovich loved and greatly respected Moysey Vainberg as an outstanding composer, and found his arrest deeply harrowing. Of course, such things could not be written about in a letter, but we discussed the event in private whenever Shostakovich was in Leningrad or I was in Moscow.

27 April 1953 Kislovodsk

Dear Isaak Davïdovich,

Warmest good wishes to you and Vera Vasiliyevna and all your family on the First of May.

I have been at Kislovodsk for eight days now, and it is very nice here. The sanatorium in which we are staying is a wonderful building, but in my view the service does leave room for improvement. Perhaps I am just being fussy, but it would be nice if they were a bit more polite to their holiday guests who have come here on holiday. I mean specifically 'more polite', because you could describe their attitude as 'polite', but not 'very polite'.[89]

Over the last few days I have been thinking about you and the orchestral musicians. I wouldn't like to be in . . .'s shoes – well, I think you can probably guess whose shoes I wouldn't like to be in.

We shall stay in Kislovodsk until 10 May. If you could write to me in time for me to get it here, it would give me great pleasure. Here is the address: Ordzhonikidze Sanatorium, Kislovodsk, for my attention. Send it airmail; it costs 1 rouble, and you should write 'Airmail' on the envelope.[90]

Moysey Vainberg returned home a few days ago, and sent me a telegram to let me know.[91]

What are your plans for the summer? How good it would be if you could come to Komarovo. Give our greetings to Vera Vasiliyevna and all your family.

I kiss you.

D. Shostakovich

6 May 1953 Kislovodsk

Dear Isaak Davïdovich,

I received your letter, thank you. I am delighted that you think of coming to Komarovo during the summer.[92]

I believe I have not brought you up to date with the state of my health.

The fact is that my stomach has effectively declined to carry out its appointed function of digesting the food that I eat. Particularly depressing is that there are a lot of delicious things (sigi, eels, garlic sausage, fish) I am now forbidden to eat.

Vodka, wine and brandy are all forbidden. All the same, I don't intend to give up drink.[93] It is true that if I do pour alcohol down my throat, I suffer pretty dreadfully from it. But the couple of hours immediately after the drink go a long way to make up for the ensuing suffering. Accordingly, when you come to Komarovo we shall have the occasional drink and something to eat, although in moderation.[94]

We leave Kislovodsk on 12 May. It is beautiful here, but I don't like sanatorium life. When the weather is clear we can see Elbrús, or as almost all the other guests here call it, *El*brus with the accent on the *El*. I suppose this is all of a piece with *port*folio, quar*ter* and *re*search fellow. I long to be in Leningrad, but I need an excuse. Best respects to all your family.

Until we meet,

D. Shostakovich

24 June 1953 Komarovo

Dear Isaak Davïdovich,

I am now at Komarovo. I should be so glad if you would telephone (the number is 35) or come up to see me.[95] In any case, please telephone my Mama if you are planning to come. She will know my movements and in particular when I am coming to Leningrad. Please give my greetings to Vera Vasiliyevna.

Looking forward to your reply.

D. Shostakovich

22 August 1953 Moscow

Dear Isaak Davïdovich,

I received your telegram yesterday. It simultaneously relieved and worried me. Evidently you did get the money, but only on the 21st although I telegraphed it on 18. I imagine the delay caused you considerable difficulties. Please forgive me, although it was not my fault.[96]

Everything is all right with me. I may come to Leningrad at the beginning of September.

I press your hand warmly.

D. Shostakovich

Contrary to his usual practice, Shostakovich did not stay at Komarovo until the end of August, but returned to Moscow in the middle of the month.

28 August 1953 Moscow

Dear Isaak Davïdovich,

I send you my warmest wishes for the start of a new academic year, and I hope that it will be even more full of joy for you than preceding ones. I am all right, but rather bored: all my family is away in Crimea until the 15th September and I am completely on my own.[97] I have been very busy with public affairs and articles for the press.[98] I'm not making much progress with the symphony. I did finish the second movement yesterday, but I'm not happy with it.[99]

I have a favour to ask of you: could you please find out where Galya Ustvolskaya is?[100] Did she come back to Leningrad, and is she in good health? I have many things to discuss with her, and I have sent her many letters and telegrams. Knowing what an efficient person she is, I am rather concerned at the lack of response. If it is not too much trouble, please find out where she is and if she is well. Give my greetings to Vera Vasiliyevna.

Your

D. Shostakovich

29 August 1953 Moscow

Dear Isaak Davïdovich,

Please forget my request. I have received a telegram and no longer have any cause for concern.

D. Shostakovich

III
Thaw
1954–1959

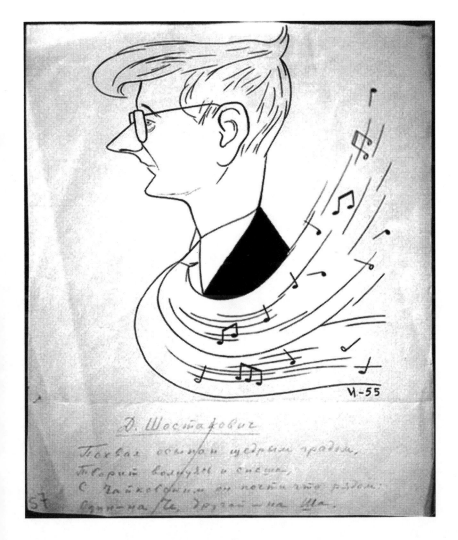

Cartoon of Shostakovich, 1955. The verse reads:

Showered with praise on all sides
He writes with white-hot inspiration;
Almost side by side with Tchaikovsky,
One starts with S, the other with T.

With Stalin dead and the unholy trio of Molotov, Malenkov and Beriya replaced by the (relatively) more moderate Khrushchov, the sense of the ice cracking was almost palpable; the title of Ilya Erenburg's 1954 novel The Thaw *symbolically encapsulated the new spirit of the times. Khrushchov's 'secret' but widely circulated revelations to the Twentieth Communist Party Congress in 1956 of the former dictator's crimes, and the progressive release from the prison camps of thousands of victims of Stalinist repression, seemed to offer artists the faint hope that a measure of freedom might soon be restored to them. The other side of the coin was still ominously present, in the shape of the Hungarian invasion, the suppression of Pasternak's* Doctor Zhivago *and its author's expulsion from the Writers' Union. Nevertheless, Shostakovich felt able to reveal to the world the Violin Concerto on which he had been at work when Zhdanov promulgated his infamous 1948 Decree and the song cycle* From Jewish Folk Poetry. *Moreover, he felt able to resume work on large-scale orchestral works which would not be pure hostages to patriotic orthodoxy: the Tenth (composed in the summer and autumn of 1953) and Eleventh Symphonies and the First Cello Concerto belong to this period, in tandem with additions to the private canon of string quartets. Even a revival of* Lady Macbeth *seemed to be not completely out of the question. In the composer's private life, the sudden death of his first wife Nina in 1954 caused, despite the complex nature of their relationship, a deep-seated grief exacerbated by the death of his mother a year later. None of the composer's friends, biographers or commentators seem able to explain his impulsive and short-lived second marriage which lasted from summer 1956 to summer 1959.*

4 January 1954 Moscow

Dear Isaak Davïdovich,

My best wishes to you and Vera Vasiliyevna for the New Year. I wish you the best in everything, and especially in health. Thank you for your letter. I read it many times; it both delighted and moved me.[1] As is well known, 'encouragement is as necessary to the artist as rosin to the virtuoso's bow' (K. Prutkov).[2] But your encouragement is too precious to me to be put into that category.[3]

I kiss you warmly.

D. Shostakovich

[53]

28 January 1954 Moscow

Dear Isaak Davïdovich,

I have been slow in replying to you. I was expecting to come to Leningrad and thus be able to answer your questions personally, but now my trip has been postponed for several days, so I decided to write to you. I am fine, and things are going well. I very much want to come to Leningrad and have a good talk with you. There have been several interesting and pleasing developments in my life.[4] They have left me in excellent spirits and full of energy, plans for future works, and so on. Please give my warmest greetings to Vera Vasiliyevna.

I kiss you warmly.

D. Shostakovich

7 April 1954 Moscow

Dear Isaak Davïdovich,

Thank you for the promised letter. I couldn't wait for it to arrive.

Everything is going well for me. There was a lively discussion and it turned out favourable to me.[5] However, things in other directions are not so rosy. The music section capitulated and deferred my symphony for another year, leaving in contention just the cantata *The Sun Shines Over Our Motherland* and the Twenty-four Preludes and Fugues.[6]

I may have to go away in two or three days' time. I will telephone you on my return.

I press your hand warmly. Give my greetings to Vera Vasiliyevna.

D. Shostakovich

25 June 1954 Komarovo

Dear Isaak Davïdovich,

I have arrived in Komarovo. I should so much like to see you. Do come, if you have time and inclination, but give me a ring first (telephone number 35). I plan to stay here all the time, although on 30 June I need to go into the city.

Give my greetings to Vera Vasiliyevna.

Awaiting your news.

D. Shostakovich

18 September 1954 Moscow

Dear Isaak Davïdovich![7]

I was kept in Moscow by some rather disagreeable and urgent matters. I shall be coming to Leningrad on 27 or 28 September.

If you are not too angry with me, please keep some time free for me. I really need to see you.

Give my greetings to Vera Vasiliyevna.

I press your hand warmly.

D. Shostakovich

After this letter, the end of the year 1954 was clouded by tragedy for Shostakovich. On 4 December, in the prime of her life, Nina Vasiliyevna, Shostakovich's wife and the mother of his children, died in Yerevan. After an emergency dash there by air, he found her still alive but in the last hours of her life.

The body was brought by air to Moscow for burial in the cemetery of the Novodevichy Monastery. I came to Moscow on 7 December to wait for Shostakovich, who travelled to Moscow by train (at Nina's request) from Yerevan with their daughter Galina. In the gloom of a December morning, a crowd of people stood waiting to greet them: relations, composers, musicians, physicist colleagues of Nina Vasiliyevna – I recall the distinguished scientist L. D. Landau among them.

In the grief-laden hours before the funeral, Shostakovich told me of Nina Vasiliyevna's last minutes, his haggard features twitching and the tears starting from his eyes. However, with an effort of will he brought his emotions under control and we abruptly turned to other, unimportant topics.

A long line of people wishing to pay their last respects filed through Shostakovich's study.[8] Lev Atovmyan had got hold of a tape recorder, and the music of the Eighth Symphony filled the room. I sat on the sofa next to Shostakovich, who wept silently.

After the interment at the snowbound Novodevichy graveyard, the Shostakoviches' housekeeper Fenya had prepared a wake, at which, besides the family, there were present Lev Atovmyan, Yury Sviridov and I.

I parted sadly from Shostakovich and returned to Leningrad, sharing a sleeping carriage with Yury Sviridov. All night long we spoke of Shostakovich, of his sublime gifts, his phenomenal and indestructible creative impulse. As Sviridov put it, however the forces of darkness might try their utmost to bend it, it would always spring back as if made of tempered steel.

21 March 1955 Bolshevo[9]

Dear Isaak Davidovich,

As soon as I arrived back in Moscow I headed straight for the dacha at Bolshevo.[10] I have been looking through the piano score of *Lady Macbeth*, and the main conclusion I have come to is that it would be a good idea to amend the text at the beginning of the second scene (pages 42–55). True, there is so much noise going on you that can't hear any of the words, but when you read it, the effect is not very pleasing to the eye. Maybe we should pay particular attention to Aksinya's lines, since hers is the only female voice in this ensemble and the part lies very high.

Perhaps we ought to do something about the frequent repetition of the word 'muzhik, muzhik'[11] on pages 109–110. Audiences of a puritanical disposition do not like such coarse naturalism.

I think that on pages 161–162 we have to find other words for Katerina Lvovna, suggesting something other than her desire for a passionate kiss. Instead of the night of rapture they have just spent or are still spending, they should reflect Sergey's brutal flogging of the previous day. So the situation could be that Sergey is still getting over his beating and Katerina Lvovna is tending to him.

Pages 169–170: again we should play down the idea of the insatiable female. Page 171: her complaint that Sergey is sleeping 'while her loving lips are so close' must also go. On the contrary she should be happy that he is asleep or going to sleep: it means that he is recovering from his thrashing. On page 178, take out the demand for a kiss. We have already discussed the text on pages 198–199. Page 280: it would be better if Sergey's reply omitted the word 'swine'.

May I ask you once again to telephone Doniyakh[12] and make sure that he includes in the full score the text which appears in the published piano score? One way and another I managed to make a good many corrections in it before it was published. It seems to me that the changes I have put in this letter are absolutely essential, but do please cast a critical eye over the complete text and if anything else strikes you as needing improvement, then go ahead and improve it.

For the present I am under the spell of *Lady Macbeth*, and have it once again vividly in my memory. And I believe that what has happened at Malegot[13] is in itself a matter for some rejoicing.

Please give my greetings to Vera Vasiliyevna.

D. Shostakovich

PS It is possible that my tour[14] will take me to Leningrad, and if it does then I will be there on 30 or 31 March. On the 31st, I should like to see *War and Peace*.[15] D. S.

I have just heard on the radio that Comrade N. A. Mikhailov has been appointed Minister of Culture of the USSR. This is great news. Everybody will remember his energetic implementation of the Historic Decrees. There will be especial rejoicing in progressive musical circles, as they have always placed the greatest hopes on Comrade Mikhailov. D.S.

This letter followed certain events, which merit a brief retelling.

On 23 December 1954, Shostakovich came to Leningrad and told me that to relieve the loneliness of this sad time he had been looking through *Lady Macbeth* and revising the part of Boris Timofeyevich. I noted down the exact words he said: 'I saw quite a lot that was wrong with it. Also, the part is awkwardly written for the singer. I am not going to touch Acts Two and Three, but I would like your advice about the Finale of the opera. Don't imagine that I am doing this with the theatre in mind. I'm no longer interested in whether the opera gets another production or not; it's had quite enough mud and abuse thrown at it already.' At this stage, nothing was said about the text of the libretto.

On 7 January 1955, Shostakovich came again to Leningrad for a viewing of the film *The Gadfly*, as he wanted to get on quickly with writing the music for it. He completed the commission in a very short time, and it has always seemed to me that the wonderful cello solo it contains mirrors his grief at the passing of Nina Vasiliyevna.

On 8 January Shostakovich came to dine with us. During a long conversation there was no mention of *Lady Macbeth*, although I had the impression that he was thinking about it all the time.

Brightening a little, he spoke of the forthcoming first performance, on 15 January, of the Jewish Songs (*From Jewish Folk Poetry*), going into raptures over the poems in the cycle. 'Ah, what magnificent poems they are!' he exclaimed. On 15 January the long-awaited première of the Jewish Songs took place in the Small Hall of the Philharmonia. Shostakovich was at the piano and the singers were Nina Dorliak, Zara Dolukhanova and Aleksey Maslennikov. It was an overwhelming success. The 'Winter' trio, the 'Cradle Song' and the final trio were all encored three times.

On 17 January we talked about the Jewish Songs. Shostakovich said: 'I was delighted with the toast you made (at Sofia Vasiliyevna's apartment after the concert) when you said that, hearing my songs, you felt yourself to be a Jew, an Armenian, a Spaniard, an Italian – in other words, a son of all mankind.' Then he added: 'In these songs I succeeded in much that I was aiming at.'

On 22 January, Shostakovich returned to Leningrad, and gave me an account of the Moscow première of the Jewish Songs which had taken place two days before. It had been an even greater success than in Leningrad, if that is possible. Crowds of people, among them even some enemies of Shostakovich had come backstage and, in his words, 'folded me in their embrace'.

At around the same time (winter 1955), the Leningrad Maly Opera, through the initiative of its director Boris Zagursky, was contemplating mounting a new production of *Lady Macbeth of Mtsensk*. This proved a difficult and complex undertaking, since it would be necessary to seek the permission of the Ministry of Culture to present an opera which had not been performed since February 1936.

Eventually, in March, Shostakovich was invited to present the changes he had incorporated into the score of *Lady Macbeth* to the Artistic Board of the Maly Opera. He arrived in Leningrad on 19 March, ready that same evening to demonstrate the new version of the opera.

About three hours before the meeting, Shostakovich began to have doubts. He said to me: 'Why should I play through an opera for them which everybody knows, and everybody has shat on? What's the point?' But the more he wavered, the clearer it became to me that he would go to the theatre and play not only the two new entr'actes but the complete opera. And so it turned out. We went together to the theatre, where we were warmly welcomed.

Dmitry Dmitriyevich played with tremendous power and *élan*, and all who heard it were deeply moved. The decision was taken to stage the opera in the 1955–6 season. We left the theatre in rather better spirits and repaired to Dmitrovsky Pereulok, where Sofia Vasiliyevna had prepared supper for us.

On 20 March Shostakovich gave me the piano score of *Lady Macbeth* and asked me, in the following words, to look through the complete text of the libretto: 'The words grew integrally with the music, they can't be separated, but when you just look with your eyes at the text in the piano score and don't listen to it with your ears, much of it appears in bad taste. Please look through the whole piano score, and make whatever corrections you judge necessary.' I promised to do this at the earliest opportunity. On 24 March I received the foregoing detailed letter in which Shostakovich identified the pages in the piano score where he specifically wanted me to make changes.

What made Shostakovich so determined to revise the libretto of *Lady Macbeth*? I shall try to answer this complex question, in order among other things to counter ill-informed conjecture that it was altered in response to external pressure rather than from inner conviction.

The truth is that when the opera was originally performed in the repertoire of the Maly Opera, the inappropriate reaction of some members of the audience to the rumbustious, vulgar and iconoclastic remarks made by Sergey and some of the other characters upset Shostakovich. For the most part, these remarks are perfectly in character, but there were times when they came at profoundly dramatic moments and were often greeted by laughter which was most painful to the composer's ears. (This was something that Shostakovich frequently mentioned to me during the run of performances at the theatre.) The libretto contained naturalistic elements which excited the disapproval of some over-sensitive listeners, described by Shostakovich as 'persons of a puritanical disposition', while other listeners on the other hand exhibited what one might call an unhealthy interest in them. Dmitry Dmitriyevich of course had no intention of simply pandering to public taste, but at the same time a man as sensitive as he was could not be altogether indifferent to the way in which his work was received. These are the reasons that lay behind his desire to revise some of the lines in the text, and they are also the reasons for my conviction that producers and conductors who defy the composer's wishes by insisting on restoring to the stage those passages from the text of the original version that were later excised, deserve censure.

21 April 1955 Moscow

Dear Isaak Davïdovich,

Very many thanks for your work.[16] I am now stitching it into my piano score, and only wish that that you had done this twenty-two years ago instead of just now.[17]

Give my warmest greetings to Vera Vasiliyevna.

I press your hand warmly.

D. Shostakovich

13 August 1955 Moscow

Dear Isaak Davïdovich,

In three hours' time we are setting off for the Crimea. Please do write to me there. This is the address: 'Miskhor' Sanatorium (that is what it is called now), Miskhor, Crimea. I should be so glad to hear from you. Give my greetings to Vera Vasiliyevna.

I press your hand warmly.

D. Shostakovich

Thank you for helping me while away the time in Komarovo.[18] D. S.

25 August 1955 Miskhor

Dear Isaak Davïdovich,

Greetings from Crimea. How are you? How are things going at the Conservatoire?[19] I wrote to you in Komarovo, but received no reply. We shall be here until 7 September. If you have time, please write to me here, at this address: 'Miskhor Sanatorium' (as it is now called), Miskhor, Crimea. Make a note of how long this card takes to reach you by airmail (the stamp costs 60 kopeks) and if there seems to be enough time then write to me

[59]

here, but if not, then to Moscow. I may come to Leningrad for a few days on 15 September.

Give my greetings to Vera Vasiliyevna. I press your hand.

D. Shostakovich

28 August 1955 Miskhor

Dear Isaak Davïdovich,

Thank you for your letter. I am always glad to hear from you. I have been following the weather in Leningrad, and am feeling sorry for you. It certainly is hot in Leningrad. It is very warm here too, but it rains sometimes. Also, one can swim.

A few days ago I heard my Ninth Symphony on the radio conducted by Aleksandr Gauk. It was not a good performance. When I switched on to listen, I was feeling quite excited, and I managed more or less to keep this up for the first movement. However by the second movement my pleasure had evaporated. It revived slightly in the third and fourth movements, but expired altogether in the fifth. The fellow is going to play it again on 24 September to open the season in the Hall of Columns[20] in Moscow. Talentless wretch![21]

You will not agree with me. You think that everybody has talent including Gauk. I don't think so.[22] I had long been dreaming of hearing the Ninth Symphony, and I was dreadfully let down by the wretched Gauk. It made me feel sick, as though I had swallowed a fly. Speaking of flies, there are thousands of them here. There are mosquitoes as well, which have bitten me to pieces.

The flies stop me sleeping, so I don't get a good night's rest. It is very hot. And I have a difficult season ahead of me.[23] If you write, please send any letters to Moscow, since we are leaving here early on the 7th.

Good music remains good music, independently of how it is played. You can play any of Bach's preludes and fugues at any tempo you fancy, with any dynamics you like or none at all, and it will still be great music. That's how music should be written, so that it is proof against ruination by some wretch playing it badly.

Give my warmest greetings to Vera Vasiliyevna. I hope we shall see one another soon.

I embrace you.

D. Shostakovich

16 November 1955 Bolshevo

Dear Isaak Davïdovich,

I am writing to give you the new telephone number at the dacha in Bolshevo, where I have come for three or four days.[24] Just in case, it is I 1–15–10, extension 93.

I sent the Concertino to R. M. Dolgoviner.[25] Give my greetings to Vera Vasiliyevna.

I press your hand warmly.

D. Shostakovich

In October 1955 Shostakovich made several visits to Leningrad, and there was therefore no need for letters. At the end of the month came the première of the First Violin Concerto, whose light, it is hard now to believe, had been hidden under a bushel for seven and a half years. The work was finished on 24 March 1948; Shostakovich showed me the date written on the final page of the score. The concerto was denied permission for performance on account of its 'pernicious formalism'. David Oistrakh, fearful of the publicity surrounding the work, learned it in secret, knowing all the while that he was dealing with music of genius, as he said to me many times. People knew of the concerto's existence, but it was wrapped in an aura of mystery almost as though it might contain a time bomb. Now, at last, the mystery was to be revealed.

On 18 October 1955 Shostakovich and Oistrakh came together to Leningrad to show the concerto to Mravinsky, who immediately started rehearsing it with the orchestra, showing the scrupulous attention to detail that was the hallmark of this great conductor. The first general rehearsal took place on 25 October, and I went with Shostakovich to hear it. Oistrakh played incomparably, and the effect was overwhelming. After the rehearsal, I went with Shostakovich to the Yevropeyskaya Hotel, where he was staying. Looking through the score and tapping it with his fingers, he said musingly (these were his exact words): 'All the same, I do deserve some credit for this.' In a fleeting remembrance of that time long ago, he was thinking less of the music's merits than of the circumstances in which it was written. In the dark days from autumn 1947 to March 1948, while he was being subjected to a hail of ridicule and defamation in the press and in countless public meetings, he continued doggedly to compose his violin concerto. Any other composer would have lost heart in such circumstances, but Shostakovich's invincible strength overcame all obstacles to express itself in music of overpowering power and beauty.

The long-awaited première took place on 29 October and was an enormous success, the finale having to be encored at the audience's insistence. After the concert, Vera Vasiliyevna and I were invited to Shostakovich's room at the Yevropeyskaya Hotel for a celebration of the concerto's première. At the table, I launched into an impassioned description of each movement at which Shostakovich, after lauding Oistrakh to the skies, suddenly said: 'To the composer's ears, and I repeat, to the composer's ears, there were places in the scherzo that sounded absolutely stunning.' (These were his exact words.) It was not a case of Shostakovich insisting that anybody, myself included, should accept this opinion of the scherzo; he was simply stating his own reaction, as the composer, to the music of this movement.

The concert was repeated the following day, and there was an even greater ovation. When the concert was over, I took the departing Shostakovich to the Moscow train. On the platform he said to me: 'You know, Oistrakh did take a few liberties here and there in the finale. Some passages were not quite as I would have wished, but even so it was very interesting. He was experimenting, and it was still interesting. What a talent!'

28 December 1955 Moscow

Dear Isaak Davïdovich,

Warmest good wishes for the New Year. I am sure that the New Year will bring you an even better life than 1955 has done.

As always, I need to ask a favour of you. Please tell me where and when, in which volume of Chekhov's Collected Works, he wrote something like this (I paraphrase): 'A writer must never assist the police or the gendarmerie.' A day or two ago I was in conversation with some representatives of progressive literary circles, to whom I quoted this thought from Chekhov. The progressive literati required proof that he had said this (in which volume of which edition, etc.) I undertook to supply the reference within a few days.

D. Shostakovich

Shostakovich's request has a history, which is worth relating briefly. During the years of Stalin's personality cult, there were certain writers who not only went along with but actively welcomed the repressive measures meted out to wholly innocent people. This naturally enraged Shostakovich and me. In the course of one gloomy conversation on this subject, I happened to mention a marvellous letter Chekhov wrote to the publisher of *Novoye Vremya* [*New Times*], Aleksey Suvorin. In this letter Chekhov springs to the defence of the slanderously accused Dreyfus, praising Zola's valiant campaign and roundly taking Suvorin's journal to task for its shamefully anti-Dreyfus stance.

When, after 1953, the time came for former orthodoxies to be reassessed, Shostakovich recalled Chekhov's letter to Suvorin while in conversation with some of the people he sarcastically calls 'representatives of progressive literary circles'. His interlocutors, most of whom had assuredly had their snouts in the trough, knew nothing of it. Although he had an extensive and detailed knowledge of Chekhov's writings, Shostakovich could not remember the date of the letter, which we had often talked about. I told him that it had been written in February 1898, when the writer was in Nice. The phrase was: 'It is not the business of writers to accuse or to prosecute ... We have enough accusers, prosecutors and gendarmes without them.' Shostakovich greatly admired this Chekhovian credo, which I had brought to his attention in troubled times.

11 January 1956 Moscow

Dear Isaak Davïdovich,

I am forwarding to you, for information, and because I may need your help, a letter I have received from Comrades Nikolayeva and Kolovsky.[26]

As it is your birthday today, I send you my very best wishes and regret that we are not spending the day together. Please give my warmest greetings to Vera Vasiliyevna.

I press your hand warmly.

D. Shostakovich

28 January 1956 Bolshevo

Dear Isaak Davïdovich,

I am writing to you having just put down the phone after our telephone conversation.[27] I forgot to tell you the following (actually, I don't really mean tell you, I mean share some thoughts with you).

I did what Boris Zagursky asked me to, and spoke to V. M. Molotov, who repeated his instructions that an authorized committee should be set up to audition *Lady Macbeth*.[28]

Yesterday I met Comrades Mikhailov, Kaftanov, Kemenov and other senior officials in the Ministry of Culture,[29] but although we had a very pleasant conversation the subject of *Lady Macbeth* was not brought up. I don't think it is appropriate for me to raise it myself. Dmitry Kabalevsky is unwell at the moment, and apparently they are waiting for him to recover before making the appropriate appointments to the committee.[30] I think that as matters stand it would be better for Zagursky to press the issue, rather than I. I don't propose to make any more enquiries about when they plan to set up an audition of *Lady Macbeth*; I think I have done enough about it already (see above).

If they do convene a committee to audition *Lady Macbeth*, I do beg you to be present not so much to defend the opera, but simply to give me the support of a friend.[31]

All my best wishes, and please give my greetings to Vera Vasiliyevna.

Your

D. Shostakovich

If you have a chance, please speak to Zagursky and explain my point of view. D. S.

29 May 1956 Moscow

Dear Isaak Davïdovich,

Very many thanks for all the trouble you went to over the shorthand notes.[32] They really were a bit of a dung heap, while you of course are no cockerel. Had you been a cockerel, I suppose you might have found a pearl in them.[33] I beg forgiveness for my secretary, who without telling me and in an excess of professional zeal dumped the dunghill on you so that you could find a pearl in it.[34]

Warmest greetings to Vera Vasiliyevna.

Your

D. Shostakovich

29 May 1956 Moscow

Dear Isaak Davïdovich,

I cannot deny myself the pleasure of sending you some cuttings from today's *Vechernyaya Moskva* [*Evening Moscow*]. Among them is an article by one Ilyin called 'Once Again In Moscow'. Reading it persuaded me yet again of the benefits of progress over reaction.[35]

D. Shostakovich

2 June 1956 Moscow

Dear Isaak Davïdovich,

Here is a little present for your friend who collects stamps. When I get letters from abroad in future I shall send you the stamps.[36]

I warmly press your hand. Greetings to Vera Vasiliyevna.

D. Shostakovich

15 June 1956 Moscow

Dear Isaak Davïdovich,

As you see, I am ignoring your request and shall go on sending you stamps. They may come in useful to your young collector.[37]

I warmly press your hand.

Your

D. Shostakovich

27 June 1956 Moscow

Dear Isaak Davïdovich,

As an Egyptologist you will no doubt be interested by this notice from *Izvestiya*, which you don't take and which I am therefore sending you herewith.[38]

I have been suffering from pneumonia for a week now, but I am getting better. It is holding up my visit to Komarovo, however.

Please give my warmest greetings to Vera Vasiliyevna.

Your

D. Shostakovich

13 September 1956 Bolshevo

Dear Isaak Davïdovich,

I am very much missing not seeing you. Please write and tell me how you are getting on, how is your health, and how goes the daily grind to earn a crust.

The day before yesterday I was speaking about you to Comrade Lapchinsky, the Deputy Director of the Higher Educational Services Executive. He was very pleasant and courteous to talk to.[39]

We have the builders in at home. At the moment my writing table and two of the bookcases are in pieces. However we have walls and ceilings of unparalleled splendour. There's nowhere to sleep. We have therefore moved out to Bolshevo, but things are not absolutely perfect here either. It is very cold, and there is no fuel. If you want anything to drink, you have to go to the other end of the world to get water. I have finished the Sixth Quartet, and am happy with it. As yet I have not acquainted the musical world with this work.

The activities connected with my jubilee are due to take place on 24 September.[40] Anosov, Gauk and Ivanov are between them going to conduct the cantata *The Sun Shines Over Our Motherland*, the Violin Concerto (with Vaiman as soloist)[41] and the Fifth Symphony. I shall be in Leningrad on 6 and 7 October: on the 6th I am playing the Quintet, and on the 7th there is going to be a 'composers' evening' at which my Sixth Quartet will be played.[42]

Please give my warmest greetings to Vera Vasiliyevna.

I kiss you warmly.

D. Shostakovich

27 December 1956 Bolshevo

Dear Isaak Davïdovich,

Best wishes to you and to Vera Vasiliyevna for the New Year. I hope that the New Year will bring you much happiness.

The old year is not ending very well for us. Maksim is ill: he got measles very badly and is still not over it. I have come to Bolshevo for three or four days; I am very tired and I need a bit of a rest.

Do write to me.

D. Shostakovich

31 March 1957 Bolshevo

Dear Isaak Davïdovich,

I miss not seeing you and am worried at hearing nothing from you for some time. I telephoned you twice, but there was no reply.[43]

I seem to be very busy rushing about at the moment, wasting a lot of time that I should be spending on my Eleventh Symphony, which I can't get on with.[44] Recently I have been at the Composer's Congress, hearing speeches by various orators. I particularly enjoyed the contribution of Comrade Lukin, who reminded the Congress of A. A. Zhdanov's inspiring directives to the effect that music should be melodious and graceful.[45] 'Sadly,' said Comrade Lukin 'we are not carrying out this inspiring directive!' The contributions of other speakers similarly contained much of value and interest.[46]

I am planning to come to Leningrad in the middle of April to meet the artistic directors of the Kirov Theatre about a production of *Lady Macbeth*.[47] I very much hope to see you then.

Kurt Sanderling[48] gave an excellent performance of my Fifth Symphony on 29 March, with the Violin Concerto (Oistrakh).

Briefly about my life: I am very busy. The phrase may be banal, but it precisely sums up my life at the moment.

Give my warmest greetings to Vera Vasiliyevna.

Your

D. Shostakovich

13 April 1957 Moscow

Dear Isaak Davïdovich,

I am sending you some stamps for your young philatelist friend.

I have been meaning to come to Leningrad, but cannot manage to do so for the time being.

If you hear Klyuzner's symphony, do please let me know your impression of it.[49]

We all send our greetings to Vera Vasiliyevna.

Your

D. Shostakovich

15 April 1957 Moscow

Dear Isaak Davïdovich,

Here are some more stamps along with my best wishes.

Life is not very good at the moment. It is hard to get the domestic situation under control with Fenya and Mariya Dmitriyevna both ill.[50]

Maksim and I both have colds. Altogether life is hard. But maybe it will all be over soon; after all, I am over fifty. Nevertheless, my blooming health and my mighty organism hardly allow much hope for an early curtailment of my earthly activities.[51]

My love belongs to all who have loved me; my curses to all who have done me ill.[52]

I kiss you warmly.

Warmest wishes to Vera Vasiliyevna.

Your

D. Shostakovich

23 April 1957 Moscow

Dear Isaak Davïdovich,

With this letter I am enclosing the list from the Anniversary Committee.

I want to send all those celebrating their jubilee a greeting, but I cannot make out one of the names.[53] The one in question is the fifth from the top, between Galperin and Livshits.[54] If you can, please find out the name and let me know. I will give you a ring in about three days' time. Also, I should be glad if you could tell me the first name and patronymic of everyone except Shalman.[55]

I am appalled at the outrageous behaviour of the Regional Housing Directorate over the room.[56] Is there anything I can do to help?

Your

D. Shostakovich

24 April 1957 Moscow

Dear Isaak Davïdovich,

The Deputy's Enquiry may do some good, and perhaps your mother's Health Centre could provide a certificate as to the state of her health.[57] But in addition I suggest that you contact the director of the Glinka Hall, Nikolai Bliznyuk (you could check the first name and patronymic with Zhenya Shneyerson: her home telephone number is A 5–81–05).[58] In the past he was very helpful over Marusya's[59] apartment swap. He is a close friend of Comrade Baranov, the head of the City Housing Department.

D. Shostakovich

15 July 1957 Moscow

Dear Isaak Davïdovich,

This is to let you know that we shall come to Komarovo on 20 July. I very much hope to see you. I have missed you.

Your

D. Shostakovich

11 September 1957 Moscow

Dear Isaak Davïdovich,

I am coming to Leningrad on 15 September. If you are going to be there at that time, please find me at Marusya's. I am coming with Mikhail Meyerovich, who has kindly agreed to partner me in a performance for piano four hands of the symphony.[60] Moysey Vainberg is seriously ill. He is suffering from heart failure and is drained of energy to the point of utter exhaustion. I feel deeply for him. Give my greetings to all your family.

Your

D. Shostakovich

10 November 1957 Moscow

Dear Isaak Davïdovich,

You may not have seen an article that gave me much pleasure in the latest issue of *Literaturnaya Gazeta*, entitled 'In the Echoing Mist', so I am sending it to you.[61] There is also a fable by Sergey Mikhalkov called 'Good Advice'. An excellent fable, ah what a truly excellent fable![62] 'Good Advice' reminded me of Barkov's[63] fable:

> Prov Kuzmich with his middle-aged spread,
> Here was a man, you'd respect what he said.
> Clever and witty, he sure has a mean
> Gift of the gab – but he's f***ing unclean!

Of course, here we have Prov Fomich, not Prov Kuzmich.

Well, such are the thoughts that came to me from reading the newspapers. If you happen to come across the journal which has the story 'The Echoing Mist' by D. Granin in it, please keep it for me. I should like to read all of it rather than just the extracts which 'Literator' generously included in his article.

I kiss you warmly.

D. Shostakovich

10 December 1957 Moscow

My dear friend Isaak Davïdovich,

I am sending you a cutting from *Soviet Sport*. You may not subscribe to this paper, in which case you would not have known about this sad event.[64] Knowing your love for outstanding people in all walks of life, I thought I should send you the cutting. It comes from *Soviet Sport* No. 214 (2950) dated 10 December 1957. It is a sad story. There once lived a man called G. I. Fedotov, and while he lived he scored goals. Now the grim reaper has taken him to his bosom. Extremely sad.

The deceased was admired throughout the world of sport, more so than many of his peers, but unfortunately, unlike the happily still with us V. Bobrov, he suffered from being somewhat apolitical. I can never forget Bobrov's description of Comrade Bashashkin as Tito's stooge at the Helsinki Olympics in 1952, when Yugoslavia seized their chance and scored after Bashashkin slipped up – you remember that Yugoslavia won 3–1 against the Combined USSR. One of their goals was indeed the result of Bashashkin's blunder, so Bobrov was naturally quite justified in calling him (Bashashkin) Tito's stooge. To this day the world of sport applauds Bobrov's patriotic impulse.

The late Fedotov, however, never did anything except score goals, so his death goes unreported except in the sporting press (*Sovetsky Sport*). Bobrov continues to thrive: he is the now the coach and political instructor of a football team. Bashashkin on the other hand was immediately fired back in 1952; good centre back he might have been but he suffered from an inadequate grounding in political understanding. Bobrov's political understanding, on the other hand, was admirably grounded.

But the only thing the late Fedotov did was score goals, an occupation well known to be apolitical.

I am going away on the 12th and shall be back in Moscow on 29 December. I hope you and Vera Vasiliyevna have both recovered and are feeling better now.

Your

D. Shostakovich

On the surface, the Yugoslavia–USSR match at the Helsinki Olympics five years previously had been a routine event in international sport, but it took on an unexpectedly powerful and shameful resonance. For Shostakovich, the hunting down and persecuting of innocent people, whether they were from his own world of musicians, writers and poets, or from the more distant fields of medicine, biology or football, provoked not only his acute sympathy on a personal level but a welling-up of rage. It took all his incredible powers of self-control to contain this rage, and the vein of grim irony exemplified in this letter was an expressive outlet for it.

A few days after the Helsinki game, I was talking to the composer Leon Khodzha-Einatov. He was bemoaning the Soviet team's defeat and saying how upset Shostakovich must have been by it. I forebore to tell him the truth, which was that the moment he heard of Yugoslavia's victory on the early morning radio, Shostakovich rushed round to my dacha in Komarovo to share the joyous news with me. In celebration we demolished a bottle of 'Finchampagne' brandy, sitting at one of the little tables out on the street near the railway station. Paradoxically, passionate supporter of the Combined USSR team though he was, Shostakovich could not help but look on its defeat at the hands of Tito's Yugoslavia as a victory for justice and a challenge to the Stalinist terror threatening that country.

In defiance of common sense, the game of football did have a political dimension. All sorts of chauvinist passions were given free rein, for Stalin had decided on a whim that Yugoslavia was an enemy country, its leader Tito a Gestapo thug, a murderer and a spy working for foreign intelligence agencies. This was how he was depicted in innumerable newspaper editorials and cartoons. Starting from this so-called premise it became a commonplace among the rabble of every class and position to explain the Soviet team's defeat as a betrayal. Shostakovich and I had considerable fellow-feeling for the Yugoslav players: we naturally wished them no ill, the more so as they represented a small country menaced by a bullying neighbour's threats. Our team was simply unlucky; they lost fair and square but in so doing provoked a campaign of incredible abuse from tub-thumping patriots. Among them, the diehard obduracy of Bobrov's voice could be heard shrieking above the rest, accusing his colleague Bashashkin of being 'Tito's stooge', no less, for having accidentally let Yugoslavia score. In those times a denunciation like this could be a serious matter for Bashashkin, and Shostakovich became seriously worried about what might be the fate of this football player, who was personally of course completely unknown to him. It also pained him that the Bobrovs and their ilk somehow managed to continue flourishing in the post-Stalin world, not only in sport but also in music and literature.

11 December 1957 Moscow

Dear Isaak Davïdovich,

Aleksandr Kholodilin returned only yesterday, and I have not managed to get hold of him yet.[65] I am leaving Moscow tomorrow (12 December) and shall not be back until the 29th. In the meantime I have written to A. A. asking him to take urgent action on Vera Vasiliyevna's application.[66] I hope you are both in good health and that all is well with you.

I press your hand warmly.

D. Shostakovich

18 December 1957 Lvov

Dear Isaak Davïdovich,

I am in the middle of a big concert tour to the following places: Kiev, Lvov, Kishinyov, Odessa.[67] I get back to Moscow on 30 December. I am playing twice in each city, each time with the same programme: *Festive Overture*, Second Piano Concerto (with me as soloist) and Eleventh Symphony. Sadly I have no time to see the sights; the rehearsals and concerts take up all the energy I have. So far the only real pleasure I have had has been in Kiev, where the orchestra is first class and Rakhlin was, to my surprise, very good indeed.[68] The orchestra in Lvov is not as good, and the conductor (Stasevich) quite poor.[69] He will also conduct in Odessa. In Kishinyov it will be the local conductor.

I am spending a lot of time on trains. After tonight's concert I have to go back to Kiev at 5 o'clock in the morning. I met several old Leningrad acquaintances in Lvov: the musicologist Kotlyarevsky,[70] the organist

Bakeyeva,[71] the singer Filatov whom I remember as a terrific football fan, the pianist Borovsky's sister,[72] and others. They are all doing pretty well, they have their apartments and salaries, but they all miss Leningrad.

I had an evening off in Kiev, and I gave in to Georgy Maiboroda's entreaties that I should spend my free evening at a performance of his opera *Milana*.[73] Having seen it, I concluded that a hopak in a Ukrainian opera always has to be a swaggering, earthy, popular sort of number.[74]

After my time in Kiev, I must say that my opinion of Rakhlin as a conductor soared.[75]

I hope that you and Vera Vasiliyevna are both well. I was very sorry you were ill.

I press your hand warmly.

Your

D. Shostakovich

24 December 1957 Odessa

Dear Isaak Davïdovich,

I learned today that Mozhaiskoye Shosse has been renamed Kutuzovsky Prospect. Therefore my home address is now: Apartment 87, 37–45 Kutuzovsky Prospect, Moscow G-151.

My tour is coming to an end, and I shall be back in Moscow on the 30th. Best wishes to you and yours for the forthcoming New Year.

Your

D. Shostakovich

I get to Moscow on the 30th, but on 3 January I fly to Bulgaria for three weeks.[76] D.S.

29 December 1957 Odessa

Dear Isaak Davïdovich,

I arrived in Odessa on the day of the nationwide holiday celebrating the 40th anniversary of the founding of Soviet Ukraine. This morning I went out in the streets; you will understand of course that on such a day as this, one cannot stay at home. In spite of the weather, which was rather gloomy and foggy, all Odessa was on the streets.[77] Everywhere were portraits of Marx, Engels, Lenin, Stalin, and also Comrades A. I. Belyayev, L. I. Brezhnev, N. A. Bulganin, K. Ye. Voroshilov, N. G. Ignatov, A. I. Kirilenko,

F. P. Kozlov, O. V. Kuusinen, A. I. Mikoyan, N. A. Mukhitdinov, M. A. Suslov, Ye. A. Furtseva, N. S. Khrushchev, N. M. Shvernik, A. A. Aristov, P. A. Pospelov, Ya. E. Kaliberzin, A. P. Kirichenko, A. N. Kosïgin, K. T. Mazurov, V. P. Mzhavanadze, M. G. Pervukhin, N. T. Kalchenko.[78]

The streets are filled with flags, slogans, banners. All around can be seen beaming smiles on radiantly happy Russian, Ukrainian and Jewish faces. On every side can be heard joyful exclamations hailing the great names of Marx, Engels, Lenin, Stalin, and also those of Comrades A. I. Belyayev, L. I. Brezhnev, N. A. Bulganin, K. Ye. Voroshilov, N. G. Ignatov, A. I. Kirichenko,[79] F. P. Kozlov, O. V. Kuusinen, A. I. Mikoyan, N. A. Mukhitdinov, M. A. Suslov, Ye. A Furtseva, N. S. Khrushchev, N. M. Shvernik, A. A. Aristov, P. A. Pospelov, Ya. E. Kaliberzin, A. P. Kirilenko, A. N. Kosïgin, K. T. Mazurov, V. P. Mzhavanadze, M. G. Pervukhin, N. T. Kalchenko, D. S. Korotchenko. Everywhere one hears the accents of Russian and Ukrainian speech, as well as from time to time the foreign tongues of those progressive representatives of mankind who have come to Odessa in order to salute Odessans on their great holiday. I myself walked the streets until, no longer able to contain my joy, I returned home and resolved to describe to you, as best I might, Odessa's National Day of Celebration.

Do not, I beg you, judge me too harshly.

I kiss you warmly,

D. Shostakovich

5 January 1958 Moscow

Dear Isaak Davïdovich,

I spoke today to Aleksandr Kholodilin. He told me that all is in order for Vera Vasiliyevna, and that the papers will be signed and sent to her on 7 January.

I kiss you warmly.

D. Shostakovich

2 February 1958 Bolshevo

Dear Isaak Davïdovich,

As soon as I returned from Bulgaria I telephoned you but could not get hold of you, or rather there was no reply. Belated congratulations on your birthday,[80] may you always be well and happy. I am very tired after my trip, and have come to Bolshevo for a day or two. If you happen to come across a novel by Leonhard Frank called *The Disciples of Jesus*, published in translation by Foreign Literature, Moscow 1957, do read it.[81] I think it is a very good book.[82]

My address has changed again as the apartment block has been renumbered. It is now: Apartment 87, 27 Kutuzov Prospect, Moscow G-151.

Give my greetings to all your family.

Your

D. Shostakovich

20 March 1958 Moscow

Dear Isaak Davïdovich,

I received the copy of your article. It is a brilliant piece of work and written with great love for our late friend. Reading it, I vividly recalled Aleksandr Semyonovich Rabinovich and saw him as clearly as if he were still alive.[83] I remembered the many other gifted, noble and idealistic words he uttered. I remembered that, he is no longer alive. I thought, I am still alive, but I am already 51.

Warmest wishes to Vera Vasiliyevna.

I kiss you warmly.

D. Shostakovich

5 May 1958 Gorky

Dear Isaak Davïdovich,

I am writing to you from Gorky where I arrived yesterday for concerts I am giving here. Gusman conducted my Eleventh Symphony.[84] Being a creative person he felt obliged to alter tempi and dynamics all over the place, resulting in a mostly very bad performance. The concert will be repeated today, and afterwards I go straight to Moscow. I am playing the solo part in the Second Piano Concerto here, and am playing badly; for some reason my right hand seems to be seriously lagging behind.[85] It seems we are going to Italy on the 7th or 8th, and then on to France.[86] We get back early in June. May is a busy time for me: Maksim's birthday is on the 10th, Galya's on the 30th. The 19th is the twenty-fifth anniversary of my marriage to Nina. And on all of these dates I shall be abroad.

I can't say I am looking forward to this trip at all. I would be better off sitting at home playing patience.[87] But if the trip really cannot be put off, then I must say goodbye to you until June. Be well and happy. Give my heartiest greetings to Vera Vasiliyevna and all your family.

I kiss you warmly,
D. Shostakovich

3 June 1958 Moscow

Dear Isaak Davïdovich,

We returned home yesterday after a difficult and exhausting trip.[88] If you have time, please write to me. I have missed you very much.

Give my greetings to all your family.

Your
D. Shostakovich

22 June 1958 Bolshevo

Dear Isaak Davïdovich,

Tomorrow I am travelling to London and then on to Oxford, where there is to be a ceremony at which I will be awarded an honorary doctorate. This will be take place on 25 June. Then on 27 June I shall return home.[89]

This time I shall go alone, as Margarita[90] is busy with examinations. Write and tell me what your plans are for the summer. For us, matters stand thus: Galya is going away to Ryabinsk on a field trip until August, the rest of us plus Marusya are going to Ruza. We are not going to Komarovo this year. My respects to all your family.

Your
D. Shostakovich

10 July 1958 Repino

Dear Isaak Davïdovich,

On 14 August[91] Margarita Andreyevna and I are coming to Leningrad for two or three days. We hope very much to see you then.

Please telephone us and we will telephone you.
D. Shostakovich

17 July 1958 [Leningrad]

Dear Isaak Davïdovich,

Margarita and I invite you and Vera Vasiliyevna to a celebratory dinner on 26 July at 5 p.m., to mark the second anniversary of our nuptials. The dinner will be at Marusya's apartment.[92] Please come without fail.

D. Shostakovich

24 August 1958 Moscow

Dear Isaak Davïdovich,

I was saying to you that whenever I see Misha Shneyerson (Zhenya's son),[93] I am reminded of Kuprin's story *The Simpleton*. Do read it. It is published in Volume One, page 508 of the Collected Works, State Literary Publishing House edition, Moscow 1957.

Tomorrow I go into hospital to have treatment for my right hand.[94]

Your

D. Shostakovich

Give my greetings to all your family. D. S.

6 September 1958 Moscow

Dear Isaak Davïdovich,

I have to stay in hospital at least until the beginning of October. The professors, those high priests of science, had a consultation yesterday, and that was their decision.[95] My right hand is really weak. I have pins and needles all the time. I can't pick up anything heavy with it. I can grip a suitcase with my fingers, but it's difficult to hang my coat on a peg, or clean my teeth. When I write, the hand gets very tired. I can only play slowly and pianissimo – I noticed this in Paris, where I could hardly get through the concerts. I didn't pay any attention at the time.

When I asked the medical high priests to give me a name for whatever it is that is wrong with me, they did not answer but simply condemned me to stay in hospital until the beginning of October. In any case, I am exercising the hand. Every day I practise writing out the letters of the alphabet and the numbers, and phrases like 'Masha eats kasha' and 'vicar scratches knicker'.[96] But my God how difficult it is. I'm not getting on very well, in fact I don't seem to be getting anywhere at all. My left hand is hopelessly

[76]

inadequate. I envy Vissarion Shebalin: he lost the use of his right hand altogether but managed to train his left, and now he can write quite fluently with it. Not just anything either: having regard to the Historic Decree that all art should be closer to life and closer to the people he has written an entire left-handed opera on the theme of our contemporaries marching forward under the banner of the Party towards the shining heights of our future, towards Communism.[97]

If you have time and inclination, please write to me. My address is: USSR Ministry of Health Hospital No. 4, 2 Granovsky Street, Moscow K-9; make sure it is marked for my attention.

The conditions are good here: I am in a quiet ward on my own. All the sisters, nurses and other hospital workers are excellent, honest and hardworking people. I see a bit of Aram Khachaturian, who has been here for two weeks with a stomach ulcer. I am feeling fine, but bored and frustrated. My treatment consists of injections three times a day into my bottom and having both hands massaged. My bottom is being punctured to an unbelievable extent; I fear I shall soon not be able to sit down.

Give my greetings to all your family, please.

I press your hand warmly. Please write.

D. Shostakovich

12 September 1958 Moscow

Dear Isaak Davïdovich,

Thank you for your letter. I am glad of its news, but I am happiest of all that you don't forget me and that you spoil me – not often enough though – with your letters. I am feeling all right. My hand is getting better, although it gets very tired when I write.[98]

There is a good library in this hospital. I have been reading, or rather re-reading, *Gulliver's Travels*, *Robinson Crusoe* and a whole series of other books[99] with real pleasure. One book I read with great interest was a collection of stories by American writers. The introduction to this anthology was particularly interesting; the author (I forget his name) writes about the difficult conditions under which progressively-minded authors in America are obliged to work. He comes right out with it: 'Howard Fast[100] has declared in his *Literature and Life* that the creation of a positive Communist hero is the most important task facing American literature.' Well said indeed, but perhaps not so easy to achieve in the degenerate and reactionary climate of the USA. I do recommend that you read this collection of *Short Stories by American Writers*, published by the State Literary Publishing House, Moscow, 1954. And I strongly urge you to read *A Long Day in a Short Life* by the progressive American writer Albert Maltz,[101] also Upton Sinclair's *The Metropolis*.[102] They are all most interesting.

I expect to be in hospital about another two weeks. Do please write to me.

I kiss you,

D. Shostakovich

19 September 1958 Moscow

Dear Isaak Davïdovich,

Thank you very much for writing. I am very bored in here, and all your letters, especially the last one, give me much pleasure.

The story about your drinking companion in Komarovo started me thinking. I have great admiration for Jesus Christ, especially in the legend (parable) of the scales. Christ, crucified between the two thieves, takes into consideration the dying thief's last-minute repentance and decides to take him with him into the heavenly kingdom. The sinner's repentance in the face of approaching death tips the balance against the weight of all his terrible crimes on the other side of the scales. You say that it was your own 'burden of lies', as you put it, that made you value the individual who was himself so heavily weighed down by them. Were you right, and was Christ right in a similar situation? Probably, you were both right. And I think I too was right at the time in seeing in this man, author of a string of melodious and graceful compositions, at least some passing resemblance to a human being, and your talk with him in the bar in Komarovo supports this. Please God at least on that occasion he wasn't lying, and won't try any of his disgusting tricks on you in the future. But I can't be sure of that. We shall have to wait and see what the future brings.[103]

My stay in hospital is coming to an end. I should be home by about the 25th of the month. My hand is better, but I don't think I shall be able to undertake much concert activity in the near future. In my spare time, of which I have plenty at the moment, I think about *Lady Macbeth* and the Fourth Symphony. I should so much like to hear both of these works performed. I cannot say that I would expect much joy from the opera; the theatres are so full of untalented, incompetent people merely taking up space – singers, producers, designers and the like. But the Fourth could perhaps be done. Actually, I don't have very high hopes of either work being performed, but I indulge myself by imagining them in my inner ear.[104]

Give my best greetings to all your family,

I warmly kiss you,

D. Shostakovich

Please write to me at home, not to the hospital. They always bring me your letters from home anyway. A few days ago I heard a symphony by Venyamin Basner; I managed to wangle a visit from him along with Moysey Vainberg and Boris Tchaikovsky, who played it through to me on four hands on the piano here. I liked the symphony very much; he is definitely a talented composer.

D.S.

11 November 1958 Moscow

Dear Isaak Davïdovich,

I received your letter. If the Malegot wants to stage my operetta, let them. They will have to apply to the Moscow Operetta Theatre in Mayakovsky Square, Moscow to obtain the performing material.[105]

Give my warmest greetings to all your family.

I very much miss not seeing you.

D. Shostakovich

19 December 1958 Moscow

Dear Isaak Davïdovich,

I am behaving very properly and attending rehearsals of my operetta. I am burning with shame. If you have any thoughts of coming to the first night, I advise you to think again. It is not worth spending time to feast your eyes and ears on my disgrace. Boring, unimaginative, stupid. This is, in confidence, all I have to tell you.[106]

I press your hand warmly.

D. Shostakovich

2 February 1959 Bolshevo

Dear Isaak Davïdovich,

I have promised to write a few words, about four typewritten sheets, for the centenary of the Leningrad Conservatoire. I should be extremely grateful if you would help me with this.

Here is a rough synopsis:

1. I was a student at the Conservatoire, receiving like other students a solid musical education. Mention Leonid Nikolayev, Maksimilian Shteynberg, Aleksandr Glazunov.

2. Anything else that comes into your head.

You will earn my heartfelt gratitude for your help.

Give my greetings to Vera Vasiliyevna.

Your

D. Shostakovich

I complied with Shostakovich's request, sticking closely to the exceptionally detailed thesis he had set out.

6 February 1959 Moscow

Dear Isaak Davïdovich,

Thank you very much for Gilels.[107]

I press your hand warmly.

Your

D. Shostakovich

20 May 1959 Moscow

Dear Isaak Davïdovich,

I have not heard from you for a long time. Do let me know how you are and what is going on. I have no particular news. The Gilels book is about to come out, and I got a fee of 4,000 roubles for the article. Well, money doesn't grow on trees, does it?

Give my greetings to Vera Vasiliyevna.

Please write, do stay in touch.

D. Shostakovich

26 May 1959 Moscow

Dear Isaak Davïdovich,

The piece about Aleksandr Rabinovich gets a separate fee.[108] This money is for the Gilels book. A famous author deserves a decent fee. On the 31st I fly to Prague for ten days. I hope to be in Leningrad in the middle of June.

D. Shostakovich

27 May 1959 Moscow

Dear Isaak Davïdovich,

I seem to have made a real muddle of my accounts.[109] You will see that item 4 in the statement I enclose herewith shows the sum of 4,000 roubles. When I enquired what this related to, they told me that it was the fee for the article, and that it had been put straight into my savings account. So, not thinking any more about it, I sent you this amount – 4,000 roubles – that I happened to have in cash because the Bolshoy Theatre had just made a final settlement with me on dispensing with my services.[110]

So when I got your letter, I sent you a postcard telling you that it was all correct. Well, apparently it wasn't. As you will see, there is also an item 1 on the statement which gives the true amount due for the article (0.56 author's sheets).[111] The 4,000 roubles is the fee for all the authors. I enclose the statement so that you can see it all laid out. Don't send the money back to me. Please keep whatever is due to you, and keep the rest until I come to Leningrad, or else give it to my sister Marusya.[112]

Forgive me.

I kiss you warmly.

D. Shostakovich

15 June 1959 Moscow

Dear Isaak Davïdovich,

Thank you for your letter. I am sorry I was not at the concert, but I did not know it was happening.[113]

It's been unbearably hot here in Moscow all the time, but now it's a little cooler and a bit easier to breathe.[114]

Let me know what your plans are for the summer. It's possible we may go to Komarovo.

Greetings to all your people.
Your
D. Shostakovich

25 August 1959 Moscow

Dear Isaak Davïdovich,

My sister Mariya tells me that the Fomins[115] have a copy of the complete works of Leonid Andreyev. If you cannot get hold of them yourself, please telephone her and make sure you read his story 'The Governor'.[116]

Please pass on my warmest greetings to all your family.
Your
D. Shostakovich

8 October 1959 Moscow

Dear Isaak Davïdovich,

Thank you very much for your telegram.
Your
D. Shostakovich

20 October 1959 Moscow

Dear Isaak Davïdovich,

I am enclosing a note to Sergey Yeltsin. I very much hope you will make use of it.[117] Please telephone him on Zh-32120.

I kiss you warmly.

Give my best greetings to Vera Vasiliyevna.
Your
D. Shostakovich

Yeltsin's name is Sergey Vitaliyevich.

IV
Public Face, Private Feelings
1960–1966

At rehearsal in the Moscow Conservatoire, 1960s

The see-saw between relaxation and repression that characterized Soviet life under Khrushchov continued alternately to stimulate and undermine the artistic community. Within the space of a few days in November and December 1962, Solzhenitsïn's epoch-making exposé of the labour camps One Day in the Life of Ivan Denisovich *was published, an exhibition of modern art in Moscow was rudely broken up and forced to close, and Shostakovich's Thirteenth Symphony, with its controversial verses by Yevgeny Yevtushenko was, to the composer's profound joy, allowed by the narrowest of calculated margins a handful of performances before being put on the blacklist for four years. The Party's coercion of the country's greatest composer to improve its image by joining its ranks was eventually success-ful in September 1961, but at what personal cost is movingly set out in this chapter, if indeed not made manifest in the autobiographical Eighth Quartet. In the com-poser's private world, Quartets 9, 10 and 11 were added to the canon, while in the public arena the momentum for the former bogeys of 'pernicious formalism' –* Lady Macbeth of Mtsensk *and the suppressed Fourth Symphony – at last to be rehabili-tated became irresistible. The Fourth Symphony was first performed a quarter of a century after its composition in December 1961, and after a similar absence* Lady Macbeth *regained the stage as* Katerina Izmailova *at the Nemirovich-Danchenko Musical Theatre in Moscow in December 1962. In this period Shostakovich married his third wife, Irina Antonovna Supinskaya, but his happiness began to be clouded by bouts of ill health, culminating in a heart attack suffered while performing in a concert of his works in Leningrad in May 1966.*

11 February 1960 Moscow

Dear Isaak Davïdovich,

Here I am in hospital again, where I am having some treatment to my right hand. I am very bored; it is really very tedious to have to be in hospital when you are feeling perfectly well. Last time I was buoyed up by the hope that the problem would be cured. Now the last iota of hope has disappeared.

Someone I know in the hospital gave me Sergey Semyonov's novel from the twenties, *Natalya Tarpova*, to read. I highly recommend this novel. Do read it if you haven't already. Its main distinction, and it is a big one, is that it gives such an extraordinarily faithful and accurate description of the times.

Re-reading *Natalya Tarpova* now, I 'empathized' very much with the characters. Please get hold of it, however difficult it may be to do so:[1] it is not a bad book and astonishingly much better it is than so much that was produced in the forties and fifties. I vaguely remember the book being criticized when it was first published: the author was accused of elevating the 'biological' above the 'party imperative'. And it is true that however earnestly the author seeks to disapprove of the Executive Secretary's marriage to the drama circle teacher although she is not a Party member, and despite his impeccably correct Party-speak rebuke to Works Committee Secretary Natalya Tarpova for picking up a non-party spets[2] to console herself with, the charges ultimately fail to convince because the 'biological urges' of Natalya and the Executive Secretary do win out over the party imperatives. And there are many other issues in *Natalya Tarpova* that we used to vex our brains with in those days. You absolutely must read this novel. If you have time, please write to me. I hate being here and most especially miss you.

Give my warmest greetings to Vera Vasiliyevna.

Your

D. Shostakovich

Shostakovich was deeply interested in new writing, but rejected most literature that appeared in the 1940s and 1950s, finding it saturated with hypocrisy and falsehood. Any exceptions merely proved the rule. The writers of the 1920s, however, being closer to the Russian literary tradition, had not yet learned these dubious skills. Such was Shostakovich's view of Sergey Semyonov, whose novel *Natalya Tarpova* was published in 1929. The book, despite its failings and weaknesses as a work of art – of which Shostakovich was fully aware – nevertheless impressed him with its fidelity to life and manifest desire to express the reality of people's daily lives, their attitudes and moral preoccupations, in the post-Revolutionary Petrograd which the adolescent Dmitry Shostakovich had himself experienced.

17 February 1960 Moscow

Dear Isaak Davïdovich,

Thank you for your letter. I do dislike being here: there's nothing worse than being in hospital when you feel completely healthy. It seems I have to stay for another week. I am so glad you share my opinion of *Natalya Tarpova*. And I entirely agree with you that it is far better, and purer, than a whole lot of other works. Do read it again. It has one other enormous virtue, in my eyes: it gives a true picture of the times in which the action takes place – twenties Petrograd, when it still was Petrograd and hadn't yet become Leningrad. It is a tremendous quality in a work of literature to give a *rounded picture* [writer's emphasis – I. G.] of the life of our country and of our people in all its variety. Only Zoshchenko, perhaps two or three other writers besides him, really succeeded in presenting a true and vivid picture of our life.[3] But if you read most contemporary works about the period you think to yourself: no, it wasn't really like that.

I haven't seen you for so long. Many things have happened, and are happening, but for too long we have had no opportunity to talk about them.[4]

Give my greetings to Vera Vasiliyevna.

Stay well.

Your

D. Shostakovich

26 February 1960 Moscow

Dear Isaak Davïdovich,

I received your letter. I think the ideal person to write the music for a film of *The Gentle Maiden*[5] would be either V. P. Solovyov-Sedoy or G. N. Nosov.[6] The important thing when writing music for the films is that composer and director should be soulmates, and that both of them should be lovers of melodious and elegant music.[7]

I don't think that Ustvolskaya would be able to give the director of the film what he needs, although she does need to earn some money. However philosophical one's attitude to poverty, in the end it does become pretty unbearable.[8] I have never thought of either self-deprecation or self-aggrandisement as being valuable personal qualities. Of course, as Comrade Stalin used to teach us, 'the finest quality of the Bolshevik is modesty'. But when all's said and done, one can forgive Beethoven for giving himself a pat on the back for the symphonies. The same applies to Grechaninov for *Dobrïnya Nikitich*.[9] But what neither of them, nor anyone else, should ever be forgiven for, is turning out work that is amoral and spiritually lickspittle. I am sure the composer of that oratorio[10] will be awarded a prize, if on no other grounds than the time he spent standing shoulder to shoulder with masters such as V. Kochetov, A. Sofronov, K. Simonov and other outstanding exponents of the art of socialist realism.[11]

[87]

Self-congratulation takes many forms, and no two of the forms are alike. But Beethoven's self-congratulation (if there were any such thing) is a very different matter from that of F. Bulgarin, the author of *Ivan Buzhigin*.[12] I trust I make myself clear?

I am going to be in hospital for quite a bit longer, at least two weeks. This was decided at the consultation three days ago. As soon as I get out I shall come to Leningrad, as I have received a letter from Georgy Korkin[13] stating that they want to stage *Lady Macbeth* at the end of the season. My presence is required for practices, rehearsals and so on. I cannot say that the prospect of this new production fills me with joy,[14] as the theatre's stock of performing talent is not on a particularly high level.

My hand seems to be getting better. But if I get depressed or worried, the feeling of weakness comes back. Answer: avoid getting depressed or worried.

Life in the hospital is intolerably boring. Please write to me. They are very good about bringing me any letters that come for me at home.

I have not yet told you of a hugely important event: I am expecting a grandson or granddaughter. Of course I am thrilled about it, but also very nervous. Galya is expecting an addition to the family in five months' time. Everything is going well, for now. Give Vera Vasiliyevna and all your family my warmest greetings.

Write, please.

Your

D. Shostakovich

14 March 1960 Moscow

Dear Isaak Davïdovich,

I am now at home and getting ready to come to Leningrad to carry out my responsibilities as a Deputy.[15] I very much hope to see you there. The moment I came out of hospital an avalanche of problems descended on my head. I simply don't know how I am going to deal with them.

D. Shostakovich

Please pass my greetings on to Vera Vasiliyevna, and thank her very much for all her trouble over the hat.[16] D. S.

21 March 1960 Moscow

Dear Isaak Davïdovich,

I plan to come to Leningrad on 28 March, and should much like to see you. I shall stay until 31.

I have the following urgent things to do while I am in Leningrad: on the 29th, constituents' surgery.[17] On the 30th, *Boris Godunov*.[18] On the 31st I shall hear Salmanov's symphony at the Philharmonia.[19] It would be good if we could meet on the 28th or 29th.

I kiss you warmly.

D. Shostakovich

8 April 1960 Moscow

Dear Isaak Davïdovich,

It is a great shame that you spent so little time in Moscow. Here are two stamps from Mexico. I should be most grateful for your help in writing the Foreword to the book about Richter.

I am coming to Leningrad for three days on 14 April.

Please give Vera Vasiliyevna my warmest wishes.

Your

D. Shostakovich

30 April 1960 Moscow

Dear Isaak Davïdovich,

Have you yet had a chance to find out anything about the artistic projects being hatched by Boris Fenster and Pavel Feldt? If so, what impression did you form of them? They are both in love with their idea of combining my ballet suites with the best and most talented poet of our epoch.[20]

If you have not yet found out how their plans are progressing, may I ask you please to do so and tell me your opinion, perhaps also sharing your thoughts with Fenster, whom I know you get on well with?[21]

I am at the moment under the spell of Moysey Vainberg's violin concerto, which was magnificently performed by the Communist–violinist Leonid Kogan.[22] It is a superlative work in the true meaning of the word. And the Communist–violinist plays it magnificently. If you see it advertised in Leningrad, make sure you find time to go to hear it.[23]

The Beethoven Quartet is now studying my Seventh Quartet. The rehearsals are giving me great joy. In general, however, life is far from easy. How I long to summon the aid of the Old Woman so inspiringly evoked by the poet in his *Horizon Beyond the Horizon*, published in the Party's Central Organ *Pravda* on 29 April 1960.[24]

I kiss you warmly. Be well and happy.

Your

D. Shostakovich

Please pass on my warmest greetings to Vera Vasiliyevna. D. S.

18 June 1960 Moscow

Dear Isaak Davïdovich,

My dacha now has a telephone.[25] The number is D 8–66–40. I am just letting you know in case you need to get in touch with me urgently.

I have been missing you very much.

Warmest greetings to Vera Vasiliyevna.

Please stay in touch, don't forget me.

Your

D. Shostakovich

19 July 1960 Zhukovka

Dear Isaak Davïdovich,

Thank you very much for helping Maksim out with money. I do hope you are enjoying your stay in Zelenogorsk, and that your holiday in that heavenly place does you good.

I am now back from my trip to Dresden, and have been to see Lev Arnshtam's film *Five Days and Five Nights*. Much of it gave me great pleasure. Lyolya's[26] goodness of heart absolutely shines through it, and that is the main quality of this film.

Dresden was an ideal set-up for getting down to creative work. I stayed in the spa town of Görlitz,[27] which is just near a little place called Köningstein, about 40 kilometres from Dresden. A place of incredible beauty – as it should be, the whole area being known as 'the Switzerland of Saxony'. The good working conditions justified themselves: I composed my Eighth Quartet. As hard as I tried to rough out the film scores which I am supposed to be doing, I still haven't managed to get anywhere; instead I wrote this ideologically flawed quartet which is of no use to anybody. I started thinking that if some day I die, nobody is likely to write a work in memory of me, so I had better write one myself. The title page could carry the dedication: 'To the memory of the composer of this quartet'.

The basic theme of the quartet is the four notes D natural, E flat, C natural, B natural – that is, my initials, D. SCH.[28] The quartet also uses themes from some of my own compositions and the Revolutionary song 'Zamuchen tyazholoy nevolyey' ['Tormented by grievous bondage']. The themes from my own works are as follows: from the First Symphony, the Eighth Symphony, the [Second Piano] Trio, the Cello Concerto, and *Lady Macbeth*. There are hints of Wagner (the Funeral March from *Götterdämmerung*) and Tchaikovsky (the second subject of the first movement of the Sixth Symphony). Oh yes, I forgot to mention that there is something else of mine as well, from the Tenth Symphony. Quite a nice little hodge-podge, really. It is a pseudo-tragic quartet, so much so that while I was composing it I shed the same amount of tears as I would have to pee after half-a-dozen beers. When I got home, I tried a couple of times to play it through, but always ended up in tears. This was of course a response not so much to the pseudo-tragedy as to my own wonder at its superlative unity of form. But here you may detect a touch of self-glorification, which no doubt will soon pass and leave in its place the usual self-critical hangover.[29] The quartet is now with the copyists, and soon I hope the Beethovens and I will be able to start work on it.[30]

So that's my news from the Switzerland of Saxony.

Please give my warm greetings to Fanya Borisovna, and my best wishes to you.

D. Shostakovich.

What follows is an account of the events preceding the composition of the Eighth Quartet.

During the last ten days of June 1960, Shostakovich came to Leningrad and stayed with his sister Mariya rather than at the Yevropeyskaya Hotel as he usually did. It became clear later that there was a reason for this.

On 28 June I paid Dmitry Dmitriyevich a short visit. He told me that he had recently written *Five Satires to Words by Sasha Chorny*, and he hoped to acquaint me with this new opus. But the following day – 29 June – Shostakovich called me early in the morning and asked me to come to see him urgently. The moment I saw him I was struck by the lines of suffering on his face, and by his whole air of distress. He hurried me straight into the little room where he had slept, crumpled down on to the bed and began to weep with great, aching sobs. I was extremely alarmed, imagining that some dreadful harm had befallen either him or someone in his family. In answer to my questioning, he managed through tears to jerk out indistinctly: 'They've been pursuing me for years, hunting me down . . .' Never before had I seen Shostakovich in such a state of hysterical collapse. I gave him a glass of cold water; he drank it down, his teeth chattering, then gradually calmed himself. However, it took about an hour for him to recover enough composure to tell me what had recently been happening in Moscow.

It had been decided on the initiative of Nikita Khrushchov to appoint Shostakovich President of the Russian Federation Union of Composers, but in order for him to take up the post he would have to become a member of the Party. The task of persuading him to take this step had been entrusted to P. N. Pospelov, a member of the Bureau of the Central Committee of the Russian Federation.

These are the exact words which Shostakovich said to me that June morning in 1960, at the height of the 'thaw': 'Pospelov tried everything he knew to persuade me to join the Party, in which, he said, these days one breathes freely and easily under Nikita Sergeyevich. Pospelov praised Khrushchov to the skies, talking about his youth – yes, youth was the word he used – telling me all about his wonderful plans, and about how it really was time I joined the ranks of a Party headed now not by Stalin but by Nikita Sergeyevich. I had almost lost the power of speech, but somehow managed to stammer out my unworthiness to accept such an honour. Clutching at straws, I said that I had never succeeding in properly grasping Marxism, and surely I ought to wait until I had. Next I pleaded my religious beliefs, and after that tried to argue that there was no overriding reason why a Composers' Union President had to be a Party member, citing Konstantin Fedin and Leonid Sobolev, who were non-Party members high up in the Writers' Union. But Pospelov would not hear of my objections, and mentioned several times Khruschchov's particular concern for the development of music, which he felt I had an obligation to support.

'This conversation completely exhausted me. Later, I had another meeting with Pospelov, when he renewed his efforts and once again simply backed me into a corner. In the end I lost my nerve, and just gave in.'

This account of what had transpired kept being interrupted by my agitated questions, and I reminded Shostakovich of the many times he had said to me that he would never join a Party that endorsed violence. After a long pause he went on: 'The Composers' Union soon got to know the outcome of my discussions with Pospelov, and someone or other cobbled together a statement which I was supposed to parrot at a meeting. But look, I absolutely decided I wasn't going to go to any meeting. I came up here to Leningrad on the quiet to stay with my sister and hide from my tormentors, still hoping that they would think better of it, they might feel some sympathy for me and leave me in peace. And I thought if that didn't happen, I could lock myself in up here and just sit it out. But then yesterday evening they sent telegrams to me demanding my return. But I'm not going, you see, they'll only get me to Moscow if they tie me up and drag me there, you understand, they'll have to tie me up.'

Saying these last words as if he were swearing an oath, Shostakovich suddenly became absolutely calm, as though by coming to this decision he had loosened the cord from around his neck. He had taken the first step: by not turning up at the session planned with so much pomp and ceremony, he would effectively neutralize it. Overjoyed at this resolve, I said goodbye and after promising to visit the recluse again in a few days' time, I went back out to the dacha my mother had rented in Zelenogorsk.

However, on 1 July, without waiting for my return visit, he suddenly arrived on the doorstep of the dacha late in the evening, clutching a bottle of vodka. It was raining. After a sleepless night with its attendant emotional upsets, he looked completely exhausted.

Dmitry Dmitriyevich had hardly crossed the threshold of our little cottage when he said: 'Please forgive me for coming so late. But I simply had to see you and share my troubles with you.' Little did I realize then that in a few weeks' time he would be pouring out the troubles gnawing at his heart and unburdening his soul in the Eighth Quartet.

Once the vodka had begun its job of thawing him out, Shostakovich began to talk, not about the ill-fated meeting, but about the power of fate. He quoted a line from Pushkin's *The Gipsies*: 'There's no escaping from one's destiny.' Listening to him, I began to wonder unhappily if he were not even now preparing to submit to his fate, having seen that resistance was vain and he would have eventually to yield. Sadly, this proved to be the case: the meeting, a tragic farce, was simply rearranged for a later date and Shostakovich, his face on fire with shame, read out the prepared statement announcing that he had been accepted into the Party. Thinking back to this episode, I cannot help remembering the title of a marvellous choral work by Shostakovich: *Song of Victory*. It could stand as an epigraph to the story of how he was forced to join the Communist Party.

The utter fearlessness Shostakovich exhibited in his creative and artistic life coexisted with the fear Stalin's terror had bred in him. Small wonder that, caught in the toils of years of spiritual enslavement, writing the autobiographical Eighth Quartet he gave such dramatic and heart-rending voice to the melody of the song 'Tormented by Grievous Bondage'.

19 August 1960 Moscow

Dear Isaak Davïdovich,

If your young friend is still interested in stamps, I hope he will like these ones.

Your

D. Shostakovich

3 November 1960 Moscow

Dear Isaak Davïdovich,

Thank you for your letter. I had a letter yesterday from my sister telling me about the death of Yury Balkashin, and then your letter arrived today. My Moscow friends concealed this terrible news from me. I heard the circumstances of the tragedy from Moysey Vainberg.[31] I did not know him very well, but I liked him for his great culture, true musicianship, kindness and warmth. Galya will, I am sure, be devastated by his death.[32] And I am sure that now she really loves him. She loved him while he was alive, but would not marry him. 'It is your suffering, not you, that I love' – I believe her character is dominated by this somewhat Dostoyevskian trait. But now I can imagine how she must be suffering. I am very worried about her future. Now that Balkashin has died, there will be a question about his living space: will they insist on moving somebody in to share with her?[33] I don't know the precise nature of their relationship, but they lived together in harmony and Galya never complained of finding him a burdensome neighbour.

Altogether, Yu. A.'s death has shaken and upset me no less, and in fact a good deal more than, any of the other circumstances of my life, including breaking my leg. The leg is very painful. They are going to change the plaster on 11 November, and then I have to keep the new plaster on for a further three weeks. After that I'll be on crutches, and I should be allowed to leave hospital at the end of December. The simplest bodily functions have become very complicated. No stool can pass without a nurse.[34] Given my combination of aestheticism, love of cleanliness[35] and modesty, this adds very little joy to my life.[36] At the moment I am abnormally dirty. Tread carefully, mind where you go.

I kiss you warmly. Warmest greetings to Vera Vasiliyevna.

Your

D. Shostakovich

Please write to me. Your letters give me such pleasure.

19 December 1960 Moscow

Dear Isaak Davïdovich,

Thank you for your letter about *Khovanshchina*.[37] How long I have to stay in hospital is now up to me: as soon as I learn to walk on crutches they will let me go home. I have been learning this skill for four days now. It is terribly difficult, and I am not having much success. All this is very lowering to the spirits. Whatever happens I am going to be an invalid until 26 January, when they will remove the plaster. Walking on one leg with crutches is horribly difficult.

Please give my warmest greetings to Vera Vasiliyevna.

D. Shostakovich

31 December 1960 Moscow

Dear Isaak Davïdovich,

A Happy New Year to you!

I left hospital on 27 December and immediately came to the dacha. I have to go back to hospital for two weeks on 21 January to have the plaster removed. After that, there will be various procedures designed to 'restore the use of the left leg'. Just now I am struggling to get about on crutches: I am hoping to avoid the need to develop total mastery of this art. I somehow don't think I shall be enjoying myself dancing the cotillion after my second stay in hospital.

In any event, I am not going to be back on my feet until the middle of February.

I am really out of sorts, but delude myself with the hope that 1961 will be an even better year than 1960.[38]

I kiss you warmly.

Please pass on my best wishes for the New Year to Vera Vasiliyevna and all your family.

D. Shostakovich

1 February 1961 Moscow

Dear Isaak Davïdovich,

Back again in hospital. I now have a 'longetka'[39] on my leg in place of the plaster. It doesn't feel all that different. They are now working on the leg, but I am not allowed to put any weight on it; I still have to hobble about on crutches. I shall soon be going home for a week, and then back again to hospital for the final treatment. I feel just wonderful, really out of sorts and incapable of doing anything; my capacity for doing useful work has entirely evaporated. Thank you for your letter. I know Basner's quartet and Chistyakov's songs,[40] and greatly admire these works.

Please write, do stay in touch.

My respects to all your people.

D. Shostakovich

26 February 1961 Moscow

Dear Isaak Davïdovich,

Thank you very much for your letter. If you have time, please go to Galina Vishnevskaya's concert in the Glinka Hall on 3 March. Her programme includes my songs to words by Sasha Chorny. I should very much like you to hear them.[41]

Give my warmest greetings to all your family.

Your

D. Shostakovich

I am walking on both legs now, but with a stick. The leg aches a bit, but as the doctors say, in six to eight months I shall be able to dance. D. S.

I left the hospital one week ago.

27 February 1961 Moscow

Dear Isaak Davïdovich,

I learned today that the concert by Galina Vishnevskaya and Mstislav Rostropovich that was supposed to have taken place on 3 March and that I asked you to go to, has been postponed until the beginning of May. However I still hope to come to Leningrad on that date for *Khovanshchina*. I hope very much to see you then.

Your

D. Shostakovich

30 April 1961 Moscow

Dear Isaak Davïdovich,

Venyamin Basner has taken with him to Leningrad a very good recording of my Sasha Chorny songs. I should be very pleased if you could find time to listen to them.[42] He has a tape-recorder and I am sure would be happy to play them for you. Unfortunately, he lives quite a long way out; here is his address: Apartment 26, 41 Altaiskaya Street, Leningrad M-142. He isn't on the phone, but you could send him a postcard.

I have written to him saying that I would like you and Galya Ustvolskaya[43] to hear the songs. I expect he will telephone you.

Give my greetings to Vera Vasiliyevna.

Your

D. Shostakovich

6 May 1961 Moscow

Dear Isaak Davïdovich,

You can take it that I am persuaded. Although I have no overwhelming desire to do so, I will write another song.[44] To this end I am planning a working session with the co-authors of the libretto.[45]

I press your hand warmly,

D. Shostakovich

14 May 1961 Moscow

Dear Isaak Davïdovich,

Many thanks for your kind words about my Sasha Chorny songs.[46] Life is very difficult for me at the moment, so much so that I seem to be losing the sense of humour that is so much part of me. As a result, all sorts of dreary thoughts come into my head.

I kiss you warmly, my friend.

D. Shostakovich

15 August 1961 Zhukovka

Dear Isaak Davïdovich,

I have heard nothing from you for ages. It worries me, although I keep in mind that French proverb you are so fond of quoting: 'No news is good news.'

My family is expanding. Maksim and Lena have had a son, whom they have decided to call Dmitry; they are all well. In the matter of the name I have maintained principles of strict neutrality. Then, Galya informed me today that in five months' time I shall have yet another grandson or granddaughter. It's all very nice, but a lot of work. I am beginning to become conscious of a certain lack of living space.[47] I comfort myself by thinking that in ten years' time I shall have quite enough space for any needs I may have, and in twenty years I probably shan't need any at all.

In a week or two I expect to finish my Twelfth Symphony. The first movement is by and large successful, the second and third almost completely so. The fourth does not look as though it is going to work. I am having great difficulty writing it.

Well, that is all my news. We have some rather acute personnel problems. Fenya is very old and feeble now. I found Mariya Terentyevna, but she is not registered to live here.[48] I jump out of my skin every time I see a policeman.[49]

Well, that really is all.

Please give my greetings to all your people, and pass on my special good wishes to Vera Vasiliyevna and Fanya Borisovna.

Your

D. Shostakovich

I am sending this to Leningrad, as by now you have presumably either returned or are about to. D. S.

20 August 1961 Moscow

Dear Isaak Davïdovich,

Three days ago[50] I sent you a letter to you in Leningrad, but yesterday I got one from you from Sestroretsk. I am glad you are still there: I hope you are going for walks, having a rest, gathering your strength for the rigours of the coming season.

I have not yet seen my new grandson. It was a very difficult birth for Lena and they have not yet signed her out of the maternity home. She has been there since 9 August, but she is getting better and we hope they will send her home soon. We were all very worried about her here, especially Maksim. But thank God, all that is over, and we are now looking forward to having her and the baby home with us.

I have finished the Twelfth Symphony, of which I gave you a preliminary critique in my last letter.[51] I am now going to do the piano reduction, after which I will throw myself at Yevgeny Aleksandrovich's feet.[52] I miss very much not seeing you. I started thinking of the summers we spent at Komarovo, when we saw so much of one another.

I press your hand warmly.

Your

D. Shostakovich

18 November 1961[53] Moscow

Dear Isaak Davïdovich,

Thank you for your letter, and for your never-failing kindness towards me. It gives me tremendous support at this particularly difficult time of my life, which has already dragged out its existence for too long.[54]

I have no news to speak of. I finished the Ninth Quartet, but was very dissatisfied with it so in an excess of healthy self-criticism I burnt it in the stove. It is the second time in my 'creative life' that I have pulled a trick like that: the first time was in 1926, when I burnt all my manuscripts.

Please give my warmest greetings to Vera Vasiliyevna, and I send my very best wishes to you.

D. Shostakovich

20 November 1961 Moscow

Dear Isaak Davïdovich,

I am sending you my opus.[55] Please confirm that you have received it. I am rather hoping there will not be any need for further additions to the score, and to that end I spoke on the telephone today to G. M. Rapoport. But he is awash with creative plans.[56]

Your

D. Shostakovich

13 December 1961 Moscow

Dear Isaak Davïdovich,

I am sending you the score and the piano reduction of the finale of the future chef-d'oeuvre of the cinema.[57] I also enclose the Eighth Quartet, which has just been delivered from the printers.

I flew back today from Sverdlovsk, where I spent eleven days, for eight of which I was ill. And I am still not feeling at all well. The organism is giving out, I am convinced of it.

I kiss you warmly.

Your

D. Shostakovich

19 December 1961 Moscow

Dear Isaak Davïdovich,

I am coming to Leningrad for one day on 23 December. I very much hope to see you. It would be good if we could meet that evening, between 8 and 9 o'clock.

Your

D. Shostakovich

Shostakovich was anxious that I should be in Moscow for the première of the Fourth Symphony, scheduled for 30 December, under the baton of Kirill Kondrashin, whose initiative the concert had been. Dmitry Dmitriyevich was in a state of great anxiety, fearing that the symphony would not be well received, after hiding its light under a bushel for twenty-five years. His anxiety communicated itself to me. After all, I had myself been a witness of the rehearsals and the clandestine banning of the symphony in the autumn of 1936. Needless to say, I did go to Moscow, and was present at the triumph of that unforgettable concert.

27 January 1962 Moscow

Dear Isaak Davïdovich,

This evening I went to see Grigory Shantïr's opera *City of Youth*, and a little later on I'll give you my brief opinion of it.[58]

But just now I must share with you my thoughts on a conversation I had with Lev Mikhailov, the chief producer of the Stanislavsky–Nemirovich-Danchenko Musical Theatre. Shantïr's opera is in three acts, so there are two intervals. During the intervals, Mikhailov took me aside and led me into his office where, waving his arms about and showering me with saliva in his excitement, he imparted to me his ideas about what should be done to *Lady Macbeth* to make it stageable. I am fairly used to this sort of thing, but on this occasion I must admit I was rather taken aback by the curious nature of his conception.

'The way to make Katerina Lvovna a warmer, more sympathetic character (?) is to play on the fact that she is pregnant. She dreams of our (that is to say, her and Sergey's) child. She must sing of the child to come, dream of the child. Therefore some of the existing arias should have their words rewritten, and you will definitely have to write two or three more.' He went on in this vein as his inspiration caught fire and took wing.

I reminded him what Ivan Sollertinsky used to say about all those Soviet operas that have ballads, arias and cavatinas about 'the infant yet unborn', *The Quiet Don*, *The Battleship Potyomkin* and *Into the Storm* among others. I can now add to this list Shantïr's *City of Youth*, which likewise includes a duet about an unborn child. But my efforts failed to produce on L. D. Mikhailov the effect I was hoping for, and he persisted in developing his theme right the way through both intervals until the second bell. I listened gloomily.[59]

City of Youth was decently, but not very interestingly staged. The conductor, Provatorov, is competent.[60] In itself Shantïr's opera is certainly better than *The Quiet Don, Into the Storm, The Decembrists, The Great Friendship, With All My Heart* and other pinnacles of Soviet operatic achievement. But he is a quiet, modest sort of person and doesn't occupy a powerful position, so obviously his opera doesn't get the same level of attention and adulation as the others.

That's what I wanted to write to you about. The grandchildren Andrey and Dmitry, Mariya Dmitriyevna and Fenya all have the flu, and now I have come down with it as well. Galya is back from the maternity hospital and brought with her a splendid little boy whom they have called Nikolai. I pray to God that she doesn't get flu as well.

Kondrashin and his orchestra are on tour to Leningrad from 8 to 12 February, and are including Vainberg's Fourth Symphony in their programme. I strongly urge you to hear this marvellous work.

Please give my warmest wishes to Vera Vasiliyevna and all your family.

I press your hand warmly.

Your

D. Shostakovich

10 April 1962 Moscow

Dear Isaak Davïdovich,

I am about to move to a new apartment. Here is the address: Apartment 23, 8–10 Nezhdanova Street, Moscow K-9. The telephone is 2-29-95-29. Nezhdanova Street is what used to be called Bryusovsky Pereulok; the late Nezhdanova was a coloratura soprano. It is terribly sad to be moving; so much is bound up with the apartment we are leaving.[61]

Give my warmest greetings to Vera Vasiliyevna and all your family.

I kiss you warmly.

D. Shostakovich

31 May 1962 Moscow

Dear Isaak Davïdovich,

Thank you for your letter and for what you say about 'Baby Yar'.[62] I am in some difficulty, however, about who could sing it. Vedernikov[63] has been in Italy where they have trained his voice to sing bel canto, and according to Galina Vishnevskaya it has lost all its qualities. Gmïrya's[64] voice is too high. Ivan Petrov is very stupid. And meanwhile I have had an idea that I could write something else along the same lines to words by Yevtushenko.

I have a collection of his poems and it has given me the idea of a symphony, the first or second movement of which would consist of 'Baby Yar'. When I see you, I will show you the poems I have chosen for two of the movements, and I hope that Yevtushenko is going to write another poem I have asked for. So, the Thirteenth Symphony is beginning to take shape. Will it work, do you think? We shall see.[65]

I may have to go into hospital in two or three days' time. The oracles of science have consulted, and decided that this is necessary for my health and general well-being.

Give my warmest greetings to Vera Vasiliyevna and all your family.

Your

D. Shostakovich

24 June 1962 Moscow

Dear Isaak Davïdovich,

Thank you for your letter. I am back in hospital, where they are going to have another try at curing my hand. I cannot say that I am overjoyed to be here,[66] especially during my honeymoon.[67] My wife's name is Irina Antonovna; I have known her for more than two years. Her only defect is that she is twenty-seven years old. In all other respects she is splendid: clever, cheerful, straightforward and very likeable. She comes to see me every day, and that gives me pleasure. She is very good to me. I think we shall get on very well, living with one another.[68]

I am making good use of the time here; I am composing. At the moment I am working on a setting of a poem by Yevtushenko called 'Humour'. I can't say yet whether it will be the second movement of the symphony, or another separate symphonic poem.[69] I have started on the third movement (or third symphonic poem): 'In the Store'. Yevtushenko promised to write something especially for the fourth movement, but he has gone off somewhere or other. I call up every day on the phone, but there is no reply. At all events there are going to be four movements, but whether they will make up a symphony or a suite for voice and orchestra only time will tell.

I wrote to Boris Gmïrya inviting him to take an interest in my new work, and am anxiously awaiting his reply.[70] I think he is probably the only bass who can sing it. As soon as I leave hospital, I want to come to Leningrad for two or three days with Irina Antonovna. I so much want to bring her to visit you and Vera Vasiliyevna. I should imagine this will be in the first half of July.[71]

I am glad you have gone to Sestroretsk. Have a good rest there and recoup your strength.

Please give my warmest greetings to Vera Vasiliyevna.

Your

D. Shostakovich

2 July 1962 Moscow

Dear Isaak Davïdovich,

I am still in hospital. I was delighted to get your letter, and long to see you. If Irina and I come to Leningrad, I will let you know in advance when we plan to come. At present our plans are as follows. When I get out of hospital, we shall come to Leningrad for two or three days. Then we will go back to Moscow and on to Irina's family near Ryazan. She assures me that it is very nice down there and that her aunt will be glad to put us up, feed and water us and so on. We shall be away for two to three weeks. After that – who knows? Apparently I will be going to Edinburgh for the Festival which takes place there.

In general, I am in rather low spirits. It is very boring in the hospital, but on the other hand I suppose the very tedium may be forcing the creative process to spring into action. I have already composed the second and third movements of the Thirteenth Symphony: the second movement is 'Humour' and the third 'In The Store'. I am not expecting this work to be fully understood, but I cannot not write it. If you can get hold of a book of Yevtushenko's poetry called 'A Wave of the Hand', do read these poems. 'Humour' is on page 121 and 'In The Store' on page 109. 'A Career' is on page 52.

Yevtushenko did promise to write another poem for the work, but he has vanished into thin air. There is no reply from his telephone. Gmïrya hasn't replied either.

I agree with you: Burns of course is a genius, while Yevtushenko is talented.[72] But Yevtushenko is still very young, and . . . well, when we meet I'll tell you what I think about Yevtushenko. At all events, I think his life is more complicated than Burns's was. What I like about his art is its life and its undoubted humanity. All the talk about him being just a fashionable poseur and a 'poet of the boudoir' is mostly envy. He is far more talented than many of his colleagues with more conventionally respectable attitudes.[73]

Irina is very nervous about meeting my friends. She is very young and modest. She works from nine to five as a literary editor with Sovetsky Kompozitor publishers. She can't say her r's and l's.[74] Her father was Polish and her mother Jewish, but they are both dead. Her father was a victim of the cult of personality and violations of revolutionary legality.[75] Her mother died. Irina was brought up by an aunt on her mother's side, the same one who is inviting us to stay with her where she lives near Ryazan – I have forgotten the name of the place. Irina was born in Leningrad. Well, that's a brief sketch of her. She was in a children's home, and for a time even in a special children's home.[76] All in all, a girl with a past.

They look after me very well here. I have had a capillaroscopy; what that exactly is isn't important. It was done by Doctor L. F. Timashuk; I expect you remember his name. I do, and was therefore interested in the procedure. L. F. Timashuk resembles the playwright Murashkin in Chekhov's story 'The Drama'. I found L.F. Timashuk very interesting, and would have liked to have a talk with him. But I didn't, I kept silent. A lot of thoughts were buzzing in my head though, after the capillaroscopy. [77]

Well, that's all for now.

Have a good rest, build up your strength and your health.

Give my greetings to Vera Vasiliyevna.

Your

D. Shostakovich

7 July 1962 Moscow

Dear Isaak Davïdovich,

Time passes, and I am still in hospital. The doctors saw me yesterday, and decided that I must stay here until 21 July. Dostoyevsky's injunction to 'humble yourself, proud man' is most appropriate for me now. I should have obeyed it right away when I first began having trouble with my right hand; if I had, perhaps I should not now be having to resign myself (i.e. wait until the 21st).

After the 21st, as soon as I finish the Thirteenth Symphony, I shall go to Kiev to see Gmïrya, from whom I got a nice letter which however stops short of making any commitments.[78]

Then I shall definitely come to Leningrad. I very much want to see you, and so I should like to agree in advance a time when we can meet. If you don't object, and if it would not be a great nuisance, Irina and I will come to visit you in Sestroretsk. In order to achieve this, could I ask you to do the following for me? Go to the bus stop and note down the buses which go between Leningrad and Sestroretsk. Send me the fruits of your researches with a note of which stop to get out at, and how to find the way to Middle Street.[79] I will send you a telegram a day or two before we come. We will stay at Marusya's.[80] If I don't find a letter from you there saying that you can't receive us at Sestroretsk, we will set off straight away to come out to you. We will spend an hour or two with you, and then come back to Leningrad and on to Moscow.

After that we shall go for two or three weeks to Solotcha, near Ryazan, where Irina wants to take me to stay with her aunt. I'll go, and I'll see what sort of a place Solotcha is and what sort of an aunt Irina has.

If it is not convenient for you for us to come to Sestroretsk, then please come into Leningrad to see us.[81] So, I shall wait for your bus timetables – but if it is better to come by train, please let me know the times of the trains. What a lot of trouble I am giving you!

Please give my warmest greetings to Vera Vasiliyevna and all your family.

Your

D. Shostakovich

Needless to say, I am very anxious to show you the Thirteenth Symphony (if it is a symphony?).[82] Three of the movements are completely finished, and I'm now writing the fourth and fifth. Perhaps all this activity is due to being in hospital and otherwise having nothing at all to do.[83]

Irina sends you her best wishes. D. S.

9 July 1962 Moscow

Dear Isaak Davïdovich,

In your last letter you had some complaints about Yevgeny Yevtush-enko's behaviour.[84] This is unjust. The poet sent me five of his poems to choose from. As it happened, none of them were quite right for what I wanted, but he had gone away to Batum, while I sat in hospital with the 'creative juices' in full spate. So I chose one of the poems, the one called 'Fears', which is rather long and a bit wordy. But the first half of it was almost exactly what I needed, although as a matter of fact there are many good things in the second half as well.[85] Anyhow, there's no need for all these explanations now; I shall see you soon after the 20th, when I shall be able to show you the whole opus. It seems it will be called the 'Thirteenth Symphony'. It would be wonderful if there could be a piano available when

I see you. I don't suppose you would be able to come into the city for a couple of hours?[86]

In any case, two days before we come to Leningrad I will send you a telegram, and then we can discuss the details of how we are going to work this out. Perhaps we shall come to see you in Sestroretsk, and then you will return the visit to us at Marusya's in Leningrad. My only reason for coming to Leningrad is my burning desire to see you, and for you to get to know a little about the Thirteenth Symphony.

I press your hand warmly.

Your

D. Shostakovich

Give my warmest greetings to Fanya Borisovna. I am so sorry to miss Vera Vasiliyevna.[87] D. S.

14 July 1962 Moscow

Dear Isaak Davïdovich,

Thank you for your letter. I am still in hospital, but I shall be out on the 20th. On the 21st I am going with Irina Antonovna to Kiev to see Gmïrya, and on the 23rd we shall fly to Leningrad. If it is not too late in the day when we arrive there, say between 12 noon and 2 o'clock, then we shall come straight out to you in Sestroretsk. I will send you a telegram from Kiev, as I won't know the timetable of the flights before then. With such serious events taking place in my life (marriage and the completion of the Thirteenth Symphony)[88] I am desperately anxious to see you, but I would hate to cause any inconvenience to you or Fanya Borisovna. Irina and I will bring half a litre of Stolichnaya[89] and a kilo and a half of lyubitelsky sausage, we'll have a drink and something to eat and then head back into Leningrad to Marusya's.[90]

I am taking a bit of a break from the symphony. It is not finished yet, but it definitely will be by the 20th, or even before.[91] 'In the Store' seems to have turned out to be the strongest movement so far. I find I am utterly transported by this poem.[92]

I should very much like to see Mravinsky when I am in Leningrad, but this probably won't be possible, as I know he is away in Ust-Narva.

I don't want to spend long in Leningrad. I should like if I can to accomplish everything in two days, visiting you, acquainting you and Mravinsky with the symphony, and then back to Moscow.[93] I want to get away to

Solotcha, near Ryazan, and have a rest. I became very tired composing the symphony in hospital. I'm getting old.

I embrace you warmly.

Your

D. Shostakovich

Thank you for the bus timetable. I may send you a telegram from Kiev telling you which bus we shall be on, and then perhaps you could meet us. If you can't, don't worry, we will manage.

Give my warmest (postal) greetings to Fanya Borisovna and Vera Vasiliyevna. D.S.

Irina is a lovely person, but when she is with my friends her nervousness is inclined to make her act a bit like a schoolgirl who suddenly finds herself among the grown-ups. Well, it will soon pass. Don't be offended if she is all embarrassed and tongue-tied. D. S.

16 July 1962 Moscow

Dear Isaak Davïdovich,

Yesterday I received a telegram from Gmïrya, asking me to go to Kiev on 21 July. I had planned to be there on the 22nd, so everything has had to be brought forward by a day. I shall be in Kiev on the 21st and will fly to Leningrad on the 22nd. I will send you a telegram from Kiev letting you know what time I expect to be in Leningrad. If it is early enough we will come out to you on the 22nd, but if it is late, then on the 23rd. In that case, if you have a chance, please telephone me at Marusya's on the evening of the 22nd.

Your

D. Shostakovich

Our meeting that had been the subject of so much meticulous planning duly took place. It is curious that Shostakovich did not think of taking a taxi to bring himself and his new wife out to Sestroretsk, all of thirty-five kilometres from the centre of Leningrad, but elected to travel on the bus. 'Like all the best people,' he said when, after saying goodbye, they squeezed on to the packed bus.

3 August 1962 Solotcha

Dear Isaak Davïdovich,

Irina and I are still talking about our wonderful visit to you in Sestroretsk. For her, and not to mention me, it was the highlight of our time in Leningrad and Ust-Narva.[94]

We are now in Solotcha, where we shall stay until 12 August. On 16 Maksim is coming with me to England, and we shall not be back, so it seems, until 15 or 20 September.

Life is very good here. It is wonderful countryside, and we go for long walks. I am working quite hard; I have orchestrated Musorgsky's *Songs and Dances of Death*[95] and have corrected the proofs of the Fourth Symphony and *Khovanshchina*, both of which are about to go to press. I am now making a four-hand piano reduction of the Thirteenth Symphony.[96]

So that's what's going on.

Give my greetings to Fanya Borisovna and my heartfelt thanks for her hospitality. Irina also sends her best wishes.

Your

D. Shostakovich

Until 12 August our address (marked for my attention) is:

Council of National Economy House, Solotcha, Ryazan District. D. S.

6 January 1963 Moscow

Dear Isaak Davïdovich,

I am sending you the 'new version' of 'Baby Yar'. The lines which the poet has revised in response to criticism are indicated by brackets.[97]

I embrace you.

D. Shostakovich

7 January 1963 Zhukovka

Dear Isaak Davïdovich,

I am bombarding you with poetry. Here is another opus by Yevgeny Yevtushenko, a poem inspired by the première of *Katerina Izmailova* and dedicated to me.[98]

When Tsar Nicholas 1 heard Glinka's opera *Ivan Susanin*, he graciously permitted himself to make the following observation:

The music is of no importance. What matters is the subject.

With reference to 'Second Birth', I feel inclined to echo this august thought, however with the difference that both Yevtushenko's poetry and the subject are very good in this work.[99]

I don't much like the title 'Second Birth'. My music did not die, and therefore did not need to be born a second time.[100] I failed to convey this thought to the poet, as he is travelling in West Germany, France and other countries for two months, and that was also the reason I was not able to tell him my reaction to the new version of 'Baby Yar'.

Your
D. Shostakovich

28 January 1963 Zhukovka

Dear Isaak Davïdovich,

On 10 and 11 February there will be regular subscription performances of the Thirteenth Symphony. I have made two changes:

instead of	I see myself a Jew of ancient days
	Wandering in ancient Egypt's distant lands,
	Upon the cross my life ebbs out its sands,
	My flesh still shows its legacy of nails.
I shall have	I stand as if beside the living wellspring
	That nourishes my faith in brotherhood,
	Here Russians and Ukrainians lie sharing
	That same earth with the Jews who once here stood.
and instead of	Above the thousand thousands buried here
	I am a mute, unuttered, wordless cry.
	I am each old man shot behind the ear,
	I am each cruelly murdered little boy.
I shall have	And then I think of Russia's victory,
	Blocking the Fascist's headlong rush to hate,
	That Russia which is ever dear to me
	To her last drop of being and of fate.[101]

The music stays as it was; the only thing that has changed is the words. As Tsar Nikolai said at some time or other: 'The music is not important. What matters is the subject.'[102]

I have a favour to ask of you. My exercise in graphomania is drawing to a close: I have almost finished sorting out the score of *Lady Macbeth*.[103] Ought I to change the Police Officer to a Police Constable? I think 'Officer' was a rank in the towns, but in the provincial districts and volosts they were called 'Constables'. If your erudition extends this far, could you please give me your opinion?

Please give my warmest greetings to Vera Vasiliyevna and all your family.

Your

D. Shostakovich

22 February 1963 Moscow

Dear Isaak Davïdovich,

I shall probably come to Leningrad early in March.

I doubt whether I can do anything to help Doniyakh. His position is a very difficult one.[104]

Your

D. Shostakovich

14 April 1963 Moscow

Dear Isaak Davïdovich,

On 13 April I drank too much, fell asleep and almost missed the train.[105] I expect that you telephoned me or called round and knocked on the door, but I did not hear anything. If this was indeed the case, for heaven's sake please forgive me.

Besides that, I am annoyed with myself that as a result of this disgraceful behaviour I did not give you the little present I had for you. It is my *Six Romances on Verses by English Poets,* one of which – 'MacPherson Before His Execution' – is dedicated to you. I wrote these songs a long time ago, but they have just been published.[106]

Once again, I implore you not to be angry with me. I am going into hospital again tomorrow to get more treatment for my hand. If you have a moment, please write to me.

Give my warmest greetings to Vera Vasiliyevna.

Your

D. Shostakovich

6 May 1963 Moscow

Dear Isaak Davïdovich,

The day after I returned from Leningrad, I went into hospital, where I have to stay until 15 May. On the 17th I shall come to Leningrad, and stay until the 20th inclusive. I hope very much to see you during that time.

I feel well, which makes me very frustrated. I am having treatment for my hand, with about the same level of success as on previous occasions.

Thinking back to my last stay in hospital, which must have been about a year ago, I remember how I spent days on end working on the Thirteenth Symphony, so caught up was I in it.[107] I remember that the moment I left hospital, Irina and I went to Kiev to meet Boris Gmïrya, and then we flew straight from there to Leningrad. Then out to see you at Sestroretsk, then on to Ust-Narva to see Mravinsky. What a wonderful time it was.[108] Now I am composing nothing; my head is absolutely empty and I am devoid of creative ideas. That is to say I do have some, but I have no strength, no 'inspiration'.[109] It's only to be expected. I am already an old man.

I shall soon be out of hospital, then I shall come to Leningrad and after that return to Moscow. 'And what then?', as the late Aleksandr Zhitomirsky used to say.[110]

So, until we meet again, which I pray will be soon.

Give my warmest greetings to Vera Vasiliyevna.

Your

D. Shostakovich

28 June 1963 Moscow

Dear Isaak Davïdovich,

I have transferred 65 roubles to you for the Mayakovsky reminiscenses.[111] When it arrives, could you please confirm receipt of the money to me at this address: Composers' House, Dilizhan, Armenian Republic. Send it airmail so that it gets here more quickly.

I press your hand warmly,

D. Shostakovich

7 July 1963 Dilizhan

Dear Isaak Davïdovich,

Thank you for your note. By the way, it was delivered within three days, so airmail gets here quicker than a train but slower than an aeroplane. As I discovered, the flight from Leningrad to Yerevan takes four hours and 15 minutes. I rejoice that the dream of the greatest and most talented people on earth has thus achieved sublime reality.[112]

We are having a wonderful time here in Dilizhan, or rather, to be precise, eight kilometres from Dilizhan, which is itself roughly halfway between Yerevan and Tbilisi. They have built twelve cottages in the middle of marvellously wild country, with all facilities. There is even gas laid on, so there is no problem with baths; you can turn on the gas at any moment day or night and take a bath or a shower. I must say, the Armenian Musical Fund has done it all splendidly. You breathe the mountain air and drink in the forests all around. It is not so easy to walk, as the ground has not been levelled, you're always going either up or down hill. All the same, we are walking a lot, difficult though it is for me taking into consideration my broken leg. I do it in a vain attempt to reduce my stomach, which is expanding relentlessly.

Having recently been in Kirghizia and now in Armenia, I have come to the conclusion that there is nothing more beautiful than the Earth. I think constantly of Mahler's *Song of the Earth*.[113] I have a *Song of the Earth* of my own, ripening somewhere inside me, but so far it is no more than vague imaginings.[114]

On 13 July we are thinking of going in to Yerevan to hear Stravinsky's *Oedipus Rex* at the Opera.[115] They are doing two consecutive performances, on the 13th and 14th – great people, these Armenians! We are staying here until the 28th, after which, rested and brimming with health, creative power and enthusiasm, we shall return home.

I am planning to celebrate the anniversary of the completion of my problematical Thirteenth Symphony on 20 July. The cottages here all have a tape recorder, and we brought a tape of it with us. We'll play it, and then have a drink accompanied by some tomatoes, cucumbers and garlic – for which I have developed a passion – and fall into bed. We'll celebrate in seclusion.

I remember how one year ago I came out of hospital and left the same day for Kiev to see Gmïrya, then we went to Leningrad and Ust-Narva to see Mravinsky, and out to you at Sestroretsk. A lot of water under the bridge since then.

I remember Nikolai Peyko objecting that one cannot call Humour a fine fellow of a man, because Humour is not a person. And also that one cannot say 'I am making a career of not making a career.' Ho, ho, ho. The world is full of clever people.[116]

All in all, I am remembering much and I am thinking many thoughts. Even so, I am taking physical exercise, going for walks on the rough, uneven terrain, because if I have a good few years still allotted to me I do not want to be an invalid. So I am getting into training, and not drinking. The weather is very changeable here, and it rains a lot. But it is not too hot, and that is good.

> And so – a toast to our career
> When we have one as full of joy
> As that of Shakespeare or Pasteur,
> Of Newton or of Lev Tolstoy![117]

Irina and I send you, Vera Vasiliyevna and all your family our very best wishes.

Your

D. Shostakovich

24 July 1963 Dilizhan

Dear Isaak Davïdovich,

I received your letter. I believe the record length of time my letter took to get to you is explained by purely local problems. The nearest post office to the Composers' House is in Dilizhan, which is eight kilometres away. The local postmen seem pretty absent-minded, so it probably languished for several days in the letter-box at the Composers' House. As for the return address I put on the envelope, I have a rule that wherever I am writing from, I always put my permanent address in Moscow on the envelope. I do this because, should for any reason my letter not get to the addressee, I want it to be sent back to me in Moscow. For example, suppose my letter from Dilizhan did not get delivered to you – perhaps because you had gone to Sestroretsk earlier than anticipated. Then my letter would have been sent back to me in Dilizhan, but I would already have left there. Then, eventually, it would have to be sent on to me in Moscow after all. And that is why I always follow the rule of putting my permanent address on the envelope.[118]

On 28 July we are flying to Moscow. I have thoroughly enjoyed my time in Dilizhan. I may have to come to Leningrad in August, in which case I will send you a wire.

Be healthy and happy.

Warmest greetings to Vera Vasiliyevna and all your family from Irina and from me.

D. Shostakovich

1 August 1963 Zhukovka

Dear Isaak Davïdovich,

Irina and I are coming to Leningrad for two days on 10 August. I should very much like to see you then. If you can, please write down the times of buses from Leningrad to Sestroretsk and send the timetable to me at the Moscow address. Then, if you will, tell me which bus you propose to meet. If possible, I should like to leave Leningrad for Sestroretsk at about 12 noon, so that I can spend some time with you and then get back to Leningrad in time for the Red Arrow[119] to Moscow.

I am hoping to achieve all this on 11 August.[120] If when you write you can let me know which bus you will meet, then that is the one we shall come on. As I said, it would be ideal if the bus left Leningrad at around 12 noon.

I have been sent a recording of Benjamin Britten's *War Requiem*. I am playing it and am thrilled with the greatness of this work, which I place on a level with Mahler's *Das Lied von der Erde* and other great works of the human spirit.[121] Hearing the *War Requiem* somehow cheers me up, makes me even more full of the joys of life.

Your

D. Shostakovich

If this letter is delayed reaching you, please reply to Leningrad poste restante D-88, as neither Marusya nor Mitya are in Leningrad at present.

Give my warmest greetings to all your family, also from Irina. D. S.

27 August 1963 Zhukovka

Dear Isaak Davïdovich,

I shall be in Leningrad on 6 and 7 September, and should very much like to see you. On 6 I shall be busy from 12 noon until 2 o'clock, and the same on the 7th. I am going to bring with me the recording of B. Britten's

Requiem, and should love to play it to you.[122] If any of your friends has a record player, we could go there and listen to it. It lasts about an hour and a half. Do let me know if this would be possible.

Your

D. Shostakovich

1 September 1963 Moscow

Dear Isaak Davïdovich,

Thank you for your reply. Unfortunately I don't know Mikhail Vaiman's address, so I wish you would give him my best wishes and ask him if we could possibly make use of his gramophone to listen to the *Requiem*.[123] The best time would be on 6 September at 7 p.m. The *Requiem* lasts an hour and a half. Do make sure you are free at that time.

Your

D. Shostakovich

Yesterday was the first performance of *Katerina Izmailova* this season.[124] It seems to have fallen to pieces a bit during the summer. D. S.

9 October 1963 Moscow

Dear Isaak Davïdovich,

I have heard rumours that Molchanov's opera *Romeo, Juliet and Darkness* has been justly and inspirationally panned in *Leningrad Pravda*.[125] I should be very grateful if you could send me the article in *Leningrad Pravda* which thus justly and inspirationally reviews Molchanov's opera.

Forgive me for troubling you with this, but as you may deduce, Molchanov's art has always interested and excited me.

Your

D. Shostakovich

31 December 1963 Zhukovka

Dear Isaak Davïdovich,

Warmest good wishes to you and to all your family for the New Year. I hope that 1964 will bring you, Vera Vasiliyevna and all of you health and happiness. On the night of 1–2 January, Irina and I are going to Zagreb in Yugoslavia, where there is a new production of *Katerina*

Izmailova opening on 7 January. I am not expecting any great artistic revelations from this trip; I am mostly going out of curiosity. I have never been to Yugoslavia, and am most interested to be going there.[126] We shall be back on 10 January, travelling by train, because there is only one direct flight a week to Belgrade.

In four hours' time it will be the New Year, and we are celebrating it simply and by ourselves at home. Galina Vishnevskaya and Mstislav Rostropovich may come over; they are our neighbours at the dacha.

I press your hand warmly.

Your

D. Shostakovich

At the start of the year 1964, during January and February, Shostakovich was often in Leningrad in connection with the film of *Hamlet* directed by Grigory Kozintsev, for which he wrote the score. In my capacity as editorial consultant for the film, I watched all the cuts twice through with Shostakovich.

Shostakovich asked me several times to write a libretto based on any of Shakespeare's plays (except *Othello*). He said (verbatim): 'Some time I really must talk to you about Shakespeare. I love and admire him although sometimes I begin to regard him with the eyes of Lev Tolstoy.' (Tolstoy held very idiosyncratic views on Shakespeare.)

During March and April of 1964 Shostakovich settled down to serious work on the *Hamlet* score. He asked me if I thought it would be a worthwhile project to make a symphonic poem from it, and on 10 April he telephoned to ask me if I could arrange for the recording of the music to be expedited. However, he soon lost interest in the further life of the magnificent music he had composed for the film, and turned his attention to the Ninth Quartet to replace the one he had destroyed. As he informed me when he came to Leningrad on 29 May, he had finished the quartet the previous day.

16 July 1964 Dilizhan

Dear Isaak Davïdovich,

Time flies. We have already been in Dilizhan for ten days, in this glorious part of the world. Everything is good here, including the most important thing – the weather.

We have to leave this divine place on the 29th. We are having a splendid time, and are very well. I have composed two movements of another quartet, the Tenth. I expect to be able to finish it before we leave Dilizhan.

All the cottages here have a tape-recorder, and every day I listen two or three times to *Songs of Kursk*. Each time I hear them I am overwhelmed by their matchless beauty.[127]

1 Dmitry Shostakovich with Ivan Sollertinsky in Novosibirsk

2 DS with Yevgeny Mravinsky in Novosibirsk

3 Isaak Glikman in 1939

5 The sculptor Gavriil Glikman (r.) in 1934 with his brother Isaak and the bust of Beethoven presented to Shostakovich. The bust is still in the study of Shostakovich's apartment in Moscow.

4 DS with his first wife, Nina Varzar, in Prague, 1946

6 DS with the conductor Natan Rakhlin in Kiev, 1957

7 DS with the conductor Nikolai Rabinovich

8 At the recording of the music for Kozinstev's film *King Lear*. Seated (l. to r.): Irina Shostakovich, Isaak Glikman, DS, Grigory Kozintsev

9 DS with the composer Boris Klyuzner at Repino

10 DS with his children Galina (Galya) and Maksim, and Isaak Glikman, Komarovo, early 1950s

11 DS with Isaak Glikman at Komarovo, 1954

12 (l. to r.): the violinist Mikhail Vaiman, DS, Irina Shostakovich, Venyamin Basner

13 DS with Irina Shostakovich at a concert, 1962

14 Galina Shostakovich with her children at Repino

After Dilizhan, Irina and I may go to Lake Balaton in Hungary, so it will be some time before you and I see one another. I regret so much that we did not meet during your stay in Moscow, but you were there such a short time.

Give our very best wishes to all your family. Please write to me, bearing in mind the time it takes for airmail to get here. We are leaving for Moscow on the 29th.

Your

D. Shostakovich

Address: Composers' House, Dilizhan, Republic of Armenia, for my attention.

21 July 1964 Dilizhan

Dear Isaak Davïdovich,

I have kept my word – another quartet, the Tenth, was finished yesterday. It is dedicated to Moysey Vainberg. He wrote nine quartets and with the last of them overtook me, since at the time I only had eight. I therefore set myself the challenge of catching up and overtaking Vainberg, which I have now done.[128]

Yesterday, in celebration of this achievement and of the anniversary of finishing the Thirteenth Symphony, we had a good old booze-up.[129] Today I feel dreadful and disgusting.

I am glad that everything is going well for you and that life in Sestroretsk is good. We return to Moscow on 29 July.

Irina and I send you and all your family our very best wishes.

Your

D. Shostakovich

15 September 1964 Zhukovka

Dear Isaak Davïdovich,

The summer is over, the time of troubles now begins. I miss you very much. I may come to Leningrad for two or three days on 20 September.

I have had something wrong with me for a few days: I got some kind of infection, and then a cold. Nevertheless, the creative diarrhoea continues unabated.[130] Yesterday I finished a large symphonic poem for bass, mixed choir and orchestra, not unlike 'Baby Yar'. It is called *The Execution of*

Stepan Razin,[131] and the poet is the same Yevgeny Yevtushenko. The piece lasts about thirty-eight minutes; although at first I did think of making something like the Thirteenth Symphony, I have now decided there is not going to be any more of it. I like Yevtushenko's poetry very much, although there are certainly things in *The Execution of Stepan Razin* that will cause Nikolai Peyko some innocent amusement.[132]

I find it interesting that when I was composing the Thirteenth Symphony, I felt myself at one with almost every word the poet had written. But in *The Execution of Stepan Razin* (please have a look at the poem) there are many lines that I object to, in fact I find myself almost engaging in polemics with them. Also, some lines are simply not very good, and these I have cut out. Yevtushenko is away from Moscow at the moment, so I am not in 'creative dialogue' with him. If he does not agree with me, and I'm sure he won't, then I shall have to leave it as it is, but at least he ought to know what I categorically don't agree with.[133] When you look at my work, please take note of the marks I have made on the text. Where lines have a cross (+), it means that I categorically don't accept them. A nought (o) means that I have cut out the line. A dash (—) means that Nikolai Peyko would, in all sincerity, find the line risible. A question mark means that the line could run into difficulties with the censor. I have made these marks in pencil, so please erase them. I may have to show the score to people when they listen to the work, and they ought just to be able to follow the text without anything to distract them.

I have written the poem in *style russe*. Critics both favourably disposed and hostile will find plenty of material to occupy them. Quite often I descend to coarse naturalism;[134] for example there is naturalistic depiction of the itching of the wanton girls' thighs and of fleas jumping from the peasants' armyaks[135] to the women's furs. Not to mention that the whole idea of the piece is essentially depraved. Anyhow, please have a look at my poem, which I enclose for you.[136]

That's all for now. Keep in good health.

Your

D. Shostakovich

Please pass on to your family our warmest greetings. D. S.

24 September 1964 Zhukovka

Dear Isaak Davïdovich,

I have to carry on writing in red ink. My black pen has finished, and there is no more ink. Thank you for your letter and for your very perceptive comments about Yevtushenko.[137] I have the greatest admiration for this poet.

What draws me above all is the ethical basis of his poetry. His brain may still have a few holes in it, through which leaks the occasional foolishness, but in time the holes will be darned.[138] It's my belief that those who reject Yevtushenko's poetry are not in fact legion; they are far fewer than that. Among them, of course, are those who reject it on aesthetic grounds. 'Call that a rhyme!' they say. Sadly, such people utterly fail to appreciate the ethical basis of the poetry, not only Yevtushenko's but that of many other poets as well. And there are educated and cultivated people among their ranks.

I well remember that clever and cultivated man Anatoly Kankarovich[139] wittily jeering at the poems by Gmïrev, Radin, Tarasov and Kots that I used for my choral settings; he did a brilliant hatchet job on them.[140] I also remember the many cultivated and intelligent people who told me that they were shocked at how dreadful the libretto of *Lady Macbeth* was.[141]

The whole phenomenon is a very complex one: the character of rhyme and the style and rapidity with which phrases modulate are highly subtle manifestations which are not easy to judge. For instance, I prefer Yevtushenko's rhyming of '*stráshny*' with '*zráchki*'[142] to Mayakovsky's '*zhízn s kovo*' with '*s Dzerzhínskovo*'[143] as he has in his 'Verses on Dzerzhinsky'.

In the old days, long, long ago, music's only mission was to entertain, and music like this has a perfect right to exist. 'Music is nice to listen to', 'a painting is nice to look at', 'a novel is nice to read'. But behind this niceness lurks the philistine, the ignoramus, the vulgarian.

Generally speaking, things are not very good nowadays.

And generally speaking, all kinds of thoughts come into one's mind on the eve of one's fifty-eighth birthday.

All the same, Yevtushenko is a true, a fine poet.[144] And those holes in the brain will mend.

On 26 September I am going for a week to Ufa. I have given *The Execution of Stepan Razin* to the copyists. After Ufa, I shall come to Leningrad to do some work with the postgraduate students. Three of them (Byelov, Okunyev and Mnatsakanian) are coming to the end of their courses and have their final exams on 17 October.

Your

D. Shostakovich

13 December 1964 Moscow

Dear Isaak Davïdovich,

I urge you to read a short story by Yury Nagibin, 'Far Away from the War'. I was most impressed by it. If you can't find it in Leningrad, I will bring it up with me. It is published by the Sovetskaya Rossiya press, and it may well be on sale now.

Rehearsals of *Stepan Razin* begin on the 22nd, and the performance is scheduled for the 28th.[145]

D. Shostakovich

27 January 1965 Moscow

Dear Isaak Davïdovich,

I was in hospital for three weeks, but came out yesterday.

I received your letter, and was so sorry to hear that Vera Vasiliyevna is ill. I hope she will soon recover, and that everything will be all right for you. There is nothing worse than illness. I had an exceedingly dull time in hospital: there is flu going about in Moscow and so no visitors were allowed. We were allowed to use the telephone only between 4 p.m. and 9 p.m., and there was only one telephone for a large number of patients.

Thank you for the news about Aleksandr Prokofiev; it was from your letter that I learned about his temporary problems. That is not a slip of the pen: I really believe that what has happened to him is not a long-term misfortune. The truth will prevail.[146] I know very little, correction I know absolutely nothing, about Dudin,[147] and have not been able to find out from anybody. I went straight to the dacha from hospital, and have no sources of information here. I have no desire to go to Moscow; after my stay in hospital I have lost all my energy and don't want to do anything, although I must buckle down to the music for the *Karl Marx* film.[148]

It looks as though Irina and I have to go to Vienna on 31 January for the première there of *Katerina Izmailova*. I don't want to go at all.

There has been a ten-day festival of Russian art in Belorussia, with performances of *The Execution of Stepan Razin* in Minsk and Gomel. Kondrashin led the orchestra, and Yurlov the choir; the soloist was Gromadsky. *Stepan* had its second Moscow performance on 5 January, and was also performed in Gorky on the 24th, conducted by Izrail Gusman. A Leningrad performance is scheduled for 27 March, as Kondrashin will be on tour there then.

Yevtushenko's 'The Bratsk Hydro-Electric Station' has been dropped from the first issue of the magazine *Youth*.[149] The poet is hysterical about this.

So, that's how life goes on.

Give my greetings and best wishes to Vera Vasiliyevna.

Your

D. Shostakovich

23 April 1965 Zhukovka

Dear Isaak Davïdovich,

Illness has chained me to the dacha. I don't go anywhere, but try to go for walks as much as I can. In life everything comes to an end. Evidently I am coming to the end of the road as a composer.[150] I simply cannot write the music to the *Karl Marx* film. Roshal[151] is furious with me. The reason for writing to you now is to tell you about an absolutely excellent article on *The Execution of Stepan Razin* by Sergey Slonimsky[152] in issue no. 4 of *Sovetskaya Muzïka*. Try to get hold of this journal and read the article.

In issue no. 4 of *Oktyabr* [*October*] there is an article by A. Dremov headed 'A Start Has Been Made. Now What . . . ?' The article contains an inspiring critique of the art of Yevtushenko, notably the speculative nature of his poem 'Baby Yar'. Do read it, it will broaden your horizons.[153]

Please pass on my warmest greetings to Vera Vasiliyevna.

Your

D. Shostakovich

19 June 1965 Moscow

Dear Isaak Davïdovich,

Excuse me for writing on this paper. I have no other at the moment.

Aram Khachaturian has given me his impressions of the scenario. He thinks it is excellent.[154] However, he does consider that not enough attention is paid to the Historic Decree concerning the opera *The Great*

Friendship.[155] He suggests adding to the scenario scenes along lines something like this: the Historic Decree is issued and put into operation, meanwhile the composer continues to work on his violin concerto and the Jewish Songs.[156] This conforms to historical accuracy.[157] Khachaturian said that he would write to you about his ideas.[158] I have not had an opportunity to speak to Chulaki, so I don't know his opinion on the scenario.

Somehow or other I seem to have got through the drudgery of writing the score for Karl Marx, and the final recording will be done on 21 June. The number of leaves added to my crown of laurels as a result of this work will be, I fear, small.

What are your plans for the summer? Irina and I are going to the Belovezh Forest at the end of July.[159]

Please pass on my warmest greetings to all your family.

I press your hand warmly.

Your

D. Shostakovich

3 July 1965 Repino

Dear Isaak Davïdovich,

I have arrived at the Composers' Rest House at Repino, where I shall stay until 12 July. It would be splendid if we could meet.

D. Shostakovich

6 July 1965 Repino

Dear Isaak Davïdovich,

I got your note.[160] I should be delighted if you could come over to Repino on Sunday. Come to lunch, which we shall have at 2 o'clock.

Do come.

D. Shostakovich

I shall be leaving on Monday. D.S.

3 August 1965 Kamenyuki

Dear Isaak Davïdovich,

We did not manage to get together before I came away.

I am here with Irina in the forests of Belovezh. We have seen bison, wild boar and deer.[161] It is all very interesting, but the weather is bad and most of the time we have to stay indoors, as the rain just pours down without stopping. However, it is very beautiful here.

We shall stay until 14 August. If you feel like dropping me a line, I should be very glad. The address is: The Hotel, Kamenyuki Postal District, Kamenetsky Region, Province of Brest. Mark letters for my attention.

Irina and I send you and all your family our very best wishes.

D. Shostakovich

16 August 1965 Moscow

Dear Isaak Davïdovich,

I received your letter. I found the Belovezh forests absolutely thrilling.[162] I should love to think that you also might come here some time. I have seen bison: they are most impressive, even I should say frightening. It was also a delight to encounter deer who did not run away in fear, taran (a breed of horse), wild boar and other animals.

I am looking forward with some excitement to the start of the new season. On 20 September my Thirteenth Symphony is to be performed, which was a pleasant surprise for me.[163] Gromadsky is brushing up his part, and Yurlov is already rehearsing the chorus. The engine has been started. Kondrashin is also under way with his preparations.

That's all the news for now.

I press your hand warmly.

Your

D. Shostakovich

I may come to Leningrad some time after the 20th of the month.

4 September 1965 Moscow

Dear Isaak Davïdovich,

There are some enjoyable snippets in *Krokodil*,[164] No. 24 (1782) of 30 August 1965. I have picked out five of them and set them to music for bass voice with piano accompaniment.[165] It may be that you don't subscribe to *Krokodil*, so I have transcribed the texts and am sending them to you.[166]

I have thought up a title for each one. The first three are taken from the 'Believe It Or Not' section, and the last two from 'Leafing Through The Pages'. There is a small domestic conflict going on here over number four, 'Irinka and the Shepherd'. Irina Antonovna wants me to substitute 'Marinka' or 'Anyutka' for 'Irinka', lest the public imagine that I am writing about her. Although this is in fact not the case, I am prepared to accept a suitable alternative, since at the end of the day the change won't make any difference.

The musical style of this opus incorporates the genius of folk idiom (the Russian folk-song 'In the Garden or the Kitchen Garden') and also our classical heritage (Tchaikovsky's opera *The Queen of Spades*). I have also made use of the '*Dies irae*'. Thus in composing these songs I have drawn on the techniques of Socialist Realism.

The demands of the concert season are almost upon us. I have to go to Kiev, and to Leningrad, where the Thirteenth Symphony will be played on 20th September.

That's all for now.

I expect you will have returned to Leningrad by now. We have torrential rain in Moscow at present, and great thunderstorms. 'I love the thunderstorm in early September.'[167]

Warmest greetings to all your family. Irina also sends her best wishes and hopes that you will succeed in persuading me to change Irinka into Marinka or Anyutka.

Your

D. Shostakovich

I am much looking to showing you my new opus.[168] D. S.

10 September 1965 Zhukovka

Dear Isaak Davïdovich,

Thank you for your letter. Irina is grateful for your solidarity in the dispute over Irinka. I remain unconvinced. If I change Irinka to Marinka, then I risk giving offence to the musicologist Marina Sabinina. On the other hand, if Irinka becomes Anyutka, Anna Karavayeva[169] might be insulted. In the same way, college registrars and chauffeurs, for example, may erroneously feel they have been slighted, as Comrades Gogol and Rumyantsev have already described in their writings.

We go to Kiev tomorrow, and will fly to Leningrad on the 15th. There has already been one rehearsal of the Thirteenth Symphony, but so far only with the orchestra. They have kept it in their memory very well, and I know they will give an excellent performance on the 20th. Kondrashin was not well today: he has lost his voice so had to take the rehearsal in a whisper. It is not serious though; the voice will come back tomorrow or the day after.

Please God Gromadsky doesn't fall ill. Yurlov told me that the chorus also has a good recall of the piece.

At all events we shall see, if we live.

I am a prey to nerves. For some reason I don't have much enthusiasm for the film version of *Katerina Izmailova* that is going to be made.[170] I am also worrying about Maksim and the Tenth Symphony.[171]

I am living at the dacha for the time being. Mariya Dmitryevna has gone into hospital to have treatment for her serious illnesses. Daily life is grinding me down. Little Mitya (Maksim's son) is without a nanny, and so gets shuttled about like a football between his grandma and his great-grandma in Vïshny Volochok. It seems very difficult to get him into a kindergarten. I miss seeing you very much.

Your

D. Shostakovich

24 September 1965 Moscow

Dear Isaak Davïdovich,

Thank you for your letter and for the newspaper cutting.

You have nothing whatever to reproach yourself for. It was all very good, and very nice.[172]

Please give my warmest greetings to Vera Vasiliyevna. I hope we shall soon see one another in Leningrad.

Your

D. Shostakovich

26 November 1965 Moscow

Dear Isaak Davïdovich,

I am terribly upset that such an awful misfortune should have befallen Olga Panteleymonovna.[173] I shall do whatever I can to ensure that Muzfond (the Musical Fund) helps her out, although one-time or occasional help won't be able to solve the general problem of her material circumstances.

I clasp your hand warmly.
D. Shostakovich

I fully agree with your opinion of the novel *The Aphis*.[174] D. S.

16 February 1966 Zhukovka

Dear Isaak Davïdovich,

Thank you for your letter, and for what you say about *The Execution of Stepan Razin*. Everything fits in with what I had intended. However I had imagined a slightly different scene at the point where the pipers, especially imported for the occasion, play their lively music. I thought the crowd on the square should not in fact be dancing, which would make it reasonable for them to be urged to do so[175] – 'Now, good people, why stand you there not merrymaking? Hats in the air, and dance!' The only people who would in fact be dancing at that point would be the professional Song and Dance Ensemble of those days – everyone else would be frozen in horror. Evidently I have not succeeded here, since you imagined the whole crowd dancing and only later freezing in horror.[176]

I am planning to go for ten days to Repino. I'll pay for it no doubt: on 19 February the Plenum of the Governing Body of the Union of Soviet Composers of the USSR opens, at which there will be a quantity of brilliant new works by composers to listen to.[177] I did promise to attend the Plenum, but I simply don't have the strength. Also, I have now begun work on the Fourteenth Symphony, and I think that perhaps I shall get on better with it in Repino than in Moscow. But I shall really catch it, I'm sure, for absconding from the Plenum.

It would be great if you could visit me in Repino. I shall be there from 19 February. But do ring up first, because I may go into the city, or back to Moscow, or perhaps not go at all.

Give my warmest greetings to Vera Vasiliyevna.

Your
D. Shostakovich

20 March 1966 Zhukovka

Dear Isaak Davïdovich,

We all congratulate you most heartily on your new home.[178] All the teething troubles will soon disappear, and all will be warmth and light.

Before long Vera Vasiliyevna will cook something magical, something fully worthy of her culinary genius, on her own gas cooker. To be able at last to go to the lavatory or the bathroom without queuing up is such a joy.[179] At all events, I do congratulate you. I am longing to come to Leningrad and inspect your new abode.

I have just crossed out your old address in my address book and written in the new one. I have a lot of addresses for you in this book, which I have had since 1944: 18 Ulyanovskaya Street, Tashkent; Apartment 57, 2 Lomansky Pereulok, Leningrad; Apartment 2, 63 Dzerzhinsky Street; Apartment 3, 6 Moskovsky Prospect, Leningrad. All these addresses hold many memories for me, and no doubt for you.

As for me, I fell ill when I returned to Moscow. My blood pressure went up, and my heart began to have problems. I am now officially classified as invalid seventh class. I expect in time to graduate to invalid first class de luxe.[180] However, I'm not depressed. I have just composed a 'Preface to the Complete Collection of my Works and a Brief Reflection upon this Preface'.[181] Words and music are by me, and you can see the text of this opus overleaf:

> I smudge the page with just a single smear
> And hear the whistling sounds with practised ear.
> I deafen the whole world with hideous clang,
> Then publish in the river Lethe. Bang!

Such a Preface could be written not just to my collected works, but to those of many, many other composers both Soviet and foreign. And here is the signature: Dmitry Shostakovich. People's Artist of the USSR. A great many other titles and honours. First Secretary of the RSFSR Union of Composers, just plain Secretary of the USSR Union of Composers, and also a great many other highly responsible commitments and appointments.

Thus acquainting you with the text of my new composition, I close my letter.

I may also inform you that I have composed another quartet, my eleventh. I am now working on a second concerto for cello and orchestra, and am on the point of finishing the first movement.

Be of good cheer.

Your

D. Shostakovich

30 March 1966 Moscow

Dear Isaak Davïdovich,

I am so glad to hear that you now have the keys to your postbox, and that correspondence will in future reach you in good time. I now wait for further good news about your new home: the gas connected, continuous electric light, telephone installed, and so on.

D. Shostakovich

5 April 1966 Moscow

Dear Isaak Davïdovich,

I shall be in Leningrad on 9 and 10 April. I badly want to come to visit you and see your new home.[182] Please telephone to Marusya's and fix a time. I am busy between 12 noon and 3 p.m. on the 9th.

D. Shostakovich

I have just discovered that I must be in Moscow on the 10th, and so shall only be in Leningrad for one day on 9 April. D. S.

19 April 1966 Moscow

Dear Isaak Davïdovich,

We are travelling to the Crimea today. We shall be back on 15 May. If you need to get in touch with me, my address will be: Nizhnyaya Oreanda United Sanatorium, Yalta, Crimea. Mark the letter for my attention.

Your

D. Shostakovich

27 April 1966 Nizhnyaya Oreanda

Dear Isaak Davïdovich,

I have got into the habit of informing you about my new compositions. I have just completed the second concerto for cello and orchestra.[183] I find it rather difficult to say anything about it in view of the fact that it has no literary text or programme. As for scale, it is quite long. It is in three movements, the second and third following one another without a break. In the second movement, and at the climax of the third, there is a theme very reminiscent of the Odessa song 'Buy my bubliki'![184] I cannot say where

[128]

on earth this came from, but it certainly is very similar. All the time I was writing the concerto, I was naturally thinking of Mstislav Rostropovich's fabulous playing. I am counting on him to perform the concerto.

On 28 and 29 May there will be two concerts devoted to my music in the Glinka Hall, with the same programme repeated:

Part One

1. Preface to the Complete Collection of my Works and a Brief Reflection on this Preface (first performance)
2. Five Humoresques[185] on Texts from *Krokodil*
   performers: Yevgeny Nesterenko and myself
3. Sonnet No. 66 of Shakespeare in the translation by Pasternak
4. 'Jennie', words by Burns in the translation by Marshak
5. Five Satires on verses by Sasha Chorny
   performers: Galina Vishnevskaya and myself (*sic*!?!)

Part Two

6. Quartet No. 1
7. Quartet No. 11 (first performance)
   performers: The Beethoven Quartet

I am terribly nervous about my part in the concert, but I very much want to try. I am afraid, though, that I shall not be able to manage 'Progeny' (Sasha Chorny) and 'Irinka and the Shepherd'. When I think that the concert is not that far off, my right hand starts to go on strike altogether.[186]

Irina and I are staying here until 13 May, and on the 14th we shall be back in Moscow.

How are you and Vera Vasiliyevna getting on in the new apartment? Have you mastered the Estonia?[187] I should so like to hear from you. Here is the address: Nizhnyaya Oreanda United Sanatorium, Yalta, Crimea, marked for my attention. We have a telephone in the room; the number is 1–53–05. But that would only be for emergencies.

I kiss you warmly.

Your

D. Shostakovich

Irina and I send our warmest greetings to you and Vera Vasiliyevna.

In *Novy Mir* No. 3 there is a story by Chingiz Aitmatov[188] entitled 'Farewell, Gulsary!' I was enormously impressed by virtually the whole novella. I urge you to read it. Obviously, Aitmatov has a huge talent. D.S.

4 May 1966 Nizhnyaya Oreanda

Dear Isaak Davïdovich,

Thank you for your letter. Our stay in Crimea is drawing to a close, and we leave on 13 May. On 24 May I am coming to Leningrad to rehearse my concert.

The thing that most worries me about the concert is that my right hand is very weak. I am afraid that platform nerves will make it even worse and it will give up altogether, and then it will be a total shambles.

As soon as I finished the concerto[189] I sent it off by post to Moscow to have it copied. I was rather worried that it might get lost and not arrive. But it arrived safely at its destination, thank you postal services. I should really sit down and write a hymn of gratitude.[190]

I agree with your opinion of the symphonies by Peyko and Ustvolskaya.[191] I regret not having heard them myself, but it seems to me that there were quite a number of other works besides these ones deserving of praise. For instance, I liked Andrey Petrov's poem[192] and Vladislav Uspensky's violin pieces, and several others.

I am feeling fine, although I am finding it difficult to walk.[193]

Crimea is very beautiful, and happily not too hot. Generally, life goes on as usual. I am revisiting the scenes of my youth, as I often used to come to Gaspra in the spring. Memories are crowding in on me, and I have become very aware of my advanced age.

Irina and I send you and Vera Vasiliyevna our very best wishes.

D. Shostakovich

8 May 1966 Nizhnyaya Oreanda

Dear Isaak Davïdovich,

Thank you for your letter and for the cutting from *Literaturnaya Gazeta*. I had actually read the speech that was printed in it before, but is a good idea to read and reread such speeches.[194]

I am glad that you found 'Farewell, Gulsary!' to your taste. I must tell you that I read it three times, and only on the fourth could I bring myself to read the passage where Gulsary is castrated. The first three times I skipped over this place, feeling that it would be unbearable to read. And so it was: I had to keep the tightest hold on myself not to break out in hysterics when I finally read the passage.[195] No doubt your reservations concerned the same passages as mine. But they are insignificant in the sweep of the novella as a whole.

A singer of intellectual pretensions once decided to sing my 'Humoresques' from *Krokodil*. He came and sang them through to me, not at all badly. Being not just a singer but a singer–philosopher, he had a question for me. Here I had better break off and quote the passage from 'Irinka and the Shepherd':

The shepherd cannot see Irinka. Thickset and broad-shouldered, he sits with his back to her peeling the shell from an egg.
Irinka desperately wants to squeeze it.[196]

The philosophically inclined singer asked me: 'I'm not quite clear exactly what it is that Irinka wishes to squeeze. Is it the shepherd or the egg?'

I answered him thus: 'Nowadays, audiences are ready and willing to play an active part in looking and listening. They will have no difficulty understanding what it is that Irinka is so anxious to squeeze.'

True, it took a little while for the intellectual singer to see my point.

It seems to me that as distinct from singer–philosophers there do exist readers who have a true understanding of what is good and what is bad. It is also my belief that writers like Chingiz Aitmatov, and a few others, write for them.

We have had a very good holiday in Crimea. On the 14th we return to Moscow, and on the 24th come to Leningrad.

Be well and happy.

D. Shostakovich

Shostakovich arrived in Leningrad on the appointed day, and we met in the Yevropeyskaya Hotel. On 27 May, the day before the first of the two concerts, he told me that he was finding it almost impossible to calm his nerves at the prospect of going on stage.

28 May was one of those stiflingly hot, sticky and humid Leningrad days that Shostakovich had always found very trying. In the Glinka Hall, the Small Hall of the Conservatoire, there seemed to be no air at all to breathe. It was uncomfortable enough in the light jacket I was wearing, but for Shostakovich, in tails and a starched shirt, it must have been unbearable. On top of this he was under tremendous stress, and when a very young Nesterenko, nervous as he might well be at being accompanied by the great composer himself, twice fluffed his entry, Shostakovich's face showed real panic. With a huge effort of will, he mastered himself and the performance continued.

Overall the concert was very successful, and the new Eleventh Quartet was encored. But the appalling heat and the extreme nervous tension had taken their toll, and Shostakovich was taken ill during the night. It was diagnosed as a heart attack.

Late the following morning, on hearing the dreadful news, I rushed to the hotel, where I found a crowd of people clustered round an ambulance at the entrance. At the sight of Shostakovich on a stretcher I was seized with mortal fear, and found it all I could do to keep back the tears. As he was being lifted into the ambulance Shostakovich caught sight of me and, smiling his characteristic smile, disengaged a hand from the blankets to give me a wave. Some of my terror immediately left me. The doors of the ambulance closed and, picking up speed, it disappeared from view.

I stood on the pavement, numb with shock, with no one to say a word to. Irina Antonovna had gone with her husband to the hospital. But suddenly there appeared at the hotel none other than Mstislav Rostropovich, clad in a summer shirt and filthy as a chimney-sweep. He had heard by telephone what had occurred, and had that instant set off from Moscow. Finding no taxis at the airport, he had flagged down a passing motorcyclist, jumped on the pillion and got himself to the Yevropeyskaya Hotel enveloped in a cloud of dust. Such was the impulsiveness and the resourcefulness of the famous cellist in his young days.

I was overjoyed to see Rostropovich and, together with Aleksandr Kholodilin, we set off to the élite Sverdlov Hospital, the Leningrad equivalent of the Kremlin Clinic in Moscow. Between us, notwithstanding it was Sunday, we succeeded in calling out from his home the eminent professor who confirmed the diagnosis.

The succeeding days and nights were spent in unremitting fear for Shostakovich's health. On 3 June, his sister Mariya told me that he had been asking after me and wanted to see me, but the doctors were unwilling to risk any disturbance to the patient. Two weeks later I received the following postcard.

14 June 1966

Dear Isaak Davïdovich,

I should be so glad if you could come to see me, on any day from 5 p.m. to 7 p.m. at the Sverdlov Hospital, in Treatment Section 1, Ward 11. Let Marusya know the day before, so that I can arrange a pass.

D. Shostakovich[197]

Dictated by D. D. – Irina Antonovna Shostakovich

29 July 1966 Leningrad

Dear Isaak Davïdovich,

If you know the first name and patronymic of the television executive M. Dubenskaya, do please let me know. She sent me a photograph taken from a programme about Ivan Sollertinsky, and I must thank her for it. [198]

D. Shostakovich

6 August 1966 Melnichy Ruchey

Dear Isaak Davïdovich,

Yesterday (5 August) we arrived safely at Melnichy Ruchey. We are very well set up here. The main telephone number is Zh 8–19–15. Our dacha No. 1 has its own extension.

I think that without private transport it might be a little difficult to get here. In the time it takes for this card to reach you, I will have found out some details. When you have a chance, please telephone me.[199] The address here is: Dacha No. 1, Communist Party District Committee Sanatorium, Melnichy Ruchey, Leningrad District.

Your

D. Shostakovich

13 August 1966 Melnichy Ruchey

Dear Isaak Davïdovich,

Thank you for your letter. This is to let you know that from 29 August for two weeks we shall be in the Composers' Rest House at Repino. After that we shall go home.[200]

Please keep me abreast of your movements. Are you going to stay for long in the Cinema House? Will you be going back to Leningrad after that, or on to somewhere else?

Your

D. Shostakovich

9 October 1966 Zhukovka

Dear Isaak Davïdovich,

Thank you for your letter, which gave me much pleasure as do all your letters – even the ones that don't contain anything cheerful.

But in any case your last letter had plenty that was cheerful. I am staying out at the dacha all the time. Summer has returned to Moscow: the thermometer shows 20 degrees during the day, and in the sun it goes up to 30 degrees. The flies and mosquitoes buzz around and poison life just as effectively as they do in July and August.

May I urge you to get hold of issues nos. 7 and 8 of the magazine *Prostor* [literally, *Free Range*] for 1966, and to read Mark Popovsky's short story 'The Thousand Days of Academician Vavilov?' The cast of characters includes Academicians I. I. Vavilov, T. D. Lysenko, B. M. Zavadovsky and a whole series of other leading figures in the biological sciences, such as I. I. Prezent and others. I read it with a good deal of emotion and I may say horror.[201]

Prostor is published in Russian in Kazakhstan, and so it may not be a simple matter to obtain it in Moscow or Leningrad. Evidently, Mark Popovsky did not find it easy to get his story published in Moscow or Leningrad either, and that is why it has been printed in a literary-artistic, socio-political illustrated monthly journal published by the Kazakhstan Union of Writers in Alma-Ata.

Slava Rostropovich telephoned me from London to tell me that he had a success playing my second cello concerto there, and I also received a kind telegram from Benjamin Britten. I was very pleased by the telegram, as I consider Britten a very good composer who has a true understanding of music.[202]

Please pass on my warmest greetings to Vera Vasiliyevna and all your family.

Your

D. Shostakovich

The bottom of the envelope is embellished with a little present I was given. It is not the value of the gift that matters, but the love behind it.[203] D. S.

10 November 1966 Zhukovka

Dear Isaak Davïdovich,

Thank you for your letter. I have not told you anything about myself for quite some time, because in fact there has not been much to tell you.

On 5 November I came out of hospital, where I had spent eighteen days. I was there at the insistence of Professor F. P. Rabotalov, who has been in charge of the treatment for my right hand since 1958. He said that it was necessary for me to have a spell in hospital in order to build up my strength again. In particular, he remarked, I would be able to walk up stairs without difficulty. There being, in the course of the eighteen days, no discernible improvement in my ability to walk up stairs, we – that is to say, Professor Rabotalov and I – thereupon agreed that I was much better and that I could go home full of joy and good cheer.

While I was in hospital I was also examined by Professors Mikhelson (surgeon) and Shmit (neurologist). They both pronounced themselves extremely satisfied with my hands and my legs. At the end of the day, the fact that I cannot play the piano and can only walk up stairs with the greatest difficulty is of no importance at all. After all, nobody is obliged to play the piano, and one can live perfectly well without going upstairs. The best thing to do is sit at home and not mess about with stairs, or for that matter slippery pavements. Quite right too: I went out for a walk yesterday, fell over and banged my knee hard. If I had sat at home, you see, nothing of the kind would have happened.

As for everything else, it is all going just as well. I have still not gone back to smoking or drinking. I used to be tempted, but my stupid fear is now stronger than the temptation. I have simply lost the craving to smoke: tobacco is no longer a temptation. I do sometimes really want a drink, but . . . (see above re fear).

There are other physical enterprises, too, that now seem to be beyond my powers. I do not think I shall be able to come to Leningrad for the première of my cello concerto[204] because of my generally weak state. Everywhere has stairs, even the Great Hall of the Conservatoire.[205] Needless to say, this makes me very sad. It looks as though I shall not be coming to Leningrad for some time; indeed it may be that I shall never come there again.[206]

I do know Bunin's Shakespeare settings,[207] and in my opinion they are good compositions to which Bunin has brought all his strengths and abilities. Overall, the piece more or less comes off and there are some passages that are excellent. God grant him health and success; he has a difficult life, and there seems to be little hope of its getting any easier.

Please come to Moscow. I miss very much not seeing you. If I start feeling better then I may come to Leningrad, but this seems rather doubtful.

Your

D. Shostakovich

2 December 1966 Zhukovka

Dear Isaak Davïdovich,

Your letter both delighted and touched me. It was a delight and a pleasure (to borrow an expression from the old days) to know that the thoughts one has expressed in sounds have reached out to people and made an impression on them.[208]

Slava Rostropovich gave me a most enthusiastic report of the marvellous playing of the student orchestra under Nikolai Rabinovich.

Everything is more or less all right with me. I am trying to live at the dacha, where everything is wonderful. Lately I have begun to share some of Yevgeny Mravinsky's traits, like a love of nature.[209] The only drawback is that I am not composing anything, and as a result my brain is rusting over. To build up my strength and my energy I am doing a lot of physical exercises and I walk three times a day: an hour in the morning, an hour in the afternoon and an hour in the evening.

Issue No. 11 of the magazine *Yunost* [*Youth*] has the first part of a short story by Nikolai Chukovsky entitled 'An Early Wound'. I liked it very much. The conclusion will appear in issue No. 12 so I can't yet tell you anything about it. But the first part was attractive, and rather sad. If you come across *Yunost* No. 11, do read the story.

Please pass on my warmest greetings to Vera Vasiliyevna.

Your

D. Shostakovich

I hope that all is in order in your household, that the gas is alight, the heating working and so on. Please let me know, otherwise I shall worry, remembering those temporary problems you had. D. S.

26 December 1966 Moscow

Dear Isaak Davïdovich,

Best wishes for the New Year. May it lift from you all the cares and disappointments of the old year, and may everything turn out well in the new.

Everything is fine with me. I was delighted with your letter and its account of the performance of the Thirteenth Symphony.[210] Yesterday's concert in the Great Hall [of the Conservatoire] by Peter Pears and Benjamin Britten was a great joy to me. They performed Schumann's *Dichterliebe*,[211] Britten's *Seven Sonnets of Michelangelo*,[212] and his own versions of English and French songs. The whole concert gave me the greatest pleasure.

Have you no plans to visit Moscow? It would be so good if you did. I am not likely to be coming to Leningrad in the near future: I am just not up to it.

Give my warmest greetings to Vera Vasiliyevna.

I press your hand warmly.

Your

D. Shostakovich

V
Failing Health
1967–1969

Sketch by Maksim Shostakovich

The end of the 1960s were dominated for Shostakovich by a string of illnesses and accidents which occupied much of his thoughts and tested to the utmost the extraordinary resilience of his inner strength. Scarcely had he recovered from the heart attack he suffered in May 1966, when his right leg (the other one) was broken in a fall in September 1967. Gradually, more and more of his time was spent in hospital or convalescing in isolation, cut off even from attending, much less participating in, the world of music performance, including those of his own new works. While there are one or two works in the patriotic, 'public' mode, like the symphonic poem October, *which somewhat routinely celebrates the fiftieth anniversary of the Revolution, the major works share an elegiac and mystical quality born of the long hours of reflection and a growing preoccupation with the end of life. These include the Second Violin Concerto, the Romances on Poems of Aleksandr Blok, the Twelfth String Quartet, the Violin Sonata and, above all, the Fourteenth Symphony.*

24 January 1967 Moscow

Dear Isaak Davïdovich,

It is a long time since I had any news from you. I hope that you are in good health and that all is going well for you. How good it would be if you could come to Moscow. It is such a long time since I have seen you, and I miss you.[1]

There are no significant changes in my life. I am feeling fine. I try to compose something every day, but nothing seems to come of it, and I do not have very high hopes. On the other hand, I think of the life of Sibelius, who wrote nothing at all for many years in the latter part of his life, but simply occupied the position of the Glory of the Finnish People.[2] This role was admirably rewarded: an apartment, a dacha, a substantial pension, and so on. Sibelius himself swilled brandy and listened to music of all kinds on gramophone records. I wouldn't mind that at all. But I am loaded down with worries. Many of them. And I have no strength.

If you can tear yourself away to come to Moscow, please come out to the dacha. The only problem is that I won't be able to share a bottle with you. I gave up drinking after the illness.[3] I am not smoking either. This abstinence has cost me a great deal, but I dare not go back to smoking and drinking because I am so idiotically afraid.

Please write to me, and come to see me.

Give my warmest greetings to Vera Vasiliyevna.

Your

D. Shostakovich

3 February 1967 Moscow

Dear Isaak Davïdovich,

I am thinking much about life, death and careers.[4] In this connection, recalling the life of certain famous (I do not say necessarily great) people, I arrive at the conclusion that not all of them died at the time they ought to have. For instance, Musorgsky died before his time. The same can be said of Pushkin, Lermontov and several others. Tchaikovsky, however, should have died earlier than he did. He lived slightly too long, and for that reason his death was a terrible one, or rather his last days were.

The same applies to Gogol, to Rossini and perhaps to Beethoven. They, like a great many other famous (great) people, and people who were not famous at all, outlived their true span and crossed over that boundary in life beyond which it (life) can no longer bring joy but only disappointment and dreadful happenings.

I expect you will read these lines and ask yourself: why is he writing such things? Well, it's because I have undoubtedly lived longer than I should have done. I have been disappointed in much, and I expect many terrible things to happen.

I am also disappointed in myself. Or rather, [I have become convinced] that I am a dull, mediocre composer. Looking down from the vantage point of my sixty years on 'the path travelled',[5] I see that I have twice in my life been the focus of publicity (*Lady Macbeth of Mtsensk* and the Thirteenth Symphony).[6] This publicity had a great effect. But when all the dust settles and you see things in their true perspective, it is clear that actually *Lady Macbeth* and the Thirteenth Symphony were nothing but '*fook*', as they say in *The Nose*.[7]

I still hope to have a chance to chat to you on this subject. But the thought which I have just expounded is a terrible one. Since I have ten years of life left,[8] the prospect of dragging this terrible thought around with me for all those years . . . No! I don't envy anyone in my shoes.

Nevertheless, the urge to compose pursues me like an unhealthy addiction. Today, I finished seven songs to words by Aleksandr Blok. If you have the two-volume edition of Blok (State Literary Publishing House, Moscow 1955) you will find 'The Song of Ophelia' on page 11 of Volume One. That is the first song. Next is 'Gamayun, The Bird of Prophecy' (page 13). Immediately after that, on the same page, is a poem beginning with the words 'We were together'. Then 'The City Sleeps' (page 17). Then 'Oh, what rage beyond the window' (also page 17). Then 'Secret Signs Flare Up' (page 74), and finally 'At Night, When Agitation Stills' (page 67).[9] The songs are scored for soprano, violin, cello and piano. I am hoping that Galina Vishnevskaya, David Oistrakh, Mstislav Rostropovich and I will perform them. In writing the piano part I have taken into consideration my very restricted capabilities.

Well, that's all for now.

Your

D. Shostakovich

18 February 1967 Moscow

Dear Isaak Davïdovich,

Thank you for going to all the trouble. I believe that S. M. Gershov is indeed that very Sasha Gershov, the friend of the artists V. V. Dmitryev, M. B. Erbshteyn and others.[10] I have written to him, but I'm not sure I know this particular Ivanovskaya Street in Leningrad. Is it the one which had its name changed to Sotsialisticheskaya, or perhaps some other Ivanovskaya? At any rate, if I do eventually hear back from S. M. Gershov, all will become clear.

I send Vera Vasiliyevna my greetings and best wishes.

Your

D. Shostakovich

The composer Boris Tishchenko paid me a visit yesterday. He showed me his Symphony No. 3. Much of it I liked tremendously.

The day before yesterday I went to see a production of Bertolt Brecht's *Galileo*. I did not really like either the play or the production.[11] D. S.

13 March 1967 Zhukovka

Dear Isaak Davïdovich,

It is a long time since I heard from you. I heard reports that you had toothache, and that you were getting treatment for it. I also heard that Gavriil is in hospital suffering from a hernia.[12] This is very sad news. Illness is a sore affliction for sufferers and their friends. Please write and let me know how you are, and how your teeth are.

Everything is more or less all right with me. I am trying to compose something, but so far have only managed one song to words by Pushkin:

Spring, spring, the time for love,
My heart sinks when you come to me
Etcetera

Evidently nothing is going to come of my attempts to set 'The Monument' – I have tried ten times, without result.[13]

I seem to have got myself into a bit of a mess, in my material circumstances. Well, probably somehow or other I will struggle out of it.

I am in rude health. The question is, is this rude health of any use to me? After all, life is given to us to enjoy. But how can I enjoy it when I can hardly walk, I gasp for breath and cannot lift anything at all heavy?

I miss not being with you.

Your

D. Shostakovich

I send my very best wishes to Vera Vasiliyevna and all your family. D. S.

22 March 1967 Zhukovka

Dear Isaak Davïdovich,

Thank you for your letter. I am sorry you are having such a wretched time from the toothache. Let us hope you are already better, all the pain and misery already in the past.

I have been thinking that perhaps I might manage to come to Repino. I am going to the town of Gorky in a couple of days; this will be my first journey of any distance since becoming ill, and if I find it does not do me any harm then I shall come to Repino in early April. I will let you know about this later on.

I very much want to see you. It would be wonderful if you could come to visit me in Repino. I am extremely nervous about the journey to Gorky. Irina and I are going by train during the day. Although the night train is very comfortable, the whole journey takes only six hours so you don't get a chance to have a proper sleep. By the time the train has started and the conductor has made up the bed, it's two o'clock in the morning before you know it, and at six o'clock the conductor is already coming round to wake you up. The daytime train leaves at 5 p.m. and gets to Gorky at 11 p.m., so you can sleep properly in the hotel. The trouble is, there is no soft class[14] on that train, and as I am so spoilt I am rather dreading it and wonder how I shall survive the journey.[15]

On the 23rd and 24th I shall be available to my constituents,[16] and on the 24th we shall return to Moscow again on the daytime train.

I send you my very best wishes.

Your

D. Shostakovich

Please pass on my warmest greetings to Vera Vasiliyevna and all your family. D. S.

8 April 1967 Zhukovka

Dear Isaak Davïdovich,

I sent you my petition concerning Nikolai Semyonovich yesterday.[17] I was in a hurry, so I did not add any note to you. I am not going to Cannes.[18] My health does not permit it, and in any case I have absolutely no desire to undertake such a taxing journey.

I still cannot decide whether or not to go to Repino. I found the journey to Gorky very tiring.

Slowly and with great difficulty, squeezing out one note after another, I am writing a violin concerto.[19] Everything else is fine.

Your

D. Shostakovich

I had a telephone call yesterday from Roman Tikhomirov.[20] He, and according to him you, want me to write a Foreword to a book, the title of which I did not catch. Perhaps you could give me an idea what the book is about?[21] D. S.

24 April 1967 Zhukovka

Dear Isaak Davïdovich,

A musician by the name of Geronimus[22] has asked me to write a reference on his musical activities. He teaches at the Conservatoire. Could you please find out his first name and patronymic for me?

Your

D. Shostakovich

6 May 1967 Leningrad

Dear Isaak Davïdovich,

Irina and I are going to the Composers' Rest House at Repino and very much hope to see you. Please telephone me at 9 a.m. or 2 p.m. or 7 p.m.

All the Musical Fund telephone numbers have changed, so please find out from them the new number.

Your

D. Shostakovich

I have found out the Composers' House telephone number. It is Repino 27–45.

14 June 1967 Zhukovka

Dear Isaak Davïdovich,

I received your letter today. I miss you very much and should dearly like to see you.

It may be that in the near future I shall come to Leningrad for about three days, although it is hard for me to make such journeys now.

I have joyous memories of our visit to your and Vera Vasiliyevna's home, and regret that I could have so little to drink.[23] I am, as before, not allowed to drink, smoke and so on. This does little for my health or my spirits.

At the moment my health is, thank God, good.

Two days ago, Galina Vishnevskaya, David Oistrakh, Mstislav Rostropovich and I had our first rehearsal of my Blok settings. For a first time it was quite respectable. The rehearsal gave me much joy, and for a time I stopped experiencing acutely painful feelings about all kinds of acutely painful events.[24]

My violin concerto has still not been copied, so I cannot yet give it to David Oistrakh for him to become acquainted with it and for one to immerse myself in its sound world.

Give my best greetings to Vera Vasiliyevna.

I press your hand warmly.

D. Shostakovich

1 July 1967 Zhukovka

Dear Isaak Davïdovich,

From 5 July we shall again be in Repino. It would be wonderful to see you. As soon as we arrive there I shall telephone you, or you could also call me at Repino 28–45.

Your

D. Shostakovich

Please call at 9 a.m., 2 p.m. or 7 p.m.

11 August 1967 Kamenyuki

Dear Isaak Davïdovich,

We shall be going home on 21 August, but in any case here is the address where we are at present: 12, Belovezh Forest Hotel, Kamenyuki, District of Brest. It is wonderful here, except that there have been several exceptionally hot days and, what is worse, nights.

I have done a lot of work here, and written a poem for symphony orchestra entitled *October*. I am now feeling very tired.

Sadly, I have only ten days left of my stay here. I have been working without a break for the past seven days.[25]

I do hope that all is going well with you, and that you are having a good time in Repino. Irina and I are very well set up here and have started going for long walks. I am much impressed by the grandeur of the bison and by the way they look at you, with a mixture of calmness and ferocity. There are lovely red deer and roe deer and wild boar, and others of the animal kingdom.[26] Hunting is categorically forbidden here, so they have little fear of man. All the same, it is a good idea to keep a prudent distance from the bison.

I am in quite a state of nerves about the prospect of returning to

[145]

Moscow, where premières of my new works are coming up. This is always a very unsettling time.[27]

Well, that is about all for now.

We shall be in Moscow from 22 August.

Irina sends her greetings.

Your

D. Shostakovich

30 August 1967 Zhukovka

Dear Isaak Davïdovich,

My best wishes for the start of the new academic year.

Two days ago I sent you a little present of my *Collected Songs*.[28] Naturally there are some rather weak ones among them, but there are also some which are by and large successful.

There is little to boast of in my life at the moment; it was much better in the Belovezh Forest. The climate is divine there, and the company of deer, wild boar and bison was a constant joy. If only I could have relaxed a bit more, it would have been a perfect stay. As it was, I worked very hard.

Now that I am home, I am a prey to anxiety with the premières that are imminent. I may be in Leningrad from 23 to 30 September for the concerts in the Music of Soviet Russia series. I am not in a particularly good state of health; in spite of a daily exercise regime and long walks, my legs seem to be getting worse. As far as the rest is concerned (heart and so on) everything is all right.

We are having some domestic problems at the moment. Irina's aunt has to go into hospital as she is in a bad way. They will take her in for a certain length of time and then let her out to come home. She is no longer responsible for her actions, so it is extremely difficult to look after her.

As far as work is concerned, Eisenstein's film *October* has been released, with a score that A. A. Kholodiliv has put together from various works of mine. I have seen the film, and believe that overall my music has by and large added to it. But the film itself does not appeal to me; I really cannot understand why Eisenstein, and for that matter Dovzhenko, are considered such geniuses. I don't much like their work. No doubt this simply reflects my lack of understanding, since the experts agree that they are geniuses.[29]

Among my recent aesthetic experiences I must single out a record Irina has bought of gypsy songs fabulously sung by Volshaninova with a gypsy choir. The songs are wonderfully beautiful, although very sad. Listening to them makes the tears flow and engenders a keen desire to imbibe strong drink with *zakusky*.[30]

Please pass on my greetings to Vera Vasiliyevna.

Your

D. Shostakovich

2 September 1967 Zhukovka

Dear Isaak Davïdovich,

I was terribly upset by your letter.[31] First and foremost I am to blame for the mistake, because I also checked the proofs. I simply cannot understand how I can have let such an outrage through. Please forgive me if you can, and throw the music out with the rubbish.

D. Shostakovich

I think I must have been concentrating mainly on Sasha Chorny,[32] but even there the eighth bar of 'Kreutzer Sonata' has an outrageous misprint. (Sasha Chorny has not been published before whereas all the others have, and that is why I did not pay so much attention to them.) D. S.

30 September 1967 Kuntsevo[33]

Dear Isaak Davïdovich,

Please excuse me for not replying to your letters, which bring me great joy and for which I am most heartily grateful.

Here is a general report. Target achieved so far: 75 per cent (right leg broken, left leg broken, right hand defective. All I need to do now is wreck the left hand and then 100 per cent of my extremities will be out of order.)

For the time being it is difficult to write, and so you must excuse me for not answering your letters. Don't be angry, but don't stop writing to me even if you don't get a reply.

Please give Vera Vasiliyevna my belated congratulations on her name day.[34]

Your

D. Shostakovich

16 October 1967 Zhukovka

Dear Isaak Davïdovich,

I received your letter, thank you very much. I have been allowed out of hospital for the holidays,[35] but afterwards I have to go back for the plaster to be taken off and to be taught how to walk again.

My Blok songs are due to be performed on 23 October, and on the 29th David Oistrakh is going to play the violin concerto.[36] Mariya Dmitriyevna was mistaken in telling you that the concerto was not going to be performed. If you plan to come, please let me know.[37]

Please give my greetings to Vera Vasiliyevna.

Your

D. Shostakovich

29 November 1967 Moscow

Dear Isaak Davïdovich,

Yesterday I learned the very sad news that Vladimir Lebedev had died. He was an absolutely wonderful artist. Although I know little about painting and my appreciation of it is not very highly developed, his work always had a profound effect on me. I had not seen him at all for twenty-five years, yet my attachment to him remained as strong as ever. He always struck me as a thoroughly good and decent person.[38]

So I was very sad about that, and then today I got your letter with its wretched news about your accident. Look after your arm, and don't rush to make it bear full weight. I hope it will soon recover and you will be able to forget all the misery it has brought you.

I am still in hospital. They have been promising to remove the plaster some time about 5 to 7 December. But today Mariya Aleksandrovna (the doctor in charge) told me that they might have to put on another plaster for a further week. She explained that this would be because the bones do not knit as quickly in someone of my age as they do in a young person.

I have heard Yureneva sing on the radio several times. I have also heard her in chamber music concerts, and I really liked her singing. I have sent her my Blok settings and asked her to consider singing them.[39]

I am a bit worried about her partners, however. I would be absolutely happy with, for instance, Mikhail Vaiman or Boris Gutnikov as violinists, but I don't know about the cellist. Is there an outstanding cellist in Leningrad anything like Rostropovich? You move in musical circles; please let me know. But of course first of all you would have to get Nadezhda Yureneva's agreement, and only then put the ensemble together. Yureneva has absolutely captivated me with her musicality, her beautiful voice and her well-nigh impeccable diction.

Life in hospital is extremely tedious.

Get better soon and look after yourself.

I kiss you warmly.

Your

D. Shostakovich

Warmest greetings to Vera Vasiliyevna. D. S.

8 December 1967 Moscow

Dear Isaak Davïdovich,

Thank you for your letter. I have the impression that you are a trifle sceptical about Yureneva as a singer.[40] I have not had the chance to hear her very often, but whenever I have her voice really appeals to me, and her diction is wonderful. (Vishnevskaya's diction is not particularly good, fabulous singer though she is.) I really appreciated Yureneva's diction when I listened to her singing works I did not know beforehand and was hearing for the first time, and I found I could understand every word.[41] As for her vow of celibacy and the preservation of her virginity, they are no doubt temporary phenomena and in any case do not have a direct bearing on her gifts.[42]

I shall be in hospital until the New Year, so please write to me more often. Your letters bring me joy.

I have been reading a lot in the press about Ivan Dzerzhinsky's opera, *The Quiet Don.* If you have seen it, do please give me a critique of it.[43]

It is very frustrating being here in hospital. I fortify myself with patience, while my broken bones slowly mend. That is what you have to do with old bones. At least I am lucky to be in a ward by myself with no neighbours, which makes me very happy. There is a television, a Spidola,[44] a record player and a tape-recorder, and Irina brings me records. As I play them, I marvel at the extraordinary beauty of some works and the crassness of others. For sheer hideousness and tedium I would instance Franz Liszt's *Via Crucis* – although, perhaps, I have not fully understood this work.[45]

As I have such a huge amount of free time, reminiscences crowd in on me. My thoughts are full of past times never to return, and of people, friends, acquaintances also gone for ever. It is much better not to have the time to think about such things, then the memories do not trouble you. But, my God, how amazing they are, these memories.[46]

Give my warmest greetings to Vera Vasiliyevna.

Your

D. Shostakovich

26 December 1967 Moscow

Dear Isaak Davïdovich,

I envied you so much when I read your letter from Repino. It is so lovely there! And at any time of year, what's more.

I send you my best wishes for the New Year 1968. 'What does the forthcoming year hold in store for us?' I believe it will be even better, even happier, than the one now coming to an end.[47]

Life carries on as usual. Not long ago, Vladimir Bragin put in an appearance, as he regularly does once every seven years or so. No matter how the years pass, he remains ablaze with his various creative inspirations. So once again, I get a long letter full of inspired creative plans.

I suppose I shall have to meet him when I leave hospital. Then, once I have ritually delivered my discouraging little speech about having no desire whatever to compose an opera, or a ballet, or a radio oratorio, or a fairy-tale for the cinema, or whatever it is that has fired him up this time, we shall part company for another seven or eight years. V. G. Bragin talks up his own artistic achievements in terms of the warmest approbation; according to him, the reason that *The Craftsman of Clamecy*[48] is Kabalevsky's best opera is because that is the one for which he, Kabalevsky, had the immense good fortune to have a libretto written for it by V. G. Bragin. All in all, despite the resolutely chirpy tone of V. G. Bragin's letter, reading it plunged me into a deep depression.[49]

I am feeling pretty well, and hope to be home on 29 December.

Please give my warmest greetings and kindest season's wishes to Vera Vasiliyevna.

I press your hand warmly.

Your

D. Shostakovich

25 January 1968 Zhukovka

Dear Isaak Davïdovich,

Thank you for your letter. I had not heard from you for some time, so I was beginning to get worried. But then your letter came, and I was so happy that you are well and in good health.

I am fine, although life is rather boring. I don't go to the theatre, nor to concerts. True, I did go to the Bolshoy Theatre not long ago, to hear *Yevgeny Onegin* conducted by Mstislav Rostropovich. Slava was very good, and once again gave proof of his phenomenal talents. I was struck by the exceptionally low standard of the singers, all of whom except Vishnevskaya as Tatyana were at best average. Lensky was extremely feeble. Maslennikov, who sang the role and was a good singer once upon a time, has evidently lost his voice either through drink or for some other reason. Gremin (Ognivtsev) was positively indecent.

On 2 February I am planning to go to Mahler's *Das Lied von der Erde* conducted by Paul Kletzki.[50] I get some pleasure from listening to short-wave radio broadcasts: yesterday I heard Dargomïzhsky's fabulous opera *The Stone Guest*.[51]

For myself, I am just staying at the dacha and hardly going anywhere. I spend a lot of time wondering how we are going to manage in the future, since my income has dropped sharply.[52]

Be well.

Your

D. Shostakovich

Give my greetings to Vera Vasiliyevna. Irina also sends her best wishes. D. S.

12 May 1968 Zhukovka

Dear Isaak Davïdovich,

Thank you for your letter. I am so glad that you spent the May holidays in Repino. It is lovely there in spring. You may congratulate me on the Grand Prix du Disque for the recording of my opera *Katerina Izmailova*. This award was made by the French Record Academy (there is such an organization). The prize is not, alas, expressed in francs or roubles; all I got was a very beautiful album.[53]

It is very hot in Moscow at the moment, and I don't feel at all well. Nevertheless, I have to go into the city quite often.

Irina sends you her greetings, and I send you my very best wishes. We both send Vera Vasiliyevna our greetings.

Your

D. Shostakovich

It is possible that I shall spend July in the Composers' Rest House at Repino. D. S.

The gap in correspondence from 25 January until 12 May is explained by the fact that Shostakovich was quite often in Leningrad for concerts, and we saw one another regularly. On 19 February, he and Irina Antonovna dined with me at home.

He stayed at the Composers' Rest House from 2 to 20 March, and there finished the Twelfth String Quartet. On 9 March, at Repino, he said to me with a smile: 'It's funny, but I always feel that whatever opus I am working on, I shall never finish it. I may die suddenly, and then the piece will be left unfinished.' But, thank God, nothing of the sort happened and on 16 March Dmitry Dmitriyevich played through the profoundly dramatic Twelfth Quartet to Venyamin Basner and me at Repino. He was in high spirits at the time.

On 17 March he attended Nadezhda Yureneva's recital in the Small Hall of the Philharmonia, in which she sang the Blok songs beautifully.

15 June 1968 Mayori

Dear Isaak Davïdovich,

Irina and I arrived today at the seaside near Riga, and we shall be here until 8 June. The heat is unbearable.[54]

My Twelfth Quartet was showcased at the Russian Federation Union of Composers yesterday. The Beethoven Quartet played it magnificently. As far as I could tell, the quartet made an impact on those present.

What are your plans for the future? Are you going anywhere, or will you be in Leningrad? Please write and tell me. This is the address (mark any letters for my attention):

Post Office Box 23, Mayori Village, Yurmala, Republic of Latvia.

From 1 August onwards, we are probably going to spend some time at the Composers' House in Komarovo.[55] It would be wonderful if you were in the vicinity.

Please pass on my warmest greetings to Vera Vasiliyevna.

I warmly press your hand.

Your

D. Shostakovich

If you telephone, you have to call the town of Yurmala. The number there is 2–49–44. D. S.

Irina sends her very best wishes.

22 June 1968 Mayori

Dear Isaak Davïdovich,

Thank you for your letter. It has been better here since the temperature dropped. For a time the heat was intolerable, and I thought I was literally not going to be able to stand it. But I did, and now it is very nice here.

I may come to the Composers' House in Repino from 1 August. How good it would be if you were in the Cinematographers' House at the same time.

We shall be here until 8 July, staying in a second-rate sanatorium. The food is awful, unappetizing and there is not much of it.[56] But this is unimportant compared with the sea and the fabulous beauty of the scenery. Of late I have become passionate about nature, I expect because so much of it has now become inaccessible to me. My poor shattered legs do not work very well, and I can walk only with difficulty. Forbidden (and inaccessible) fruits are the sweetest. So now I am ecstatic about all the little streams, glades, breezes, flowers and berries. Once or twice, I have drunk some Kristall here, which in its taste, colour, smell and price (3 roubles, 7 kopeks) reminds me of Stolichnaya.

Keep well. I long to see you again.

Your

D. Shostakovich

Post Office Box 23, Mayori, Yurmala, Republic of Latvia.

5 July 1968 Mayori

Dear Isaak Davïdovich,

We shall be at home from 9 July. Please write and tell me your address for the summer. We may be in Repino during August.

Your

D. Shostakovich

20 July 1968 Zhukovka

Dear Isaak Davïdovich,

Thank you for your letter. We shall be in Repino from 1 August at the Composers' House. There is a telephone there: Zelenogorsk 28–45. Telephone at 9 a.m. or 2 p.m. or 7 p.m., because those are the times when we shall be within reach of the phone. Much looking forward to seeing you.

Your

D. Shostakovich

From 27 July onwards our phone numbers in Moscow will change: 2–29–95–29 (town) and 1–58–66–40 (dacha). D. S.

2 August 1968 Repino

Dear Isaak Davïdovich,

We are at the Composers' House. Telephone us on 28–45, either at 9 a.m. or 2 p.m. or 7 p.m.

D. Shostakovich

Shostakovich stayed at the Composers' House throughout August and the beginning of September. I was staying two kilometres away, at the Cinematographers' House. We met almost every day, although he was much occupied with writing the Violin Sonata.

One day he came to fetch me in the car, and we drove out to Sestroretsk to visit Zoshchenko's grave on the tenth anniversary of the great writer's death.[57] Shostakovich loved Zoshchenko's writing, and our conversations often turned to his wonderful stories.

24 September 1968 Zhukovka

Dear Isaak Davïdovich,

My thanks to you for your letter with its description of the concert in the Leningrad Concert Hall.[58] The student choir of the Conservatoire does sing very well, and I am glad that they impressed you.[59]

Irina is getting on well with her chauffeuring duties. She now drives quite expertly not only in the suburbs but even in the centre of Moscow. I am very pleased about this. Time was when she suffered from a mixture of laziness and terror. But that's all over now.

Tomorrow is my sixty-second birthday. At such an age, people are apt to reply coquettishly to questions such as 'If you could be born over again, would you live your sixty-two years in the same way?' 'Yes,' they say, 'not everything was perfect of course, there were some disappointments, but on the whole I would do much the same again.'

If I were ever to be asked this question, my reply would be: 'No! A thousand times no!'[60]

It looks as though I shall be coming to Leningrad at the beginning of November, for the opening of the season in the Small Hall of the Philharmonia. Please give my warmest greetings to Vera Vasiliyevna.

Your

D. Shostakovich

9 October 1968 Zhukovka

Dear Isaak Davïdovich,

I have been approached by the violinist M. G. Simkin about his obtaining an appointment as professor.[61] Can you help me? He did not give me his first name and patronymic. I remembered that you know him, and I think were even a guest at his birthday party.[62] If this is so, please let me know his first name and patronymic.

D. Shostakovich

26 October 1968 Zhukovka

Dear Isaak Davïdovich,

I have finished the Violin Sonata, which I started work on at Repino.[63] There are going to be performances of the Twelfth Quartet on 3, 4 and 5 November in Leningrad, and I should very much like you to hear it.

I shall not come to Leningrad myself, as I am feeling rather mediocre. The concert on 3 will be in the Composers' House, on 4 and 5 in the Small Hall of the Philharmonia. If you have any problems getting tickets, please get in touch with my sister (15–75–05) as she should have my tickets for the Small Hall. And please for the time being don't mention to anyone about my not coming to Leningrad.[64]

Give my warmest greetings to Vera Vasiliyevna.

Your

D. Shostakovich

10 November 1968 Zhukovka

Dear Isaak Davïdovich,

Please excuse me for writing to you on such a scrappy piece of paper. It is all I have at the moment; I must go to the shop and get some more.

Things are not very good at home just now. My grandsons Andrey and Nikolai have contracted whooping-cough, and their father Zhenya[65] has caught it from them. It is a rather disagreeable illness when you are grown up, and can lead to all sorts of unpleasant complications. Irina has also got a cold and feels wretched. All in all, home is more or less a hospital.

I have got to know Basner's violin concerto. I find it an excellent work.

Myself, I am hard at work, making corrections to the piano reduction of my opera *The Nose*, which is going to be published. I was being very careless at the time when I originally made it, so I am now having to put it into some sort of decent shape.[66]

I watched a film on television called *You Cannot Pass Through Fire*. I liked it very much, and I especially liked Bibergan's music.[67]

Please write, do stay in touch.

Please pass on my greetings to Vera Vasiliyevna.

Your

D. Shostakovich

4 December 1968 Moscow

Dear Isaak Davïdovich,

Forgive me for bothering you with the following.

On my return to Moscow after a ten-day absence, I found a letter from M. G. Simkin waiting for me. Do you perhaps know his address? If you do, please let me know what it is. He forgot to put it either on the envelope or on the letter. Forgive me once again.

Please pass on my greetings to Vera Vasiliyevna.

Your

D. Shostakovich

19 December 1968 Moscow

Dear Isaak Davïdovich,

I am sorry to have been slow answering your letter and thanking you for Simkin's address. He has an earnest desire to become a professor, and as a result he and I have embarked on a very active correspondence.

[156]

David Oistrakh has returned to Moscow and has had a go at my violin sonata. The question now arises of who his partner should be. Probably it will be his regular partner Frida Bauer.

There is to be a performance of my Second Cello Concerto today, but Mstislav Rostropovich is ill and Natalya Gutman will play it instead of him. She is a prizewinner of national and international competitions.[68]

Day after day I have been sitting at the composers' congress, and in the evenings listening to premières of the outstanding new musical compositions which are part of the festival.[69] But somehow these festivals do not always turn out to be very festive for me.

Stay well and happy.

Your

D. Shostakovich

Give my warmest greetings to Vera Vasiliyevna. D. S.

I was terribly shocked by the dreadful news of G. Yu. Blazhkova's death.[70] D. S.

2 January 1969 Moscow

Dear Isaak Davïdovich,

Heartfelt good wishes to you and to all those dear to you for the New Year. Irina also sends warm wishes.

You probably know that the greatest high-jump athlete of our age, Valery Brumel, broke his leg three years ago. For two and a half years he was treated by the greatest medical luminaries of our age, but alas 'he wasn't ever going to jump again.'[71] He was permanently on crutches. Today he has commenced training again and has every intention of setting new records: for the past two and a half months he has been under the care of a little-known doctor from Kurgan.[72]

It is not my intention to go in for high jumping, or long jumping for that matter. But I would like to be able to walk up stairs more or less normally, and up gentle hills. I long not to think of myself as an invalid. Sometimes I get really depressed.[73] So I am thinking of making a trip to Kurgan in about two weeks' time, and maybe this will do some good. This doctor might even be able to make my right hand serviceable again. Wouldn't that be wonderful!

David Oistrakh and Sviatoslav Richter will play my sonata on 3 and 4 May in Moscow. Alas, it cannot be before then, since that is the earliest that they will both be in Moscow at the same time. Oistrakh is already getting to grips with the sonata. He has been working with Gennady Rozhdestvensky, Richter and . . . myself as accompanists. I could manage the easy passages all right, but the difficult ones were awful.

Please pass on my warmest greetings to Vera Vasiliyevna.

Your

D. Shostakovich

1 February 1969 Moscow

Dear Isaak Davïdovich,

Thank you for your letter. It brought great joy to my lonely hospital existence. Influenza is rampant throughout Moscow at the moment, so the hospital is quarantined and no visits are allowed.

I have made contact with Doctor Ilizarov (not Yelizarov, as I wrongly told you). He is not in Kurgan at the moment, but is touring round the district. He is a real worker–doctor, helping the people on his own patch and living religiously up to his Hippocratic oath. I am afraid that my legs do not really fit his 'profile': he is an orthopaedic surgeon and bone-setter. But my bones, so my doctors tell me, grew back splendidly after they were broken, and therefore it seems there is not much that G. A. Ilizarov can do for them. The problem with my legs is some kind of affliction of the nerves. (?) All the same, when I come out of hospital on 15 I intend to go to Kurgan. After all, Brumel the high jumper was also [conventionally] treated for two and a half years and during that time the only thing he could do was walk on crutches. After meeting Ilizarov he went back into training and is already chalking up great successes.

I don't particularly want to jump. But I should like to be able to get on to a bus or a trolley-bus or a tram. I should like not to drop dead with fright every time I step on to the escalator in the Metro. I should like to be able to walk up stairs easily. These are not extravagant desires. Here they promise to make my legs and my right hand stronger. Well, maybe I shall live to see the day.

I have been composing a lot recently. In one sense it is 'an addiction, like a disease', in another evidently a sort of senile graphomania.[74] I am now writing an oratorio for soprano, bass and chamber orchestra (like Barshai's)[75] to words by Federico García Lorca, Guillaume Apollinaire, Rainer Maria Rilke and Wilhelm Küchelbecker. It's quite an interesting idea, I think. One way and another, I'm finding this occupation keeps me happy and amused.

If Barshai's orchestra comes on tour to Leningrad, and if his programmes include Vainberg's Symphony No. 10 or Boris Tchaikovsky's Sinfonietta, do make sure you go and hear them. They are incredibly beautiful pieces. In general, they are both composers you should take note of. If you have time, please write to me.

Give my warmest greetings to Vera Vasiliyevna.

Irina sends her regards (on the telephone).

Your

D. Shostakovich

17 February 1969 Moscow

Dear Isaak Davïdovich,

On 10 February I remembered Ivan Ivanovich. It is incredible to think that twenty-five years have passed since he died.[76] Thank you for describing so fully the evening held in his memory at the Union of Composers. However I do I think that in his memoirs and 'oral histories' of Ivan Ivanovich the highly qualified Andronikov allowed himself to play the clown rather too much.[77]

Obviously the buffoon element was prominent in the proceedings in the hall of the Composers' House, and you did something very important in reminding everyone that Ivan Ivanovich Sollertinsky was one of the most dedicated and tragic personalities of the century as well as one of the wittiest. He was never, ever, a buffoon.[78]

It looks as though I shall be discharged from hospital in about ten days' time. I finished the piano score of my new work yesterday.[79] It cannot really be called an oratorio, since an oratorio is supposed to have a chorus, and mine doesn't. It does have soloists though – a soprano and a bass.

When I get home, I shall type out the poems that I used for the new work. It shouldn't really be called a symphony either. For the first time in my life, I really do not know what to call one of my compositions.[80]

How many truly great artists there are among poets who are not geniuses. I am thinking here of Küchelbecker, whose contemporaries (including Pushkin) were inclined to laugh at him. When I get out of hospital I am going to make a study of writers and poets who were not geniuses.[81]

I have a rather daring plan: I want to go to Komarovo for a week or two.

But you must absolutely come to visit me there, and when you do, bring a bottle of Stolichnaya. I'll pay.[82]

In general, I'll keep you abreast of my plans.

Thank you for not forgetting me.

Give my greetings to Vera Vasiliyevna.

Irina also sends her greetings.

Your

D. Shostakovich

19 March 1969 Moscow

Dear Isaak Davïdovich,

Thank you for your letter. I am sending you the poems which I used for my Fourteenth Symphony for soprano, bass and chamber orchestra, which is to be conducted by Barshai. I very much hope that the soprano will be Vishnevskaya. The bass has not yet been chosen.

This is how the selection of the poems came about. It came into my head that there exist certain eternal themes, eternal problems. Among them are love and death. In the past I have turned my attention to the question of love, if only in my setting of Sasha Chorny's 'Kreutzer Sonata',[83] but up to now I haven't tackled death. The day before I went into hospital I was listening to Musorgsky's *Songs and Dances of Death*, and idea of addressing the question of death finally came to fruition in me.[84]

I cannot say that I am wholly resigned to this event. So I settled down to make my choice of the poems. And while the choice of poems may appear to be random, it seems to me that the music gives them a unity.[85] I composed the work very quickly, fearing that while I was occupied with it something might happen to me, for example my right hand might finally cease to work altogether, or I might suddenly go blind, or something like that. I was quite tormented by such thoughts.[86] But in the end everything turned out all right; the hand still works, more or less, and the eyes continue to see. To conclude the subject of health, I should inform you that my legs are a little better, but my right hand is noticeably worse.

Dr Ilizarov (not Yelizarov as I wrongly told you) is coming to Moscow at the end of the month. He has promised to see me and give me his opinion. However, I think it is unlikely that he will be able to help me; my trouble is not really within his field. His field is splicing bones, and my bones are already spliced.

The Fourteenth Symphony (this is what I have decided to call it) seems to me a turning point in my work in that everything that I have written for many years now has been in preparation for it. Of course, I may be mistaken in this.[87]

In the poem 'Malagueña' I changed the words 'they smelled of salt and women's blood' to 'they smelled of salt and burning blood'. 'Women's blood' would probably have a menstrual and gynaecological association for poetry-lovers like N. I. Peyko.[88]

I envy you being able now and then to go to parties and similar celebrations. I have almost completely stopped going to such events; I find, to my intense dismay, that alcohol now gives me no pleasure at all. This is terrible.[89]

I have not seen you for such a long time. I miss you very much.

Your

D. Shostakovich

Please pass on my warmest wishes to Vera Vasiliyevna.

19 March 1969 Moscow

Dear Isaak Davïdovich,

I have just sent you the poems that I am using in the Fourteenth Symphony, and now as a postscript I want to ask you a few questions.

1. In the first poem, am I correct in having set it like this:

They are covered with red sand,
The roads of Andalusía

that is to say with the accent on the penultimate, not on the third, syllable? [90]

2. In the fifth poem, 'On Watch', can you help me with an alternative version of the fourth line from the end, 'The hour of love then sounded, and feverish neurosis'? I find the medical overtones of 'neurosis' very awkward; in the original the poet speaks about a kind of fever. Can you think of something like: 'The hour of love then sounded, and the thunderous crash of war'?[91]

3. 'In Prison at the Sante Jail'. Apollinaire has a great many verses, from which I have chosen sometimes one and sometimes two quatrains. I am explaining this to you so that you will not be put out by the apparent formlessness of the poem as I have set it.[92]

[161]

You should also know that:

Nos. 2, 3 and 4 are played without a break.
Nos. 6 and 7 are played without a break.
Nos. 8 and 9 are played without a break.
Nos. 10 and 11 are played without a break.
No. 1 is sung by the bass.
No. 2 – soprano.
No. 3 – duet for soprano and bass.
No. 4 – soprano.
No. 5 – soprano.
No. 6 – duet for soprano and bass.
Nos. 7, 8 and 9 – bass.
No. 10 – soprano.
No. 11 – duet for soprano and bass.

I don't suppose this will clarify anything much for you, but somehow I wanted you to know these details.

Give my greetings to Vera Vasiliyevna.

Your

D. Shostakovich

25 March 1969 Moscow

Dear Isaak Davïdovich,

Thank you for your letter, and for your help in liquidating the problem of 'neurosis'. Your amendment is very good: 'The hour of love then sounded, the hour of fateful fever.'

Today I received the piano score of the Fourteenth Symphony from the copyists, and before long I shall get the full score. After that, as soon as I have proofread it, I shall send it off to have the parts copied. I don't expect this will take long. The orchestra is small: ten violins, four violas, 3 cellos, two double-basses and percussion. I am very worried about the bass soloist, and because of this I am going to a lot of opera performances, where perhaps I shall succeed in finding a suitable one.

I did not quite understand the points you made about the 'Malagueña' poem. Why between

Black stallions and dark souls
Wander in the ravines of the guitar.

Smelling of salt and of black blood,[93]
Clustered blossoms of nervous ripples

should there be dots? Well, you can explain this to me when we meet, which I long to be soon.

I very much want to see you.

Give my greetings to Vera Vasiliyevna.

Your

D. Shostakovich

28 April 1969 Zhukovka

Dear Isaak Davïdovich,

Of course I am very sorry that you are not coming.[94] On the other hand, it may be all to the good: I get extremely nervous before a première, and an anxious man is egotistical and bad company for all who are forced to associate with him. Also, I do want you to have a good rest over the May holidays.

I am rather surprised myself by my own anxiety. After all, it is not as if I haven't been through plenty of premières in my time. Some of them have been good, some of them bad. David Oistrakh and Sviatoslav Richter play [the work] extremely well. So well, in fact, that perhaps there is no point in being anxious about it.

There is little to boast of in my general state. My organism is approaching old age. Add to that my broken legs, my inadequately performing stomach and so on, and life is generally pretty miserable. On top of that there is my anxiety, not only about the première, but about a lot of other things as well.

My sonata is going to be performed in Leningrad in September, but Richter will not be taking part then. Oistrakh will play it with Frida Bauer, a very good pianist who is his regular sonata partner.[95]

The May holidays are going to be very difficult for me. I dream of a holiday, but it seems hard to achieve: I have no peace and quiet and don't look like getting any.[96] Maksim gave me great joy not long ago: he gave a very good performance of Mahler's Symphony No. 2.[97]

I have found a bass soloist for the Fourteenth Symphony: a singer on Moscow radio by name Yevgeny Vladimirov. The voice is strong and beautiful, and the only problem is his physical appearance. He is small, weedy, and somewhat unprepossessing. But he is musical, and he is studying his part with enthusiasm.[98]

[163]

It is a shame that you still do not know my new symphony at all. When we were all together in Repino, I had to retire early from the fray.[99]

Please pass on my greetings to Vera Vasiliyevna and all your family. Irina joins her greetings to mine.

Your

D. Shostakovich

12 May 1969 Moscow

Dear Isaak Davïdovich,

Your letter both delighted and distressed me – delighted by your warm regard for me, and distressed by the hypochondria you are suffering. I hope that over the summer you will be able to have a rest, and all your hypochondria will vanish of its own accord.

David Oistrakh and Sviatoslav Richter will play my Sonata in Leningrad on 21 and 22 September, 21 in the Small Hall and 22 in the Great Hall of the Philharmonia.[100] I was thrilled with this news, since Richter is magnificent in his part. In all probability Barshai will start studying my Fourteenth Symphony in a week's time. The orchestral parts are being copied now, and they will soon be ready. I am in a state of great nervous excitement about it, wondering how will it sound?

Be well. Your

D. Shostakovich

Give my greetings to Vera Vasiliyevna. D.S.

10 June 1969 Moscow

Dear Isaak Davïdovich,

I am sorry for the long delay in replying to your letter. I was completely knocked off balance by the death of Nina Basner. She was a most admirable person. Her illness simply broke her spirit; she has left behind her family, her home and her children.[101]

Yefim Galanter died yesterday at the age of 83. He was the Director of the Great Hall of the Conservatoire, and had worked in the administration there all his life. He refused to give out complimentary tickets when none were available, and endured all manner of threats and insults from important people when he had to say no to them. He swept up the dust, and worried when the tickets didn't sell.[102]

Barshai has begun rehearsals of my Fourteenth Symphony. The orchestra is playing magnificently but the singers are not yet fully prepared. The orchestra goes on holiday on 22 July, and comes back to work on 1 September. Barshai wants to arrange the première for the end of September.

We shall be in Dilizhan from 1 July.

Please write, keep in touch.

Give my greetings to Vera Vasiliyevna.

Your

D. Shostakovich

Irina sends her greetings.

24 June 1969 Moscow

Dear Isaak Davïdovich,

Thank you for your letter. I much regret not having been at *Benvenuto Cellini*. I know this opera a little, and worship its composer.[103] Perhaps I shall be able to hear it in the autumn.

On the 21st there was what amounted to a play-through of my Fourteenth Symphony in the Small Hall of the Conservatoire. The performance was absolutely first class. Barshai and his orchestra are phenomenal, and the singers Miroshnikova and Vladimirov not at all bad. Since Vishnevskaya has not yet learned her part and I could not find another bass in time, they were, in a way, guinea-pigs. I believe that Miroshnikova, in addition to a good voice, possesses talent and understanding.

Some sad events have occurred in Moscow. The chief producer of the Circus, Arnold Arnold, has died. He was a splendid man.[104] And then the musicologist Pavel Apostolov was taken ill during the fifth movement of my symphony.[105] He managed to get out of the packed hall, but died a little while later.[106]

We are flying to Yerevan on 1 July, going on from there to Dilizhan (or Delezhan). 'I' is actually more correct, but I have seen this little place spelt with an 'e' in several references. My address will be: Composers' House, Dilizhan, Republic of Armenia. It would be very nice to hear from you. We shall stay in Dilizhan until 20 July and then perhaps go to Lake Baikal. Give my warmest greetings to Vera Vasiliyevna.

Your

D. Shostakovich

PS The symphony made a very strong impression on those present, myself included.

I have written to Ilya Kiselyov about *The Young Girl and the Hooligan*, giving him my consent.[107] D. S.

22 July 1969 Moscow

Dear Isaak Davïdovich,

We are now back in Moscow after an enjoyable time in Dilizhan. On 28 July we shall take the train to Irkutsk, where from 1 to 24 August our address will be: Sanatorium 'Baikal', Listvinichnoye Settlement, Irkutsk Oblast.[108] I have never been to Lake Baikal, and am very excited about going there.

My legs still just about carry me about, although a little worse than last year. My right hand is even less use than it was.

While we were in Dilizhan the composer Avset Terterian acquainted me with some of his compositions. He seems very talented to me. Apart from these pieces, I heard no other works new to me, although I did hear a gramophone record of Edgar Oganesian's Saxophone Concerto and also Aleksandr Glazunov's Saxophone Concerto. I liked the Oganesian; Glazunov's concerto was so bad it made me want to cry.[109]

I should so much like to have a line from you. Please be sure to write to me.

Give my greetings to Vera Vasiliyevna, Fanya Borisovna, and all your family.

Your

D. Shostakovich

18 August 1969 Baikal

Dear Isaak Davïdovich,

I was most distressed by your letter. I think it is the very first time in our long friendship that you have complained of your nerves. Do please take care of yourself. Take Valokordin[110] and generally look after your heart. Go to the doctor. You may need some treatment for your heart. Don't drink too much, and cut down on your smoking, perhaps even give it up altogether.

I am deficient in literary talent, so I cannot do justice in words to the incredible beauty of Baikal, which Irina and I are so fortunate as to witness just now.[111] We are staying in an excellent and well-run sanatorium, built just where the river Angara flows out of Baikal. It is indescribably beautiful.

We shall leave here on the morning of 24 and cross Lake Baikal by motor-launch to the Buryatiya shore-line. Then we shall go by road to the town of Ulan-Ude, where we have been invited to stay with some Buryat friends. Then we return overland (not by air) to Moscow – we took the train coming here as well. It was very pleasant. The only hard part was the last day or two, when it became incredibly hot.[112] We have been twice to Irkutsk, a very beautiful town.

In the sanatorium I met my cousin Sergey Shostakovich, a somewhat decrepit old man. He is four years older than I, and the last time we saw one another was 55 years ago.[113] It was however good news that he has no plans to come and stay with us in Moscow, nor to billet his son on us, who sometimes goes there on business. For the rest, he is a rather ordinary old man, whose existence principally serves to remind me that I shall soon be 63 and that my legs don't work too well. Even so, I am walking a lot here. Baikal is so wonderful that it will be very hard to leave it.

David Oistrakh and Sviatoslav Richter will play my Sonata on 21 and 22 September in Leningrad, and Barshai is planning to preview my Fourteenth Symphony on 25 and 26 September in the Capella Concert Hall.

Give my warmest greetings to Vera Vasiliyevna, who I suppose has already returned from her trip.

Irina sends her greetings.

Your

D. Shostakovich

10 September 1969 Zhukovka

Dear Isaak Davïdovich,

The dates of the concerts in Leningrad have changed. David Oistrakh and Sviatoslav Richter will play the Sonata on the 23rd in the Small Hall and 24 in the Great Hall of the Philharmonia.

The Fourteenth Symphony will be performed on the 28th and 29th in the Capella Hall.

We shall arrive on 22 September.[114] Tickets for all the concerts will be arranged for you. Thank you for your letter.

Irina sends her greetings. My respects to Vera Vasiliyevna.

Your

D. Shostakovich

6 October 1969 Moscow

Dear Isaak Davïdovich,

Thank you for transferring the money, although you really need not have troubled. In a few hours' time I am going to the Great Hall of the Conservatoire to hear the Fourteenth Symphony sung by Galina Vishnevskaya and Mark Reshetin.[115] The last few days have been devoted to rehearsals.

Yesterday I went to the opening of the concert season, where I heard Prokofiev's *Zdravitsa* and his Classical Symphony. The second half of the concert was Beethoven's Ninth Symphony.[116] Unfortunately the whole programme (conducted by Yevgeny Svetlanov) was rather indifferently done, and afforded me little pleasure.

Give my greetings please to Vera Vasiliyevna.

Your

D. Shostakovich

7 October 1969 Zhukovka

Dear Isaak Davïdovich,

From the outside, it seemed as though the Moscow première of the Fourteenth Symphony went very well. There were lots of people there, and lots of applause at the end of the performance. But sadly the performance was not as good as in Leningrad. Galina Vishnevskaya got completely lost on two occasions, and once the orchestra fell apart and it was Barshai's (!) fault.[117] Mark Reshetin sang his part very well. The printed programmes contained the texts of the poems I had used, so the audience was able to follow the words. This is a good thing, since diction is sometimes not very good.

I am terribly tired, and am thinking of taking some days off to do absolutely nothing.

Please give my greetings to Vera Vasiliyevna.

Your

D. Shostakovich

26 October 1969 Zhukovka

Dear Isaak Davïdovich,

Thank you for your letter. All is more or less well with me, although my right hand and both legs are not much use.

Thank you for all the kind things you said about the Fourteenth Symphony. Barshai and his orchestra will soon return from the tour they are carrying out at present, and it seems that the symphony is to be played again in Moscow on 26 November.

I telephoned you several times, but did not manage to catch either you or Vera Vasiliyevna at home. I listened to Venyamin Basner's quartet on a recording which he gave me, and I liked it. Yesterday I heard Sergey Slominsky's opera, *Virineya*; I did not find all of it good. And it is rather long, although there is some good music in it.[118]

I very much miss not seeing you.

Your

D. Shostakovich

Please give our greetings to Vera Vasiliyevna.

23 November 1969 Moscow

Dear Isaak Davïdovich,

I am in hospital once again because my legs and my hands (especially my right hand) are in a bad way. Some light has been shed on why my extremities function so badly: strange as it may seem, the cause is poliomyelitis. This is usually a young person's malady but, although rare, it is not unknown among the elderly. As a result I am not going to Kurgan to Dr Ilizarov. Surgery would be of no use in this case.[119]

They are treating me, or perhaps I should say tending to me, with injections, physiotherapy, massage and oxygen. I do feel a bit better now, I feel as though I have more strength. I have to stay in hospital at least until the middle of December and possibly until the New Year.

There will be performances of the Fourteenth Symphony on 21 or 23 December and there will also be one at the University on 18 December.

I am keeping issue eleven of *October* magazine for you. Unfortunately the end of Kochetov's novel falls off considerably compared to the beginning: there is much less fighting spirit and less development of the ideas that can be traced back to *The Aphis* (not *The Moth*, as you called it in your letter). Of course, Kochetov is not the only writer to draw on the *Aphis* heritage; other books you might perhaps come across include Oles Bendokh's *In the Jaws of the Locusts* or V. Fyodorov's *The Battle for Olympus*. I urge you to read these novels.[120]

I agree with your remarks on the subject of whether directors [in the theatre] can be geniuses. In my opinion this is not a profession which often offers the wherewithal for genius.[121] It is true that I recently saw *St Petersburg Dreams*, directed by Yu. A Zavadsky, and although I have no idea why this staging of Dostoyevsky's *Crime and Punishment* was given this title, as a production it did produce the most stunning impression on me.[122]

I will let you know when I get out of hospital, and then I hope you will come to see me. I very much miss not seeing you.

Please pass on my greetings to Vera Vasiliyevna.

Your

D. Shostakovich

26 December 1969 Zhukovka

Dear Isaak Davïdovich,

Irina Antonovna and I send our warmest good wishes to you, Vera Vasiliyevna and all those near and dear to you for the New Year. I very much hope that the New Year 1970 will bring us all much joy.

I came out of hospital the day before yesterday. My legs and hands are a little stronger than they were, but they get tired very quickly. Professor Rabotalov, who has been treating me (tending to me, rather) since 1955, told me: 'At least twice a year you must spend two to three months with us' (he meant the Neurology Department). I expect he is right.

Yesterday the Moscow luminaries gathered for a so-called consultation on my case. The chief luminary (I have forgotten his first name, patronymic and surname) said that I was perfectly well, and that there was nothing at all remarkable in the fact that my hands and my legs don't work. 'If X-ray photographs were to be taken of me,' he said, 'they would be scarcely be any different from ones taken of you. However, I can move about with ease, while this is very difficult for you. All this merely goes to show that no two organisms on earth are the same. In one organism the abnormality you present would be quite trivial, while in another, for example yours, it seriously inhibits movements and weakens muscles.' Having delivered himself of this verdict, the luminary, his colleagues and accompanying train left my house waving away the fees which had been specially prepared in envelopes for them. I had devoted much effort and cunning to getting the fees into their hands, but they resisted with ox-like stubbornness.[123]

I am not at all steady when I stand up. My hands are not functioning very well either; however I went to the Great Hall of the Conservatoire on 23 December to hear Haydn's 46th symphony and my 14th. There are to be further performances of my symphony on 28 December in the House of Scholars and on the 30th in the Great Hall of the Conservatoire; if I feel strong enough I shall attend these concerts.[124]

It seems to me that Miroshnikova and Yevgeny Vladimirov sing better than their opposite numbers (Vishnevskaya and Reshetin).[125] Barshai's orchestra is simply superb.

I may come to Leningrad after the New Year to do some work on the music for *King Lear*.[126]

I embrace you. Give my greetings to Vera Vasiliyevna.

Your

D. Shostakovich

VI
Intimations of Mortality
1970–1975

The last photograph, May 1975

In search of a cure for his steadily worsening condition, Shostakovich spent long stretches of time in Dr Gavriil Ilizarov's clinic in the remote town of Kurgan in Siberia. As he underwent the unconventional treatment regime, he experienced the emotional swings between hope and despair that only a sick man with an indomitable will to create can know. The progressive crumbling of the exhausted body went hand in hand with an unquenchable desire to write music; indeed, the year-long caesura after the Fifteenth Symphony seemed to cause the composer even more grief than any of his physical ills. The relief when the flow started again is almost palpable from the letters. There was little respite in the public demands that continued to beset the iconic figure Shostakovich had, involuntarily, become: ritual pronouncements, official appearances, awards, journeys far and near to receive honours, obligations to write a work celebrating Lenin's centenary. For all those – and there were many – who were dismayed at his apparent failure to cross the ethical Rubicon and speak out for Sakharov and Solzhenitsïn, it is safe to say that none were more dismayed or suffered more acutely from it than the beleaguered composer himself. Such was the background to the inner world from which came the Fifteenth Symphony, the last three quartets, the Tsvetayeva Songs, the Suite on Verses of Michelangelo *and the final Viola Sonata.*

In the last letter Shostakovich wrote to his friend Isaak Glikman, he sums up his distillation of Michelangelo's essence as

Wisdom, Love, Creation, Death, Immortality.

It could have been his own epitaph.

25 January 1970 Zhukovka

Dear Isaak Davïdovich,

On 26 January, Irina and I are going to stay at the Composers' House in Repino. We shall be there for about ten days. I should be so glad if you could come to visit us there. If you can, please telephone Zelenogorsk 28–45 at 9 a.m., 2 p.m. or 7 p.m.[1]

Give my greetings to Vera Vasiliyevna.

D. Shostakovich

27 February 1970 Kurgan

Dear Isaak Davïdovich,

Here I am at last in Kurgan, in Dr Gavriil Ilizarov's hospital. Irina has come out here with me, and we are staying together as we did in the Sverdlov Hospital in Leningrad.[2]

This is my address while I am here: Poste Restante, Kurgan 5. The post office for this postal district (No. 5) is actually in the hospital building, and all patients here have the above-mentioned address. Please write to me. I have a telephone in the ward, the number is 97465. I mention this just in case you should want to ring me.[3]

I arrived today, 27 February, and the main treatment will start on 2 March. I am absolutely counting on this treatment. I shall be here in the hospital for at least a month and a half.

Please write.

Give my greetings to Vera Vasiliyevna. Irina sends her regards.

Your

D. Shostakovich

28 March 1970 Kurgan

Dear Isaak Davïdovich,

I was delighted to hear your voice on the phone, it was so good of you to ring me. I forgot to tell you when we were speaking that a book has recently appeared called *The Day of Poetry*, published by the Soviet Writer press, Moscow, 1969. On page 52 of this book there is a poem by Yevgeny Yevtushenko that I liked very much. I should like you to read it too.[4]

As well as this, I hope you will read the story by Chingiz Aitmatov called 'The White Steamer'. It appeared in the magazine *Novy Mir*, issue 1 for 1970. I think it is a magnificent piece of work; it seems to me that Aitmatov must be one of the most powerful prose writers in our country, perhaps in the world.[5]

Our life here goes like this. We rise at seven o'clock, and from seven to eight I follow my morning regime: wash, shave, physical exercises, listen to the latest news. Breakfast at 8.30. At 9.15 I walk for an hour in the woods. From 11 to 12.30 – violent gymnastics which bring me out in a sweat, then massage. Lunch at 1.30. At 3.30 another walk in the woods. 5 o'clock: return to the hospital. All this seems to be doing some good: my hands and legs are getting stronger. But by evening I am so tired that I cannot think even of *King Lear*, let alone other things.[6]

On top of this, I have an injection every three days, and I have had a simple operation as well. Everything I have seen in the hospital relating to the medical treatment it offers has impressed me very much, and fills me with admiration, delight and wonder at the power of human genius. I am speaking here of Gavriil Ilizarov; when we meet I will tell you of the things he has achieved.

Please give my warmest greetings to Vera Vasiliyevna. Irina sends her regards.

Your

D. Shostakovich

I shall be here at least until 15 April.

11 May 1970 Kurgan

Dear Isaak Davïdovich,

I hope to be discharged from the hospital early in June. I have achieved a lot: I can play the piano, go up and down stairs and get on a bus – admittedly this last not very easily. Gavriil Ilizarov has restored my strength; now what I have to do is build up my various techniques again. Many of my functions are already rehabilitated: I can shave with my right hand, do up buttons, put a spoon into my mouth without completely missing it, and so on.[7]

Irina Antonovna and I would be very grateful if you would pass on the enclosed article about my Blok songs to the literary critic Professor V. N. Orlov. The article was written by a very serious and gifted musicologist and theorist, Yelizaveta Mnatsakanova. It would be most important and valuable to her to have V. N. Orlov's appraisal of her work, and so it would be much appreciated if he would write a review of it.[8]

I miss you very much. Please write to me at Municipal Hospital No. 2, Kurgan 5 (or you can equally well send it to Poste Restante, Kurgan 5).

Irina and I send you and Vera Vasiliyevna our warmest greetings.

D. Shostakovich

2 June 1970 Kurgan

Dear Isaak Davïdovich,

I am coming out of hospital on 10 June and shall go straight to Moscow. From 18 June until 18 July, I hope to be in Repino.[9] After that I shall come back to Kurgan in order that Dr Ilizarov can, as he puts it, dot the i's on the treatment. This second visit to Kurgan will not be a long one: ten to fifteen days.

I hope very much to see you before long.

Your

D. Shostakovich

Warmest greetings to Vera Vasiliyevna.

16 August 1970 Zhukovka

Dear Isaak Davïdovich,

I have a great favour to ask of you. Comrades Krastin and Sarkisov[10] have approached me with a request to write an introduction (or foreword) to a commemorative album being brought out to celebrate the fiftieth jubilee of the Leningrad Philharmonia. I should be most grateful if you could write something in a highly laudatory tone, mentioning Ivan Sollertinsky, Yevgeny Mravinsky and Afanasy Ponomaryov.[11] I simply cannot write it myself, because I am incompetent and lack the literary skills to find elegant constructions to express such things.[12] Please come to my rescue and write it for me. You can send it to my Moscow address, and if I go to Kurgan in the near future it will be sent on to me there.

I hope you will have a very good time in Repino. Please give my warmest greetings to Vera Vasiliyevna and my most grateful thanks to Gavriil Davïdovich.[13]

Your

D. Shostakovich

24 August 1970 Zhukovka

Dear Isaak Davïdovich,

Tomorrow (24 August) I go to Kurgan. My address will be: Poste Restante, Kurgan 5. I should be so happy to have a line from you. I expect to be at the hospital until the middle of September, or possibly not quite as long.

Give my greetings to Vera Vasiliyevna.
Your
D. Shostakovich

I have composed a quartet, which will be my number 13. D. S.[14]

7 August 1970 Kurgan

Dear Isaak Davïdovich,

Here we are once again in Kurgan, and back in the same ward. The address and telephone number are the same: Poste Restante, Kurgan 5, tel. 97205. It seems we shall be here at least a month, or so Dr Ilizarov said when he saw me today.

Did you get a letter from me asking for your help in writing a salutation in honour of the fiftieth anniversary of the Leningrad Philharmonia? If you did not receive the letter, do please help me out with this.

Irina joins me in sending greetings. Give my regards to Vera Vasiliyevna.
D. Shostakovich

21 September 1970 Kurgan

Dear Isaak Davïdovich,

Warmest thanks for your help over the Philharmonia business. As always, your assistance was effective and ideal for the purpose.

In all probability I shall be home by the end of October. Give my greetings to Vera Vasiliyevna.
Your
D. Shostakovich

25 October 1970 Kurgan

Dear Isaak Davïdovich,

I have been stuck out here in Kurgan for an inordinately long time. However, I shall be getting the train home on 30 October and shall arrive in Moscow on 1 November. I am feeling fine, and Dr Ilizarov's treatment has done me good.

I have been missing you very much, and pray God we shall soon see one another.[15]

Give my greetings to Vera Vasiliyevna.

Your
D. Shostakovich

Irina sends her greetings.

22 February 1971 Moscow

Dear Isaak Davïdovich,
Thank you for your letter.[16] This is to let you know how my address should now be correctly written: for letters, Moscow 103009. For telegrams: Moscow–9, nothing else needed.
With best wishes
Your
D. Shostakovich

2 June 1971 Moscow

Dear Isaak Davïdovich,
We are flying to Kurgan tonight. This is the address: Poste Restante, Kurgan 5. If I have access to a telephone there, I shall let you know the number when I get to Kurgan. I think we shall probably be there for two weeks.
Your
D. Shostakovich

3 June 1971 Kurgan

Dear Isaak Davïdovich,
We arrived safely in Kurgan today, and are once again installed in the hospital.[17] The number of the telephone in our ward is 97439. Address, as before, is Poste Restante, Kurgan 5.
I was so happy to get back here. After the 35 to 40 degree heat in Moscow, it is very pleasant indeed to be in the cool of Kurgan, where the temperature drops to between 3 and 5 degrees at night.
Your
D. Shostakovich

Warmest greetings to Vera Vasiliyevna.

15 Première of the First Violin Concerto (composed 1947– 48), in the Great Hall of the Leningrad Philharmonia, 29 October 1955. Yevgeny Mravinsky (far l.), David Oistrakh (centre), DS (far r.), members of the Leningrad Philharmonic Orchestra

16 DS with the composer Moisey Vainberg after the première of the Fifteenth Symphony

17 DS with two of his students, Revol Bunin (l.) and Kara Karayev

18 Maksim Shostakovich with his son Dmitry at the keyboard

19 DS with Mstislav Rostropovich and
Yevgeny Svetlanov after the première of
the Second Cello Concerto

20 Dr Gavriil Ilizarov

21 DS with Irina Antonovna Shostakovich at Kurgan

22 DS with Isaak Glikman in 1968, visiting the grave of Mikhail Zoshchenko on the tenth anniversary of the writer's death.
23 DS on board ship at Kizhi

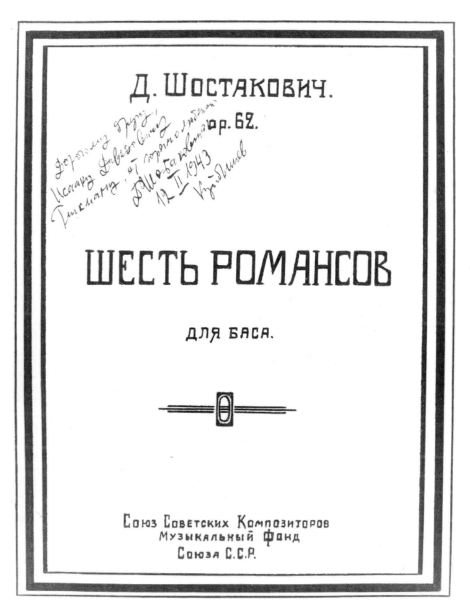

24 Title page of the 1943 Music Fund 'steklograf' edition of the Six Romances, Op. 62.
The inscription reads: 'To my dear friend Isaak Davïdovich Glikman from D.
Shostakovich, who loves him dearly. 12.2.43, Kuybïshev'

25 First page of the 1943 edition of 'MacPherson Before his Execution', with dedication to Isaak Glikman. The translation of the Burns poem is by Samuil Marshak.

26 Isaak Glikman, Venyamin Basner and Yevgeny Mravinsky in the conductor's green room at the Leningrad Philharmonia

28 DS with the film director Lev Arnshtam at a rehearsal of *The Nose* when it was revived in 1975.

27 Vera Vasiliyevna Antonova-Glikman, 1976

29 DS with the writer Chingiz Aitmatov, November 1971. An inscription on the back of the photograph reads: 'I needed so much to sit beside you, Dmitry Dmitriyevich. Ch. Aitmatov, Barvikha, 21 November 1971'

30 At the première of Vainberg's opera Madonna and the Soldier, Maly Opera, Leningrad, 17 March 1975. (l. to r.) DS, Boris Tishchenko, Irina Bogachova Isaak Glikman

9 September 1971 Moscow

Dear Isaak Davïdovich,

I very much miss not seeing you. Your letter came at just the right time, and gave me great pleasure. Thank you for your kind words about my Sixth Symphony.[18]

I completely agree with your assessment of Stravinsky's *Dialogues.* Some of his opinions can only be excused by assuming that he was rambling on without thinking what he was saying, and then signed them without taking much trouble to check exactly what he was putting his name to, merely so as to be left in peace. He is not the only person to whom such things have happened.

Stravinsky the composer I worship. Stravinsky the thinker I despise.[19]

My Fifteenth Symphony is presently with the copyists. As soon as there is news of when and where it is to be performed, I will let you know.

You didn't tell me anything about that source of great concern to you: the article usually delicately referred to as the 'toilet'.[20] Has it been repaired?

Please give my warmest greetings to Vera Vasiliyevna. Irina sends her regards.

Your

D. Shostakovich

Please tell me your new postal code. D.S.

A few days after writing this letter, which is dated 9 September, misfortune struck Shostakovich once again, when he was diagnosed with another heart attack and taken into hospital. It was five years since, on the eve of his sixtieth birthday, he had suffered his first serious attack, and now it had happened again. Only on 28 November, after two months of constant worry, was I able to breathe freely again on hearing his voice on the telephone from the Barvikha sanatorium, where he had been sent to recuperate. Soon afterwards, I received a letter from him.

28 November 1971 Barvikha

Dear Isaak Davïdovich,

Thank you very much for your phone calls. After two months in hospital I am now in this sanatorium. Irina is here with me. My heart condition is very much better, but my hands and legs are much weaker than they were. Everything that was gaining strength before I became ill has now deteriorated sharply. It looks as though I shall have to begin all over again. I may have to go back to Kurgan.

I have been warned to cut out alcohol, nicotine, strong tea and strong coffee completely from my diet. This is most distressing to me.

Please take good care of your health; it is a hard thing to bear when you lose it.[21] And there are all kinds of heart diseases that can creep up on you unseen. All the same, if you start noticing that the first shot of vodka fails to give you any pleasure, this can be a bad sign. I noticed in Repino that vodka was not doing anything for me, and it was a signal that a heart attack was on its way.[22] If this happens to you, do consult a doctor straight away. Better still, don't drink at all, or at least only in strict moderation.

We are staying in Barvikha, which is not far from our dacha. After the hospital, it seems like heaven to me. We shall be in the sanatorium until 17 December, and then go to the dacha. The première of my Fifteenth Symphony is scheduled for 8 January, and it will be conducted by Maksim, who has made great strides recently.

Irina and I send Vera Vasiliyevna and you warmest greetings.

Your

D. Shostakovich

Please look carefully at the envelope and make sure you write the postal code correctly.

We have a telephone in the ward: 241–05–24, extension 581. Or you can write to the Moscow address. Please don't fail to write. D. S.

30 December 1971 Zhukovka

Dear Isaak Davïdovich,

I send you my best wishes for the New Year. May you be always healthy and happy. Please give my warmest wishes also to Vera Vasiliyevna and all those near to you.

During 1971 death carried off several friends and acquaintances, among them the composer Sabitov, Professor Boris Votchal, who treated me in 1966, the film directors Mikhail Shapiro[23] and Mikhail Romm. Zinaida Gayamova, my secretary, has also died, and Aleksandr Kholodilin. I now have a new secretary, Rita Kornblyum. She is the widow of the proletarian playwright V. M. Kirshon, who was well known in his day.[24]

After the month I spent in hospital, I am now ensconced in my dacha, but I go in to the city to attend rehearsals of my Fifteenth Symphony, which Maksim is doing very well. The première is on 8 January, and if Maksim is on form, as I hope he will be, the symphony should sound as it was intended to.

Today we had three rehearsals in the recording studio; from 5 January on the rehearsals move to the Great Hall [of the Conservatoire]. Everything has been sounding wonderful in the studio, and now after a break the orchestra will have to adapt to a new acoustic. Studio and Great Hall – two big differences, as they say in Odessa.

Maksim has made great strides recently. He has become a real conductor, and in five years' time he will achieve even more: he will be older, more experienced, wiser.

It would be very good if you could come on 8 January.[25]

I feel well, but my hands and legs are extremely weak after my illness. Stairs are practically impossible for me, although I can manage fairly well on a level surface. I may have to go back to Ilizarov at Kurgan.

From 10 January we shall be in Ruza, where there is a Composers' Rest House, much like the one at Repino.

Irina sends you and Vera Vasiliyevna her warmest New Year greetings and best wishes.

Your

D. Shostakovich

20 February 1972 Zhukovka

Dear Isaak Davïdovich,

Thank you for your letter, which I have received, but the earlier letter you refer to has not arrived yet.

You ask me how the revival of *Katerina Izmailova* went. My answer is: extremely badly. So badly, in fact, that I suffered heart pains during the performance. It is obvious that nobody currently in the Stanislavsky–Nemirovich-Danchenko Theatre pays the slightest attention to the letter of the musical score. The singers were as shamelessly inaccurate as they were when Provatorov was on the podium.[26] The conductor now is Kitayenko, a Karajan Competition prizewinner.

To the shamelessly sloppy singing he added equally shameless, obscenely sloppy orchestral playing. The whole thing was an unprecedented insult to *Katerina Izmailova*.[27]

The opera was done in the edition that was used in the Mikhailovsky

Theatre.[28] There are some differences from the one used for the 1962 Stanislavsky–Nemirovich-Danchenko Theatre production.

I was deeply saddened by the death of Gavriil Popov.[29]

The composer Vladimir Yurovsky died not long ago. 'And yet another's hour is near at hand.'[30]

Please pass on to Vera Vasiliyevna our warmest greetings.

I press your hand warmly.

Your

D. Shostakovich

21 February 1972 Zhukovka

Dear Isaak Davïdovich,

Your letter previous to the one you wrote recently arrived today.

I warmly press your hand.

Your

D. Shostakovich

3 April 1972 Zhukovka

Dear Isaak Davïdovich,

Would you please do me a great favour? I want to summon up all my strength and come to Leningrad to hear the performance of my Fifteenth Symphony.

I should like you, please, *tactfully* to find out if and when it is due to be performed. It is rather awkward for me to do it myself.[31] I am worried that Yevgeny Mravinsky's creative personality may not be in complete sympathy with the work, and that he may therefore treat it as cavalierly as he did the Thirteenth Symphony and the Second Cello Concerto.[32] And so I should like you to find out everything you can about this matter. Then I would plan to come up five days or so before the first performance, attend the rehearsals, and afterwards go for about 7 or 8 days to Repino. I will wait for your news.

Irina and I send our greetings to Vera Vasiliyevna.

Your

D. Shostakovich.

PS My health has really gone. If I come, I shall bring my own car, so that I won't have to depend on the kindness of car-owners and can go where I want to in mine.

[184]

I miss you very much, and, strange to say, I miss Leningrad as well. Whenever I see the Neva or St Isaac's Cathedral etc. on television or at the cinema, tears come to my eyes.[33]

Anyway, find out what you can, and please don't mention that I am in any way concerned about this. D.S.

I don't get up stairs very well these days. Even a short walk leaves me gasping for breath. I am finding it hard to keep going. D.S.

Please look carefully at the envelope, it gives the correct postal address. D.S.

The worries expressed in this letter were soon allayed. Shostakovich telephoned me from Repino on 24 April and asked me to tell him what I had discovered. The première of the Fifteenth Symphony had been scheduled for 5 and 6 May.

Shostakovich came from Repino for the rehearsals. He was delighted with all that Mravinsky did, saying that it combined profundity with extraordinary attention to detail.

On 1 May, Dmitry Dmitriyevich and Irina Antonovna came to supper with us. Half in jest, half seriously, he complained that his recent illness had left him a poor trencherman and taken away one of life's great pleasures. His dream was that by the autumn he might again be able to enjoy a glass of vodka, which he hoped would restore both health and optimism, the absence of which made it hard to live in a world otherwise so imperfectly arranged. He then turned to the mastery with which Mravinsky was conducting the rehearsals for the symphony.

The first performance of the Fifteenth Symphony took place on 5 May. The Great Hall of the Philharmonia was filled to capacity, and every eye was turned to the box in which Shostakovich sat. It seemed to me as though many people had come not only to hear the symphony but to see its much-loved composer. He wore a black suit with a snow-white shirt and from a distance he looked his old self, youthful and handsome.

The end of the symphony brought forth an ovation, and Shostakovich's appearance on the platform stirred the audience to wild applause. In the wings, he said to me: 'If only you knew how tired going out to bow makes my legs.' His face was drawn with the pain he was suffering.

The symphony was repeated the following day, when the reception was, if anything, even more tumultuous than at the première. I clearly remember the state of exaltation in which Marietta Shaginyan, who had come up from Moscow, rushed into the Artists' Room, embraced Shostakovich and made the sign of the cross over him. Shouting because she was deaf, she cried: 'You must not say, Dmitry Dmitriyevich, that you are not well. You *are* well, because you have made us happy!' To this impulsive cry from the heart Shostakovich, smiling politely, replied: 'Where did you get the idea that I am not well? I always tell people I am well!' I overheard this little exchange, and marvelled at Shostakovich's unfailing poise in such situations.

On 8 May, I went myself to Repino; Shostakovich was to return to Moscow the following day. Before him lay a journey to Berlin for the première there of the

Fifteenth Symphony, and in the autumn he was due to go London. He simply did not have the strength for these obligations. He began to speak with sadness about his 'lost health', but did not linger long on this subject and quickly turned to reminiscences of the composer Gavriil Popov. 'Now there was a talent. His First Symphony, which had a lot of magnificent stuff in it, was banned at the time by the Fighters against Formalism. I have been appointed chairman of the Popov Memorial Committee; it is essential that his works are played.'

We then turned to the subject of the Thirteenth Symphony, which had also at that time been under threat of proscription. Shostakovich said: 'I was sure that the symphony would be banned, but evidently Khrushchov changed his mind, and it was performed, and you were there at the concert . . .'

Shostakovich spoke warmly about Sergey Slonimsky's opera *The Master and Margarita* and said he could not understand why it had not yet been produced on stage. In March 1971 he had listened, with a score, to a play-through of the opera by the composer, but the text, which was written in pencil, was very hard to make out. Shostakovich observed: 'The text does play a major role, as our orators of today are fond of saying', and laughed quietly to himself.

On 9 May, Shostakovich went back to Moscow.

12 May 1972 Moscow

Dear Isaak Davïdovich,

We are flying to Berlin today, and will be back some time after 10 June. I will let you know as soon as we return.[34]

Yesterday Maksim conducted the Fifteenth Symphony very well indeed. And the cellist David Geringas, substituting for Rostropovich who was ill, also played my first Cello Concerto very well.

I press your hand warmly.

D. Shostakovich

19 July 1972 Leningrad

Dear Isaak Davïdovich,

I have unfortunately mislaid your address in Sestroretsk. I gave your razor to Galya, who is at present staying in Komarovo.[35] Her telephone number is 317–35, so please give her a call and make arrangements to get it from her.

Your

D. Shostakovich

15 August 1972 Zhukovka

Dear Isaak Davïdovich,

I still cannot come to terms with the dreadful news of Nikolai Semyonovich's death.[36] He was a wonderful and pure-hearted man, who lived a wonderful and pure-hearted life. I shall treasure his memory.

My friend Vadim Borisovsky has also died. He was an excellent man who if you remember recently gave up his position as viola player of the Beethoven Quartet.

In general, life has become very hard. Fate has dealt many heavy blows and grievous losses. I continue to toil in the sweatshop of life, as Ivan Sollertinsky used to say. My hands and legs don't function very well, and apparently there is not much hope of improvement.

I do envy you being at Repino. I am sure it is wonderful there. The awful heat even we have been suffering here seems to have passed over. Autumn will soon be upon us. The season will begin. Musical life will start to boil and bubble.

I embrace you.

Your

D. Shostakovich

Please give warmest greetings from Irina and from me to Vera Vasiliyevna.

19 October 1972 Barvikha

Dear Isaak Davïdovich,

Here is a small addendum to the article about Ivan Ivanovich.[37] Please give it to Lyudmila Mikheyeva;[38] if it should come in useful, I would be very pleased.

At the moment I am having some treatment in the Barvikha Sanatorium just outside Moscow. On 8 November I have to go to London because my Fifteenth Symphony and some other works are being performed. It would be so good not to have to go.

I have very little strength, but that is not taken into account and they still say that I must go.[39] I recently had to go to Baku. It was terribly hot there, so hot that when I returned home I was taken into hospital. I must get better before going to England.[40] What worries me most of all is this: I have not written a note since the Fifteenth Symphony. Surely this last modest pleasure is not to be denied me now? I have never before gone so long without writing anything.[41]

I kiss you warmly.
Your
D. Shostakovich

Please give our warmest greetings to Vera Vasiliyevna. D. S.

16 January 1973 Moscow

Dear Isaak Davïdovich,

I don't remember in the past ever having to admit that I don't enjoy reading letters I receive. In any case, this does not apply to letters from you.[42]

I have almost forgotten what it is like to be at home. I am either away on some extended journey, or in hospital. For instance, I have now been in hospital here since 3 December. It started with stones in my kidneys. They were extremely painful, but I suppose they must eventually have passed out of my body. After that I was going to be sent home, but in the end they decided that they had better give me a complete check-up, 'just in case'. As a result of this they found a cyst on my left lung, and I am now getting radiation treatment to destroy it. The cyst is gradually reducing, so that in about three to four weeks I shall be the proud possessor of two immaculately cyst-free lungs. On the other hand, my hands and legs are weaker, since all attention is now centred on the lung.

I am feeling better now, so I can reply to your letter.

Please take good care of your health. I have lost mine, and am wretched because of it.[43] I am almost completely helpless in the ordinary business of life; I can no longer do things like dress myself or wash myself on my own. Some kind of spring has broken in my brain. I have not written a note since the Fifteenth Symphony. This is a terrible state of affairs for me.[44]

Irina and I send you and Vera Vasiliyevna our greetings and best wishes.

D. Shostakovich

I shall be in hospital for about another month. It is very frustrating to have to stay here.

9 March 1973 Moscow

Dear Isaak Davïdovich,

Thank you for your letter. After my Berlin visit I had to come back to hospital once more, as they explained it, in order to observe what effect my last stay in this sainted institution had had on me.

I have a great favour to ask of you: could you please try to find out the first name and patronymic, and the address, of Vladimir Lebedev's widow?[45] I must reply to her letter, which I have lost along with her address. I think she still lives in the same place, that is to say on Belinsky Street, but I don't remember the number of the building or the apartment. Please find out and let me know.

Warm greetings to Vera Vasiliyevna.

Your

D. Shostakovich

There is a telephone in the ward where I am: 141–43–31.[46]

17 July 1973 Zhukovka

Dear Isaak Davïdovich,

Thank you for your letter.

I shall miss very much not coming to Repino this summer and not being able to see you. Irina and I are, it seems, going to Pärnu[47] where we are promised an idyllic life.

On my last journey, the ocean made the most profound impression on me. It is an indescribably sublime sight. I will tell you in more detail about my trip to Denmark and America when we meet.[48]

My hands and legs are in a very bad state. There seems to be no hope of any improvement in them.

I embrace you.

Your

D. Shostakovich

Irina and I send our warmest greetings to all of you. D.S.

PS Death continues to cut down all around us. About five days ago, the composer Aleksandr Mosolov died. You may remember him. D.S.

1 August 1973 Moscow

Dear Isaak Davïdovich,

Irina and I are spending August in Pärnu. Here is our address until 1 September, in case you would like to write to me: 12 Merepujeste Street, 203601 Pärnu.

Please give my warmest greetings to Vera Vasiliyevna.

Your

D. Shostakovich

14 August 1973 Pärnu

Dear Isaak Davïdovich,

Do forgive me for writing to you on such an unattractive piece of paper. It has been torn out of a notepad, a feat calling for a mighty effort of physical strength and native cunning. The pad is after all a product of the town of Chernigov.[49]

I am worried that I have not heard from you. I am sending this letter to your Leningrad address; I wrote to you to Sestroretsk and again to Repino, but had no reply from either.

Irina and I are enjoying ourselves here. It is very quiet and peaceful, although Irina has to do the housework, cook, go to market and so on. I am feeling well, although I suffer much from my hands and legs. Time was, when I was informing you about my vocal works, I would write out the texts for you. Now it is very difficult to write out words, music notation and so on.

While I have been here, I have written six songs to poems of Marina Tsvetayeva. The poems came from the book: *Marina Tsvetayeva, Selected Works*, published by Sovetsky Pisatel [Soviet Writer], Moscow–Leningrad, 1965. If you come across this book, have a look at pages 57 (the first poem), 75 (the second poem), 240 ('Hamlet's Dialogue with his Conscience'), 288 ('The Poet and the Tsar'), 289 (the sixth poem) and 103 (the first poem).

The work is written for contralto and piano, and I have been thinking about interpreters. Vocally speaking, the best to my mind would be Bogachova.[50] And it needs a very good pianist, because I myself couldn't play 'Three Blind Mice' now, and I simply don't know whom to ask.

We shall return to Moscow early in September, and then I will get on with organizing the duo. It is a problem that Bogachova comes from Leningrad; the Moscow singers Obraztsova and Sinyavskaya don't appeal to me quite as much. It's true that Bogachova is somewhat of an enigma to me: I recently heard her on the radio singing something by Pushkov or Novikov or some such, but I was simply knocked out by the beauty of her voice. I don't know her first name and patronymic. If it is not too much trouble, could you please find out for me her first name, patronymic, address and telephone number?

Until 30 August our address will be: 12 Merepujesta Street, 203600 Pärnu, telephone 56135. After that we shall be in Moscow. Before my long and arduous trip to Denmark and the USA I wrote my Fourteenth Quartet, but the first performance has had to be put off for some considerable time because Nikolai Zabavnikov, the second violin, has hurt his left leg rather badly.

Please give our warmest greetings to Vera Vasiliyevna and all your family. Do write to me, even if only a few words.

Your

D. Shostakovich

20 September 1973 Moscow

Dear Isaak Davïdovich,

I received your letter, for which many thanks. I also got the one you sent to Pärnu.

I do have the score of Britten's *War Requiem*, and if you need it I will send it to you. Or perhaps I will bring it with me, because I plan to come to Leningrad at the beginning of October, if my by now much enfeebled powers permit.[51]

So far I have no definite news to tell you about a performance of my Tsvetayeva songs. Tamara Sinyavskaya has the score and is studying it. I also wrote to Irina Bogachova asking her to consider singing them, but this was some time ago and I have not heard from her. I expect she is away.[52] I can't possibly play them myself. Things are very bad with my right hand: I couldn't even play 'Three Blind Mice'.

Give my greetings to Vera Vasiliyevna.

Your

D. Shostakovich

On 4 January 1974 Dmitry Dmitriyevich and Irina Antonovna arrived in Repino. As usual, they telephoned me straight away and asked me to come over to see them as soon as possible.

I visited them on 7 January. My first impression was that Shostakovich was not looking at all bad. When he was sitting down, at table, for instance, there was almost no trace of his illness. We dined in the cottage and talked of this and that, among other things of his plans to use his leisure time at Repino to make an orchestral version of the Tsvetayeva Songs.

During those January days, Shostakovich was lively and talkative in my presence, and often the cottage pleasantly resounded to his laughter. But suddenly the laughter would be interrupted by a severe and melancholy look.

He wanted to discuss certain matters which would have been difficult to confide to paper: 'After all,' he said with a meaningful smile, 'there are often problems with paper,' meaning that letters were always liable to be opened and inspected.

Some of his conversations with me amounted to what I might style 'oral letters'. On the day in question, 7 January, Shostakovich was reminiscing about Meyerhold, with whom he was closely connected in his youth and for whom all his life he retained the warmest feelings. He had enormous respect for Meyerhold, and suffered greatly over the terrible fate inflicted on the director in Stalin's torture-chambers.

Shostakovich said: 'Next month will be the centenary of Vsevolod Emilievich's birth, and there is talk of a celebration. What for? Do you think they will mention his arrest, or announce that he was an innocent victim of Stalin's bloodlust, or refer to the tragedy of his death? Will anything be said about the brutal murder of his wife, Zinaïda Raikh? Of course not. They will go on about what a good director he was. But we know that already. Now they are suggesting that I dedicate my Fourth Symphony to his memory, but that strikes me as a clumsy idea. After all, such was not my intention [when I wrote it] in 1936. And now . . . so long after the fact, what good would it do?'

After thinking about it, Shostakovich declined to make the requested dedication, and his instincts were quite right: the jubilee celebrations were pointless, and the truth about Meyerhold's fate ignored. The actual centenary of his birth was duly celebrated in February 1974 in the former Aleksandrinsky Theatre, where he had once had such a brilliant career. I was present – indeed, I had acted as consultant on the musical part of the programme. Just as Shostakovich had predicted, G. A. Tovstonogov made a fine speech honouring Meyerhold as a great director, but said not one word about his arrest and excruciating fate. He had been forbidden to mention it, and the resulting lacuna (much against Tovstonogov's will) seemed like a blasphemy against Meyerhold's memory. Sitting in the hall, I thought how we would feel if for instance the poet Rïleyev[53] were to be remembered with no mention of his arrest and execution. It would be an inconceivable profanation of the truth, and yet here we were in the Brezhnev era routinely witnessing the torments of Stalin's victims being trampled on by equally shameful distortions and manipulations.

Shostakovich sent a telegram to be read out, which he used to make a plea for the Aleksandrinsky Theatre to revive Meyerhold's masterpiece – Lermontov's *Masquerade*. For the finale of the concert, at my suggestion, Yury Temirkanov conducted the orchestra in the third movement (Largo) of Shostakovich's Fifth

Symphony. The emotional charge of the magnificent lament sounded as a requiem to Meyerhold and spoke directly to everyone present of his tragic end.

From speaking about Meyerhold, Shostakovich turned to Prokofiev. He, of course, had lived an entirely different life, but had also endured much, not least over the staging of *Romeo and Juliet* at the Maryinsky Theatre. We recalled our pre-war attendance together at a rehearsal of the ballet not long before the première, and how impressed we had been by the magnificent music. In this connection Shostakovich said: 'I was told that one of the leading prima donnas of the theatre announced in a voice loud enough for all to hear, "The production is all right, but how much better it would have been if it had had music by someone other than Prokofiev." If this is true, how do you think Sergey Sergeyevich would have enjoyed hearing the comment? If you haven't read it already, do please read Gennady Rozhdestvensky's open letter to *Sovetskaya Muzïka* on *Romeo and Juliet*. He sticks up for Prokofiev and accuses the choreographer, Lavrovsky, of being stubborn and arbitrary, and of course this is true. But all the same, Lavrovsky is no longer with us and it may be that he did not wish Prokofiev any harm, he simply did not know what he was doing.'

10 January 1974

Shostakovich had interesting things to say about his most recent visit to America, a country he had already visited twice before. He said: 'It is a wonderful country, however much you find people here spitting on it. I found there to be a very great and very deep interest in music. There is a great deal of music going on in both capitals all the time, and many other places as well. Pierre Boulez, who has taken over from Leonard Bernstein in New York, does much to promote both classical and contemporary music. By the way, I got into a slightly tricky situation with him at a banquet: imagine the arch-apostle of modernism coming up to me, seizing my hand and kissing it! I was so taken aback I didn't manage to snatch it away in time.'

18 January 1974

I accompanied Shostakovich and Irina Antonovna to a concert in the Small Hall of the Philharmonia. On their way back to Repino in the car, before dropping me off at my home on Bolshaya Pushkarskaya Street, Shostakovich said, *à propos* the concert we had just heard: 'That C minor Quartet of Brahms is such a wishy-washy piece. But on the other hand what magnificent symphonies he wrote! It often happens that feeble things come from the same hand as other things that are incredibly strong. Also, I find Beethoven's Ninth Quartet has lost none of its power to transport me.'

21 January 1974

Dmitry Dmitriyevich and Irina Antonovna came to dinner. For the savouries to go with the vodka, my wife had baked potatoes in their jackets, and it was touching to see the enthusiasm with which Shostakovich fell on this far from sophisticated dish. His obvious enjoyment of good food was quite like old times, and as I told him it made me quite envious. His response was: 'You know, there is an old saying that there are those who eat to live, and those who live to eat. I must belong in the first camp: if I didn't eat, I wouldn't be able to write music!'

After this sally, the talk turned to the fate of Aleksandr Solzhenitsïn, whose 'One Day in the Life of Ivan Denisovich' and 'Matryona's House'[54] Shostakovich had found remarkable for their great artistic power and truthfulness to life. He wanted to meet the author. It appeared that the feeling was mutual, and I was there when Solzhenitsïn came to the apartment on Nezhdanova Street. As he hurried into Shostakovich's study next door, I had a fleeting impression of a formidably severe face with a scar on the forehead. At one point Shostakovich emerged briefly from the study and asked me if I would like to make the celebrated writer's acquaintance, but I was seized with unaccountable shyness and declined the honour.

24 January 1974

Shostakovich, his wife and I went to the Maly Opera to see the ballet *Coppélia*. After the performance, Shostakovich said: 'I love Delibes's ballet music. It is written with such taste and refinement, as well as mastery. Tchaikovsky greatly admired it and went so far as to say that it was much better than his own *Swan Lake*.'

29 January 1974

Vera Vasiliyevna and I went out to Repino for supper. Shostakovich wanted us to drink a commemorative glass of vodka together to mark the sad, even tragic, thirty-eighth anniversary of the devastating article 'Muddle Instead of Music' published in *Pravda* on 28 January 1936.

Every word of it was imprinted on our memory, for scars like that do not heal. We could recall every detail associated with the article; we remembered all those terrified musicians who joined in the abject chorus excoriating *Lady Macbeth of Mtsensk,* and we had a special word for those who indulged in their frenzied denunciations specifically in order to parade the exceptional purity of their allegiance to the regime.

Shostakovich said: 'That article no longer has its power to frighten, but all through those years it was a source of alarm and fear to people. Stalin got what he wanted. It was not simply that you could not disagree with the article; you were forbidden to have the merest scintilla of doubt about anything whatsoever in it. He who doubted was guilty of a crime against Stalin's regime, and the sinner could save himself only by repenting. And, as you remember, after "Muddle Instead of Music", the authorities tried everything they knew to get me to repent and expiate my sin. But I refused. I was young then, and had my physical strength. Instead of repenting, I composed my Fourth Symphony.'

7 February 1974

Today I received a recording of the Fourteenth Symphony which Shostakovich had inscribed to me. The conductor on this recording was Rostropovich, the soloists Galina Vishnevskaya and Mark Reshetin. I was particularly impressed by 'Lorelei', 'The Suicide' and 'On Watch', but the other movements also sounded superb. The whole performance was permeated with the extraordinary expressivity that is the hallmark of Rostropovich the cellist and Rostropovich the conductor.

11 February 1974

Shostakovich telephoned from Moscow, anxious to know my reaction to the Rostropovich recording. Although he had the highest regard for Rudolf Barshai and his chamber orchestra, who were the first interpreters of the Fourteenth Symphony, he had found new things in Rostropovich's account.

25 March 1974 Zhukovka

Dear Isaak Davïdovich,

I enclose a label from a bottle of Extra brand vodka. You will see that I have drawn an arrow on the label pointing to the quality mark. Experts say that if you can find this mark on the label, it means that the bottle contains a superior grade of Extra vodka. My advice to you is, therefore: whenever you buy a bottle of Extra, check carefully to see whether or not the quality mark is there.

Be healthy and happy.

Warmest greetings from us to Vera Vasiliyevna.

Your

D. Shostakovich

This letter could be subtitled: Shostakovich smiles. Ordinarily speaking, Extra brand vodka was terrible stuff, but apparently one could occasionally come across a bottle with good-quality spirit in it. I deduced – correctly as it turned out – that Shostakovich must be in a sunny mood, and that he must be composing. On 2 May he telephoned from Moscow and announced that he was writing a new quartet.

12 May 1974 Moscow

Dear Isaak Davïdovich,

Thank you for your letters.

At the moment I am in hospital: my hands (especially the right hand) and legs are very weak. I hope to be away from here at the end of May.

I press your hand warmly.

D. Shostakovich

This time, Dmitry Dmitriyevich stayed in hospital for about two weeks, and on 1 June he went to Repino. I visited him there on 3 June. He told me: 'I have finished my Fifteenth Quartet. I don't know how good it is, but I had some joy in writing it.'

9 June 1974

I went to see Shostakovich in Repino. We talked for a long time about this and that, discussing among other things the extraordinary talent of Rostropovich and his imminent departure from the Soviet Union.

When Irina Antonovna went out of the room and we were left alone, Shostakovich spoke of the suffering he was enduring from his hands and legs. As he jerked out his abrupt phrases, his eyes filled with tears. Then, pulling himself together, he said: 'Anyhow, I don't like people who grouse, and I don't like grousing myself.' It was all I could do not to burst into tears.

23 June 1974

Dmitry Dmitriyevich and Irina Antonovna came to dinner with us. We spoke of the ballet, and discussed the forthcoming première of Boris Tishchenko's ballet *Yaroslavna* at the Maly Opera. Shostakovich said: 'When I was younger I wrote three ballets to completely rubbishy librettos. Why don't you settle down and write me one? But keep away from philosophical problems, make sure it is continuously entertaining and has a happy ending. When you are writing it, tell me how many bars you need me to compose for such and such a piece of action. Apparently that is how Petipa and Tchaikovsky worked on *The Sleeping Beauty*.'

23 August 1974 Zhukovka

Dear Isaak Davïdovich,

I have been composing quite a lot recently, and so I decided to inform you about my new works.

After the Fifteenth Quartet I made eleven settings of sonnets by Michelangelo. See if you can track down the book called *Michelangelo* in the edition published by Isskustvo, Moscow, 1964. Leafing through this book and looking at the reproductions of Michelangelo's great creations, I found a series of his poems. These are the ones I selected for my 'cycle'. (All the poems and sonnets are numbered.)

> Page 126, No. 4
> Page 127, No. 8
> Page 136, No. 35
> Page 128, No. 12
> Page 128, No. 11
> Page 166, No. 75
> Page 166, No. 77
> Page 139, No. 38
> Page 163, Nos. 67, 68
> Page 178, No. 100
> Page 155, Nos. 16, 12

The sonnets appear in this order. Where two are shown, for example 67 and 68 or 16 and 12, they are combined in one [piece of music].

My next opus was Verses of Captain Lebyadkin, to words by Fyodor Dostoyevsky:

No. 1   The Love of Captain Lebyadkin
No. 2   The Cockroach
No. 3   The Ball for the Benefit of Governesses
No. 4   A Shining Personality[55]

Both cycles are written for bass and piano.

The character of Captain Lebyadkin has something of the buffoon, but there is also something that is much more sinister about him.[56] I think I have achieved a very sinister composition.

I find it hard to make any judgement about Michelangelo, but it does appear to me that the essence has come through. And by the essence of these sonnets, I had in mind:

Wisdom, Love, Creation, Death, Immortality.

The translations by Abram Efros are not always successful, however the immense creative power of Michelangelo shines through even an inadequate translation.

Irina and I send to Vera Vasiliyevna and to you our very best wishes.
Your
D. Shostakovich

The was the last letter that I received from Dmitry Shostakovich. On 12 September he invited me to attend the première of *The Nose* in the Musical Chamber Theatre in Moscow. Some hours before the performance Shostakovich and I came in to the city from Zhukovka to hear Moysey Vainberg play through the Michelangelo Sonnets on the piano, which he did magnificently. I listened to the Suite with a rare feeling of excitement, and Shostakovich similarly found it hard to control his emotions. Afterwards, we left for the theatre. (The inexplicably inept scene in the recently released film about Shostakovich, *Viola Sonata*, according to which the composer is unable to walk to the première and has to be carried to it from his Moscow apartment, is completely fictitious.)

The atmosphere in the theatre was electric. Small wonder: after forty-four years of black disgrace the once reviled opera was returning to the stage in triumph. In the foyer I bumped into David Oistrakh, carrying a tape recorder: he was planning to record the whole performance. But there was an embarrassing moment: just before the conductor raised his hands to begin the performance, a sudden burst of unexplained music coming from somewhere filled the air, and as suddenly died. The opera then began in all its glory.

In the interval, Oistrakh told me that he had pressed the wrong button on his tape recorder. He was mortified at the mistake, and could not get over it. To console the great violinist, I told him that the accident which had so upset him was entirely in the spirit of *The Nose*, filled as it was with bizarre and unexpected events. We had a good laugh about it.

At the end of the performance, an ovation began that seemed as though it would never end, and the composer became exhausted from all the bows he had to take. He embraced Gennady Rozhdestvensky and warmly shook the hand of the director Boris Pokrovsky in acknowledgement of their work.

Shostakovich decided not to mark this première by inviting a large party of guests, and so the three of us went out to Zhukovka by ourselves. During supper, we had a lively discussion about the production, singling out the most successful parts of the performance. Shostakovich bestowed high praise on the orchestral playing under Rozhdestvensky, and on the singers. He said: 'What a wonderful, original story the young Gogol came up with. He was only twenty-five or twenty-six when he wrote it, and I was even younger when I composed my opera. Everything in the story is amazing, but the passage I most often think about is when Kovalyov asks the doctor to restore his nose. You remember what he replies: "Of course it can be put back again, but I assure you, you will be the worse for it." Only Gogol could have written that. Let Kovalyov stay without his nose. He would be worse with it back on. And my God, I've had to deal with doctors like that myself.'

14 November 1974
This morning, Dmitry Dmitriyevich telephoned me on arrival in Leningrad. He said: 'I decided to be daring and risk it, so here I am. I'm at the Yevropeyskaya Hotel. Come and have dinner with me, and bring Vera Vasiliyevna.'

It was a quiet dinner. We had a drink to celebrate our meeting. When Shostakovich was sitting at the table, he looked well, and when he laughed it was as though his youth had returned. His words, together with his mimicry and his gestures, brought back the Dmitry Dmitriyevich Shostakovich I remembered from long ago. We talked of David Oistrakh, who had recently died. Shostakovich said: 'In life, Oistrakh's features were not very clearly defined, but when he lay in his coffin his face took on a formidably severe expression. He did the right thing, carrying on working – travelling, playing, conducting – until the last minute. That's what one should do. He died with his boots on, in Amsterdam, in the same way as the cellist Sergey Shirinsky died in Moscow on 18 October. That morning he was rehearsing, in the evening he was no more. If you remember, I telephoned you straight away to tell you what had happened, and I think I quoted Pushkin's "And yet another's hour is near at hand". Pushkin was a young man when he wrote that fateful phrase.' I had a strong feeling that in speaking of how Oistrakh and Shirinsky had conducted themselves, Shostakovich was thinking of himself.

Shostakovich asked me to sit next to him at the following day's concert in the Small Hall of the Philharmonia and had made special arrangements with the Artistic Director of the Hall, Irina Semyonova, that this should happen. He was concerned that the presence of television cameramen would be an irritation, but thought my presence alongside him would be a calming influence. Maybe he hoped that the detested television would at least film us sitting together. I cannot swear to this, but cannot otherwise explain his insistence.

15 November 1974

The Fifteenth Quartet received its first performance today. About twenty minutes before the concert, Shostakovich handed me a note on which he had written the key signature and the headings of the movements. This is what it said:

> Quartet No. 15 in E flat minor.
>   Elegy
>   Serenade, leading without a break to
>   Intermezzo
>   Nocturne
>   Funeral March
>   Epilogue

This is the last document that I possess in Shostakovich's hand. The penultimate one, received not long before, consisted of a copy of his *Vocal Works*, inscribed as follows:

> To dear Isaak Davïdovich Glikman from his warmly loving friend Shostakovich. 25 October 1974, Moscow.

An unforeseen development prevented me from fulfilling his request to sit next to him during the concert. After the concert, which had an enormous success, Shostakovich told me what had happened: 'Just when you went out into the foyer to smoke, Mravinsky appeared and Irina Nikolayevna [Semyonova], ignoring my request, seated the distinguished guest in your place. I ought to have said: "Yevgeny Aleksandrovich, this is Isaak Davï-dovich's seat," but I didn't say anything. I didn't have the courage, and was afraid of offending Mravinsky. So I sat there, quietly angry with myself, with you for going out to smoke, and with Irina Nikolayevna for not heeding my request.' This confession, trivial as it may appear, is a paradigm of Shostakovich's psychological make-up and of the way he behaved to people.

23 December 1974

Shostakovich and Irina Antonovna came to Leningrad today. He invited me to dinner at the Yevropeyskaya Hotel before the concert, greeting me with the words: 'Well, as you see, the old cripple's managed to get here.' It was the first time I had heard him use the harsh, old-fashioned word to describe his condition, and it saddened me.

Soon after dinner, we made our way to the Small Hall of the Philharmonia, where Yevgeny Nesterenko sang the Michelangelo Sonnets, to my mind with great feeling. The whole audience rose to its feet and applauded the composer. Afterwards, before returning to Moscow, Shostakovich said: 'Nesterenko sang well, I might even say powerfully, but I think he has more work to do on this piece. It is far from simple.'

16 February 1975

I visited Shostakovich in Repino, where he had come for a month to be treated by a woman doctor. He revealed this in a gloomy tone of voice, but over dinner he cheered up and started to tell me about a revival of *Katerina Izmailova* at the Kiev Opera House. He said: 'This production was like a holiday for me. Orchestra, singers, conductor and even the producer were all splendid. Although Simeonov does not have a particularly original personality, he is a fine conductor. By a strange, and I am sure quite fortuitous circumstance, the performance they gave on 28 January was on the anniversary of the "Muddle Instead of Music" article on the same day in 1936.'

24 February 1975

I went out to Repino. With her usual generous hospitality, Irina Antonovna provided food and drink for supper. Before my arrival, Shostakovich had been listening to Boris Tishchenko play through his gigantic new Fourth Symphony. Shostakovich had praise for the third, fourth and fifth movements, but was rather more reserved about the first and second movements. He said: 'I'm not generally very talkative. I don't like engaging in analysis and conversation about works I have heard, and I'm not good at it. All I do is listen to music that is presented to me. I either like it, or I don't. That's all.'

After this, Shostakovich told me something about the treatment he was having. 'You'd think she was giving me singing lessons,' he said with a somewhat rueful smile. 'She says it is all in the breath.' His superficial raillery masked the tragic hopelessness of the situation.

5 March 1975

Shostakovich had moved from Repino and was now installed at the Yevropeyskaya Hotel. He had come there to be treated by some kind of quack – a female psychic who by the simple laying-on of hands, so it was said, induced healing burns on the skin. Dmitry Dmitriyevich called her a witch.

After a few days, rolling up the sleeves of his shirt and smiling vaguely, he showed me the burns. His suffering was such that he was ready to believe in miracles.

That evening, we went, accompanied by Irina Antonovna, to a concert at the Philharmonia. The programme included Ravel's *Daphnis and Chloë* Suite, Arapov's *Piece for Piano, Violin and Percussion*, and Stravinsky's *Symphony of Psalms*. During the interval we reminisced about how before the war Shostakovich had made a piano transcription of the *Symphony of Psalms* which he showed to his students, and for which during the shameful era of the 'war against cosmopolitans' he had subsequently been castigated. At one general assembly, a Leningrad Conservatoire teacher, swelling with righteous indignation, was heard to shriek: 'How dare Shostakovich defile the walls of this Conservatoire with Stravinsky's vile music? Such an action could only be the work of a cosmopolitan, an enemy of our own patriotic music.' (I was myself present at this meeting, a horrified spectator at the mob in full cry against so-called cosmopolitanism.)

Shostakovich said: 'I was forced to believe that these subhumans were ready to damn not only Stravinsky but their own mothers and fathers to please the authorities.' Then he changed the subject abruptly to talk of Johann Strauss, regretting that his music was not much to be heard at the Philharmonia these days. He said: 'What a delight his polkas, galops and waltzes are! And how witty he is, wonderful Strauss! Do you remember his *Perpetuum Mobile*, or *Der Jäger* where the conductor has to join in the fun and fire a pistol whenever the hunt is on?' I should mention here that when shortly before the war Boris Khaikin put on a production of *The Gypsy Baron* at the Maly Opera, he asked Shostakovich to orchestrate one of Strauss's polkas which he thought it would be a good idea to insert into the action. At first Shostakovich resisted, on the grounds of not wanting to tinker with Strauss's own mastery which he deeply admired, but eventually he yielded to the conductor's insistent pleas. The resulting polka blazed like a rocket through the third act of the operetta, a miracle of orchestral colour that defied analysis. For years to come, conductors including Gennady Rozhdestvensky and Mstislav Rostropovich would include this brilliant number in their programmes as an encore.

7 March 1975

I dined today with Shostakovich in Room 106 of the Yevropeyskaya Hotel. We discussed Boris Tishchenko's ballet *Yaroslavna*, which had recently been produced at the Maly Theatre. Shostakovich said: 'I saw the production several times. The music is generally good, but I did not like the choreography at all.'

13 March 1975
I had supper today with Dmitry Dmitriyevich at the Yevropeyskaya Hotel. He was very worried about Moysey Vainberg's opera *Zosya* [*Madonna and the Soldier*], which was scheduled to open at the Maly Opera on 17 March. Shostakovich told me: 'The production is almost ready, but it is threatened with a ban. Bogomolov, the author of the original book on which it is based, has been whipping up a storm about the opera, which he claims is a perversion of his story. Vainberg is terribly worried, and so am I. I have sent a telegram to the Ministry of Culture asking them to protect the opera, but I am still waiting to hear anything positive from them. So far, all we know is that the dress rehearsal is going to take place as planned tomorrow. Please be sure to come and put in a word for this opera, which has some very good music in it.'

14 March 1975
The dress rehearsal of *Madonna and the Soldier* took place today. The production was quite an interesting one, but the Polish producer, Danuta Badushkova, in an evident attempt to ratchet up the audience's sense of fear, had introduced the figure of Death. Death roamed aimlessly around the stage in a manner unrelated to either the music or the action. Shostakovich considered this to be an inept director's conceit, and I shared his opinion. He said: 'Please explain to me why it is that directors are so arrogant that they feel obliged to meddle like this with an opera? Whatever is the point of this *danse macabre*? There's not a note in Vainberg's score calling for it.'

After the rehearsal, Shostakovich insisted on making his painful way up to the third floor of the theatre for a meeting of the Artistic Committee. In a short speech he described *Madonna and the Soldier* as 'a great opera'. I also added some laudatory comments. But we did strongly suggest that the Death figure be removed.

17 March 1975
Vainberg's *Madonna and the Soldier* opened as planned this evening, due in no small measure to the energetic defence Shostakovich had mounted against the writer Bogomolov's attempts to have it banned. The producer

of the opera rejected Shostakovich's advice and left in the Dance of Death scenes. In my naïvety I had supposed that she would regard the sheer fact of the great composer's having come to the production and said kind words about it as an honour, and would take notice of any recommendations he made, but not a bit of it. The obscure Danuta Badushkova clearly set herself above Shostakovich, as is often the way with producers today, swelled with self-importance and megalomania. Shostakovich had reason to view the majority of their kind critically, having come across them in the various cities and countries where *Katerina Izmailova* had been staged. This time, he said: 'Why ever was that *danse macabre* put in? It was hideous.' This was the performance at which Shostakovich indignantly dismissed the suggestion that he might want to write reminiscences of people he had known, whoever they were, on the grounds that he was not a writer, merely a musician (see the Preface).

1 May 1975
Shostakovich telephoned today to tell me that he planned to go to Repino on 11 May.

11 May 1975
Shostakovich telephoned from Repino, announcing that he was going to have more sessions with the 'witch'. He asked me to visit him.

15 May 1975
I went out to Repino to see Shostakovich. According to what was by now a tradition, we sat down to a modest repast. Shostakovich said: 'A few days ago, on 10 May, we heard Nesterenko's concert in Moscow. He sang my *Four Verses of Captain Lebyadkin* and the songs from *Krokodil*. I thought he sang extremely well. The *Krokodil* songs were encored. It may be immodest of me, but I much enjoyed hearing my little things from *Krokodil*.' So saying, Shostakovich smiled that glorious smile of his.

22 May 1975
Shostakovich telephoned from Repino and sorrowfully informed me of the unexpected death (in Komarovo) of the composer Boris Klyuzner. Shostakovich had been fond of him as a person and rated his talents highly.

25 May 1975
Dmitry Dmitriyevich and Irina Antonovna came to dinner with us. I was

thrilled by his cheerful appearance and mood, and his appetite for the food and drink.

We talked of general matters. Shostakovich said: 'I have been hearing about the Uzbek composer Mukhtar Ashrafi's boorish attacks on the teachers at the Tashkent Conservatoire. When I get back to Moscow I intend to come to the defence of the professors he has insulted and humiliated in this way. This won't be easy, because Ashrafi is the darling of the Uzbek authorities. Do you remember my going to Tashkent many years ago to do something similar, and those rogues in the local Union of Composers all but succeeded in poisoning me and despatching me there and then to the next world?'

For some reason Shostakovich told this story, which could well have ended in tragedy, in high good humour. What was the reason for the broad smile? Could it have been the quiet satisfaction of knowing that, despite the best efforts of poisoners of all ranks from highest to lowest starting with Stalin, he, Shostakovich, was still alive, still at work, and still actively coming to the aid of others in their misfortune?

It never entered my head that that spring day in May would be my last meeting with Dmitry Dmitriyevich. It was the last time he was ever to be in Leningrad.

15 June 1975

Shostakovich telephoned me from Moscow, but not catching me at home spoke to Vera Vasiliyevna and then called back. He said: 'Don't be too surprised, but I have a request to make of you. I want you to write and give me your impressions of Andrey Petrov's opera *Peter The First* at the Maryinsky Theatre. I'd like to know how Tsars are depicted in operas these days . . . in any case, if you could write to me, I'll respond by ringing you up. It's hard for me to write letters now. Please don't be angry with me, and do please write.' I was amused by the charmingly innocent way in which Shostakovich expressed his curiosity about the treatment of Tsars in Soviet opera. To tell the truth, he was not much enamoured of the way in which, for example, Ivan the Terrible or Peter the Great were portrayed in the cinema.

Shostakovich did not ring.

To begin with, this did not worry me, since I kept thinking how well he had been looking at dinner on 25 May. As the days lengthened into weeks I did begin to get alarmed at the continuing silence from him, however I suppressed all my anxieties, clinging to the French proverb that

Shostakovich was fond of quoting on all sorts of occasions: 'No news is good news'. In general I seldom telephoned him, preferring to write letters which I had reason to believe he liked reading. But towards the end of July I broke my self-imposed rule and did make a phone call.

29 July 1975

I rang Shostakovich today in hospital. Irina Antonovna answered her anxiety making her speak in a remote, toneless voice: 'Dmitry Dmitriyevich will speak to you now.' Shostakovich greeted me and then said: 'I'm feeling better now, coughing less and not so breathless. Write to me at home. The whole town seems to be here.' After a long pause he continued: 'They are keeping me here until 10 August. I may come to Repino about the 1st of September.'

His voice was dull, as if covered with a kind of shroud. I was suddenly alarmed, but clung to the belief that what he said might really be so: he was not complaining of anything specific, he was hoping to go home soon and would then be coming to his beloved Repino.

No doubt Shostakovich, his physical strength ebbing, was refusing to give up; like Beethoven he was 'grasping fate by the throat'. But death, whose features he had limned in his music with such overwhelming power, was silently stalking his victim. Death finally took him on 9 August, on the eve of the date he had told me in our telephone conversation he would be going home.

The 9 August 1975 left me bereaved for ever, the threads of gold that bound me to Dmitry Dmitriyevich for more than forty years irrevocably sundered. I loved this man with all the tenderness and passion of which my soul was capable. His memory is sacred to me. In my heart I have treasured every word he let fall, from his pen or from his lips. And I believe that these words will resonate in the hearts of all who loved and to this day love the genius that was Shostakovich.

It is now seventeen years since the death of Dmitry Dmitriyevich Shostakovich – no small passage of time in our changing and fast-moving world. Happily, his music is still with us, its undying message sounding still as pledge and consolation. It was ever thus, even in the dark times and grievous ordeals through which every one of our countrymen, his and mine, lived. Shostakovich's tragic muse is irradiated with particles of light and joy which illuminate the hope that springs eternal.

Whenever I reflect on the towering role that Shostakovich played in our individual lives and the life of our country, I call to mind Herzen's wonderful description of Pushkin, which with apologies to literary purists I now take the liberty of adapting to my friend: 'Only the boundless, vibrant song of Shostakovich sounds through the valleys of slavery and torment; a song which carries through from ages now past, which fills the present with its valiant melodies, and which sends its voice ringing far into the distant future.'

August 1991

Appendices

Satirical Songs by Isaak Glikman

Kaganovich's Travel Song

Refrain from the Song of the Iron and Steel Commissar Nikolay Ivanovich Yezhov

Panegyric in honour of the glorious pea-farmers and bean-planters who after being received at the Kremlin achieved unprecedented harvests

More peas! More beans! (contemporary slogans)

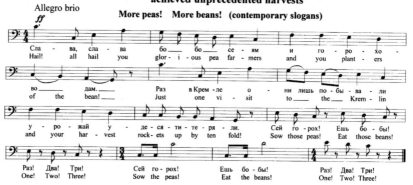

Historic Pronouncement by J. V. Stalin on Gorky's Story *Death and the Maiden*

On the article 'Muddle Instead of Music',
and other matters

Immediately after the première in Leningrad of *Lady Macbeth of the Mtsensk District*, which took place on 22 January 1934, there was a flood of enthusiastic reviews, reactions and critiques in the Leningrad and Moscow press, and also abroad. *Pravda*, for example, noted with pride the opening of the opera in New York's Metropolitan Opera under the baton of the famous conductor Artur Rodzinsky.

At the time, it would have been an uncommonly perspicacious person who could have foreseen that before long the pages of the selfsame newspaper would carry a crushingly condemnatory article, the very title of which – 'Muddle Instead of Music' – would serve as a model for the desecration that was about to be unleashed on an opera hitherto widely regarded as a work of genius.

The article appeared on 28 January 1936, on the second anniversary almost to the day of the famous opera's première. At that time the Moscow papers were not generally available in Leningrad until the day after their publication in the capital, and so most Leningraders would not have the opportunity to read the notorious *Pravda* piece until 29 January. As luck would have it, however, I was among those who tasted the bitter pill on the day the article appeared.

Late in the morning of 28 January I went to call on Sofya Shostakovich in the apartment on Dmitrovsky Pereulok, and just as I arrived the telephone rang. It was Mariya Dmitriyevna's husband, the composer's brother-in-law, on the line from Moscow. Misfortune had struck out of the blue. I took the receiver and as I asked him to read the complete text of the article, I listened in horror. It felt as though someone were dripping poison into my ears. The article was unsigned. In those days, not many people understood the full import of a '*Pravda* editorial'. I remember that during the discussion that dragged on for days in the Leningrad Union of Composers, one composer – I. Ya. Pustïlnik – naïvely enquired why the writer had been afraid to put his name to it. For this lapse of understanding he was torn to pieces without mercy in the press reports of the discussion.

But on that memorable morning of 28 January, I knew full well that 'the thunderclap came not from the dungheap but the cloud'¹ and that the only one who could have dared to raise his hand to destroy so celebrated a work would be Stalin. And so it proved.²

Shostakovich was not in Leningrad that the time. He was on tour with Viktor Kubatsky in Arkhangelsk, performing in his First Piano Concerto and Cello Sonata. All of us – Ivan Sollertinsky, I, and all his friends – were extremely worried as to how his health and his nerves would stand up under the shock, but when the fateful news actually reached him, what he did was something utterly astonishing. He sent me a telegram asking me to subscribe to a newspaper cutting service at the Central Post Office, targeted on all references to him and his compositions. Here I must explain that it never normally occurred to Shostakovich to collect or keep favourable articles or reviews, but having read 'Muddle Instead of Music', he perceptively understood sooner and better than anyone that critics who had formerly praised him would now sharply be changing their tune; an avalanche of abuse and censure was about to descend on the head of the composer of *Lady Macbeth*. Naturally I carried out his request, and saw his forebodings fully justified. As soon as he returned to Leningrad he acquired a large scrapbook and doggedly proceeded to stick in the vast quantity of clippings that soon accumulated.

Parroting Moscow and Leningrad, the musical establishment in all major cities started to cry foul not just on *Lady Macbeth* but on almost all of Shostakovich's compositions. On the first page of the scrapbook the *Pravda* article stared out in all its glory; when I reproached Shostakovich for what I regarded as a self-indulgent piece of masochism, he replied unsmilingly, 'It has to be there, it has to be there.' The scrapbook soon filled up with cuttings; Shostakovich generally read them without comment. Occasionally the expression on his face seemed to say 'they know not what they do.' I do remember him being stung by the name of a very famous pianist who published a long and censorious article on *Lady Macbeth* in, I think, *Izvestiya*, but this article joined all the others in the scrapbook.

In predictable fashion, writer after writer rushed into print to beat his or her breast for a grievous lapse of judgement in having been initially taken in by *Lady Macbeth*. One by one they 'confessed' that only through the spotlight of 'Muddle Instead of Music' had the glaring defects of the opera been shown up in all their disgraceful relief. Even reputable people, so it seemed, abandoned all shame and threw elementary dignity to the winds.

Let us return to February 1936. Dmitry Dmitriyevich returned to

Leningrad from Moscow, whither he had gone from Arkhangelsk. On a freezing cold morning, Ivan Sollertinsky and I went to meet him at the Moscow station. The train was late. We were extremely nervous, wondering how our friend would appear before us now that he had been thus unceremoniously thrust into a completely new era. We both had a strong feeling that the publication of the *Pravda* article had irrevocably split Shostakovich's creative life into two halves. His former well-earned reputation had vanished into oblivion, and now there would begin a new era of pitiless darkness in which the spark of his unique talent would not, of course, be extinguished altogether, but would be hidden from view. This is how it seemed to us then, and we were anxious and afraid. We had not reckoned on the tremendous strength of will and inexhaustible reserves of creative power that the twenty-nine-year-old Shostakovich, despite his apparent lack of resolve, had at his command. I believe that his very youth helped him to withstand the savage abuse on a national scale to which he began to be subjected.

Shostakovich emerged from his carriage slim, elegant, handsome. I remember the somewhat set expression on his face, no trace of the flashing white smile with which he usually greeted friends. We embraced and set off for Dmitrovsky Pereulok. Not once did he lose his phenomenal reserve: there was no outpouring of emotion, no anguished sighing, no voice raised in angry complaint. He did not need to say much; the pain in his eyes was eloquent enough.

Once home, Shostakovich said little more, except that he gave us an account of his meetings with the President of the Committee for Cultural Affairs, Platon Kerzhentsev, and with Marshal Mikhail Tukhachevsky. From what they had said he understood clearly that there could be no question of any request or appeal altering the verdict handed down by the *Pravda* editorial. Shostakovich, in any case, made no such request or appeal. Kerzhentsev – a highly cultivated and courteous man – insisted that the only course open to Shostakovich was openly to acknowledge the errors into which the excesses of youth had led him when composing the opera *Lady Macbeth*.[3]

Tukhachevsky, a devoted admirer of Shostakovich's talent, sat down to write a letter to Stalin, a task he undertook with the greatest difficulty. Shostakovich had to look on with compassion as the poor Marshal, gripped by anxiety and fear, mopped with a snow-white handkerchief the perspiration that broke out on the back of his head. The letter needless to say had no effect whatever.

Some supporters of Shostakovich seemed to think that the situation, dramatic though it seemed, was not necessarily beyond redress. The unknown author of the article could have somehow misread Stalin's intentions; after all the Great Leader could hardly have dismissed as 'muddle' music that was admired all over the world, hence the article must be the result of a misunderstanding. According to this interpretation, the thing to do was immediately to seek clarification and once this was done to leap to the defence of the young genius beloved by all, the pride and ornament of Soviet culture. This would be the way, it was felt, to dissipate the nightmare.

No doubt some such belief had motivated Marshal Tukhachevsky when he took his courage in both hands and sat down to write his letter. I met Tukhachevsky that same spring of 1936, on one occasion when Shostakovich had asked me to dinner, as he regularly did. When I entered the apartment, Dmitry Dmitriyevich told me that another guest from Moscow, who was staying at the Yevropeyskaya Hotel, would be joining us for dinner. He did not tell me who it was: Shostakovich did not like his companions to be over-inquisitive and for his own part always refrained from idle curiosity, which he regarded as a mark of poor upbringing.

About five o'clock we went out on to the balcony of No. 14, Kirovsky Prospect. It was raining, and rather cold. A few minutes later a taxi drew up and a man in a grey military greatcoat got out, whom I recognized instantly from his portraits. It was Tukhachevsky. He quickly turned up the collar of the coat, emblazoned with its Marshal's stars, presumably not simply to protect himself from the rain but in order not to attract the attention of passers-by. In 1936 it was quite something to see a real live Marshal, for the rank had only recently been created.

Shostakovich greeted his guest with an affectionate smile of pleasure, but naturally, without fuss or awkwardness. I was introduced to Tukhachevsky, who probably did not catch my surname, but, as became clear the moment we sat down to dinner, he had immediately retained my first name and patronymic.[4] Mikhail Nikolayevich was a man of great education and intelligence. He treated me as an equal, not questioning who I might be or what I might do for a living, or anything of that nature. He was good-looking, with an attractively open expression on his well-bred features. I remember his slightly protuberant, almond-shaped grey eyes which frequently glinted with humour. I noted the meticulously polished nails on his well-groomed hands. He showed himself to be a man who enjoyed life and good company. The conversation flowed easily, steering clear of disagreeable topics so as not to darken the mood. Tukhachevsky gave a lively and enjoyable account of his recent visit to France, where he had met high-ranking officers of the armed forces; among other enlightening revelations they had instructed him in the art of drinking champagne without suffering the accompanying hangover. Apparently it was all a matter of choosing the right hors-d'oeuvre.

Turning to me, Tukhachevsky suddenly asked my opinion of Alexandre Dumas. I replied that I had loved the *Musketeers* trilogy since childhood, and also many chapters of *The Count of Monte Cristo*. He seemed to be delighted with this response, and observed that Dumas' writing was a continual delight to him, and that in a bookstall at the Yevropeyskaya Hotel he had happened on a brilliantly written book by him on a gastronomic theme, entitled *Grande dictionnaire de cuisine*. He rolled the sonorous title expertly round his tongue, laughing cheerfully.

The conversation turned to the Bolshoy Theatre. Tukhachevsky was loud in his praises of the ballerina Olga Lepeshinskaya, seeking backing for his opinion from Shostakovich, which the latter granted more out of politeness than conviction. In fact, Shostakovich had by this time cooled towards the art of Terpsichore, its high priests and priestesses, to whom he had made obeisance in the days of his early youth.

Much later in life, this indifference to ballet, or more precisely to balletomanes, grew into active dislike. Shostakovich said to me that he did not consider Tukhachevsky a balletomane; he simply enjoyed Lepeshinskaya's dancing and Shostakovich's ballet *The Limpid Stream*, which was then having a tremendous success in Moscow. But this success was short-lived, for the tireless *Pravda* followed up the *Lady Macbeth* article with another editorial heaping abuse on *The Limpid Stream*.[5] The anonymous author, whose sensitivities would naturally be outraged by the merest hint of anything false, headed his diatribe 'Ballet Falsity'. But however avidly it was pored over in ballet circles this second article did not gain much currency in the wider field, and Shostakovich could afford to react dispassionately to it.

A digression on the Ballet
In the summer of 1936, Ivan Sollertinsky, completely ignoring the 'Ballet Falsity' article, proposed to Shostakovich that he should write a fourth ballet.[6] But this time it ought to be one on a subject with an unimpeachable artistic and literary provenance: Cervantes's *Don Quixote*. Sollertinsky had a deep knowledge of Spain, and quickly set about sketching a libretto.

The idea initially attracted Shostakovich, and I also supported it, for I could imagine no one better than he to translate into music the unique blend of humour and pathos that permeates Cervantes' great novel. After a while, however, Shostakovich's interest in the project declined: he said half seriously and half in jest that he did not feel equal to contending with Minkus, whose *Don Quixote* had been a successful staple of the ballet stage for more than half a century. In fact he was shrewd enough to realize in advance that dancers would be unlikely to accept a new ballet score on this subject by him with any great enthusiasm, and might indeed be actively hostile, comfortably accommodated as they had long been to Minkus's music.[7]

Indeed, this was more or less what happened some years later with Sergey Prokofiev's *Romeo and Juliet*. The Bolshoy Theatre rejected it outright, while the Maryinsky accepted it only through gritted teeth. I well remember in the autumn of 1940 being with Shostakovich at one of the dress rehearsals of *Romeo*.[8] Prokofiev was also present, making comments about the orchestra in a loud voice. Next he found something to displease him in the dancing. After a moment's pause for reflection, the tall figure of the composer got up from the stalls and crossed over the passerelle on to the stage. Shostakovich, somewhat surprised at the great composer's behaviour, whispered to me: 'Perhaps it's all right for a composer to do that, but I simply would never be able to.' In fact at the time there were not many people in the auditorium, and most of them were friends and colleagues, so probably Prokofiev felt he had no need to hide his dissatisfaction with certain aspects of the production. In the event, the première of the ballet scored a phenomenal success. Sergey Sergeyevich was, as I could see for myself, entirely happy with it and thrilled with the performance as a whole. Shostakovich also liked it, and said to me that whatever else he had, Prokofiev had a rare gift for melody. He repeated this opinion after hearing *War and Peace* at the Maly Opera Theatre and *The Betrothal in a Monastery* at the Maryinsky Theatre.

Auto-da-fé

Let us return to the memorable events of February 1936. The Union of Composers on Rossi Street organized a debate on 'Muddle Instead of Music' that lasted for several days. The organizers were most anxious that Shostakovich should attend. They didn't want much, merely that he should publicly state his agreement with the article and objectly repent. In those days (and for long afterwards) great importance was attached to confession and repentance; these central postulates of Christianity had been lifted bodily out of the church and translated into the social and political life of the country. Dmitry Dmitriyevich determined to have nothing to do with this tragic farce, and could not be budged from this position. Having extracted an undertaking from me to write to him daily with a report of the proceedings, he departed to Moscow where he had a pied-à-terre. It was not so much the character of the discussions – this was already, he knew, a settled issue – that interested him, but the revealing details that would serve to throw the psychological ground plan into relief. I did as I had promised, reporting as objectively as I could and allowing myself the luxury of commenting only on the speeches that had particularly incensed me. Later, Shostakovich regretted that in accordance with his long-standing practice he had destroyed my reports, which, had they survived, would have yielded an unrivalled conspectus of the times. (Only in the rarest of circumstances did Shostakovich keep any letters from his correspondents.) I wrote my letters early in the morning, since the sessions lasted until late in the evening, and after they finished Ivan Sollertinsky and I repaired (on foot, of course) to the 'Chvanova' Restaurant[9] on Bolshoy Prospekt in the Petrogradsky district, a favourite haunt of Sollertinsky's where incidentally not long before these events Yury Sviridov had held down a job as pianist. It was quite a long way, and there was time, as we walked along in the cold night air, to calm down. Once in the restaurant we could cleanse with vodka all the disgusting verbal filth we had endured. Long after midnight we parted to make our separate ways home.

The man in charge of this protracted debate was the Executive Secretary of the Union of Composers, Vladimir Iokhelson, a great favourite of the Smolny.[10] Beside him sat his assistant, the composer Lev Kruts. His job was to keep his boss on track with the developing situation, since Iokhelson's sight was so poor he could hardly see anything at all. In a vigorous, ringing tenor voice Iokhelson urged all present to speak up honestly, directly, and most important of all, courageously. The example of courage he adduced was *Pravda* which, he said, had not shrunk from the duty of unmasking Shostakovich's opera despite the exaggerated celebrity it had enjoyed for two years.

And so one bold spirit after another took to the rostrum.

Some shed crocodile tears as they confessed to having been led astray by the devil, so that even though as professionals they ought to have known better, they had nevertheless been seduced into mistaking for good music what was now so obviously nothing but muddle.

Others professed sympathy for the young composer who had shown such early promise but who had now fallen into the mire of formalism, from whose baleful influence it was so very hard to escape.

Still others castigated themselves for their previous tolerance of the grievous formalistic errors perpetrated by Shostakovich in his earlier opera, *The Nose*. This work was, as could now be seen, nothing more than a 'formalist offspring of the devil'.

When the bold spirits touched on Shostakovich's early works, like *The Nose* or the Second or Third Symphonies, their voices swelled with indignation. The level of zeal with which the speakers at the rostrum poured out their denunciations rose and fell in line with their true feelings. It was a rather more difficult task to work up an equivalent degree of fury over *Lady Macbeth*, but several of the brave spirits managed it with impressive conviction.

That detestable, lying word 'formalism' was on every speaker's lips; it hung over the discussions like an evil prophecy. A correspondent from *Pravda* was in the hall, sending back daily reports to his paper. Whenever he wanted particularly to plunge the knife into Sollertinsky, he referred to him as 'the troubadour of formalism'. This bizarre appellation caused Ivan Ivanovich a great many problems. Several of the institutions with whom he had had relationships over the years now told him: 'It's enough of a disgrace to be branded a formalist, but it's a hundred times worse to be a troubadour of formalism!' Several speakers denounced Sollertinsky as Shostakovich's evil genius, his seducer from the path of true virtue. There were calls for the critic to be punished for his sins.

Before the Resolution was put to the floor and voted upon, Sollertinsky was in an agony of apprehension. He called me out into the corridor several times to talk through what he should do when the time came to vote.[11] I was myself pretty much in a state of confusion, but I said to him: 'Since it is beginning to look as though you yourself are going to be included in the Resolution, you can hardly be expected to vote in favour of it and thereby endorse your own condemnation. That would make no sense at all.' I did not then fully understand that so absurdly illogical an action would actually be seen as the most heroic form of expiation.

Sollertinsky wavered, sometimes agreeing and sometimes disagreeing with me. Then he suddenly blurted out in a whisper: 'Did you know that before he went off to Moscow, Dmitry Dmitriyevich gave me permission, in case of dire necessity, to vote for any Resolution whatsoever?' I had not known this, but naturally did not doubt Sollertinsky's words: I am sure that, with the supreme generosity I knew to be characteristic of Shostakovich, he would have done anything to avoid his friend suffering on his account, the more so as the suffering would have been quite useless – if not from a spiritual, at least from a practical point of view. For one lone voice to be raised in opposition, only to be drowned out in the general chorus of acclamation for the Resolution, would have been a useless gesture. While I was certain that deep in his heart Shostakovich would have been happy to learn that Sollertinsky had *not* voted for the Resolution, had *not* had his dignity as a human being dragged through the mud, had *not* compromised his good name, at the same time he was perfectly well aware that this course of action could entail risks that were simply beyond his friend's powers to cope with. So without a backward glance he had given him carte blanche to do whatever he needed.

For Shostakovich's offer to have any meaning, whatever decision Sollertinsky came to would give rise to no blame from that quarter because Shostakovich had pre-empted any such possibility. Sollertinsky was thus left with the responsibility of avoiding any action that might independently be construed as meriting it. It was a hideously difficult position to be in, and an unfair one. Why? Because despite all the hullabaloo, Shostakovich felt himself to be strong, even invincibly strong, while Sollertinsky felt himself so weak at the end of this degrading assembly that he could see no way out of his predicament. Fear lay at the root of his weakness. I felt profoundly sorry for Ivan Ivanovich, whom I sincerely loved.

The Resolution was passed unanimously, with one abstention. This proved to be the well-known composer Vladimir Shcherbachov. Confusion reigned on the presidium of the assembly; I can remember as if it were yesterday Vladimir Iokhelson starting to his feet with enough belligerence to start a war. He called on Shcherbachov to join in solidarity with his colleagues, all of whom had in friendly accord cast their votes in support of the Resolution. Three or four times, separated by brief intervals, the voice of Iokhelson gaunt, unprepossessing figure with its fanatical air urgently pressed its cause, while all eyes were on the recalcitrant dissenter. But he simply stood silently in the enormous room, nervously fingering the hole in his chin that was the legacy of a First World War wound – an involuntary gesture that with him always signalled inner tension.

Why did Iokhelson make these pauses between his appeals to Shcherbachov? Presumably to give him a chance to reconsider. But Shcherbachov would not be moved. My God, how pregnant with drama those pauses were! Shcherbachov stuck to his guns with dignity and refused to vote for the Resolution. He was too frightened actually to cast his vote against it, but he abstained, and I consider that the act of a truly brave man.

I knew Shcherbachov quite well. He had always struck me as a proud man, uncompromising and intractable, a composer of the old school. While he fully appreciated Shostakovich's enormous talent, he had not subscribed to the generally ecstatic response to *Lady Macbeth* when it exploded upon the scene. He gave it what he considered its due. In this connection I call to mind the following episode.

In autumn 1935 an exhibition opened in the Foyer of the Great Hall of the Philharmonia which, in my capacity as head of the Philharmonia's Mass Education Department, I had had a hand in organizing. Behind the glass of the display cases were busts of Bach, Beethoven and Tchaikovsky. In thrall as I was to Shostakovich's music, I conceived the notion of placing a bust of him alongside the others. Sollertinsky encouraged the idea, and the Artistic Director of the Philharmonia, A. V. Ossovsky, raised no objection. No sooner said than done! My brother, the sculptor Gavriil Glikman, quickly made a splendid head of the young composer of *Lady Macbeth* which took its place in the exhibition. (This sculpture is now in the Library of the Philharmonia.)

Many musicians came to the private view of the exhibition, among them Vladimir Shcherbachov. He took one look at the exhibits, then came up to me and said, entirely without rancour: 'Why has a bust of Mitya Shostakovich been included? Surely it's a bit early to place him with the greats!' I did not argue with the eminent composer, although I was upset by a rebuke which at the time seemed to me offensive and uncalled-for.

All the more admirable, then, his conduct at the Composers' Union assembly.

And so the campaign against Shostakovich as the composer of *Lady Macbeth* proceeded on its seamlessly successful way not only in Leningrad but all over the country. The musical community brilliantly learned the part assigned to it, and earned top marks in subservience and anti-sedition witch-hunts. It abdicated from all opinions and convictions of its own, accepting a newspaper article inspired by Stalin as the fount of unquestionable truth which rapidly acquired the status of holy writ. The disgraceful diatribe found its way into Conservatoire courses on the history of music. Teachers quoted from it, expounded on its significance, analysed its content, bowed down in superstitious reverence before its superior wisdom. It continued to resonate far beyond its time.

Twelve or thirteen years after the publication, a professor of music-ology at the Leningrad Conservatoire was heard to say in a lecture that 'the composer Shostakovich, in writing his opera *Muddle Instead of Music*, committed an irreparable mistake.' Constant repetition of the newspaper article's title had given this educated, and not by the way notably ill-intentioned man such a callus on his tongue that it had become a synonym for the opera. I actually heard this lecture, and was amazed that the professor's farcical slip failed to evoke so much as a titter in the auditorium. Perhaps, I thought to myself, the collective hal-lucination is now so universal that the members of this audience are already accustomed to the idea that Shostakovich really wrote an opera called *Muddle Instead of Music* and not *Lady Macbeth of the Mtsensk District*!

Stalin could be well satisfied with the first of his experiments in total domination of his subjects, which he inaugurated with the artistic intelli-gentsia. Musicians all over the country were made to learn that the wielder of absolute power was by the same token the arbiter of absolute and infallible taste in their art. The same lesson was soon absorbed by the practitioners of other professions: writers, poets, film-makers, linguists, biologists, etc., etc.

Even Louis XIV, an absolute monarch if ever there was one, was careful to acknowledge the pre-eminence of musicians and poets in their fields. One day, in the Court at Versailles, the Sun King remarked: 'M. Despréaux (Boileau) has a better understanding of poetry than I do.' I doubt if Stalin was aware of this interesting exchange, but even if he was his response would no doubt have been to rebuke the Sun King for 'decadent liberalism' (a widely used phrase in the 1930s).

Even after the death of its progenitor, 'Muddle Instead of Music' con-tinued to exert its baleful influence. Shostakovich was made painfully aware of this in March 1956 during a discussion chaired by Dmitry Kaba-levsky about the possibility of a new edition of *Lady Macbeth*. When I tried to speak up for the opera's artistic power and magnificence, I was cut short in turn by Kabalevsky and Georgy Khubov, and by Vasily Tseliko-vsky from the Ministry of Culture. They reminded me (and of course Shos-takovich) in strenuous and imperious accents that the article 'Muddle Instead of Music' had not been officially withdrawn, and that in praising the opera I was appearing to gainsay its undoubted and continuing exist-ence. 'Not so!' wailed the ophidian musicians, 'the article is still relevant and in force.' Unhappy people! With what incredible zeal did they stand guard over the discredited sanctity of a newspaper article published some twenty years before! For them, to doubt it in the absence of the express permission from higher authority would mean falling into heresy, and they knew that heretics were apt to have an uncomfortable time of it![12]

Notes

Preface

1 It is interesting to note that at this time Pushkin was himself writing his own memoirs, which he subsequently burnt.
2 Pushkin, A. S., *Letters of A. S. Pushkin*, (*Perepiska A. S. Pushkina v 2 T*), Moscow, vol. 1, 237.
3 Pushkin, A. S., *Collected Works* (*Polnoye sobraniye sochineny v 10 T*), Moscow, 1978, vol. 7, 410.
4 Hume, David, *My Own Life*, 1777.
5 The Philharmonia was (and is) an institution in all major cities of Russia and the former Soviet Union. It is a musical umbrella organization embracing a range of responsibilities and activities: promoting concerts, employing orchestras, ensembles, conductors and soloists on contract, running concert halls and other venues. The Leningrad Philharmonia was in existence before the Revolution (as the St Petersburg Philharmonia, to which title along with its constituent and affiliated organizations it has now reverted) and was the first to be established in the Soviet era, as the Petrograd Philharmonia, in 1921. The official title of the Leningrad Philharmonic Orchestra, the orchestra of Cooper, Malko, Stiedry, Mravinsky and currently Temirkanov, was 'The Leningrad Academic Symphony Orchestra of the Leningrad Philharmonia'. (Translator's Note)
6 Shcherbachov, Shaporin, Deshevov, Arapov, Zhivotov, Pashchenko and Zhelobinsky were composers; Nikolayev and Sofronitsky pianists; Gauk, Rabinovich and Mravinsky conductors; Druskin a musicologist and critic. (Translator's Note)
7 'Die Feder des Genius ist immer größer als er selber.' (Translator's Note)
8 '. . . He [Beaumarchais] was a genius,
   As you, and I, are. Genius and evil
   Are two things incompatible. You agree?'

   Pushkin, A. S., *Mozart and Salieri, Collected Works* (*Mozart i Salieri, Polnoye sobraniye sochineny v 17 T*), vol. 7, Moscow, 1994, 132. (Translator's Note)
9 His daughter Galina was born that night.
10 Shostakovich, D. D., 'Thoughts on the path travelled' ('*Dumï o proydyonnom puti*'), *Sovetskaya muzïka* 9, 1956, 14. (Translator's Note)
11 i.e. Symphonies 5 to 12, not to mention the First Cello Concerto, the First Violin Concerto and the Second Piano Concerto. (Translator's Note)
12 Controversy about the true reasons behind the cancellation of the performance

and withdrawal of the symphony continues, and because of the many contradictory statements and theories is unlikely to be resolved for some time, if ever. Glikman's view is clearly stated here. Gauk and Kondrashin, and the composer himself in some (but not all) interviews, concur with the thesis that Stiedry was not competent, while Stiedry (who left the Soviet Union in 1937 and hence could perhaps have been seen as a conveniently immune scapegoat) contends that it was the composer who objected to some of the orchestral playing and cancelled the performance after an altercation with the players and the Philharmonia administration. Stiedry's version is backed up by Rodion Shchedrin's account of what he says the composer told him, and by some orchestral musicians. Flora Litvinova, a family friend, says that Shostakovich's later explanation, years after the fact, was that to save the face of Stiedry and the orchestra, who had not prepared the work properly, he announced that he wanted to rework unsatisfactory material and was therefore withdrawing it. In 1942 Nina Varzar stated that the composer had been unhappy with the orchestration of part of the Finale and could not at the time contemplate revising it. See Fay, L. E., *Shostakovich: A Life*, Oxford, 2000, 96–7, 306 nn. 38, 40; Wilson, E., *Shostakovich: A Life Remembered*, London, 1994, 115–16. (Translator's Note)

13 Some biographies, articles and memoirs of Shostakovich contain such a welter of conjectures and suppositions that it seems beyond anyone's powers to set them right. I shall briefly touch on some of these wrong-headed notions, as they relate to the Leningrad première of the Fifth Symphony. *Ogonyok* readers will have gained the impression from Yury Yelagin's interesting memoirs 'The Taming of Art' in that journal (1990, No. 43) that the first performance of the symphony took place on 21 December 1937 in the Hall of the former Chamber Music Association. Contrary to a story that has found its way into at least one biography of Shostakovich, Vsevolod Meyerhold was not among the audience for the première of the Fifth Symphony.

I have no idea of the reason, and quite possibly it was with no malicious intent, but the author of these reminiscences has distorted the truth. The editors of *Ogonyok* printed the account without comment, regardless of the fact that any listener aware of the huge forces called for by the Fifth Symphony would realize that the orchestra could not possibly have fitted on to the tiny stage of the Chamber Music Association hall. In fact the first performance of the Fifth Symphony was given by the Leningrad Philharmonic Orchestra on 21 November (not December) 1937 in the Great Hall of the Leningrad Philharmonia. The conductor was Yevgeny Mravinsky, who on that unforgettable evening inaugurated his own personal ascent to Mount Olympus. After the symphony's triumphant first performance, A. N. Tolstoy hosted a supper party in the Writers' House on the Neva Embankment, not in the Astoria Hotel as Yelagin writes.

14 See letter of 26 December 1967. (Translator's Note)

15 Evidence of press reports, a letter of Shostakovich to Lev Atovmyan dated 20 November and the Philharmonia's files and concert programmes, all suggest

the date was 21 November. See Fay, L. E., *Shostakovich: A Life*, Oxford, 2000, 312 n. 45. (Translator's Note)

16 Nina Vasiliyevna had provided me with a quantity of food, sorely needed in starving Tashkent.

17 Khlestakov is the hero of Gogol's farce *The Inspector-General*. (Translator's Note)

18 Some time later, he did set Shakespeare's 66th Sonnet and dedicated it to Ivan Sollertinsky.

Chapter I War and Separation, 1941–1945

1 Literary critic and scholar, at that time Chairman of the Cultural Affairs Committee of the USSR.

2 President of the USSR Council of People's Commissars, later reorganized as the USSR Council of Ministers.

3 Shostakovich would have liked to move to Tashkent, where the Leningrad Conservatoire, of which he was a professor, had been evacuated. In the event, this plan could not be realized.

4 Sofya Vasiliyevna Shostakovich.

5 Mariya Dmitriyevna Shostakovich, piano teacher.

6 See preface, pp. xxvii–xxviii.

7 Conductor, later professor at the Leningrad Conservatoire.

8 Musicologist, professor at the Leningrad Conservatoire and Artistic Director of the Leningrad Philharmonia.

9 The subtext of 'other friends' indicates that the relationship was less close than with Lev Oborin.

10 Reporter on the Leningrad newspaper *Krasnyaya Vechernyaya Gazeta* (*Red Evening News*), who often published reports on football matches. Klyachkin was a resourceful journalist, and his name [in Russian something like 'little old worn-out nag' – Translator's Note] amused Shostakovich with its inappropriateness to its owner's ebullient character.

11 My first wife, Tatyana Ivanovna Glikman, who later died in Tashkent of typhus on 4 April 1943.

12 Nina Vasiliyevna Shostakovich, née Varzar, astrophysicist, Shostakovich's first wife; Galina: his five-year-old daughter; Maksim: his three-year-old son.

13 Literary critic.

14 There is a further PS to the letter, written by Nina Vasiliyevna: 'Dear Isaak Davïdovich, first of all I must make a correction: Klyachkin is not as cheerful as all that, although he is certainly full of beans: he has been suffering from shell shock and is having problems with his balance. Secondly, I send you my best wishes. N. Shostakovich.' (Klyachkin recovered from his shell shock and lived to a ripe old age, writing after the war for *Vecherny* (*Evening*) *Leningrad* and other papers.)

15 Musicologist.

16 Musicologist.

17 Composer and military band conductor.

18 Musicologist.
19 Composer.
20 Composer.
21 Composer.
22 Composer.
23 Composer.
24 Czech composer and historian, later Chairman of the Czechoslovak Academy of Sciences.
25 Yury Levitin, composer and student of Shostakovich. He must have told Shostakovich about the food shortages in Tashkent.
26 Shostakovich thought this such an uninteresting detail that he makes a joke of it, completely indifferent to the fact that later biographers might find it genuinely important to know where he finished writing the Seventh Symphony. He was much more concerned to point out, in a pleasing modulation to the realities of everyday life, that the two-roomed flat had a bathroom, a kitchen and lavatory.
27 Chief Conductor of the Bolshoy Theatre. He had suggested commissioning some verses glorifying Stalin to be sung by soloists and chorus, but Shostakovich strenuously resisted the idea. Such a refusal, which meant in effect declining to praise the 'Inspired General and Leader' in an overtly war-related work, called for great courage, a quality with which Shostakovich was abundantly endowed. The letter does not go into details of this conversation, but I heard more about it from the composer himself when I visited him in Kuybïshev.

    Generally speaking, whenever Shostakovich was offered advice which ran counter to his convictions or his conception of a work, he would listen politely but avoid entering into anything resembling a polemical debate. He never took any action which was not guided exclusively by his own artistic conscience and his sense of responsibility to himself and his art. One of his favourite quotations was Pushkin's implacable maxim: 'Art thou, self-critical artist, contented with thy work?' Shostakovich was naturally irritated by the inept criticisms levelled at the Finale of his symphony, but the extraordinary restraint which was one of his most striking traits prevented him from giving full rein to his exasperation.

28 Soso Begiashvili, described ironically as a 'friend', was a former student at the Leningrad Conservatoire. Before the war, he had worked as an economist, an occupation in which he had succeeded in enriching himself. In Kuybïshev he had somehow wormed himself into the Shostakovich household, where his importunate visits were reluctantly tolerated. I later got to know Begiashvili myself in Tashkent: he always had an eye to the main chance and a slew of irons in the fire, generally of a dubious nature. Shostakovich obviously did not take Soso's strictures on the Finale of the Seventh Symphony at all seriously. In this caustic pen-portrait of an all-too-recognizable type of self-satisfied, dull-witted and routinely unimaginative musical yes-man, Shostakovich's reference to Begiashvili as a 'splendid fellow' calls to mind Erasmus's sarcastic *Celebrations of Stupidity*, a device Shostakovich often resorted to in letters and conversation.

29 Shostakovich placed a high value on the opinion of Lev Oborin, whom he considered an outstanding musician. He also took the judgements of Rabinovich and Shlifshteyn seriously.

30 Bass-baritone soloist of the Bolshoy Theatre.

31 A plan, alas, that did not materialize.

32 Shostakovich admired Samosud as an opera conductor. He considered his performance of *Katerina Izmailova* (*Lady Macbeth of the Mtsensk District*) not just irreproachable but definitive, an opinion he never wavered from. The highest praise he could bestow on any conductor he heard performing the opera, whether Soviet or foreign, was: 'He reminds me of Samosud.' At this time Shostakovich had had few opportunities to hear Samosud as a symphonic conductor since he did not often appear in that role, a circumstance which must have been the cause of his misgivings about the fate of the first performance of his Seventh Symphony. As it turned out, his fears were groundless.

33 Shostakovich suffered agonies over the horrors of war and especially the unimaginable privations undergone by the victims of the Leningrad blockade. He unburdened himself to me, naturally with his usual reserve, during my subsequent stay in Kuybïshev.

34 The listing of Leningrad football players known to us both gives a strong hint of Shostakovich's homesickness for the city of his birth. They were woven into the fabric of his memories, which gained in poignancy the nearer he drew to the end of his days.

35 Although this letter as a whole presents a rather gloomy picture, it is pierced from time to time by brighter rays which lend it an unexpected interplay of light and shade, to my mind very characteristic of the man and the music. The cheerless 'things are not good with me' introduction modulates to the amusing and rather touching episode of the stray dog the children have adopted and called 'Ginger'. And the middle of the letter is suffused with the joy of hearing the orchestra play through the first two movements of the Seventh Symphony, a joy which however fades almost as soon as it has come.

36 A lawyer, the composer's father-in-law.

37 Alla Efros, née Varzar, sister of the composer's wife Nina.

38 My mother, Fanya Borisovna Glikman, survived a full winter and spring of the blockade working in a chemistry laboratory. Shostakovich went to enormous trouble to secure her eventual evacuation from the city.

39 A. N. Tolstoy and several other acquaintances urged Shostakovich to move to Tashkent; he would sometimes consider this but in the end always rejected the proposal. Tolstoy was a Deputy of the USSR Supreme Soviet and the author of *Peter the First*, a novel extremely popular at the time, and was therefore very well set up in Tashkent. I sometimes went to visit him in the detached house surrounded by a garden which had been provided for him.

40 Even concerns over the forthcoming première of the new symphony receded into the background compared with Shostakovich's worries about the fate of his mother, his sister and his other relatives. This would account for the dismissal of the rehearsals as a 'saga', the only epithet he can find to describe the work being the distinctly unflattering 'rather long'.

41 Whenever I accompanied Shostakovich to a rehearsal of a new work, symphonic or chamber, he would talk about the effect produced on a composer by hearing with the 'outer ear', as he called it, what he had previously heard only in the mind. The effect may be positive or negative, depending on the quality of the music, but it is in any case an inescapable part of the compositional experience. Shostakovich mourned that Beethoven, conducting the Ninth Symphony, was denied this experience. Hearing two movements of his Seventh Symphony at Samosud's rehearsal was cause for rejoicing, but as Shostakovich bleakly points out, the joyful feelings lasted no more than half a day.

42 It was in fact quite a long time before the Bolshoy Theatre returned to Moscow. They were certainly still in Kuybïshev in April–May 1942, because I myself went to a performance there by the Bolshoy Ballet in which I saw Marina Semyonova dance.

43 Several Government institutions that had been evacuated to Kuybïshev in October 1941 were at this time returning to Moscow.

44 A pun on the Russian word '*dvor*', one meaning of which is 'yard' or 'street', and another the 'court' as in 'at court', so the street-urchin mongrel is neatly transformed into a '*dvoryanin*' or courtier. (Translator's Note)

45 See Preface, pp. xxxv–xxxvi.

46 Because of the continual noise and interference, our conversation consisted mainly of disjointed responses, interjections and cries of joy.

47 The planned visit to Tashkent did not take place.

48 Travelling by train at that time entailed considerable risk of infection from a typhus epidemic.

49 In the spring of 1940 Shostakovich had been travelling in the south, where he had met and become friendly with a woman from Kuybïshev, the same Yelena Pavlovna.

50 I had sent Shostakovich a congratulatory telegram the day after listening to the radio broadcast on 5 March 1942 of the first performance of the Seventh Symphony conducted in Kuybïshev by Samuil Samosud.

51 Mariya Dmitriyevna Shostakovich, the composer's elder sister.

52 Dmitri Vsevolodovich Frederiks, Mariya's son and the composer's nephew. He later became a physicist.

53 Sofya Mikhailovna Varzar, astronomer, the composer's mother-in-law.

54 Vasily Vasilyyevich Varzar, lawyer, the composer's father-in-law.

55 Irina Vasiliyevna Varzar, book illustrator, the composer's sister-in-law.

56 Gerasim Grigoriyevich Efros, artist and cartoonist, Irina's husband.

57 Alla Gerasimovna Efros, Irina's daughter. She later became an architect.

58 Pavel Serebryakov, pianist and director of the Leningrad Conservatoire.

59 Dmitry Dmitriyevich had been invited to fly to Moscow for the première of his Seventh Symphony.

60 The performance conducted by Samuil Samosud took place in Moscow on 29 March 1942.

61 Shostakovich, aware of the straitened circumstances in which I, like other teachers at the Conservatoire, was living, had sent me money.

62 A slip of the pen. The dates should be April, not March. With his habitual extreme reserve and modesty, Shostakovich says not a word about the triumphant success with which the Seventh Symphony was received both in Kuybïshev and Moscow. Shostakovich seemed completely unmoved by the enormous and worldwide reputation the Seventh Symphony soon acquired. During my stay in Kuybïshev, such few details as he vouchsafed had to be prised out of him; he made no mention whatsoever of the extraordinary success the work had been. Much more important to him was his inner satisfaction that the symphony, wrought from the irresistible demands of his artistic soul, had elicited a passionate response in the hearts and minds of its listeners.

63 In his younger days, Shostakovich suffered from great embarrassment whenever he had to speak in public, something he had to endure repeatedly in Moscow at this time. His melancholy mood was exacerbated by having recently seen his mother, who was barely clinging to life, and his father-in-law, whose appearance was a great shock to Shostakovich. He had also just had the news from Leningrad of the death of several composers, victims of the war.

64 Vasily Varzar soon recovered from his condition.

65 Pasha was Nina Varzar Shostakovich's old nurse; Fenya the Shostakoviches' domestic help in Leningrad.

66 Valery Bogdanov-Berezovsky, composer, musicologist and friend of Shostakovich's youth.

67 Boris Golts, composer.

68 Vasily Kalafati, composer.

69 Mikhail Fradkin, composer.

70 Andrey Budyakovsky, composer.

71 A colonel in the Soviet Information Bureau. He had brought me a parcel from Shostakovich containing real coffee beans, a rare treat in the privations of wartime.

72 Plans for the composer's visit to Novosibirsk for the rehearsals and local première of the Seventh Symphony to be conducted by Yevgeny Mravinsky had been initiated in telephone discussions between Shostakovich and Ivan Sollertinsky – in his capacity as Artistic Director of the Leningrad Philharmonia – during my stay in Kuybïshev.

73 Yelena Konstantinovskaya was a foreign-language teacher at the Leningrad Conservatoire and therefore living in Tashkent.

74 Sollertinsky.

75 Georgy (Yury) Sviridov, Shostakovich's much-loved student from the Leningrad Conservatoire.

76 Dobchinsky's phrase from Gogol's *The Inspector-General*, quoted here ironically.

77 Matvey Blanter, composer.

78 Vladimir Shcherbachov, composer and professor at the Leningrad Conservatoire. Shostakovich held Shcherbachov in particular esteem, but while he was on good terms with both him and Blanter, neither could be considered close friends.

79 Again, the theme of nostalgia for Leningrad and the football culture that was a feature of life in the city can be heard in this letter to the faithful companion of his pilgrimages to the stadia.

80 My mother, Fanya Borisovna Glikman, was evacuated from Leningrad at the end of June 1942, thanks to Shostakovich's interventions on her behalf.

81 Sollertinsky wrote to me in Tashkent about the extraordinary success Shostakovich had enjoyed in Novisibirsk following Mravinsky's performance there of the Seventh Symphony. True to form, Shostakovich saw no occasion to mention it to me.

82 A Leningrad footballer.

83 Glikman would have undoubtedly been aware of Shostakovich's year-long love affair with Yelena Konstantinovskaya in Leningrad eight years or so before, and that he had considered marrying her at the time. (Translator's Note)

84 See note 65 to the letter of 31 March 1942.

85 With his usual deadpan humour, Shostakovich refers to the tremendous burden now placed on his shoulders by all the relations and other people who had descended on Kuybïshev and whose welfare would henceforward depend on him.

86 The creative collaboration between Shostakovich and the Moscow-based Beethoven Quartet, which had begun before the war in parallel with the Glazunov Quartet in Leningrad, continued to the end of the composer's life.

87 The Central Song and Dance Ensemble of the NKVD of the USSR under the direction of Zinovy Dunayevsky, for whom in October 1942 Shostakovich created the substantial composition *My Native Land*.

88 Several of Shostakovich's works (the First Symphony, the First Piano Concerto, the Ballet Suites from *The Golden Age* and *Bolt*, and *Lady Macbeth of Mtsensk*) already enjoyed wide popularity among American audiences in the mid-1930s, but after the New York première of the Seventh Symphony conducted by Arturo Toscanini (19 July 1942), his popularity soared to new heights. This was obviously why the New York Philharmonic had invited the composer to conduct a cycle of performances.

89 An artless and strikingly modest admission. Shostakovich frequently bemoaned the lack of confidence that prevented him from mounting the conductor's podium. Citing Tchaikovsky – who did succeed in overcoming his terror and conducting his own works – he used to say to me, 'How I wish I could do that!' Shostakovich did in fact subsequently once agree to take up the baton, on 12 November 1962 in Gorky, when he conducted the Festive Overture and the First Cello Concerto.

90 Chief Conductor of the State Symphony Orchestra of the USSR from 1946 onwards.

91 Shostakovich did not publicize his dissatisfaction with Ivanov's account of the Seventh Symphony, but privately flavours his discouraging assessment with the variety of bittersweet wit of which he was a past master.

92 There was, apparently, some justification for the sarcastic tone in which Shostakovich answers my enquiry about his father- and mother-in-law.

93 Iosif Utkin, the poet, wrote lyric verses and war poetry during the Civil War and the First World War. He was killed at the front in 1944.

94 In the Moskva Hotel, where Shostakovich was living.

95 Leonid Nikolayev, piano professor at the Leningrad Conservatoire, in whose class Shostakovich studied. He died on 11 October 1942 in Tashkent, from typhoid fever. Dmitry Dmitriyevich not only loved him but admired him as a first-class musician and man of great wisdom and learning.

   Shostakovich's sombre reflections doubtless owed much to his memory of the – to him incomprehensible – zeal for administrative activity that overcame Nikolayev in the mid-1930s, when he accepted the position of director of the Leningrad Conservatoire. After a short time he was removed from office, finding himself thereupon in an impossible position. Shostakovich was probably thinking about this when grieving for his beloved teacher, as he had mentioned it in several conversations we had before the war on Nikolayev's fate.

96 Pyotr Ryazanov, composer and professor at the Leningrad Conservatoire, who died on 11 October 1942.

97 Aleksandr Solodovnikov had visited Tashkent in his capacity as Deputy Chairman of the Cultural Committee of the USSR, which oversaw the work of the Leningrad Conservatoire. He came to inform himself as to the state of affairs with the Conservatoire, but I did not have occasion to meet him.

98 Utkin did indeed give me the letter. I was very pleasantly impressed with the poet's handsome appearance and intelligence. At the time, he was still under forty years of age.

99 Ivan Sollertinsky had hatched a plan for Shostakovich to move to Novosibirsk, which, thanks to the Leningrad Philharmonia's temporary relocation there, had become a powerhouse of musical culture. Sollertinsky planned that I should also move to Novisibirsk, along with a mutual friend of ours, [the critic and musicologist] Mikhail Druskin. The plan was never realized.

100 Zoya Dmitriyevna Shostakovich, the composer's younger sister.

101 Professor Grigory Khrushchov.

102 See note 10 to letter of 30 November 1941. For Shostakovich, Arkady Klyachkin represented the archetypal image of the irrepressible 'good sport', to use an expression of the 1930s. Shostakovich had a Chekhovian appreciation of unusual or strange surnames and enjoyed juxtaposing them with their owners, especially when, as in this case, they formed such an inappropriate contrast.

103 In Leningrad before the war, Shostakovich and I often talked about social and political matters as well as artistic life. Whenever we heard Stalin speak, shared feelings of implacable revulsion instantly passed between us.

104 I naturally answered all of Shostakovich's letters, but apparently not everything I sent reached him. The same was true of his communications to me in Tashkent, which he why he was always so anxious to take advantage of any opportunity to send messages by means other than the post.

105 The hint of irritation betrays the burden Shostakovich felt at having to look after such a numerous family.

106 Shostakovich asked me, in a letter I have lost, to meet Sofya Vasiliyevna at Tashkent Station, a request he also made of one of his Leningrad acquaintances N. N. Kostromitin.

107 Pavel Serebryakov, Director of the Leningrad Conservatoire.

108 Shostakovich's article in the *Educational Gazette* had upset Serebryakov because it was a matter of pride for him that the Conservatoire orchestra had performed the Seventh Symphony in Tashkent. This performance took place on 22 June 1942, following the March premières in Kuybïshev and Moscow.

109 Shostakovich actively engaged in the fight against Fascism, taking part in several rallies and meetings held in Moscow. He never wrote to me about the nature or content of speeches he made, assuming that I would read about them in the press.

110 During my stay in Kuybïshev, Shostakovich and I ate in the restaurant of the National Hotel. Supplies for the rest of the family were what is known as dry rations. The food we ate was simple, but there was plenty of it.

111 Boleslav Yavorsky, musicologist, composer and professor at the Moscow Conservatoire.

112 I had written to Dmitry Dmitriyevich about my mother's and my wife's emaciated condition, brought on by our life of semi-starvation.

113 Kostromitin had some professional connections with the Tashkent railway, and he and I had gone together to the station to meet Sofya Vasiliyevna. When we got there however we discovered that the timetable was in a state of complete chaos, and so had no way of fulfilling Shostakovich's request.

114 Shostakovich refers to a song I had written entitled 'Kaganovich's Travel Song', dedicated to Stalin's comrade-in-arms, the People's Commissar of Transport and Communications, Lazar Moyseyevich Kaganovich. Needless to say, I wrote it under the influence of Shostakovich, the master of musical parody. His well-known penchant for taking a melody and then wittily tweaking it, examples of which are profusely scattered throughout his youthful ballets *The Golden Age* and *Bolt*, was never completely eliminated from the great composer's arsenal even in his maturity. In the 1930s, whenever he was assaulted by the detestable stream of announcements, slogans and maxims by Stalin that 'progressive' elements delighted in learning by rote and endlessly spouting, Shostakovich almost literally itched to parody them in musical terms. He fulfilled this ambition many years later in his lampoon *Rayok*.

   The many conversations Shostakovich and I had on this highly seditious topic impelled me to try my own extremely modest talents in the composition of a cycle of satirical songs 'in praise of stupidity', sarcastically celebrating Stalin and his immediate entourage. Discovery would naturally have resulted in the ultimate penalty, so the songs remained secret and not committed to paper; however, they were in circulation among a small group of friends led by Shostakovich, who enjoyed singing them to his own accompaniment on the piano. Taking a huge risk, he secretly transcribed words and music (without the accompaniment), noting on the score the date: 1937. When in this letter he gives vent to his irritation at the chaos on the railways that prevented me from meeting his mother at the station, he was calling to mind the refrain of my 'Travel Song', which goes like this:

> Lazar Moyseyich, our Driver and Guide,
> Through crash, bank and whistle you captain our ride.
> Lazar Moyseyich, we raise a grateful glass
> To our luxury train that is – Bolshevik, First Class!

The complete text of the song can be seen in Appendix 1.

115 Isaak Dunayevsky, conductor and composer of popular music.

116 An ironic inclusion of my name among well-known and not so well known composers of music for the masses.

117 Shostakovich's good spirits were due in part to satisfactory progress on the opera *The Gamblers*.

118 An interesting indication of the widespread fame the Seventh Symphony had gained in so short a time after its first performance – not that Shostakovich says so directly, but the implication is clear. Even in this small and remote Bashkir town, the local wind band had taken the trouble to unravel the complexities of the symphony's first movement and courageously elected to play it through to the distinguished composer. Shostakovich was obviously impressed and touched by the Belebey musicians' enthusiasm, but tactfully refrains from commenting on the calibre of the performance.

119 The previous month Dmitry Dmitriyevich had sent me a collection of his songs printed from a glass master by the Composers' Union Musical Fund, with an affectionate inscription to me. [The technique known as '*steklograf*' (literally, 'writing from glass') involves spreading an adhesive substance over a piece of frosted glass and thereby producing an impression of an original placed upon it. (Translator's Note)] It was the *Six Romances on words of W. Raleigh, R. Burns and W. Shakespeare*, Op. 62. One of the songs, 'MacPherson Before his Execution', to words by Robert Burns in the translation by Samuil Marshak, was dedicated to me. The theme of this song was later used in the Scherzo of the Thirteenth Symphony. I was thrilled and flattered by the dedication, and had said as much in my telegram to Shostakovich.

120 It is true that Shostakovich usually wrote about a huge range of subjects, trivial and important, in a consistently unemotional, businesslike style. He did not particularly single out important topics, for example by a new paragraph or with emphases, but simply wrote straight on in the general context of the letter. Despite this, from time to time he did feel the need to pour out his soul, and this need would sometimes find expression in his letters.

121 Shostakovich had been ill for some time with typhoid fever.

122 A deliberate use of standard phraseology, a cliché of the 1930s and 1940s.

123 The composer Vissarion Shebalin was a close friend of Shostakovich, a professor and at that time Director of the Moscow Conservatoire.

124 Shostakovich paid little attention to domestic matters, distancing himself from them as far as possible. However, to his annoyance, wartime living conditions sometimes impinged on his attention, giving rise to this sardonic sally.

125 From the very first, Shostakovich had been certain of victory over Fascist Germany, and this belief found vivid expression in the Finale of the Seventh Symphony.

126 Shostakovich dedicated this wonderful sonata to the memory of his teacher Leonid Nikolayev.

127 Work on the opera had not been revealed to anyone outside a close circle of the composer's friends.

128 See the preface for the reasons why Shostakovich abandoned work on *The Gamblers*.

129 Sollertinsky.

130 Aleksandr Yegolin, influential literary critic and scholar in the 1940s.

131 The reference is to a little comic chorale which I perpetrated shortly before the war on a (slightly adapted) note that Stalin had written on a copy of Gorky's poem *Death and the Maiden*. Stalin's aperçu had become a crucial source for exhaustive analysis of Goethe's *Faust*. This revolting blot on Soviet literature had nevertheless caused a great stir among certain composers, who rushed to cobble together operas based on Gorky's *Death and the Maiden*, recognizing that it was now by infallible resolution of Stalin far superior to Goethe's masterpiece. Needless to say, Shostakovich had not the slightest intention of writing an opera on this subject, other than to make a joke. My song, together with the Stalin text, as notated by Shostakovich, can be seen in Appendix 1.

132 A deep attachment to Leningrad, the city in which Shostakovich had spent the first thirty-five years of his life, was the cause of much soul-searching over the move to Moscow. But as was in fact inevitable, he became a Muscovite. Within a short space of time he had been allocated a flat on Kirov Street, opposite the post office, where I first visited him at the end of April 1945.

133 My wife Tatyana Ivanovna died of typhus on 4 April 1943. The death of a wonderful and beloved young woman plunged me into boundless and inconsolable grief.

134 Shostakovich learned of the death of my wife from Colonel Boltin, who was serving in the Frunze Military Academy, which had been evacuated to Tashkent. There would not in fact have been much time for the exchange of letters.

135 I did receive the money after Tatyana had died.

136 Shostakovich showed a degree of heartfelt sympathy for me that I found deeply touching.

137 The pianist Emil Gilels was in Tashkent in April 1943 and showed me much kindness and sympathy during my time of trial. On his return to Moscow, he volunteered to take my letter to Dmitry Dmitriyevich by hand.

138 Sent without any request on my part, out of pure goodness of heart and concern for my welfare.

139 Only in the rarest cases did Shostakovich invite people outside the family, even those he found congenial, to stay with him. He felt constrained by anybody's presence if it went on too long. In my case, however, he made an exception; I visited Moscow on many occasions and Shostakovich would never hear of my staying in a hotel, insisting that I stay at his home. This continued until his death. Moreover, until the time when he fell seriously ill, he always came to meet me at the railway station. I mention this simply to illustrate the nature of our relationship.

140 Boltin had presumably given Shostakovich news of the circumstances of my life and how I was getting on. Originally from Moscow, he was a professional soldier, but we had many literary and musical interests in common. Although his tour of duty in Tashkent was not a long one, I was captivated by his love for Shostakovich. We became friends, and the evenings I spent enjoying the hospitality of his apartment were bright spots of my life. It had all begun on the evening when he had brought me Shostakovich's present of coffee beans.

141 The plans for my visit to Moscow collapsed of their own accord. My mother's precarious state of health meant that I could not leave her.

142 I was in such a state of depression that I had not written to Shostakovich.

143 Boltin and his family had moved to Moscow.

144 Shostakovich had often complained of the boredom, isolation and provincialism of life in Kuybïshev.

145 Shostakovich clearly considered acquaintance with the Metropolitan something of a curiosity, and an indication of the unexpectedly wider range of people he was now encountering.

146 Boris Klyuzner, composer then serving in the army.

147 Aleksandr Kamensky, pianist and professor at the Leningrad Conservatoire. His wife Aleksandra Bushen was a musicologist.

148 Nikolai Timofeyev, composer.

149 Pianist as well as composer, Zhelobinsky had partnered Shostakovich in the two-piano preview of the Fourth Symphony at the Composers' Union. (Translator's Note)

150 I heard the Piano Sonata in Tashkent later that autumn, played by Pavel Serebryakov. It made a great impression on me.

151 Presumably I had not yet written to tell Dmitry Dmitriyevich that I did not think it would be possible for me to spend time away from Tashkent then.

152 Natan Perelman, pianist and professor at the Leningrad Conservatoire, and a former fellow-student of Shostakovich in Nikolayev's class. Nonya was the diminutive form of his name by which he was known to his friends in his student years.

153 It is hard to say what in my letter had upset Shostakovich. Most likely it was my somewhat tactless reference to his endemic dislike of burdensome obligations. He must have misunderstood my sententious remarks on this subject as an indirect reproach to him for indifference towards me, and with truly astonishing forbearance and magnanimity hastened to accept a wholly unmerited element of blame, knowing in his heart all the while that this was unjust.

154 For some reason, Shostakovich seemed (a year after the fact!) to think that I

had been dissatisfied with the welcome he gave me in Kuybïshev. This is extraordinary, for from the moment of his warm greeting at the station to the hour of my departure I was surrounded by every expression of a true friend's touching concern for my welfare.

155 This is an appropriate moment to mention an important characteristic of Shostakovich's psychology. Throughout his life, he avoided turning the spotlight on any misunderstanding that might have arisen with people close to him, considering it pointless to do so. If ever this happened, he would withdraw into silent seclusion, making clear his opinion that the incident was closed and it was unnecessary to refer to it again, because he would have expunged all traces of it from his memory. I do remember that on very rare occasions he felt impelled to speak out about some rash step a friend might be planning, but usually inner delicacy or bashfulness would prevent him doing so. But once any misunderstanding with someone he was on friendly terms with, or even a close friend, crossed the line into what he regarded as a genuine breach of manners or morality, Shostakovich would break off relations altogether. In that case he would make no attempt whatsoever to 'explain' or 'clarify'. In this letter, while as a matter of fact his conduct towards me had no need at all to be explained or defended since it was in every respect irreproachable, Shostakovich seems exceptionally to have felt the need to offer an explanation, albeit in the plainest possible language.

156 I had long ago abandoned all thought of visiting Moscow, but Shostakovich continued with extraordinary persistence to write to me about it.

157 I did in fact know this, since Shostakovich had told me of his work on the symphony in letters that are now lost. Despite the laconic nature of the information, I had a clear sense of the speed and white-hot inspiration with which he had composed the symphony.

158 A typical Shostakovich formulation: a pro-forma statement of the number of movements lacking even the barest description of the nature of the new work.

159 The première of the Eighth Symphony took place in Moscow on 4 November 1943. It was performed by the State Symphony Orchestra of the USSR, conducted by Yevgeny Mravinsky.

160 Before the first performance of any new work, Shostakovich always succumbed to a deep anxiety that, however acute its torments, he always strove to hide. Reserve was a fundamental trait of his character. Only once the performance was over could emotional equilibrium return.

161 Tatyana Litvinova, the daughter of Maksim Litvinov, was an English-language interpreter. What film it was has slipped my mind – perhaps it was referred to in one or other of the letters that were lost – but Shostakovich's praise is somewhat barbed.

162 Reference to the key phrase in Lensky's aria from Tchaikovsky's *Eugene Onegin*, in which the poet apologizes to his prospective mother-in-law for causing a scandal 'in your house'. (Translator's Note)

163 Not for the first time, Shostakovich wraps up in grotesquely ironic terms his foreboding of the bullying criticism likely to be unleashed on the composition he had written with his heart's blood.

164 The wonderful Trio Op. 62 was subsequently dedicated to the memory of Ivan Sollertinsky, who died in Novosibirsk on 11 February 1944.

165 Shostakovich's detestation of Hitler's fanatical tyranny coexisted with equal loathing for the Stalinist terror of the 1930s. In the later stages of the war, when unbridled paeans of praise for the 'Great General', to whom the army and the whole nation naturally owed all victories, began blaring out with renewed force everywhere, Shostakovich reflected with apprehension on what was likely to happen once the long-awaited victory actually came about. He feared a resurgence of the random terror that had been the reality of life 'under the sun of Stalin's constitution', the canonical phrase which in reality existed only on the pages of the newspapers. Hence the bitter irony of the reference to the 'unalloyed joy' with which he looked forward to a return to pre-war life and times.

166 Shostakovich regarded *Rothschild's Violin*, an opera based on Chekhov's short story written by Venyamin Fleishman, very highly. Fleishman had been a gifted member of his composition class, and after he was killed serving at the Front, Shostakovich completed and orchestrated his opera. After the war Shostakovich tried to persuade the Bolshoy Theatre to produce *Rothschild's Violin*, but without success. A concert performance was given on 20 June 1960 at the All-Union House of Composers in Moscow.

167 Tamara Samoznayeva (Bryanskaya) subsequently worked as a picture researcher at Lenfilm, the Leningrad film production studios.

168 Yury Bryansky was an acquaintance of Dmitry Dmitriyevich. Before the war he had worked in the Leningrad Repertoire Committee (Repertkom).

169 Ivan Sollertinsky's sudden death was for Shostakovich, as for me, a crushing blow and an irreplaceable loss. Sollertinsky was a very sociable individual with a wide circle of friends, but Shostakovich always considered that he and I were Sollertinsky's closest, most loyal and loving friends, although I also knew that he also enjoyed an extremely close and affectionate relationship with the well-known Leningrad musicologist Mikhail Druskin.

170 Shostakovich paid great attention to the observance of traditional rites and customs, such as this proposal that we should drink a glass at a prescribed time in memory of our departed friend. I was glad to honour Shostakovich's suggestion, although it was indeed extraordinarily difficult to procure the virtually unobtainable vodka.

171 The conductor Nikolai Rabinovich, one of my closest friends, was living temporarily in Tashkent. He had applied to the director of the Conservatoire, Pavel Serebryakov, to be reinstated as a professor, having relinquished the position in August 1941 in order to remain for a further year in Leningrad during the blockade of the city.

172 Igor Grabar was a well-known artist and critic. My brother, a sculptor in the fifth year of a course at the Academy of Arts, refused to take advantage of the exemption to which he was entitled and volunteered for military service. He graduated from the Artillery Institute with the rank of lieutenant, took command of an artillery battery and went to Germany, where he was wounded and awarded the Order of the Red Star.

In the spring of 1944, once it had become clear that the Red Army was well on the way to a decisive victory, I asked Shostakovich for his assistance in seeing whether Gavriil could be demobilized in order to finish his training at the Academy of Arts. Shostakovich made representations to Igor Grabar, but without result. Gavriil was eventually demobilized at the end of June 1945, after the war was over.

173 Shostakovich was anything but valetudinarian, although his health was far from perfect during the war. The spot on the lung must in fact have been quite serious, although at the age of thirty-seven he felt able to indulge in a typical joke about it.

174 The perceived creative block had no basis in reality. Only a few months before this *cri de coeur*, Shostakovich had written a great masterpiece in the Second Piano Trio. But whenever there was even the briefest interruption in the creative stream, Shostakovich endured agonies of doubt and alarm; it was in his nature to be thus, and in this he was one of a company of great artists for whom life and creative work were one and the same thing.

In later life he was several times prey to such feelings, and letter after letter to me complained of his fear of having dried up as an artist, whenever for any reason at all, or even for no reason, there was a hiatus in his production. The feelings were real enough, but the catalyst for them was entirely imaginary, since the oeuvre continued to grow with astonishing and consistent regularity despite the bouts of illness which so often kept him confined to bed for long periods.

175 Maksimilian Shteynberg, composer and professor at the Leningrad Conservatoire, with whom Shostakovich had studied composition. The work in question was the *Symphony-Rhapsody on Uzbek Folk Songs*, which Shteynberg had written in 1942 in Tashkent. Shostakovich refrains from actually revealing his opinion of the work, but manages to convey that it had not made a very strong impression on him.

Generally speaking, Shostakovich did not feel particularly drawn to his former teacher's music, although he respected him for other qualities. Nevertheless, he was always ready to lend his support to performances of his work, for instance enthusiastically backing my proposal to produce Shteynberg's musically worthwhile ballet *Till Eulenspiegel* in the Leningrad Maly Opera Theatre, where I served as dramaturg from the autumn of 1944. Sadly this plan, which at its instigation had brought great satisfaction to Shteynberg, could not in the end be realized partly owing to the composer's unexpected death.

Shostakovich treated his teacher with invariable courtesy and respect, visiting him from time to time and sometimes taking me with him. I was struck with the measured decorum and propriety that reigned in the home of Rimsky-Korsakov's son-in-law. The great composer's precepts were, it seemed to me, religiously observed not only in Shteynberg's artistic ideas but also in his way of life. But for Shostakovich there was something alienating in the way Shteynberg – a man of great culture – clung to traditional norms and rules, allied to a certain pedantry and parochialism.

176 The trip to Tashkent did not take place.

177 Gavriil had had a short leave during which he had visited Moscow and had called on Shostakovich. They had not hitherto had much personal contact with one another, but Shostakovich subsequently grew to admire him as a painter and sculptor and Gavriil's large bust of Beethoven adorns the study in his Moscow apartment to this day.

178 Needless to say, this description of my brother, drawn in the hackneyed officialese of propaganda, is not only totally unrecognizable as a portrait of Gavriil but the direct opposite of his feelings at this time. He and Shostakovich were alike repelled by the current rash of hypocritical clichés about optimism and 'positive belief in the splendid future of our country and our people'. As was frequently the case in our conversations and correspondence, I was expected to infer the direct opposite of what was written.

179 Matvey Manizer, sculptor and professor at the Academy of Arts, with whom Gavriil had studied. Although he was a famous artist in the 1930s, Shostakovich disliked him as a man and as a sculptor.

180 The Conservatoire's move back to Leningrad after its evacuation to Tashkent was planned for August, which explains Shostakovich's concern that his letter might not reach me in time. In fact the move to Leningrad did not take place until September.

181 Shostakovich may really have been thinking of moving back to Leningrad at this time. But as it turned out, he remained in Moscow, although business brought him often to the Leningrad Conservatoire so that we were able to see one another in the flesh. In summer we stayed together at Komarovo and met without fail every day that God gave. As a consequence of this, and that enemy of the art of letter-writing, the telephone, the fount of correspondence ran relatively dry. Even so, Shostakovich still continued to write to me, albeit with long interruptions caused either by our meetings, or by his frequent bouts of illness, or by emotional turmoil that stopped him from taking up his pen.

The fact remained that Shostakovich was a man with an unquenchable need to write letters, and every one of them, whether brief and drily factual or garnished with detail, was precious to me. The life of the times we lived in pulsed through them, revealing the unique contours of his personality, and in them can still be heard the authentic voice, the richly idiosyncratic vocabulary and subtext of the Shostakovich lexicon.

182 It is characteristic of Shostakovich that at the age of thirty-eight he begins to talk about approaching old age. This topic was to recur many times in the future.

183 Shostakovich found it difficult, even nerve-racking, to relate to strangers whom he found unsympathetic, and generally reacted by lapsing into protracted periods of silence.

184 This is not entirely true. During the 1944–5 holiday period, Shostakovich was mentally at work on the Ninth Symphony. As was usual with him, it was composed in his mind before the task began of fixing the mature opus on paper. In this sense, he was in fact working at this time.

At the end of April 1945, I came to Moscow for talks with the playwright N. A. Aduyev about the libretto of Shcherbachov's comic opera *The Tobacco Ship Captain*, which in my capacity as Head of Literature at the Maly Opera I had decided with my colleagues to stage there. I stayed with Shostakovich at 21 Kirov Street for about two weeks, the apartment having by that time been put in order. Shostakovich did not mention the Ninth Symphony then, but one evening he decided to show me some sketches of the first movement, magnificent in its sweep, its pathos and its irresistible movement. He played me about ten minutes of it, and then announced that there was much in the symphony with which he was not happy, in particular its number in the canon, which might suggest to many people an inevitable but misleading comparison with Beethoven's Ninth.

He did not mention his misgivings again, but some time later abandoned work on the symphony. I cannot say why he did so, as I never questioned him about it, but on 25 September 1945 I was present at the Union of Composers in Leningrad when he played through a completely different Ninth Symphony, the one we know today. It provoked a hostile response among some of those present, among whom, regrettably, was Boris Asafyev. As 25 September was also Shostakovich's birthday, we toasted the double event afterwards at Shostakovich's mother's apartment on Dmitrovsky Pereulok.

185 A dramatic confession. Shostakovich suffered all his life from nerves, and they may well have been the source of the serious problems he later suffered from in his hands and legs.

186 I was also at the time reading and enjoying Blok in Tashkent, and had written to Shostakovich about this. Among the verses that so struck Shostakovich was probably 'Gamayun', for this was one of the poems he often quoted lines from. More than twenty years later, in the early stages of recovering from a heart attack, Shostakovich composed his wonderful cycle of songs on poems of Blok and invited me to Moscow to hear it. The cycle includes the tragic 'Gamayun', the Bird of Prophecy, and it ends with the serenity and incomparable beauty of the sublime appeal 'To Music'.

187 Aron Ostrovsky, senior lecturer and later professor at the Leningrad Conservatoire, resigned his position as vice-rector but continued his teaching work.

188 Aleksandr Ossovsky, professor at the Leningrad Conservatoire. The information about his appointment as vice-rector was not correct.

189 My niece Lina was the daughter of my elder brother, who had been killed at the Front.

190 On one of his regular visits to Leningrad, Shostakovich had lent me some money and I, taking my cue from his own extreme punctiliousness in money matters, had hastened to return it to him.

191 Shostakovich had renewed his efforts to intercede on my brother Gavriil's behalf in his desire to be released from active service in the army to finish his final year at the Academy of Arts. Gavriil was a lieutenant in the artillery, and Shostakovich had turned to no less a person than Marshal Nikolai Voronov, the senior officer of that branch of the service.

192 In fact it was not, and Gavriil remained in the army.

193 See note 114 to the letter of 23 December 1942 [to savour this barbed
     suggestion – Translator's Note].

194 The promised song never saw the light of day.

Chapter II Zhdanovschina and After, 1946–1953

1 This statement is hardly to be taken at face value, since Shostakovich
   frequently felt unwell and his moods were very variable, sometimes equable
   but equally sometimes depressed and anxious.

2 In conversation with me, Shostakovich lavished praise not only on Sviridov's
   First String Quartet but also his Piano Trio. He did much to obtain a Stalin
   Prize for the latter in 1946.

3 Shostakovich means that he was writing for the cinema. While much of the
   music that he wrote for the films was excellent, in his mind he separated it
   from the mainstream of his creative work.

4 A facetious use of a most uncharacteristic salutation.

5 Needless to say, Shostakovich's declaration that he loved and valued my
   friendship was not only flattering in the highest degree, but also something to
   treasure. I worshipped his music, and his feelings of friendship – to which I
   could lay no claims whatsoever as of right – were a powerful source of support
   to me in the dark days of my life. I was always boundlessly grateful to
   Shostakovich for this.

   The background to this letter is as follows. During one of our conversations
   Shostakovich suggested that as he and I had been two of Ivan Sollertinsky's
   closest friends, we ought to compose a brief sketch of his life and publish it in,
   a journal like *Sovetskaya muzïka*. I thought this an excellent plan, so, wanting
   to get on with the job, I wrote and submitted an article under our joint names
   without taking the trouble to show it to Shostakovich. It was negligent of me,
   but I assumed he would see it in proof.

   This thoughtless and inconsiderate action elicited a letter from Shostakovich
   containing a stinging rebuke which I fully deserved. The article was taken out
   of the magazine, and I wrote to Shostakovich, apologizing. This in turn stirred
   his sensitive, delicate soul to regret the allegedly unjustified hurt I had suffered
   from his criticism of my actions, and was the cause of my most dearly loved
   friend describing his own character as hateful and bad. I knew then and I know
   now that Shostakovich's character, given as it was to severe self-criticism, was
   of the very noblest and most sensitive.

6 Whenever Shostakovich made bold statements about his 'fabulous mood', it
   was a sure sign that the exact opposite was the case: it was his way of avoiding
   the need to go into details.

7 Shostakovich's interest was aroused by the lives of these unknown toilers in
   the arts. The entire theatrical establishment from top to bottom rested on
   these armies of Ivanovs and Ivanovas, dismissively referred to by number.
   Shostakovich was astonished to realize from his reading of the *Yearbook* that
   it was thought possible to sum up the whole of the late Mr Ivanov No. 7's life
   in the ten lines of his obituary.

8 Shostakovich often revealed in this way the anxious state of his inner feelings and his pessimistic outlook about what might be in store for him in ten years' time when he would be fifty. Such irruptions of gloom were countered and his spirits rose in proportion to the state of his belief in his own creative powers.

9 Aram Khachaturian was at the time Chairman of the Executive Committee of the Composers' Union.

10 At this time Shostakovich was deeply concerned with the troubles that had befallen Mikhail Zoshchenko, who had been the subject of two viciously destructive attacks in recently published proclamations: first, the Resolution by the Central Committee of the All-Union Communist Party of 14 August 1946 entitled 'On the *Star* and *Leningrad* Newspapers', and second, the article by Andrey Zhdanov published in *Pravda* on 21 September 1946. Shostakovich much admired Zoshchenko's talent, and had great affection for him as a person.

The Resolution called for a critical reappraisal of musical values, and Ogolevets was one of the first critics to begin tilling this fertile-seeming soil. In his article 'The need to reconstruct the work of the Union of Soviet Composers', published on 20 September in *Sovetskoye Isskustvo* [*Soviet Art*], the author unleashed a torrent of lickspittle abuse on great musicians.

11 Shostakovich's description of the speeches at the plenum as 'interesting' is naturally at odds with his real objection to the manner and content of many of them. Under the banner of 'Reappraisal', the opening of the plenum was specifically timed to coincide with a hostile review by the critic Izrail Nestyev of Shostakovich's Ninth Symphony, published on 30 September 1946 in the influential and combative journal *Kultura i Zhizn* [*Culture and Life*]. The composer was found guilty of coarse buffoonery, inept stylization and other mortal sins. Needless to say, Shostakovich was deeply hurt by this obvious distortion of his intentions in this work, but he says nothing about it in this letter, already knowing how indignant I was at Nestyev's article. He confines himself to the oblique phrase about advancing age (at forty!) making 'experiences harder to deal with'.

12 Yury Sviridov's wife.

13 Shostakovich had been quite ill with diphtheria.

14 At the beginning of June 1946, while I was Head of the Repertoire Department of the Maly Opera Theatre in Leningrad, the theatre mounted the première production of Prokofiev's opera *War and Peace*, conducted by Samuil Samosud and produced by Boris Pokrovsky. I was therefore there to witness the huge success of this magnificent opera, which grew visibly from performance to performance.

Five months later, the Kirov Theatre presented a brilliant production of another wonderful opera by Prokofiev, *The Duenna*, conducted by Boris Khaikin and produced by I. Yu. Shlepyanov. This première was, however, greeted with markedly less enthusiasm than *War and Peace* had aroused. In less then six months, there had been a radical change in the attitude of composers and critics in Leningrad. Some of them based their new approach on the Reappraisal mentioned in note 11 above and called the opera a failure, branding it as tedious, written in an ultra-sophisticated idiom, inaccessible to the general public and therefore irrelevant. Fearing that the whole production was about to come to grief, I urged Shostakovich to come to Leningrad to see *The Duenna* for himself, which he did in December 1946. He liked the opera and its staging very much indeed, and said that he wanted to write a review of the production.

Being pressed for time, he asked me to draft a short article for the press. Naturally I fulfilled the request, and a review under Shostakovich's name (after he had read and corrected it) duly appeared in *Sovetskoye Isskustvo*. However, in my haste I had forgotten to mention the singer Leopold Solomyak, who sang the role of Don Carlos. This omission greatly distressed Dmitry Dmitriyevich.

The error was entirely mine, but his extreme delicacy of feeling did not allow him to take me to task for it, and in any case he felt himself responsible for inadvertently slighting the artist, whom he hardly knew at all personally. Concern over the fate of others was a fundamental element in Shostakovich's make-up.

15 I had written to Shostakovich, telling him of the powerful impression made on me by hearing his song cycle *From Jewish Folk Poetry*.

16 Usually Shostakovich was able to write film music with great rapidity, but work on *Meeting on the Elbe* was proving a heavy burden, partly because he was feeling so unwell and partly because the film was of such wretched quality artistically.

17 This unattractive self-portrait is, needless to say, vastly overstated. Shostakovich was a virtuoso at this sort of unjustified and merciless self-criticism, on the moral and spiritual plane as well as the physical, as can be seen from his letter to me of 11 February 1946. At the time this letter was written Shostakovich was forty-two years old. Then, and for many years thereafter, his physical appearance in fact preserved the charm and beauty of his youth, although the series of 'body blows', as he used to call them, that he had endured began to leave their mark on his features, lending to them a careworn and suffering expression that he found very unappealing.

This, then, is how Shostakovich appeared in January 1948. In Leningrad for a visit, he gave me an account of the meeting at the Central Committee which had debated Vano Muradeli's opera *The Great Friendship*, and told me how much this meeting had upset him. He said: 'Twelve years ago [at the time of the *Pravda* 'Muddle Instead of Music' article] I was younger and more equipped to withstand body blows like that. Now I am getting old, and I can't take it . . .' (transcribed from my notes at the time.)

My reading of this confession was that it was not fear of getting old that was the core of the problem, since it would be many years before this was a reality. Rather, it was a reflection of the tormented disequilibrium into which his nerves had clearly fallen. Then he said something else which demonstrated the courage of his character and the strength of his artistic integrity: 'In the evenings, when those disgusting, shameful debates [at the sessions] were over for the day, I would come home and work on the third movement of the violin concerto. I finished it and I think it turned out well.' (transcribed from my notes).

I often think of this modest assessment of the greatest, most inspired movement of the concerto, in which a mood of restrained grief coexists with majestic grandeur. It seems to me that in this movement the innermost feelings of the composer find their ideal expression, obliterating completely the barrier between the inner and the outer world. To my mind, the Passacaglia stands on a level with the Largo from the Fifth Symphony.

18 Shostakovich refers to the films *The Storm*, *Pirogov*, *The Young Guard* and *Meeting on the Elbe*.

19 Izrail Trauberg, film director, the younger brother of Leonid Trauberg, who collaborated with Grigory Kozintsev on many films. He was actually born in 1905.

20 A somewhat relative term, seeing that Shostakovich last wrote to me on 12 December and we saw one another regularly on his monthly visits to Leningrad to teach at the Conservatoire.

21 Sofya Shostakovich adored her 'incomparable' Mitya and her pride in him knew no bounds. In contrast, for example, to Igor Stravinsky's mother, she responded with delight to every note that he wrote and I recall her radiant happiness whenever her son's compositions were performed. A naturally gregarious person, Sofya Vasiliyevna would hold court in the Blue Salon after concerts in the Philharmonia, surrounded by her son's admirers and giving full reign to her ardent and utterly spontaneous delight. Shostakovich himself was embarrassed by such unbridled exultation, which he considered excessive, but he could never allow himself to offer the slightest hint of a rebuke to his mother; as so often happened, he chose silence over candour. He often told me how much he wished his mother would not say such things, but he could never bring himself to tell her so for fear of hurting her feelings.

His mother's welfare was always a matter of great concern to Shostakovich. He was most distressed all the time she was forced to endure the privations of the siege of Leningrad, as he frequently wrote in his letters to me at the time. Yet in the relationship of mother and son there was always a lack of those countless nuances that spell true familiarity, and indeed there existed between them a kind of respectful formality, coupled with the thoroughbred simplicity that comes naturally to intelligent people.

Sofia Vasiliyevna shrank from the thought of causing any distress to her beloved son, and was indeed concealing her true condition from him. Shostakovich knew this perfectly well, hence his request that I should visit his mother at her home on Dmitrovsky Pereulok. I did so many times, and wrote to him after each visit.

22 Shostakovich's elder sister, Mariya.

23 A sanatorium near Moscow.

24 As was his habit, Shostakovich set out his plans for visiting Leningrad and Komarovo in great detail. For many years after the war, he spent the summer months at Komarovo, first in a government dacha and subsequently, after this privilege was taken away from him, in the dacha of his father-in-law Vasily Varzar.

25 During the 1930s, as I have mentioned elsewhere, I was Shostakovich's

inseparable companion at football matches. The war cured me, but although his interest declined somewhat Shostakovich never completely conquered his addiction and from time to time when in Leningrad he would hark back to the old days and ask me to accompany him.

26 I had spent the second half of July and the first half of August in Kabarda, on a collective sheep farm in the Khulamsky Gorge. I had been invited there by a Kabarda student of mine, Leonid Erkenov, whose father was the manager of the farm. I sent Shostakovich a detailed description of my extravagant lifestyle in the mountain gorge, which he read together with Yury Sviridov, and in reply I received this postcard sent to Nalchik.

27 At the time, Sviridov's fate as a composer and as a man meant a great deal to Shostakovich. The relationship of the older composer to his former student was that of a colleague, entirely free of condescension or prescriptiveness.

28 Levon Atovmyan, composer and close friend of Shostakovich. If memory serves me right, Atovmyan was experiencing severe problems connected with his official position as director of the Musical Fund.

29 The adjective 'talented' should be interpreted as meaning that Shostakovich considered Dolmatovsky at best a professional versifier. Shostakovich wrote the oratorio *Song of the Forests* at speed and with great technical mastery, to see it greeted by the world of musical criticism with precisely the acclaim it denied to his symphonic masterpieces. The oratorio was nominated for a Stalin Prize first class, but Shostakovich was not particularly fond of it and was uncomfortable at all the praise heaped upon it. He had a particular aversion to the passages in the text that mentioned Stalin; at the end of the general rehearsal, I said to him: 'Suppose, instead of Stalin, your oratorio had featured, for example, Queen Wilhelmina of the Netherlands? She is said to be a keen forester.' Shostakovich exclaimed: 'Oh, how wonderful that would be. I do take responsibility for the music, but the words??!' The première of *Song of the Forests* took place with enormous success in Leningrad on 15 December 1949, conducted by Yevgeny Mravinsky.

30 Leonid Trauberg, the film director.

31 A birthday telegram for his forty-third birthday.

32 Shostakovich attached great importance to traditional observances, including the celebration of birthdays, and kept this up during his stay at the 'Pravda' sanatorium in Sochi.

33 At one time Sviridov certainly had a problem with his drinking. Shostakovich took this seriously, fearing that it would damage his huge talent. Dmitry Dmitriyevich did not really know how to bring influence to bear on his favourite former student. The fact was that he lacked skills in persuasion, exhortation or advocacy. His natural style was to express an opinion on any given fact or situation once and once only and, imbued as he was by respect for the autonomy of the individual, he was always reluctant to encroach on another person's private life. 'Those that have ears to hear . . .' he liked to say, but there were many who would or could not hear, or who failed to draw the right conclusions from what they heard.

During the period of his life that he lived in Leningrad, it is no exaggeration to say that I was a very close friend of Sviridov, and we saw one another almost every day. I was as captivated by Sviridov's music as I was by the depth and acuteness of his intelligence, and I suppose he also found in me a good friend and companion. Shostakovich was well aware of this relationship and hoped that I could be effective in weaning Sviridov from the arms of Bacchus. Unfortunately I was not very successful in this, first because whenever I found myself in company I was not myself a very good advertisement for sobriety, and secondly because Sviridov found my attempts at edification comic. Fortunately, however, in time he succeeded without help from anyone in freeing himself from his potentially damaging predilections.

34 A return to the subject of the previous letter. Shostakovich turns in an apt and witty quotation from Pushkin's *Mozart and Salieri*, where Pushkin has Beaumarchais addressing Salieri:

> . . . come now, good brother Salieri,
> When burdened with dark thoughts that cloud your brow.
> The choice is yours: uncork the champagne bottle
> Or read again *The Marriage of Figaro.*

The lighthearted tone fails to mask Shostakovich's real concern for Sviridov, of whose talent, as we have seen, he writes in the most glowing terms. Artists of genius do not hold back from saluting their colleagues' gifts: Pushkin, and Pushkin's Mozart, were fully capable of doing so.

35 While Shostakovich was a young man in the prime of physical strength, he often complained of the onset of old age, writing in his letters about his indispositions; but when in his sixties he became prey to truly serious illnesses, he avoided all details in letters and conversation.

36 Shostakovich, obviously, was not overly fond of his parents-in-law.

37 It is likely that Shostakovich was referring to the Eighth Symphony. Not very long before writing this letter, he had talked with me about it in a manner which left no doubt that he was satisfied with this work. At about the same time, he spoke in similarly warm terms of *Lady Macbeth of Mtsensk*. Shostakovich's attitude to his compositions varied at different times. Sometimes in conversation he would castigate himself for what he considered unsuccessful passages in one work or another. But on the rarest of occasions he would be moved to clap his hands together on finishing a piece and say of himself, in the famous exclamation of Pushkin after reading through *Boris Godunov*, 'Ah yes, Puskhin, ah yes, you clever son of a bitch!' All the same, this letter is the first time I know of that he gave such powerful expression to his belief and pride in himself as a composer.

It is my opinion that such a highly uncharacteristic avowal may be explained as a psychological reaction to the humiliating attacks to which the whole of his oeuvre had recently been subjected. One thinks particularly of countless criticisms in the press, like the series of articles in *Sovetskaya muzïka* in one of which the writer concluded his assassination with the abusive comment that 'for many years the engine of Shostakovich's creativity has done little more than tick over'.

Of course it never occurred to Shostakovich to defend himself from such attacks; in any case it would have been quite useless for all practical purposes. And so, writing to me at the turn of the year, he felt impelled to turn on his tormentors, to express exactly what he felt about their judgements and their criticisms and their denunciations, and what he truly felt about himself. I shall never forget the emotion with which I read this trusting heart's *confession de foi*.

38 A highly idiosyncratic view of correspondence. Shostakovich lays stress on his need to share with his correspondents his problems and sorrows, of which he had more than his fair share, but he seems to have forgotten that he also often wrote to me about happy events in his difficult life.

39 The energetic repetition betokens sarcasm. This was a particularly difficult time for Shostakovich.

40 Shostakovich was usually polite about my rather humble teaching duties at the Conservatoire, but here with this reference to 'scholarship' allows himself to poke gentle fun at me.

41 I was delighted with the plan, and about a month later put it into action.

42 A reference to the enthusiasm I had declared for the vocal cycle *On Jewish Folk Poetry* and my appreciation of the dinner Shostakovich had given me in Leningrad.

43 The plans changed, and I went to Moscow on 15 March.

44 After spending a week (15 to 22 March) in Moscow, as usual at the Shostakoviches' apartment on Mozhaiskoye Shosse, I returned home. As was his custom, he had met me at the station, but on this occasion, his driver being off sick, he had elected to drive the car himself. On the way home, he committed a minor traffic offence: sounding his horn in a place where this was not allowed. In the blink of an eye, to Shostakovich's great consternation, an intimidating guardian of public order appeared. Naturally, it did not occur to him to show the policeman his credentials as a Deputy of the Supreme Soviet: this would have broken a lifetime's rule. Instead he produced his ordinary driver's licence. The policeman read the offender a stern lecture and then read the name on the document, at which he enquired if he was the composer. Shostakovich diffidently satisfied his curiosity, whereupon he was waved on his way. This trifling incident completely upset a nervous Shostakovich's equilibrium.

Wishing to entertain me in style, Shostakovich took me to dinner in a private room at the Aragvi restaurant, which I had never been to before. Before we set out, my solicitous host enquired slyly of me whether I knew what 'tobacco-chicken' was. I replied that I knew what a chicken was and I knew what tobacco was. Shostakovich laughed kindly and said: 'Now you are going to find out what happens when they are put together. You don't get dishes like this in Leningrad. It will be a gastronomic novelty for you.' Where food was concerned, Shostakovich knew what he was talking about, although often enough he was content with a piece of bread and sausage.

45 Before the war, Shostakovich used to buy two season tickets for the games at the Lenin Stadium, one of which was for my use. The next seat along from us in the central stand was, as I have already related, occupied by the artist and

boxing referee Vladimir Lebedev. After the war, I rather lost interest in football; Shostakovich was aware of this and probably because of this left open the delicate question of who the second season ticket was intended for.

46 At the time Leonid Trauberg, co-producer with Grigory Kozintsev of the *Maksim* film trilogy, had been accused of 'cosmopolitanism' and had in consequence been dismissed from the Lenfilm studios, so was living in conditions of great poverty. He had written the libretto for an operetta entitled *Sparks* [subtitled *The Zanarva Pickets* – Translator's note], a live theatre version of the film scenario of *The Youth of Maksim*. He approached Shostakovich to ask him if he would write the music. Out of sympathy for Trauberg's plight Shostakovich formally agreed in order to smooth the way for Trauberg to secure a contract for his libretto with the Leningrad Musical Comedy Theatre. The ploy worked, and Shostakovich's agreement played an important role in the libretto's acceptance. But once he had helped Trauberg in this way, Shostakovich never had any real intention of actually writing the music for this operetta, and suggested to Sviridov that he should undertake the commission. This he did, with his distinctive talents, and the première took place with great success at the Musical Comedy Theatre. At Shostakovich's request, I acted as intermediary in the discussions between Trauberg and Sviridov.

47 The involuntarily assumed obligation proved to be a heavier burden on Shostakovich than he had intended. Having apparently achieved his goal of a creative association with the great composer, Trauberg exerted considerable pressure on him, so that when Sviridov agreed to write the music for *Sparks* Shostakovich was only too happy to relinquish the task. Trauberg, however, took offence, evidently not valuing Shostakovich's magnanimous gesture for what it was.

48 In ordinary affairs, in contrast to artistic matters, Shostakovich was hardly a model of organization. On 3 April he had specifically wanted season tickets, and had sent me the money for them. Now he was quite ready to abandon the object he had, to all intents and purposes, secured.

49 The reference is to the song cycle *Land of the Fathers*, which had been the subject of savage criticism at the Union of Composers. Three years later, Shostakovich and I were both present in the Small Hall of the Leningrad Philharmonia for the première of this outstanding work. Shostakovich was enthralled by it, and I recall that he arranged a supper in the composer's honour in a room at the Yevropeyskaya Hotel afterwards.

50 For my reaction to the *Jewish Songs*. On 25 September 1950, I came to Moscow at Shostakovich's invitation to celebrate his birthday. I sat next to Samuil Marshak at the supper table, and in the intervals between toasts we exchanged extravagant compliments aimed at Shostakovich. The highlight of the evening was a performance in the composer's study of his song cycle *From Jewish Folk Poetry*. The singers were the soprano Nina Dorliak, the mezzo-soprano Tamara Yanko and the tenor Belugin. Shostakovich played the piano. Although the singers had not had time to put the final gloss on their interpretations, the effect was overwhelming. Marshak said to me with tears in

his eyes that the cycle was on a Shakespearean level, and that he felt he had been wrong in his criticisms of the translations, since the music had inspired and raised the texts of the songs to great heights. Many years were to pass before these songs received their first public performance, in the Small Hall of the Leningrad Philharmonia.

51 Aleksandr Anisimov, a chorus master by profession, held the position of Deputy Chairman of the Committee for Cultural Affairs.

52 Isai Sherman was a conductor at the Maly and Kirov Opera Theatres, and also taught at the Leningrad Conservatoire. Problems at work had forced him to leave Leningrad, and I asked Shostakovich to do what he could to help a distinguished musician who had conducted the première of Prokofiev's *Romeo and Juliet* at the Kirov Theatre. As can be seen from the letter, Dmitry Dmitriyevich responded immediately to my request.

53 I saw a good deal of Shostakovich at Komarovo where he had rented a dacha during the summer of 1950, so there was no need for correspondence. He had recently attended the celebrations in Leipzig commemorating the two hundredth anniversary of the death of Bach, and was still very much under Bach's spell. He talked endlessly to me of his love for Bach as a rare human being, a phenomenal craftsman – Shostakovich insisted on this – and musician of genius. Shostakovich's admiration had also been fired by the pianist Tatyana Nikolayeva, who had brilliantly performed the cycle of Bach's Preludes and Fugues at the celebrations. This was the genesis of Shostakovich's own conception of a set of twenty-four preludes and fugues, on which he worked in the summer of 1950.

54 Shostakovich continued to work on the Preludes and Fugues, a composition to which he attached great importance. In parallel to them he was writing the cycle *Ten Poems on Texts by Revolutionary Poets*.

55 The 'choice' had been made by Vera Vasiliyevna Antonova, a singer who had graduated from the Leningrad Conservatoire in 1949.

56 Shostakovich makes a typically understated announcement of the completion of this enormous cycle.

57 After Walt Whitman. (Translator's Note)

58 This wonderful work, shot through with dramatic power and fiery protest against all forms of tyranny, rang out at the beginning of the 1950s an acutely contemporary message. Shostakovich here gives a strictly formal description of the work, merely listing the names of the authors.

59 The letter is wrongly dated: it should have been 4 April.

60 Shostakovich always presented his compositions to the judgement of his colleagues at the Union of Composers, patiently listening – invariably in silence – to whatever criticisms were levelled at them, even the most patently unjust.

61 With the Beethoven Quartet.

62 Shostakovich had been appointed a Deputy of the RSFSR Supreme Soviet in February 1951.

63 The joke depends on the fact that the Russian word for tonsils is 'glands'. (Translator's Note)

64 Shostakovich's sense of humour never deserted him, even when later in life he became seriously ill. Although he tended to view his own state of health alternately through the prism of light and shade, stoicism usually prevailed over the terrors he so often made light of.

65 My wife and I had moved to a new apartment on what was then Stalin Prospect, formerly known as International Prospect and today as Moscow Prospect, near the Fontanka river.

66 Even in dread of the forthcoming operation, the after-effects of which he describes in such gruesome detail, Shostakovich can take pleasure in looking forward to seeing my new abode. His moods were always volatile: sadness would quickly be followed by a bright smile.

67 Shostakovich usually set out the dates of his travel plans firmly and unequivocally, eschewing any such Tolstoyan qualification as 'd.v.' – 'God willing'.

68 Normally Shostakovich was quite equable about such things, but July 1951 was exceptionally hot in Moscow and he must have felt very frustrated cooped up in hospital 'feeling perfectly well' with such sultry weather outside.

69 In the middle of July, my wife and I went for a month to Anapa and Shostakovich wanted to know what life was like there.

70 I had not suggested this, but Shostakovich generously wanted me to break the journey back from Anapa in Moscow at his apartment.

71 Shostakovich left with Lev Atovmyan a special ticket requisition form for Deputies of the RSFSR Supreme Soviet, which Shostakovich was.

72 I returned to Leningrad in the middle of July. My wife and I had been given a hearty welcome in Moscow by the Shostakoviches' housekeeper Fenya, a wonderful person who adored Shostakovich and consequently would do anything for his friends.

73 It was some time before I saw Shostakovich again, as a result of the angina which I had suffered in Anapa.

74 My brother, the sculptor, was having difficulty in finding a studio for his work.

75 Shostakovich usually wrote to me on the eve of his birthday or on the day itself, whenever I could not go to Moscow to join in the celebrations. Depending on circumstances, these could be very modest affairs, but sometimes quite elaborate, with a large guest list.

76 Aleksandr Svyeshnikov, chorus master. Shostakovich's *Ten Poems* were premièred under his direction on 10 October 1951 in the Great Hall of the Moscow Conservatoire.

77 The anniversary of the October Revolution. (Translator's Note)

78 Shostakovich admired my brother's painting and sculpture. He particularly liked the bust of Beethoven that my brother had presented to him and that he kept in his study.

79 Generally, Shostakovich did not like contrived or elaborate titles for musical compositions.

80 A white freshwater fish of the salmon family. (Translator's Note)

81 Shostakovich was not an especially fussy eater, generally being happy with whatever God sent him, but he did have some favourite foods. He was partial

to pelmeny [a kind of stuffed ravioli filled with meat – Translator's Note] which his mother Sofia Vasiliyevna made to perfection, smoked sigi and eel. On his frequent trips to Leningrad, if he was in the mood he would always buy smoked sigi. They were plentiful in Leningrad, but a rarity in Moscow.

As can be seen, Shostakovich could be pedantic in the way in which he wanted things done, for instance defining the precise time at which the fish should be bought. Whenever he decided to involve himself in any undertaking, large or small, there was no such thing as a trifle, so all details had to be fully explained.

82 Specifying the hour at which dinner would be served was not incidental. Shostakovich would allow fifteen or twenty minutes' grace, after which the table would be spread and proceedings begin. Guests who were seriously late had only themselves to blame.

83 The background to the summaries is as follows. The Union of Composers, concerned about Shostakovich's ideological development, decided in its wisdom to relieve him of the obligation to attend seminars and to afford him instead the opportunity of individual tuition in the works of Stalin: *Marxism and Questions of Linguistics*, also *Economic Problems of Socialism in the USSR*. These tomes were published in 1950 and 1952, and were assiduously pored over in every corner of the country, for at this time the cult of Stalin had reached dizzying proportions.

In order to help Shostakovich achieve deeper understanding of these works, a tutor was assigned to visit him at home in order to enlighten him about the revelations they contained. This was, needless to say, an act of great generosity on the part of the Union of Composers.

I happened to be staying with Shostakovich when he was awaiting, not without a certain nervousness, the arrival of his mentor. At the appointed hour the doorbell rang, and into the study came a man of venerable years who began by making a determined effort – so it seemed to me – to ingratiate himself with the new recruit to the cause. Conversation on general topics soon languished however, the weather not providing material for sustained discourse. There was a strong sense of tragi-comedy in the whole situation.

Shostakovich assumed an expression of deep seriousness and settled himself to absorb the insights and guidance of his uninvited guest. He in turn, all too evidently sensible of the importance of his mission, was flattered by the trust that had been reposed in him. The occasion drew from him his most eloquent and inspired phrases: Shostakovich was of course a famous composer, but his creative output still contained grievous ideological errors. In order to avoid any repetition of such errors, it was essential to raise the level of the composer's ideological comprehension, to which end he – the tutor – stood ready to assist in whatever way he could.

The visitor carefully surveyed the composer's study and praised its general arrangement, but then with an apologetic smile voiced his surprise that there was no portrait of Comrade Stalin to be seen on the walls. Time stood still. Shostakovich, embarrassed by the terrible solecism he had committed, began to pace nervously up and down the room, stammering something to the effect that he would immediately acquire a portrait of Comrade Stalin. (The promise was not fulfilled, if for no other reason than that before long portraits of Stalin had rather gone out of fashion.)

'Well, that's fine. Now, let's get down to business,' said the tutor, mollified by so evident a desire to please. As soon as the homily began, I judged that my presence was no longer required, and made my escape into the adjoining room.

When the visit was over, we discussed the situation. It seemed Shostakovich now had a duty to make periodic précis of the insights he had imbibed from Stalin's oeuvre, and submit them to the tutor. This was not a task that Shostakovich found very diverting so I promised, once I was back in Leningrad, to prepare and send him abstracts of the books in question, for 'critical assimilation', as the current jargon had it. Naturally I did as I had promised, and Dmitry Dmitriyevich was duly grateful.

But this was only the beginning. About a month later, in November 1952, there arose the further urgent necessity to study and summarize the pronouncements of G. M. Malenkov on 'The Characteristics of Creativity in Art', which had formed part of his address to the Nineteenth Party Congress. The arbiters of moral and cultural values had studied these pronouncements attentively, because obviously without a profound grasp of their significance there was no hope of creating a work of art that would be of any value.

Such was the story of the summaries that enlivened the year 1952.

84 As has been mentioned before, whenever Shostakovich made this somewhat defiant-sounding statement in one of his letters to me, it meant the opposite. A less well-informed reader would, of course, take it at face value.

85 Nina Vasiliyevna was an astrophysicist and participated in many scientific expeditions to Armenia which took her away from home for prolonged periods.

86 Shostakovich loved travel and always welcomed a change of scene. Curiously, this seemed to calm his nerves and give him peace of mind.

87 The trip was postponed until November.

88 As a Deputy of the Supreme Soviet of the RSFSR, Shostakovich had actively intervened in the matter of the award of the title 'Honoured Doctor of the RSFSR' to Dr V. A. Tarasov. Tarasov worked alongside me in the Maly Opera Theatre; he had survived the whole of the blockade of Leningrad and had been severely wounded. I was anxious that he should receive this honour. However the Leningrad Department of Health turned down Shostakovich's petition, and the letter referred to was their letter of rejection.

89 Shostakovich was extremely sensitive to nuances of discourtesy, because his own manners were impeccable, never permitting himself either bluff familiarity or obsequiousness.

90 Reminiscent of the solicitous exactitude with which Chekhov used to advise his correspondents how to address letters or telegrams to him at Melikhovo or Yalta.

91 Moysey (or Mieczyslav) Vainberg was well aware how concerned Shostakovich had been at his fate, and one of the first things he did on regaining his freedom was to let him know of his release.

92 From 1952 onwards, I took to spending my summer holidays at Komarovo. Shostakovich was deeply attached to the city of Leningrad and its surrounding countryside and often spent his summers at Komarovo. In 1947 he installed himself in a government-owned dacha, but when in 1950 he lost the privilege of renting this one, he took a property belonging to his father-in-law Vasily Varzar, who had built himself a two-storey wooden house near the railway station in a wide ravine – more of a precipice really – surrounded by a vast colony of straight-standing fir trees and pines. You could almost say that the piece of land on which the house stood had been reclaimed from the forest.

The house had no facilities at all, no bathroom or lavatory. The ever-resourceful Shostakovich would once or twice a week take the train to the city and go to his mother's apartment for a bath. Shostakovich and his family had the upper floor, consisting of three rooms and a small glassed-in verandah which did duty as his study. It contained a rough home-made table and some chairs. We would sit here and endlessly pour out our hearts in conversation – the 1950s were after all not short of incident, and there was always something pressing to talk about. Occasionally, visitors would come from Leningrad or Moscow. This verandah saw the composition of the first movement of the Tenth Symphony, and later the First Cello Concerto and many other works.

Shostakovich used to laugh as he told the story of how one morning a crow had flown into the room through an open window and in its fright had defecated all over the score of the Tenth Symphony, which happened to be lying on the table. My mother and Vera Vasiliyevna were convinced that the bird's indelicate surprise gift had ensured the new symphony's success. Shostakovich shook his head thoughtfully, then said with a smile: 'Please God you're right.'

The dacha that I rented every summer for seven years was about a kilometre away from Shostakovich's, and we met every day either at his house or mine, but more often at his. He liked to leave me to eat my supper on my own on the little verandah on the ground floor, next to the kitchen. At the end of August, the ravine was often cloaked in mist and would take on an unfamiliar air of hidden mystery. Shostakovich would accompany me up the hill to the road that led to my home.

In the 1950s the little hamlet was still a quiet, remote place that cars found difficult to get to, and the air was sweet and fresh. On the main street that led to the station, past the grocery store, there were kiosks selling beer and newspapers. Regularly, every morning, Shostakovich would walk up to buy the papers, and in the afternoons we would sip beer at the little round tables next to the blue kiosk. Such was life at Komarovo, where we were perfectly content with our summer quarters and not a whit disturbed by the total lack of creature comforts.

Shostakovich was at the time awaiting the premières, due to take place that winter, of two magnificent works which it had not been possible to perform in previous years because of the official block placed on them. These were the First Violin Concerto and the song cycle *From Jewish Folk Poetry*.

93 At one time there were rumours current in musical circles that Shostakovich

drank heavily. This was not the case; these rumours were the work of enemies and philistines. At the same time, I should make it clear that Shostakovich was no ascetic. He much enjoyed a glass or two in the company of friends.

94 Shostakovich liked to quote Chekhov, saying that wine taken in moderation 'gladdens the heart and stimulates the mind'.

95 I usually waited until after the annual round of examinations before moving up to Komarovo at the beginning of July, but Shostakovich wanted us to meet before then.

96 Shostakovich was extraordinarily scrupulous about money matters. If he ever had to borrow money, he repaid it at once and in full. In this case I had lent him a sum and there had been a small delay in my getting it back in Komarovo. It caused me no difficulties whatsoever, but Shostakovich was discomfited by it, feeling it necessary to apologize and explain the mistake for which he was in no way responsible.

97 Observation of Shostakovich over many years led me to the conclusion that he was philosophical about being on his own; solitude did not as a rule distress him unduly. In fact, he preferred the luxury of filling his time with reflection about music and many other things to being in the company of people in whom he was not particularly interested.

98 I sometimes became irritated with Shostakovich's journalistic activities, and when I told him frankly what I thought he did not disagree with me. Glib journalists would lay siege to him and, pretending not to want to trouble the famous composer, would badger him just to sign his name to articles they had already written and which most conveniently lay ready to hand on the table. Thus it sometimes happened that a piece of journalism would appear under Shostakovich's name when he had merely been anxious to get rid of an importunate hack.

99 It is hard to understand how the composer of the second movement of the Tenth Symphony could possibly be dissatisfied with it. Perhaps the only explanation for it would be 'divine dissatisfaction', for I have always considered this scintillating, menacing, whirlwind scherzo to be one of the unquestionable masterpieces of Shostakovich's symphonic output.

100 The composer Galina Ustvolskaya. She had been a student in Shostakovich's class at the Leningrad Conservatoire.

Chapter III Thaw, 1954-1959

1 I had written to Shostakovich about his Fifth Quartet and about the performance I had recently heard of the Tenth Symphony by the Leningrad Philharmonic Orchestra conducted by Mravinsky.

2 Kozma Prutkov was a fictitious writer concocted by the Zhemchuzhnikov brothers and A. K. Tolstoy. Prutkov, whose 'collected works' appeared in 1884, is a Pooterish government clerk turned Sunday writer, given to sententious platitudes which often neatly parody contemporary poetry. (Translator's Note)

3 Malicious whisperings about the Tenth Symphony had reached Shostakovich's

ears, and no doubt my enthusiastic reaction to this wonderful work was genuinely welcome moral support.

Before receiving this letter I had had an opportunity to express my admiration for the new work publicly. This was at a dinner in a private room at the Yevropeyskaya Hotel arranged by Shostakovich after the première of the Tenth Symphony on 17 December 1953. Aram Khachaturian, who was also present, enthusiastically seconded my toast. But within a few months, during the spring of 1954, a critical battle was raging over the symphony, and Shostakovich took it badly. Pessimism, gloom, hysteria, formalism – the malicious defenders of orthodoxy dug out all their old destructive flag-waving phrases to brand the new symphony as suffering from mortal sins. The 'depravity' of the new symphony was compared unfavourably with the optimistic tone of *The Song of the Forests*, a work Shostakovich had little time for. As criticism this sort of thing was, of course, nothing but a bad joke.

4 Shostakovich had been throwing himself with tremendous energy into the rehabilitation of people he knew who had been sentenced on trumped-up charges to exile and the camps. To his immense satisfaction his efforts had met with success. Shostakovich's sympathy for the sufferings of these innocent victims and his tireless representations on their behalf is one of the most luminous pages in his biography.

5 The discussion was of the Tenth Symphony. In 1936 and 1948, while Shostakovich was being subjected to savage criticism as a 'formalist' composer producing 'music hostile to the people', it would have impossible for any of his colleagues to rise to his defence. But in spring 1954, when the Tenth Symphony was being evaluated, it found strong support from Aram Khachaturian and many other leading musicians. Times had changed, and for the better. However, the opera *Lady Macbeth of Mtsensk* (*Katerina Izmailova*), anathematized in 1936, was still on the proscribed list.

6 The Tenth Symphony had been nominated for a Stalin Prize, but the Music Section of the Prize Committee had rejected it.

7 This letter, unlike Shostakovich's usual practice, bears an exclamation mark after the salutation. I took this as a sign of emotion, brought on by the 'disagreeable' circumstances to which he refers in the letter.

8 The Russian custom is for the body to lie before interment for a period of time in an open coffin in order that relations, friends and colleagues may take their leave, and this can take place at the home, or place of work, or anywhere associated with the deceased. (Translator's Note)

9 This letter was written on a letterhead from the 1952 Congress for Peace in Vienna, which Shostakovich had attended as a delegate.

10 For several years, Shostakovich spent periods of time at a dacha in Bolshevo which had been allocated to him by the State. It was a small, brick-built house on a tiny, rather bare piece of ground; I went there several times. Later, Shostakovich gave up this perquisite and acquired his own dacha at Zhukovka, though this purchase involved him in enormous financial problems.

11 The Russian word means 'peasant', but with distinct overtones of 'clod' or 'bumpkin'. (Translator's Note)

12 Georgy Doniyakh was the Chief Conductor of the Maly Opera Theatre, and would have been the conductor of *Lady Macbeth* had it been produced at the time.

13 'Malegot' is an acronym for MAly [literally 'small' – as opposed to Bolshoy, meaning 'big' – Translator's Note] LEningradsky Gosudarstvenny Operny Teatr (State Opera Theatre). Also known simply as the Maly Opera, the company had been in existence for several decades. Shostakovich believed that *Lady Macbeth* was to be staged there during the 1955–6 season, as had been decided by the theatre's Artistic Directorate at a meeting on 19 March. However, in the event the promised première had to wait another ten years, until 1965.

14 Shostakovich was planning a concert tour at the end of March 1955.

15 On 31 March Shostakovich and I went together to the Maly Opera to see the recently revived production of *War and Peace* in a composite version consisting of eleven scenes. The conductor was E. P. Grikurov. Nine years earlier, in 1946, in the same theatre, Shostakovich had seen Part One of the opera, consisting of eight scenes, in a production conducted by Samuil Samosud. Part Two of the opera, which had been scheduled for production in 1947, was withdrawn from the repertoire and never produced, owing to the viciousness of the attacks to which it was subjected.

During this performance in March 1955, Shostakovich several times remarked: 'What a marvellous gift for melody Prokofiev had!' Generally he approved very much of this opera, although he was less enthusiastic about the Fili and Napoleon scenes.

16 On 15 April, in his mother's apartment on Dmitrovsky Pereulok, I showed Shostakovich the amendments I had made to the text of *Lady Macbeth of Mtsensk*. I had gone over all four acts, and while I was doing so never ceased to wonder at how complete had been the young composer's understanding of, and power to express, the barbarous cruelty of life, and the unquenchable longing for happiness that led the unpretentious young merchant's wife to moral degradation and to tragic greatness.

Shostakovich eagerly leafed through the piano score, his eyes burning as they devoured what I had written. He said: 'I am excited and agitated to see again this opera that I know so well.' He was pleased with my textual amendments, and commented: 'What you have done is very good. Thank you.'

17 That is, in 1933, when Shostakovich was preparing *Lady Macbeth* for its production in the Maly Opera Theatre.

18 We both spent the summer of 1955 in Komarovo, meeting every day, and sometimes more than once a day. In many of our conversations we returned to the theme of the new opera that Shostakovich wanted to write. He was thinking of Shakespeare, whose plays interested and attracted, but at the same time perplexed him. He used to say: 'Couldn't you help me find something from Shakespeare?'

19 Shostakovich knew that plans were afoot to cut staff in the opera faculty at the Conservatoire, in which I was a senior lecturer, and that these plans might affect my teaching career.

20 Moscow's oldest concert hall, built at the end of the eighteenth century and known before the Revolution as the Hall of the Nobility. (Translator's Note)

21 Shostakovich had been friendly with Aleksandr Gauk for many years (they addressed one another in the intimate style). Gauk had given the first performances of the Third Symphony, the ballet *The Golden Age* and many other works by Shostakovich, who admired him for his professionalism and his wide knowledge of the orchestral repertoire. However, he sometimes had doubts about Gauk's purely artistic gifts. These doubts were never expressed to anyone outside a close circle of friends, but especially in Sollertinsky's presence he could refer caustically to one or other of the conductor's more bizarre pronouncements that proclaimed his naïvety or intellectual limitations. Shostakovich was also critical of Gauk's reading of various works. But as I have said, such things were said only in private and among friends.

As for the Ninth Symphony, a particular favourite of Shostakovich, it is well known to demand a refinement and detailed understanding of its nuances that were simply beyond Gauk's powers to penetrate. As Shostakovich says, he could manage the first, third and fourth movements, but the second and fifth disappointed the composer. I well remember how in this deeply enigmatic work even Mravinsky could fall short in some respects: in the autumn of 1945, when the Ninth Symphony was being rehearsed in the Leningrad Philharmonia, the composer whispered to me that 'Mravinsky was getting lost in the fog'. His inner ear never let the slightest thing pass. At the first performance itself, however, everything was in place.

Shostakovich's irritable comments about Gauk were evidently made in the heat of the moment, and did not truly reflect Shostakovich's feelings towards the esteemed conductor.

22 In conversation with Shostakovich, inadequate as my powers were, musically speaking, I often found myself defending Gauk's conducting.

23 The première of the First Violin Concerto was scheduled for October 1955.

24 Shostakovich was not particularly fond of his dacha at Bolshevo. It was in a poor area on a tiny, bare patch of land, and therefore he only went there occasionally.

25 I had asked Shostakovich to send a copy of the Concertino for Two Pianos to R. M. Dolgoviner, a teacher of piano, which he did with a personal note on the score.

26 I. K. Nikolayeva was the Director of the Leningrad branch of Muzgiz [Muzïkalnoe Gosudarstvennoe Izdatelstvo, the State Music Publishing House – Translator's Note], and O. P. Kolovsky the Senior Editor. They had approached Shostakovich asking him to contribute an introduction to the collection of Sollertinsky's articles they were preparing for publication under the title *Studies in Music and History*, compiled and edited by Mikhail Druskin. Shostakovich wanted very much to write an article about his friend, and asked for my help in this task. I naturally agreed, and Shostakovich later acknowledged the help I gave him in a telegram which I appear to have lost. The book appeared at the end of 1956, complete with Shostakovich's introduction.

27 Telephone conversations with Shostakovich were usually extremely brief. I used to joke that his laconic style would have been the envy of Julius Caesar.

28 As mentioned earlier, the director of the Maly Opera, Boris Zagursky, was in the process of seeking permission from the authorities to stage a production of *Lady Macbeth* (*Katerina Izmailova*). Without such permission, the disgraced opera could not be put on the stage, and with this in mind he had been urging Shostakovich to make a personal approach to Vyacheslav Molotov, the First Deputy President of the USSR Council of Ministers.

Shostakovich did as he was asked, albeit with great reluctance, because he had the strongest aversion to being forced into pursuing his own interests or to push himself forward, especially with people of power and influence. His meeting with Molotov resulted in the politician's ordering a committee to be set up and charged with examining the revised version of *Lady Macbeth*.

29 N. A. Mikhailov was at that time Minister of Culture of the USSR.

30 Dmitry Kabalevsky, as a member of the Collegium of the Ministry of Culture of the USSR, was appointed chairman of this committee, the other members of which were the composer Mikhail Chulaki, the musicologist Georgy Khubov, and Vasily Tselikovsky, a conductor who was head of the Lyric Theatres Department of the Ministry of Culture. Also invited from Leningrad to attend the committee meeting were Zagursky, Georgy Doniyakh – the Chief Conductor of the Maly Opera – and myself, as the person responsible for the revised text of the opera.

Shostakovich was much concerned about the proposed review of *Lady Macbeth*. He asked me to come to Moscow at the beginning of February 1956 to talk through the procedure, and while I was there to attend the Moscow première of the First Violin Concerto performed by David Oistrakh – which had a huge success.

At length, on 11 or 12 March, the *Lady Macbeth* audition duly took place, the Ministry of Culture having taken approximately three months to organize the event. This delay was no accident; I am sure that the eventual outcome was already a foregone conclusion.

It was probably Kabalevsky who suggested that as a mark of respect to the celebrated composer, the meeting should convene not in the Ministry of Culture or the Union of Composers, but at Shostakovich's own apartment, No. 87 in 37–45 Mozhaiskoye Shosse. The committee assembled in Shostakovich's study at the appointed hour, a little after noon. Cordial greetings were exchanged with the host; there was, as far as I could detect, no indication whatever that the whole enterprise was doomed from the start.

Shostakovich was excessively nervous. He had prepared and now handed round typed copies of the revised version of the libretto. He wanted to make sure that this new version of *Katerina Izmailova*, both music and words, should be regarded as definitive, and that henceforward there would be no reversion to the original version. Some time afterwards, in order that conductors and producers should be in no possible doubt about this, he specifically added a note to that effect to the title page of the score of *Katerina Izmailova*.

The new texts being distributed, Shostakovich sat down at the piano and played right through the opera, superbly. There followed a short pause, during which the members of the committee composed themselves into attitudes of aloof severity. Then the discussion began.

The opera was savagely criticized, in terms recalling the notorious 'Muddle instead of Music' article in *Pravda*. Zagursky and Doniyakh, appalled by the tenor of the discussion, kept silent as the grave. Shostakovich sat alone on the big sofa, listening to his work being judged, shrinking back into its broad back as if seeking support there (this sofa is still in the study of his apartment in Nezhdanova Street). Eyes closed, he simply could not bear to look at his colleagues vying with one other to condemn his work. From time to time a grimace of pain crossed his face.

To the evident displeasure of the committee, I raised my voice on two occasions. I spoke, in some agitation and heat, of the need to have no more delay in staging this great opera, twenty years after its music had been dismissed as 'muddle'. Khubov tried to wear me down, continually interrupting me with shrill interjections; he did not succeed, although for all the good it did, mine was a voice crying in the wilderness.

The committee's unanimous resolution was not to recommend a new production of *Lady Macbeth* on the grounds of its serious ideological and artistic defects.

On 14 March I left Moscow and went home, still unable to come to terms with this second execution of *Lady Macbeth*, this time at the hands of trained musicians. Before my memory had time to cool, I wrote a short account of what had transpired at this memorable gathering, details of which are, in all probability, unknown to biographers of Shostakovich. I take the liberty of reproducing my note here, although I have moderated here and there some of the language which flowed in fury from my pen. I have also made one or two cuts in what I wrote at the time.

> The discussion of *Lady Macbeth* can only be described as shameful. Khubov, Kabalevsky and Chulaki kept harking back to the 'Muddle instead of Music' article, Khubov and Kabalevsky displaying particularly fanatical zeal. They picked out specific passages from the opera and tied them to abusive paragraphs from the article, repeating over and over again that since nobody had yet revoked the article it must still retain its authority and significance. (And how! After all, where else could we have derived the information that the music of the opera 'crashes, quacks, pants and gasps'?)
>
> Kabalevsky praised some parts of the opera, and this was probably the most disagreeable aspect of his remarks. Summing up as chairman of the committee, he said that the opera could not be staged since it constituted an apologia for a debauched murderess, something found offensive. I spoke up for it with as much conviction as I could, but all my arguments ran into the sand against the famous article, which Kabalevsky and Khubov kept waving about like a truncheon.
>
> At the end of the debate, Kabalevsky, addressing the composer as Mitya

in affectionate intimacy, invited Shostakovich to have his say, but he declined to speak and with astounding self-control thanked his colleagues 'for their criticisms'. He must have felt as though cats were sharpening their claws on his soul. He and I left the apartment together, went to a restaurant and got royally drunk, more from disgust than from despair. We were by ourselves in a private room in the 'Aragvi' restaurant, and when Shostakovich got up from the table he came over to me and said: 'You are my first, most loyal and dearest friend. Thank you.' He was referring of course to the stand I had taken at the meeting earlier in the day.

31 I naturally did what I did from friendship, but in any case under no circumstances could I have refrained from speaking up in defence of *Lady Macbeth* when it was under attack. To act in any other way would have been to do violence to my conscience and my duty. I have always loved this wonderful opera, and still do.

32 I never worked out which notes Shostakovich was referring to.

33 A reference to the well-known fable by Ivan Krïlov. (Translator's Note)

34 Shostakovich's secretary did quite often send me, at his request, various writings of his that needed editing.

35 Ilyin's article dealt with the return to Moscow from the USA after thirty-eight years of the seventy-four-year-old painter and writer David Burlyuk and his wife Mariya. According to the article, Burlyuk was ecstatic about the number of shops in the capital, about the riot of colour in the First of May parades, and especially about the reconstruction in the centre of Moscow. 'So many buildings! All so magnificently done!' It amused Shostakovich that Burlyuk, evidently insane with rapture, had completely lost sight of the wealth of architectural treasures that had been ripped out of Moscow during the past forty years – churches, cathedrals, houses – and that he was now so impressed with the pretentious character of the Stalinist architecture that had disfigured the unique beauty of old Moscow.

36 A typically kindly gesture from Shostakovich on learning that among my neighbours was a little boy who was passionate about collecting stamps.

37 The young collector had been misbehaving himself, and I had asked Shostakovich not to trouble sending any more stamps. He took no notice and continued to send them.

38 'Egyptologist' because, to Shostakovich's amusement, I had become interested in events in Egypt following the overthrow of the King.

39 Shostakovich was using his influence to try to get me appointed to the permanent staff of the Leningrad Conservatoire; at the time I was being paid an hourly rate for the classes I was teaching.

40 Preparations were afoot in Moscow for Shostakovich's birthday, which he was anticipating with a mixture of boredom, depression and irritation. He was already dreading the flood of congratulatory speeches, awash with hypocritical insincerity. As he confided to me when I came to Moscow the day before his birthday, he knew that the very people who had tormented him would throng to kiss him, contorting their features into a mask of devoted

admiration. The celebration took place on the evening of 24 September in the Hall of the Conservatoire. Shostakovich sat on the stage surrounded by bouquets of flowers, his face resembling that of a man condemned to death by verbal assault. He did his best to look interested while speaker after speaker droned on with addresses which were, to him, devoid of interest or value. At the conclusion of each peroration the orator attempted to kiss the hero, but I observed the dexterity with which, apparently accidentally, he contrived to elbow away all those who particularly repelled him. Needless to say, there were also some speakers who genuinely loved and honoured Shostakovich as man and composer.

The following morning, Dmitry Dmitriyevich seemed miserable and discomfited by the mountain of useless and boring souvenirs with which he had been presented. Drinking tea, we resolved not to speak of the previous evening even though nothing actually bad had happened.

The next day, 25 September, Shostakovich had an intimate gathering at home for friends, and here he felt happy and at ease. Finally, the next evening, he hosted a banquet for a hundred and forty people at the 'Praga' restaurant; again, there were no official guests and the atmosphere was relaxed and informal.

41 Mikhail Vaiman was, after David Oistrakh, one of the greatest interpreters of Shostakovich's First Violin Concerto.

42 These concerts in the Small Hall of the Leningrad Philharmonia were an enormous success. When Shostakovich appeared on stage, the ecstatic audience erupted in a sustained ovation.

43 I did not write to Shostakovich for two months, probably because we had seen one another in January and February in Leningrad.

44 Shostakovich attached great importance to his plans for the Eleventh Symphony. He felt that its programme was timely and to the point. He came to Leningrad on 10 January and told me that he had begun work on a symphony with the theme of 1905, and significantly added (verbatim): 'No, it won't be anything like *The Song of The Forests*!' On 24 February he told me that he had written the first movement, or 'more accurately the introduction to the new symphony' (his words). This wonderful work received its première in Moscow under the direction of Natan Rakhlin on 30 October 1957. Shostakovich told me with pride that he had completed the work within the timescale he had privately imposed on himself.

45 Shostakovich knew better than anyone the power of melody in music, but whenever the words 'melodious' or 'melodiousness' crossed his lips, it was with an expression of amused contempt, since they had been so completely devalued and corrupted by Zhdanov and his adherents. The same applied to 'graceful'.

46 Shostakovich hoped that, four years after Stalin's death, Zhdanov's dogmas on the proper way to compose music would have been consigned to history, but evidently this was not the case and he listened with revulsion to the speeches of Comrade Lukin and others like him at the Composers' Congress.

47 There was talk of reviving *Lady Macbeth* at the Kirov Theatre, and I was

present when Shostakovich played the opera right through, magnificently, to the assembled company. But the notion of mounting a production collapsed, since the Leningrad authorities would not approve it.

48 Kurt Sanderling, at that time a conductor with the Leningrad Philharmonia, later returned to his homeland in the German Democratic Republic.

49 The reference is to the Second Symphony of Boris Klyuzner, in whose music Shostakovich had become interested.

50 Shostakovich's much-loved housekeepers, who took turns to look after the household.

51 Gallows humour on the subject of death, which tended to preoccupy Shostakovich at times when he was emotionally upset or excessively tired.

52 Shostakovich did not always take this line with the enemies who surrounded him. He often said to me that 'ordinary' people who had done him harm 'knew not what they did' and therefore deserved Christian forgiveness. In the heat of the Eleventh Symphony's composition, he laid his curses on the aggressors not only of history (1905) but of the immediate past.

53 The Anniversary Committee of the Leningrad Philharmonia was preparing to honour those musicians who had served in the Leningrad Philharmonic Orchestra for twenty-five years, and had asked Shostakovich to take part in the ceremony, which was due to take place on 28 April.

54 The name was that of the violinist T. N. Yerishe, whose name on the invitation had been rather carelessly handwritten.

55 Boris Shalman was the Philharmonia's chief librarian and well known to Shostakovich. He had made copies of Shostakovich's scores with great care and fidelity.

56 The RHD had decided 'in the interests of consolidating tenants' to repossess one of the two rooms my mother Fanya Borisovna occupied with her grown-up granddaughter. Shostakovich took the disaster that threatened to overtake my mother very much to heart.

57 Shostakovich, concerned about my mother's fate, had sent a formal Deputy's Enquiry to Leningrad in his capacity as a Deputy of the Supreme Soviet of the RSFSR. However, sceptical as to the effective authority this would command, he also recommended applying to someone he thought would be more influential than himself, the Director of the Small Hall of the Philharmonia. Shostakovich had an objective and exceptionally penetrating understanding of the true workings of the administrative machine.

58 Yevgeniya Shneyerson, a close friend of Shostakovich and the artistic director of the Small Hall.

59 Shostakovich's sister.

60 Mikhail Meyerovich, composer and an excellent pianist. Shostakovich planned to play through the Eleventh Symphony, which he had finished in August, in Leningrad.

61 Shostakovich was in the habit of sending me newspaper clippings that had aroused his ire, but he generally couched his reaction to them in terms of ironic praise, knowing that I would immediately interpret his true meaning. The article in question was published over the signature of one 'Literator' in the

Literary Gazette, which was at that time edited by V. A. Kochetov. Its purpose was to savage a story by Daniil Granin called 'The Echoing Mist'. A practised exponent of the teeth-grinding critical style of the Stalin era, 'Literator' weighed into the unfortunate D. A. Granin with a familiar litany of accusations: decadence, petty bourgeois vulgarity, and other heinous crimes. The crowning thrust amounted to a political denunciation of the *Leningrad Almanac* for having dared to publish the story in its November issue, especially as it was an issue 'dedicated to the fortieth anniversary of the Great October Socialist Revolution. A nice present!'

62 Mikhalkov's fable appalled Shostakovich with its threadbare banality. But not long ago this same Mikhalkov had done something far worse than committing even the worst stylistic solecisms. In his 1949 play *Ilya Golovin*, Mikhalkov had overtly entered the service of the Zhdanovite persecutors who were carrying out a pogrom of great musicians, first and foremost Prokofiev and Shostakovich.

63 Ivan Barkov, eighteenth-century poet, translator and author of many scabrous verses.

64 The death of the football star G. I. Fedotov. The use of 'my dear friend' in addition to the usual name and patronymic indicates that Shostakovich was impelled to share with me something about which he felt very deeply.

65 Director of the Music Department of the USSR Ministry of Culture, whom Shostakovich knew well.

66 My wife was a singer employed by the Concert Bureau of the Leningrad Philharmonia and had applied to have her concert fee upgraded.

67 From his earliest years Shostakovich enjoyed touring; the road held an irresistible attraction for him. Hardly ever did he complain about awful hotels or grubby railway carriages; he considered all such inconveniences to be an inevitable part of travel. Whenever he visited a town or city anywhere in the country, musicians well known and not so well known vied with one another to meet him. This was often a burden, however much he forced himself not to show it, and occasionally the politeness of his good manners had a strained air about it.

68 Natan Rakhlin, an outstanding conductor. On 30 October 1957 he had directed the first performance of Shostakovich's Eleventh Symphony in Moscow. Typically, Shostakovich makes no mention whatsoever of the success the concerts on this tour enjoyed, not even the performances of the piano concerto in which he was the soloist. Perhaps there would have been little point in telling me about a triumph in Kiev or Odessa, since he was already well known in those cities, but he does not even talk about it in Kishinyov or Lvov. It always seemed to him unnecessary and even indecent to tell me about his successes, but in the unlikely event of a concert going badly, I would be sure to hear about it immediately.

69 Abram Stasevich. Subsequently Shostakovich revised his opinion of this conductor upwards.

70 Arseny Kotlyarevsky.

71 Vera Bakeyeva.

72 Aleksandr Borovsky, a celebrated pianist.

73 Georgy Maiboroda, whose *Milana* was staged in Kiev in 1957.

74 Shostakovich had great admiration for the orchestra and singers of the Kiev opera, and especially its conductor Konstantin Simeonov, but was less enthusiastic about the composers who wrote works for it.

75 At the première of the Eleventh Symphony on 30 October, which was conducted by Rakhlin, Shostakovich had been critical of what he saw as a number of failings. These criticisms were, however, confined to a very narrow circle of intimates.

76 After the shortest possible break following an exhausting tour of the Ukraine, Shostakovich was off again on a tour of Bulgaria in which he was to appear as soloist in his Second Piano Concerto.

77 The paragraph parodies the typical newspaper reports of the day.

78 The 'iconostasis' of monstrously large portraits of Politburo members, which were displayed year in, year out before the May and October holidays in towns and cities up and down the country so that the public could feast their eyes and marvel at them, always provoked a reaction from Shostakovich. 'What is it all for, and in whose name is it done?' he used to ask. Even the death of Stalin failed to put an end to these crass displays of official propaganda. The 'iconostasis' was constantly renewed, in that as one individual political nonentity disappeared from view, he would be replaced by another equally unknown.

   Shostakovich lists all the *nomenklatura*'s names in alphabetical order, including with deliberate and comic pedantry their full initials. [In fact, they are not quite listed in the order of either the Russian or the English alphabet – Translator's Note.]

79 Richard Taruskin has illuminatingly pointed out the Tweedledum–Tweedledee joke of transposing Kirilenko and Kirichenko, presenting the two Ukrainian apparatchiks as clones of one another like the Dobchinsky – Bobchinsky bureaucrats in Gogol's *The Inspector-General*. Taruskin, R., 'Shostakovich and Us' in *Shostakovich In Context*, ed. Rosamund Bartlett, Oxford, 2000 – Translator's Note.

80 On 11 January; Shostakovich never failed to wish me happy returns of the day.

81 The German writer Leonhard Frank's novel *Die Jünger Jesu* was published in 1949, while he was still living in the USA, having fled from Nazi Germany during the war. He returned to Germany in 1950 and lived and worked there until his death in 1961. (Translator's Note)

82 Shostakovich read widely and discriminatingly both Russian and foreign classics, and also kept up with contemporary literature. He frequently recommended newly published works by a variety of authors, knowing that my taste was likely to accord with his. This case was no exception: I read the novel and was deeply engaged by it.

83 Early in 1958 a collection of essays and articles by the remarkable Leningrad critic and writer on music, Aleksandr Rabinovich, the late brother of my dear friend the conductor Nikolai Rabinovich, was being prepared for publication. Shostakovich agreed to write an introduction to the collection (published as

Selected Articles and Materials, Moscow, 1959) and asked me to help him in this task. I agreed with alacrity, and in the middle of March sent him a piece I had written about Rabinovich, for whom I had great affection. Rabinovich died at the early age of forty-three in 1943.

84 Izrail Gusman from Gorky loved and admired Shostakovich's music, but did not escape being awarded the ironic epithet 'creative' for the self-indulgent way in which in his account of the symphony he strove to demonstrate his special affinity with it.

85 The problem eventually passed off, but as it turned out not without after-effects.

86 In the spring of 1958 a cornucopia of honours cascaded on to Shostakovich. He was awarded the Lenin Prize on 22 April, and on 12 May, in Italy, membership of the Accademia di Santa Cecilia. On 30 May, in Paris, he became a Commandeur de l'Ordre des arts et lettres. From the lack of information he gave me about these events in his letters, it can be correctly inferred that Shostakovich attached little importance to them; he was the least ambitious of men in worldly terms. (Whenever he spoke of honours, he would often quote from Ecclesiastes: 'all is vanity and vexation of spirit'.) He had little taste for these foreign trips to receive honours.

87 A favourite occupation, inherited from his mother Sofia Vasiliyevna.

88 It is revealing that the only reference to a trip full of honours done to Shostakovich in the grandest and most prestigious of circumstances is a remark about the difficulty and exhaustion undergone. Any other person would have derived at least some measure of enjoyment and satisfaction from such glory, but to Shostakovich all the pomp and display was merely so much 'vanity and vexation of spirit', as he said to me when we met.

89 Barely three weeks after returning from the journey to Italy and France, Shostakovich was due to fly to England, once again to receive an honour. But this time it gave him much pleasure, and not only because he became a doctor *honoris causae* of Oxford University, a distinction he valued highly in itself. It was also because he was much taken with Oxford's traditions and customs that had existed since time immemorial. Smiling, he showed me the ceremonial doctor's gown in which he had been robed. He said: 'Yes, in England they know how to preserve their ancient traditions, which is something one cannot say about our country.'

90 Margarita Andreyevna Kainova, Shostakovich's second wife, to whom he was married for three years from 1956 until 1959.

91 A slip of the pen. Shostakovich meant 14 July.

92 Shostakovich sometimes stayed at his sister Mariya's apartment when he came to Leningrad for a short visit. He was punctilious about observing the niceties of social intercourse, never neglecting to issue proper invitations for all occasions, large or small, to even the most modest of which he attached great importance. This accounts for the somewhat formal tone of the invitation, which typically was sent in good time to allow guests to arrange their diaries.

The dinner duly took place at the appointed time and place, and among others present was the film director Friedrich Ermler, with whom Shostakovich had been friendly since 1932, when he wrote the music for the film *Counterplan*, which contained the popular *Song of the Meeting*. [Also known as *Morning Light* – Translator's Note]

93 The mentally handicapped son of Yevgeniya Shneyerson, artistic director of the Small Hall of the Leningrad Philharmonia and a close friend of Shostakovich's first wife Nina Varzar.

94 Shostakovich simply announces the fact of needing treatment for his right hand. At this stage there seems no particular sense of alarm, but the clouds were to gather much later over the weakness in his right hand, the first signs of which inexplicably began to develop this year.

95 Shostakovich had a low opinion of doctors, especially famous ones attached to the high-profile clinics reserved for the élite. He referred to them sarcastically as the high priests or luminaries of science.

96 The (sonically untranslatable) Russian is pithy and slightly scabrous: '*pop chéshet poop*', meaning literally, 'the priest scratches his navel'. (Translator's Note)

97 Shostakovich pokes fun at the nauseating propaganda stock phrases and rallying slogans that poured out ceaselessly, orally and in print, after the death of Stalin.

98 In fact, when he came out of hospital, Shostakovich wrote a good deal and overcame the problems with his hand even to the extent of a considerable amount of piano playing.

99 Shostakovich loved to reread books he had read many years before, invariably discovering new virtues in them, as he did with Swift and Defoe. These wonderful writers evoked the kind of enthusiastic response in him that he failed to find in the type of contemporary American author who in those days was lauded as 'progressive'.

100 Howard Fast's books were at the time widely published and disseminated with official support in the Soviet Union, mainly on account of their critical approach to the American way of life. He was awarded an International Stalin Prize in 1953, the citation being 'For his work for Peace among Nations'. However, he subsequently fell from favour in the Soviet Union and incurred censure for his criticisms of Soviet society.

101 Albert Maltz enjoyed a certain vogue in the Soviet Union because of his polemics against the American capitalist system. [He became better known as a Hollywood scriptwriter than as a novelist, and was one of the 'Hollywood Ten' who refused to answer questions when summoned by Senator McCarthy's House Un-American Activities Committee, incurring a fine, a prison sentence and naturally a blacklisting for his stand. He died in 1985 – Translator's Note]

102 There was much outraged posturing at the time about Upton Sinclair's having adopted, after the war, a 'reactionary stance'. Shostakovich took a caustic pleasure in such reverses of fortune among the American 'progessive' literary establishment.

103 Shostakovich knew his Bible, and the account I had given him in my letter of an incident when a prominent Leningrad composer invited me for a drink and

a chat in a restaurant in Komarovo, reminded him of the Gospel story. In the course of a conversation about nothing in particular, my companion suddenly brought up the subject of lying and then, in an even more unexpected modulation, confessed that during the dark days of the campaign against 'cosmopolitans', he had yielded to pressure and publicly denounced me for various heinous crimes. For this act of treachery he was now belatedly asking my forgiveness.

I had been touched by this unprompted confession, as it appeared to me proof that pangs of conscience had been gnawing at my accuser. Shostakovich, however, reserved judgment on the moral qualities of the man he disparaged as 'author of a string of melodious and graceful compositions'. Nevertheless, he approved of the idea of the lie – handmaiden to evil – being put to rest.

In the course of a life beset by troubles enough, Shostakovich was never interested in avenging wrongs done to him. He treated enemies with a mixture of contempt and compassion, especially the latter, and was fond of quoting Jan Huss: 'They do not know what wrong they do'. His hatred was directed at those he held principally responsible for the evil that was endemic throughout the whole of society in his country, and the informers who destroyed the lives of innocent people.

104 Even though five years had passed since Stalin's death and the 'thaw' was in the air, Shostakovich understood how fragile and unreliable it was. Another three long years were to drag by before the triumphant première in Moscow of the Fourth Symphony under Kirill Kondrashin, at which I was present. Returning home after the concert, still under the powerful influence of the performance, a deeply moved Shostakovich said to me that he considered the Fourth Symphony to be among his very best works, superior even to the Eighth. As a remark made in the emotion of the moment, it probably does not bear searching analysis, even if it were possible to compare two musical works of such great distinction. Nevertheless, here was a composer of legendary modesty showering praise on a work that had long lain in disgrace. Not once in the intervening twenty-five years since it was taken out of rehearsal in autumn 1936 had Shostakovich said anything to contradict or disavow the story that it was he himself who had voluntarily withdrawn the symphony. Indeed, twenty years after the event, in an article 'Thoughts on the Path I have Travelled' (*'Dumï o proydonnyom puti'*) (*Sovetskaya Muzïka*, 1956 No. 9) Shostakovich seemed to add fuel to the legend by describing the symphony as suffering from defects and delusions of grandeur.

In fact, things were quite otherwise, and they were much more complex. The thought of his unheard symphony was burning into Shostakovich's soul, but he was powerless to do anything except replay it in his imagination; nowhere could he hear it except in his inner ear. It was a dramatic situation, yet Shostakovich treats it as no more than an ordinary misfortune about which nothing can be done. Hence the dispassionate, uncomplaining tone of his letter.

105 The operetta was *Moscow – Cheryomushki*, which Shostakovich had

somewhat grudgingly written in response to insistent requests by the director of the Moscow Operetta Theatre, G. A. Stolyarov. Shostakovich's eventual agreement owed something to his previous creative collaboration with Stolyarov, who had conducted the Moscow première of *Katerina Izmailova* in the Nemirovich-Danchenko Theatre. Not wishing to offend Stolyarov, Shostakovich had dashed off *Moscow – Cheryomushki*, on a subject which had little appeal for him. The Maly Opera had conceived the idea of mounting another production of the operetta and had asked me to help them obtain the score and performing material.

106 The cruelly self-flagellating tone of this letter alarmed me, and I hastened to Moscow to see what I could do to keep up my friend's spirits. A leading conductor once said that Shostakovich was constitutionally incapable of writing bad music: as soon as I entered the theatre, I was convinced once again of the truth of this statement. I found the music to be lyrical, witty and attractive. The highlight of the show was an extended suite of vocal and dance numbers, written with great wit and verve and, of course, brilliantly orchestrated. The principal role of Lidochka, notable for the complexity and range of her emotional states, was marvellously taken by the talented actress Tatyana Schmïga.

My reaction did not finally reconcile Shostakovich to what he still saw as the work's defects, but at least he began to look at the production with a slightly less jaundiced eye. While still broadly critical of the music, he reserved his greatest displeasure for the dialogue, which was indeed full of tasteless, slangy expressions and vulgarisms. In this I was at one with him.

The reviews were laudatory, but the production was later dropped from the repertoire, a development which in no way displeased the composer.

About two years later, I proposed to Lenfilm that they should make a film based on the operetta. The proposal was accepted and Shostakovich gave his consent; the resulting film was superbly directed by Gerbert Rapoport and was called simply *Cheryomushki*. Rapoport had simply fallen in love with the music, and the sound track was masterfully recorded under the baton of Nikolai Rabinovich. I acted as consulting editor of the film. We made significant cuts to the dialogue, and some minor ones to the score, as a result of which the film gained considerably in coherence and expressivity. While the shooting of the film was under way, Shostakovich composed some splendid additional pieces of music at the request of the director. Just before the film was released in 1963, I watched a preview with Shostakovich in the Lenfilm viewing suite. He leant over to me several times and whispered: 'Interesting! Splendid!', clearly enjoying what he was hearing and seeing. Later, he publicly endorsed and applauded the movie.

In so strikingly modifying his opinion of his own work, Shostakovich never of course got near to overstating the merits of his operetta, but at least the bitter disappointment he experienced at its rehearsals in the theatre in Moscow gave place to warmer feelings. This was because the film version of *Moscow – Cheryomushki* is genuinely a more convincing and artistically valid entity than its theatrical cousin; a better, tighter form had rescued content that was always intrinsically worthwhile.

107 I was friendly with Emil Gilels, who very much wanted Shostakovich to contribute a foreword to a book that was currently in preparation about him (Gilels). He mentioned this to me on several occasions. Shostakovich admired Gilels as a great pianist and turned to me for help in composing a short foreword. When the book came out, Gilels was moved and grateful that such flattering words about him should have come not from a musicologist but from a great composer.

108 See chapter 3, note 83 to the letter of 20 March 1958.

109 Shostakovich had been delighted to be able to send 'the famous author' four thousand roubles, under the impression that this not inconsiderable sum (this was before the 1961 devaluation) was payment for the little article about Emil Gilels that I had helped him to write. But this was a mistake: as this letter explains, it turned out a day or two later that the money was in fact due to Shostakovich from another of the sources of his modest income. In the letter to which his postcard of 26 June was a reply, I had suggested that the fee for the Gilels article seemed much more generous than would normally be expected. I naturally returned the proportion of the money not due to me, and the next time we met we had a good laugh about this financial imbroglio.

110 Shostakovich had been acting as consultant to the Bolshoy Theatre, and when this job was taken away from him he accepted it with good grace, as one of those things.

111 Writers' fees in Russia are calculated according to the number of 'author's sheets'. One author's sheet is twenty-four single-spaced typewritten pages – with a standard number of key-strokes on it – therefore 0.56 author's sheets is the equivalent of about thirteen pages. (Translator's Note)

112 Although it was quite unnecessary, I was not in the least surprised that Shostakovich sent me the statement, as he was always meticulously correct to the letter of any financial matter.

113 I do not remember what concert this was.

114 Shostakovich always found hot weather insupportable. It frightened him.

115 The architect Igor Fomin, whose daughter was married to Shostakovich's nephew Dmitry Frederiks.

116 We had talked the previous month of the great impression that reading this story had made on Shostakovich. He always wanted to know if I shared his opinion of literary works which had left their mark on his soul and his memory. By the same token, he was interested in my tentative judgements on music.

117 In the autumn of 1959 the Kirov Opera was in the throes of producing Musorgsky's *Boris Godunov* in the reworked orchestration that Shostakovich had lovingly completed before the war. Shostakovich wanted me to attend rehearsals and pass on to him my impressions of the conductor Sergey Yeltsin and the performance of the singers. Fearing (wrongly as it proved) that I might have some difficulty in gaining access to the theatre, he

wrote a request to the conductor, who at that time was also the principal conductor of the Kirov Theatre, asking him to let me have a rehearsal pass. I attended the première in November 1959, sitting in the stalls next to Shostakovich. He was passionate about Musorgsky's music and we listened together in great emotion to the brilliant new colours in which it now appeared.

Chapter IV Public Face, Private Feelings, 1960–1966

1 Shostakovich was unusually insistent that I should read *Natalya Tarpova*, clearly hoping that I would share his opinion of it and that it would store up fuel for debates about the vicissitudes of Soviet literature when we met (it did).

   Reading the novel in 1960 excited in Shostakovich a mixture of pleasure and feelings of nostalgia for the past. He saw himself in some ways as the young contemporary of that 'non-party spets' who aroused in Works Committee Secretary Natalya Tarpova the desire to console herself with him. And once again he saw in his mind's eye the charmless features of those critics who had taken up arms against the novelist and succeeded in fanning the flames of their war for several decades.

2 In the early years of Soviet power, the 'spets' was a skilled worker or professional in any sphere whose experience was needed to keep the wheels turning even though he may (as Ozhegov's 1949 *Dictionary of the Russian Language* delicately puts it) 'have come from non-proletarian circles'. (Translator's Note)

3 Shostakovich loved and admired the writings of Mikhail Zoshchenko. He avidly collected all his stories, indeed everything that this outstanding writer produced, and was deeply shocked by the horrific punishment meted out in August 1946 when, on a vicious whim of Stalin, Zoshchenko was declared a living corpse, that is to say banned from the Writers' Union and from the Literary Fund. The Union was the source of all earnings from writing, and the ration card without which it was impossible to buy food came from the Fund. All mention of Zoshchenko's name was forbidden; neither his name nor that of Anna Akhmatova appears in the Encyclopaedia of 1953–4.

   On the tenth anniversary of Zoschenko's death, Dmitry Dmitriyevich came to collect me in his car and we drove to Sestroretsk to honour the writer at his graveside. I have a photograph taken there of us both, plunged in melancholy thought. I distinctly recall how in the distance we suddenly heard, coming through loudspeakers, Tchaikovsky's First Piano Concerto. Shostakovich said: 'How appropriate to hear this music; in its way it is an affirmation of Mikhail Mikhailovich. He died before his time, but at least he outlived the men who murdered him, Stalin and Zhdanov.'

   These were Shostakovich's sincere and revealing words at the graveside of the great writer who had endured so much. It would be stretching a point to claim that the two were close friends; they were certainly on friendly terms, but their intercourse was generally limited to larger gatherings and meetings. For this reason I do not think that Zoshchenko had an intimate knowledge of the complex inner world of Shostakovich, for all his unique powers of insight and for all his admiration for the composer. I remember how moved Shostakovich had been at Zoshchenko's instinctively generous reaction to the disgraceful *Pravda* article 'Muddle not Music' in January 1936. Zoshchenko had not long before published his *Blue Book*, and on reading the *Pravda* article rushed round to Sofya Vasiliyevna's apartment before Shostakovich had returned from his tour to Archangelsk. He brought a copy of the book with him, in which he had written a dedicatory inscription and underlined an impassioned passage calling Shostakovich 'this composer of genius'. Zoshchenko was not exactly noted for purple prose, so it could only have been distress at the article that prompted him to go beyond his customary laconic phraseology.

[Zoshchenko may have understood more than is suggested here. See his extraordinarily perceptive sketch of Shostakovich in a letter to Marietta Shaginyan of 4 January 1941, quoted in Laurel Fay's recent biography:

> 'It seemed to you that he is "frail, fragile, withdrawn, an infinitely direct, pure child". That is so. But if it were only so, then great art (as with him) would never be obtained. He is exactly what you say he is, plus something else – he is hard, acid, extremely intelligent, strong perhaps, despotic and not altogether good-natured (although cerebrally good-natured).
>
> That is the combination in which he must be seen. And then it may be possible to understand his art to some degree.
>
> In him there are great contradictions. In him, one quality obliterates the other. It is conflict in the highest degree. It is almost a catastrophe.' See Fay, L. E., *Shostakovich: A Life*, Oxford, 2000, 121 – Translator's Note]

4   We had not seen one another for two months. On 12 December the previous year he had come to Leningrad on his way back from America, bringing me presents of a gold watch from the famous maker Schaffhausen and a leather-bound five-year diary. I was particularly touched that he had written out all the days of the week for the whole five years, telling me: 'I sat down in the evenings and wrote them out. I enjoy that kind of work.'

We went together to the Philharmonia on 18 December and heard a performance of the Eighth Symphony, which thrilled me to the core of my being. Afterwards we talked long about the spiritual essence of the work. Then Shostakovich went to Moscow and shortly after entered hospital.

5   In 1960, Lenfilm was making a film of 'The Gentle Maiden' based on the short story by Dostoyevsky. I was consulting editor on the film and the director, the well-known actor A. F. Borisov, delegated to me the job of engaging a composer to write music suitable to accompany this complex narrative. My choice first fell on Galina Ustvolskaya, whose gifts were much prized by her former teacher Shostakovich. I thought that both her talent and her musical style would be suitable for Dostoyevsky's story, with its refined psychological insights. I had written to Shostakovich about my proposal.

6   A joke. Both these composers are as wildly inappropriate as it is possible to imagine for anything written by Dostoyevsky.

7 A sarcastic reference to the widely repeated phrase, originally from the notorious decree 'On the opera *The Great Friendship* by V. I. Muradeli'.

8 Galina Ustvolskaya was at the time living in very straitened circumstances. Her refusal to participate in the film stemmed from a degree of innate modesty bordering on self-abnegation. In the end the score was composed by Lutsian Prigozhin.

9 An ironic comparison. Shostakovich regarded Grechaninov as a mediocre composer.

10 Unfortunately I cannot recall what oratorio Shostakovich is referring to.

11 These writers symbolized to Shostakovich the most odious and reactionary position in the country's social and literary world.

12 Faddey Bulgarin, reactionary and informer, whose yellow-press novel *Ivan Buzhigin* was published in 1829.

13 Georgy Korkin, director of the Kirov Opera and Ballet Theatre.

14 The plan to present *Lady Macbeth of Mtsensk* was aborted by fiat of the Smolny [Headquarters of Leningrad City Communist Party – Translator's Note]. The Secretary of the Regional Party Committee, Comrade Bogdanov, made it clear to me that *Lady Macbeth* should be presented at the Maly Opera and not at the Kirov.

15 Shostakovich was a Deputy of the Supreme Soviet of the Russian Federation and later of the Soviet Union.

16 My wife had managed to obtain for Shostakovich a good-quality fur hat which he needed.

17 Constituents' surgeries for Deputies to the Supreme Soviet were always an ordeal for Shostakovich, since he was acutely conscious of his powerlessness to help people who came to him, in the main, with housing problems. In the overwhelming majority of cases, as recorded on the official casework forms provided to Deputies, his efforts proved ineffectual.

18 The Kirov Opera production of *Boris Godunov* in Shostakovich's orchestral reworking of Musorgsky's score.

19 V. N. Salmanov's Second Symphony was premièred on 30 March, conducted by Mravinsky.

20 Shostakovich avoids mentioning Mayakovsky by name but ironically repeats the sobriquet awarded him by Stalin which inevitably for many years enjoyed incontrovertible and canonic status. The choreographer Boris Fenster and the conductor Pavel Feldt had the notion of mounting a one-act ballet with a libretto based on Mayakovsky's 'The Young Girl and the Hooligan' to Shostakovich's music. Shostakovich was not much attracted to this enterprise, but reluctantly agreed to the creation of the ballet. He had asked me to keep an eye on what they were planning to make sure that the authors did not perpetrate, as he put it, a production that was 'a vulgar outrage'.

21 Shostakovich knew Feldt, who had been a fellow student at the Conservatoire, but not Fenster. Fenster was a colleague of mine; while I was the head of the literary department of the Maly Opera, he was the chief choreographer of the ballet company. I admired Boris Aleksandrovich's talent and liked him very much as a person. The production did not take place as planned owing to

Fenster's untimely death, but the original idea had not been in vain for the ballet was ultimately brilliantly choreographed by K. F. Boyarsky, and enjoyed a long-running success at the Maly Theatre. The Theatre then asked me to devise a libretto for another one-act ballet to the music of the Ninth Symphony, entitled *Meeting*, and the two Boyarsky ballets were performed as a double bill.

22 Kogan was not at all reticent about advertising his membership of the party, hence the tongue-in-cheek description of him.

23 Shostakovich had the highest opinion of Vainberg's gifts, and continually said so verbally and in print, the last occasion on which he did so being a review of Vainberg's opera *Madonna and the Soldier*, which was produced at the Maly Opera Theatre.

24 The Old Woman, as depicted by Aleksandr Tvardovsky in the chapter called 'So it Was' from his poem 'Horizon Beyond the Horizon', is an image of death. No doubt the idea of death as a release from earthly travail did from time to time have its attractions for Shostakovich, and reading this poem – quite independently of the context of this letter – induced thoughts of calling on the Old Woman for help. Such dark thoughts were not uncommon to Shostakovich even in his youth, and they became more common when he began to suffer serious illness.

25 Shostakovich had given back the government-allocated dacha at Bolshevo, which was not very conducive either to rest or work, and had taken out an instalment plan to buy a better one in Zhukovka, a picturesque place not far from Moscow.

On 29 March earlier the same year, Shostakovich was in Leningrad and told me the story of how he managed to purchase the dacha without any money. Smiling dreamily, he said (his exact words): 'I did a rather naughty thing. I signed two contracts for film scores and one for the ballet *The Gadfly*. *The Gadfly* seemed to be limping along somewhat, and as you know that's no good for a ballet! So I was planning to put some of the film music into *The Gadfly*.' But later he thought better of this idea, which on reflection seemed rather absurd to him, and somehow or other managed to make ends meet so as to pay for the dacha.

26 Shostakovich always called his friend, the musician and film-maker Lev Arnshtam, by the pet name of their young days together.

27 In fact Gohrisch – Glikman has transcribed the place-name erroneously. (Translator's Note)

28 In the German transliteration of these notes, D, E flat (Es), C, B (H). (Translator's Note)

29 This mockery of the artist's tendency to 'self-glorification' calls to mind N. D. Kraskin's account of going with Tchaikovsky to a performance of *Yevgeny Onegin*. When, at the end of the Letter Scene Tatyana's love theme appears in C major over a cello tremolo, Kraskin reports Tchaikovsky as murmuring: 'How glad I am that it is dark in here. I love this so much, I cannot hold back my tears.'

30 The members of the Beethoven Quartet, who had given the first performances

of all Shostakovich's previous String Quartets except No. 1, and whom the composer numbered among his close personal friends. (Translator's Note)

31 The Leningrad composer Yury Balkashin died suddenly in the throes of an epileptic attack, at the age of thirty-eight.

32 Galina Ustvolskaya.

33 From his work as a Deputy, Shostakovich was all too aware of the harsh rules governing the allocation of living space.

34 There is a pun here: Shostakovich uses the Russian word '*sidelka*' for nurse that literally means 'sitter' (as in babysitter); the word '*stul*' has two meanings, the usual one being 'chair', the other in a medical context derived from a rather obvious borrowing. (Translator's Note)

35 Shostakovich was always extremely fastidious and detested being exposed to people whose standards of hygiene fell short of his own.

36 When I visited Shostakovich in hospital, I was struck by the tone of patient resignation with which he spoke of his injured leg. He repeated several times: 'Probably God is punishing me for my sins, for instance, joining the Party.'

37 I had written giving Shostakovich my impressions of *Khovanshchina* in his orchestration, which the Kirov Theatre had performed under the direction of the conductor Sergey Yeltsin.

38 After the misery of a long spell in hospital, to suggest that 1960 was a good year smacks of gallows humour.

39 A kind of long, elasticated surgical support stocking. (Translator's Note)

40 Probably Basner's Third Quartet (1960) and Vladlen Chistyakov's song cycle *Songs of Courage* to words by N. Khikmet (1958).

41 In Leningrad on 28 June, Shostakovich told me that he had just written some settings of words by Sasha Chorny, and that he had been attracted not only by the poet's texts but also by his biography. He said (verbatim): 'I was very impressed by Sasha Chorny's death. He was in the act of putting out a fire of some sort, and then he upped and died. An excellent death.' This was said in a tone of voice that clearly suggested envy. Four days later, in his sister Mariya's apartment, Shostakovich played through to me the song cycle, to which he gave the title *Satires (Pictures of the Past)*. I found the songs most witty and brilliant.

42 Shostakovich wanted me to hear the songs not just in a play-through by the composer as I had already done, but in the performance by Galina Vishnevskaya masterfully accompanied by Mstislav Rostropovich. Shostakovich greatly admired Vishnevskaya's talent as singer and actress. She invariably had a great success with the Sasha Chorny songs, and generally had to repeat the whole cycle as an encore.

43 Shostakovich trusted Ustvolskaya's opinion on artistic matters.

44 As a consultant to Lenfilm, I had proposed a film version of Shostakovich's operetta *Moscow – Cheryomushki* (the eventual title of the film was simply *Cheryomushki*). The proposal was accepted, and the director, Gerbert Rapoport, had requested the composer (through me) to compose an additional vocal number.

45 The libretto and screenplay were by the playwrights V. Mass and M. Chervinsky.

46 Kind words were at this time welcome to Shostakovich about the Sasha Chorny songs, which I felt had about them something of Zoshchenko's wonderful stories. A storm was brewing about the songs, *sotto voce*, but a storm none the less. The authorities were most unhappy about one of them, 'Descendants', and the dried-up pedants who had in their day attacked Zoshchenko were tut-tutting at Shostakovich for his frivolous and mischievous lapse into inadmissibly bad taste. These critical comments may not have found their way into print, but they were certainly reaching Shostakovich's ears.

47 At the time Shostakovich was living with his family in apartment No. 87 at 27 Kutuzovsky Prospect.

48 By law everyone residing in any city in the Soviet Union had to be registered as residing at a specific address. Getting such a permit could be extremely difficult. (Translator's Note)

49 Shostakovich was not married at this time, and was therefore burdened with family and domestic worries which he found very trying. His fear of policemen, janitors and the like had been with him since childhood. His appointment as a Deputy did nothing to diminish this fear, which he mentioned to me many times.

50 Actually five days previously.

51 It was rare for Shostakovich to divulge even the couple of lines in his letter of 15 August he dignifies as a 'critique'. He generally disliked speaking about the content, style or form of a forthcoming composition. These ought, in his view, to remain private to the composer.

52 Mravinsky. He in turn was of course ready to throw himself at Shostakovich's feet to have the privilege of receiving the new composition from the composer's hands, as had happened year on year since the Fifth Symphony.

53 Laurel Fay has pointed out that in the summer of 1962 Shostakovich was still telling Dmitry Tsïganov of the Beethoven Quartet as well as the press that a new quartet (No. 9) was on the stocks, and not until the summer of 1964 did he acknowledge that the now-finished Ninth Quartet was a completely different work, the first No. 9 having been destroyed. It seems more plausible that Glikman has misdated this letter a year earlier than it was actually written, than that Shostakovich destroyed *two* unsatisfactory Ninth Quartets. See Fay, L. E., *Shostakovich: A Life*, Oxford, 2000, 337, n. 92. (Translator's Note)

54 Shostakovich was in the depths of depression when he wrote this letter, occasioned perhaps by the extreme act of consigning his Ninth Quartet to the flames. The second time in his life that he had done such a thing, it no doubt resulted from fears that his creative powers were beginning to fail with age.

Such doubts oppressed Shostakovich again and again, at times to such an extent that they darkened his life, as he wrote to me more than once. It was a heavy burden which never left him so long as he obeyed the call 'to make the holy sacrifice to Apollo'.

55 Part of the new music Shostakovich had composed at the request of the film director Georgy Rapoport for the film of the operetta *Cheryomushki*, for which I was acting as consulting editor. Shostakovich had been reluctant to undertake the work, but had nevertheless done it admirably and the extra pieces represented a substantial enrichment of the original stage operetta *Moscow – Cheryomushki*.

56 Despite the ironic tone, Shostakovich genuinely admired the film director's mastery of his medium and his knowledge of music.

57 The film of the operetta *Cheryomushki*.

58 The première took place on 17 December 1960 in the Stanislavsky–Nemirovich-Danchenko Theatre, directed by Lev Mikhailov and Pavel Zlatogorov, and conducted by Kemal Abdullayev. The production was designed by A. Lushin.

59 In 1961 the Stanislavsky–Nemirovich-Danchenko Theatre resolved to be the first theatre in the country to revive *Lady Macbeth of Mtsensk* after its twenty-five-year proscription. L. D. Mikhailov, who had a good reputation as an opera producer, had undertaken responsibility for the production. But Shostakovich, accustomed as he had been all his life to 'innovative' directors and their wild ideas, was shocked and depressed by this conversation. He could not wait to share with me the news of this memorable exchange. Clearly, instead of following Kochkarev's advice in Gogol's 'The Wedding', which is to shout: 'Get out of here, you idiots!', he adopted his usual restrained manner and tried reasoning with Mikhailov, invoking Sollertinsky's ironic dismissal of the 'unborn child' cliché. But this was obviously no time for subtlety: the unfortunate Shostakovich had no option but to go on listening patiently while Mikhailov wove his flights of fancy. Full of good intentions, and not really knowing the kind of man with whom he was dealing, Mikhailov sought to make the character of Katerina 'deeper', 'richer', more 'sympathetic'. According to his perspective, the composer was blind to where the problem lay with her: she was not fully rounded and needed to be filled out. He as producer could see this so clearly, much clearer than the author, who should in any case be full of gratitude that his opera had been chosen for production.

   There were and are too many producers who subscribe to the belief, long ingrained in Soviet opera, that composers must bow to the will of any producer who has agreed to stage their opera. I need hardly say that this particular conversation led nowhere, and *Lady Macbeth* was in due course admirably staged in full accordance with Shostakovich's score. He had protected his child. [The street has now reverted to its former name – Translator's Note.]

60 Gennady Provatorov was also scheduled to conduct *Lady Macbeth*.

61 This was the third and last of Shostakovich's Moscow apartments. Previously he had lived in Kirov Street and then in Mozhaiskoye Shosse, later renamed Kutuzovsky Prospect.

62 On 16 April in Leningrad, Shostakovich told me that he had composed 'Baby Yar', at that time existing only in a piano score. 'It's turned out not badly,' he said musingly, before passing on to other things. On 24 May he was in

Leningrad again and played through to me the completed score. Both music and words moved me to tears. We speculated about who might sing the solo part, running through all the names of basses whom we knew but not alighting on any of them. 'This is no part for a singer who's a fool,' said Dmitry Dmitriyevich, forcefully.

The genesis of the Thirteenth Symphony lay back in September 1961. Shostakovich was staying in the Yevropeyskaya Hotel, and on 20 or 21 September I brought him a poem by Yevgeny Yevtushenko that had electrified me with its dramatic power. The poem was 'Baby Yar', and it was published on 19 September in *Literaturnaya Gazeta*. We were dining in his room in the hotel, and Shostakovich promised to read it later. That evening he telephoned me and told me that he shared my feelings for the poem, and that he had conceived an immediate desire to write a symphonic vocal poem based on the text. This is indeed what resulted in the first instance.

63 Aleksandr Vedernikov, bass soloist of the Bolshoy Opera.

64 Boris Gmïrya, soloist of the Kiev Opera, whose voice and musicianship Shostakovich admired.

65 Writing at the end of May 1962, Shostakovich could have had no idea of the obstacles that were to lie in the path of the magnificent Thirteenth Symphony that was taking shape in his mind.

66 This further incarceration in hospital was mitigated for Shostakovich by the compositional frenzy with which his inspiration was driving along the Thirteenth Symphony – hence the comparatively resigned tone of the letter.

67 On 16 June Shostakovich had telephoned me from Moscow with the sensational news of his marriage – sensational because no more than a month before he had told me that he had no intention of ever marrying again. But quick and unexpected decisions were always his style. This is (verbatim) what he said to me: 'I've got married! I want to come to Leningrad and show you the person I've chosen. Of course I ought to have done that before the wedding, but all's well that ends well. I think I am happy.' The only thing remaining for me was to congratulate the newly-wed over the phone.

68 He was not mistaken. This was indeed the case.

69 In his previous letter Shostakovich had written of his firm intention to write a symphony, but as the work progressed, doubts surfaced as to the form the work should in fact take.

70 These hopes were dashed. When Gmïrya was in Leningrad appearing at the Philharmonia, he told me how much he admired Shostakovich. He frequently performed the *Five Romances on Verses of Dolmatovsky*, but when it came to the Thirteenth Symphony, he took fright and bowed to the authorities in the Ukraine, who advised him not to have anything to do with the symphony owing to the seditious nature of 'Baby Yar'. The singer, whose reputation was not entirely spotless (he had stayed on in Kiev throughout the German occupation), obediently complied.

During a banquet on 20 September 1962 to celebrate the centenary of the Leningrad Conservatoire, Shostakovich silently passed me (we were sitting next to one another) Gmïrya's letter of refusal, which according to him had been forced upon him. I was saddened by this, Shostakovich of course still more so.

71 Shostakovich came to Sestroretsk, where I was staying with my mother; Vera Vasiliyevna was away in the south at the time. My mother and I both took immediately to Shostakovich's bride: she was an exceptionally attractive and charming person.

72 In my letter I had enthused about Yevtushenko's poem 'Humour', which I suggested had something in common with Robert Burns's immortal ballad 'John Barleycorn'.

73 Shostakovich reacted angrily to the sarcastic carping of obsessive pedants who criticized the texts of the Thirteenth Symphony. He regarded the symphony as an indivisible unity of words and music and defended Yevtushenko. But when the poet himself violated this unity by unilaterally making alterations to the text of 'Baby Yar', he provoked a strongly hostile reaction from Shostakovich.

74 Shostakovich forebore to add that Irina Antonovna has an attractive burr to her voice. Overall, this portrait of his young wife is drawn with his customary reserve.

75 Ironic use of the banal formulas which after Stalin's death were routinely used to describe the reign of arbitrary terror.

76 A special orphanage for the children of 'enemies of the people'.

77 A sinister figure, Timashuk had acted as *agent provocateur* in the appalling affair of the 'Doctors' Plot'. He reminded Shostakovich of the dreadful Murashkin in Chekhov's story, 'with his fleshy red face and his manly tenor voice'. After Stalin's death, Timashuk was stripped of the decorations he had received for his part in the Doctors' Plot, but was allowed to keep his job at the Kremlin Hospital, a decision which offended Shostakovich as a good citizen and man of integrity.

78 Gmïrya had not yet contacted the Kiev authorities for permission to sing the Thirteenth Symphony including the 'Baby Yar' section, as he did a little later.

79 I was staying at No. 30, Middle (Sredny) Street.

80 The composer's sister.

81 Lying in hospital, Shostakovich was evidently longing to acquaint me with both Irina Antonovna and the Thirteenth Symphony, on which his work was approaching completion. Sestroretsk is to all intents and purposes a suburb of Leningrad, and it is hardly a great journey to get there; all the anxiety about the visit can probably be explained by his excitement at the prospect of seeing me and sharing these experiences.

82 Doubts about the form of the work persisted even after three of the movements had been composed.

83 Shostakovich of course does not mention the immense creative energy by which he was possessed at the time of the Thirteenth Symphony's composition.

84 Although I very much admired Yevtushenko's gifts, I considered that he was guilty of disrespect towards Shostakovich, who was having to pursue him for work he had promised to deliver. I thought Yevtushenko should have had more understanding of the genius of the person he was dealing with.

85 Shostakovich loved this poem for its description of the ever-present fear with which people lived under Stalin.

86 For many years Shostakovich always showed me his newly composed works. If this was for him a kind of rite of passage, for me it was the height of pleasure. But why, given his habitual extreme reserve, was he now insisting so passionately on acquainting me with the Thirteenth Symphony? It seems to me that it can only have been because of its unconventional form and original subject-matter. What Shostakovich had done, with startling artistic boldness, was to build texts of the most evocative, vividly topical language into the fabric of a symphonic work; it was a completely new idea, and probably he wanted to try out on me the powerful effect the symphony would have.

87 My wife was away in the south at the time.

88 However unrelated they were to one another, Shostakovich's marriage and his Thirteenth Symphony both seemed to need my approval. My impressions of Irina Antonovna I have already recorded in chapter 4, note 71 to the letter dated 24 June 1962; my first hearing of the symphony produced an overwhelming effect on me.

89 The classic Russian vodka. (Translator's Note)

90 I was amused and touched by the delicacy of Shostakovich, who could not bear to think that he might be imposing even on his oldest friends. So he would bring to Sestroretsk 'dry rations' of vodka and a piece of his favourite *lyubitelsky*, that humble and eminently democratic variety of garlic sausage. My mother of course paid no attention to this curious version of student-life payment in kind, as she called it, and made a superb dinner at which there was no room for the *lyubitelsky* sausage. At this Shostakovich laughed shyly, while Irina Antonovna, who had not yet fully got the measure of her husband's character, smiled politely.

91 Shostakovich was very precise about his timetable. The Thirteenth Symphony was finished on 20 July 1962.

92 Some critics took a different view about the merits of Yevtushenko's verses. They castigated the poet, and to some extent the composer, for stooping to such low-life verismo. Lines like 'the smell of onions, gherkins, pungent "Kabul" sauce' shocked literary purists.

93 After some hesitation, Shostakovich went to Ust-Narva to see Mravinsky and show him the Thirteenth Symphony. Judging by what later transpired, the conductor was not over-impressed. Either he did not understand the form in which the new work was cast, or he was not sympathetic to the essential spirit it breathed. The reasons are not easy to gauge, but his behaviour over the following weeks, during which he remained silent and aloof, was far from exemplary. On 7 October Shostakovich telephoned me from Moscow to ask me to find out from Mravinsky whether or not he wished to receive the score of the Thirteenth. When I spoke to Yevgeny Aleksandrovich, he was so evasive that I hardly recognized the man I knew. He talked about his forthcoming tour of America, and about a whole range of unimportant matters, but nothing at all concrete about the symphony. I was shocked by the turn of events.

Shostakovich's demeanour throughout this puzzling situation was impeccable. He said not a word against Mravinsky, but decided to give the symphony instead to Kirill Kondrashin, who was delighted to accept.

94 The visit to Mravinsky. Shostakovich was very fond of the dacha we rented in Sestroretsk. It was a riverside 'hut on fowl's legs' in the Razliv, that same Razliv depicted in the second movement of the Twelfth Symphony. Gazing out of the window at the huge expanse of water, Shostakovich observed with a smile: 'What a job it would be to express that in sound!'

He enjoyed the dinner, but most of all the talk, of which we had both been starved. It flowed in a spontaneous stream, sometimes serious and sometimes with that wit of which Shostakovich was such a master.

95 In the serene beauty of the Russian countryside and in the happiness of his new marriage, there could hardly be a greater contrast for Shostakovich than Musorgsky's tragic song cycle of the triumph of death. His interest was not merely contemplative: he wanted to bury himself in the songs and produce an orchestral version of them. Who is to say whether in the recesses of his own heart he was harbouring dark thoughts and forebodings of his own?

96 Exhausted though he was by the labour of producing the Thirteenth Symphony, Shostakovich did not stop working for a moment, even on his short holiday. It is hard to take seriously his protestations about the effects of old age.

97 In December 1962, just before the scheduled première of the Thirteenth Symphony on 18 December, Shostakovich and Yevtushenko were both present at a meeting of the artistic intelligentsia addressed by Nikita Khrushchov. Khrushchov referred in critical terms to 'some sort of "Baby Yar" symphony' produced by the composer Shostakovich, which according to him raised wholly unnecessary issues connected with the 'Jewish question' although there had been other victims of the Fascist atrocities as well as Jews.

At that time there were virtually no limits to Khrushchov's power, and so any critical observation he cared to make effectively had the force of law. As Pushkin said, 'thunder rolled from out the cloud, not from a pile of dung'. The first performance of the symphony, which was the talk of Moscow, was on the brink of prohibition.

I came to Moscow for the première. The morning of 18 December was an anxious time. The general rehearsal had been suspended but not cancelled. For Shostakovich, the tense hours of waiting were an agony of suspense. It was painful to see his drawn face, his quivering lips and the suffering in his eyes.

About noon, the call came from the Party bosses. The rehearsal could go ahead, consequently the performance would be permitted. Permission, however, was of the most grudging kind, extracted only from fear of the negative reaction in the West if the symphony were to be banned: members of the international diplomatic corps and press were expected to be in the Great Hall of the Conservatoire for the performance.

Before setting out for the concert, Shostakovich gripped my left hand with his left hand 'for luck' and said: 'If there are catcalls after the symphony and the public spits on me, don't try to defend me. I can stand it.' (These were his exact words.) I knew of course that no such thing would happen, but the morning war of nerves had told on us, and we left for the Conservatoire a prey to anxious thoughts.

It is hard to find words to describe what actually happened in the hall. The music was nothing less than an exalted liturgy, shot through with brilliant shafts of humour. At the end of the finale the audience rose as one man and erupted in tempestuous applause, which seemed to go on for ever. The Moscow press devoted not a single word to the concert: word had gone out that the seditious work was to be greeted with the silence of the grave. [This is not strictly accurate. *Pravda* carried a brief and partial report of the performance on the following day, and Kondrashin published an enthusiastic article in a Leningrad paper. See Fay, L. E., *Shostakovich: A Life*, Oxford, 2000, 235, nn. 44, 45. [Translator's Note]

However it is interesting to note that *L'Humanité*, a paper famous for its unswerving loyalty to our rules of conduct, published an article on 20 December which I happened to come across in Moscow. It was headed '*Succès triomphale de la 13e symphonie de Shostakovitch*'.

Also on 20 December, the Thirteenth was repeated with the same shattering success. On both occasions Yevtushenko appeared on the platform with Shostakovich, to be greeted with a storm of applause. The poet was greatly loved, and not without reason.

But what happened after the première of the Thirteenth was more troubling. Mindful of Khrushchov's critical remarks, and without consulting Shostakovich, Yevtushenko inserted forty new lines into the text of 'Baby Yar' [No such extensive body of additional verse has come to light. Shostakovich did not alter his score to include the two new verses, and it was performed in its original version in Minsk two months later. See Fay, L. E., *Shostakovich: A Life*, Oxford, 2000, 236. Yevtushenko, in an article published in 1999, has specifically denied writing the extra 40 lines – Translator's Note]. In them he joined Russians and Ukrainians to the memory of the Jews who had been massacred. One of the inserted strophes reads thus:

> I stand as if beside the living wellspring
> That nourishes my faith in brotherhood,
> Here Russians and Ukrainians lie sharing
> That same earth with the Jews who once here stood.

Yevtushenko calculated that his revision would meet Khrushchov's demands, but it signally failed to meet with the approval of Shostakovich, who could not stand by and see the form of his first movement violated in this way. He was forced into a dispute on artistic grounds with the poet, although it was necessarily carried on *in absentia*.

98 The poem is called 'Second Birth'. The première of *Katerina Izmailova* took place on 26 December 1962 in the Stanislavsky–Danchenko Theatre.

99 There are certainly some excellent lines in the poem, which was written immediately after hearing the opera. For example, the second verse:

> The music crucified within the score,
> Where dust had lain for nigh on thirty years,
> At dead of night would cry in pain once more
> In anguished search of willing listeners' ears.

100   This is an extremely important insight, which does not seem to have occurred to anybody except the composer. For all his preternatural modesty, he never harboured any doubts of the value of *Katerina Izmailova*, one of the works dearest to his heart. It is impossible to destroy music. If it outlives its time it can grow old and die; indeed, there are many examples of this. But *Katerina Izmailova* was evergreen, full of the inexhaustible strength of youth, and its creator knew this. This is what he wanted to explain to the gifted poet who had celebrated its return.

101   The two subscription performances took place on the appointed days. Shostakovich wanted me to know of the changes to the text so that they would not take me by surprise. I attended both concerts and deeply regretted the loss of eight lines of rare beauty, but it was clear that the fate of the whole symphony depended on the new lines, composed to orders from on high.

102   Shostakovich had made the enforced changes with a heavy heart, but covers this with characteristically bitter humour.

103   By his own admission, Shostakovich was an obsessive lover of mechanical tasks like copying scores, finding them a welcome relief from the worries that constantly invaded his thoughts. Despite his injured hand, he made a complete new fair copy of the full score of *Lady Macbeth*.

104   The conductor of the Maly Opera Theatre, Georgy Doniyakh, who had been sacked as a result of an adultery scandal. I had asked Shostakovich if he could do anything to help Doniyakh.

105   Shostakovich was no puritan where alcohol was concerned, but he did not like drunkards and had no time for them. If it happened that he himself overstepped the mark, the following day he would be very hard on himself and condemn as disgraceful what would normally be considered unexceptionable behaviour, as in the present case.

106   The Musical Fund had previously printed the *Six Romances* in copies printed from glass during the war; Shostakovich had sent a copy to me in Tashkent with a dedicatory inscription.

107   In the letters he had written from hospital at that time, in between bouts of feverish work on the symphony, Shostakovich soberly recounted, movement by movement, the progress of the work. A year later, and he is already looking back on this time through rose-tinted glasses as a golden age of creativity.

108   In retrospect, the whole period leading up to the première of the Thirteenth Symphony is suffused with a rosy glow of varied and productive vitality; it has become a 'wonderful time'. Shostakovich had put out of his mind Gmïrya's craven behaviour and the disingenuous way in which Mravinsky evaded the issues the controversial symphony brought in its train. These were

now all submerged in the ebb and flow of daily life, above which soared the Thirteenth Symphony itself.

109 The inverted commas are significant. Shostakovich always avoided high-sounding words on the rare occasions when he would talk about the compositional process. Here, 'inspiration' has to be distanced within quotation marks.

110 A professor at the Leningrad Conservatoire who had himself been a student of Rimsky-Korsakov. In conversation he was wont to say: 'Well, so I'm a professor – and what then?' He had no illusions whatsoever about the future, and the way he put the question inevitably suggested the reply: 'Then – nothing.' In May 1963 Shostakovich evidently felt that this gloomy analysis reflected his own situation: if he was not engaged in composition, life stretched monotonously before him, meaningless and – nothing. Generally, moods like this did not last long, and were soon replaced by the opposite, a surge of mental energy.

111 Punctilious to a fault about money matters, Shostakovich hastened to pass on to me the fee for an article about Mayakovsky which in a small way I had helped him with.

112 The kind of jingoistic bragging that used endlessly to fill the newspapers.

113 Shostakovich loved all Mahler, but worshipped *Das Lied von der Erde*.

114 It is hard to say what particular work Shostakovich may have been thinking of when he wrote this. At all events the hypochondria which had gripped him at the beginning of May had given way to a cheerful optimism. On leaving hospital in the middle of the month, he came to Leningrad, and during dinner on 18 May told me that he was planning to write a new work to poems by Yevgeny Yevtushenko. He said (verbatim): 'I don't yet know what form this work will take, but it will be about conscience, the conscience of man.' Might it be that he was thinking of the final movement of *Das Lied*, with its theme of isolation and death? At all events, there was no mention of Mahler during this conversation.

115 Shostakovich greatly admired the music of Stravinsky, much as he disliked the composer as a person.

116 Shostakovich often laughed at the pompous and pedantic criticism directed at the lyrics of the Thirteenth Symphony. Nikolai Peyko, for all the tactless naïvety of his person, was a composer whose music Shostakovich rather liked.

117 A proud, and to my mind triumphant, quotation from the final movement of the Thirteenth Symphony to round off the happy memories of its completion one year previously.

118 My enquiry as to why the delayed letter had the Moscow address on the envelope hardly seems important enough to warrant this detailed explanation. But Shostakovich had a whole series of rules and customs in daily life which he considered important to maintain, and it was characteristic of him that he would always answer any question, however trivial it may have seemed.

119 The famous night train between Moscow and Leningrad. (Translator's Note)

120 Shostakovich came as planned, and we followed exactly the same procedure as in the previous year. While we dined, we talked of the dramatic events surrounding the Thirteenth Symphony, with which Shostakovich was preoccupied to an extraordinary degree. He then turned to the tragic fate of Schumann, whom he regarded as a composer of genius, and explained why he had felt impelled to re-orchestrate the Cello Concerto. He said (verbatim): 'I have the impression that at the time when Schumann orchestrated the concerto he was suffering from a deep depression, so much so that he was actually ill. That is why I felt justified in taking such a liberty.'

121 The deep affection Shostakovich felt for Benjamin Britten lasted until the end of his life. It was no accident that he dedicated to the Englishman his Fourteenth Symphony, the most spiritual of all his compositions.

122 So anxious was Shostakovich that I should share his feelings about this work that two and a half years later, on 9 April 1966, he brought me a present of the wonderful English recording of the *War Requiem*, signing a presentation note to me on it.

123 The outstanding Leningrad violinist Mikhail Vaiman gladly agreed to Shostakovich's proposal that we should listen to the recording in his apartment. He told that he considered it an honour to offer hospitality to Dmitry Dmitriyevich, whose First Violin Concerto he played with extreme pleasure.

124 At the Stanislavsky–Nemirovich-Danchenko Theatre.

125 The première of Kirill Molchanov's *Romeo, Juliet and Darkness* took place in the Maly Opera Theatre on 27 May 1963, conducted by Asen Naidyenov, produced by Yu. Petrov, designed by E. Shtenberg. On 9 June, *Leningrad Pravda* carried a review of the production by A. Vladimirovskaya under the elegant heading 'Why did darkness win?' The writer sharply criticized both composer and theatre for the darkly pessimistic treatment of the subject, and for the absence of melody in the music.

126 There were many foreign productions of *Katerina Izmailova*, but Shostakovich seldom derived much satisfaction from the various producers' conceptions of the opera. However, he had been interested in Tito since the Yugoslav leader became the subject of virulent attacks by Stalin.

127 Sviridov's cantata of that name for choir and symphony orchestra. [Kursk folk-song is the richest survivor of the tradition of multipart singing from the rural areas of the black earth belt of the Southern Russia steppe – Translator's Note]

128 Shostakovich admired Vainberg's talent without reservation, placing him without a hint of ulterior motive on a level with himself.

129 Shostakovich's particular love for the Thirteenth Symphony was only strengthened by the disfavour into which it had fallen: performances of it were effectively proscribed by the authorities.

130 Shostakovich frequently adopted the spirit of Pushkin's Mozart when, as he does here, he dismisses his own creative work in deliberately disparaging terminology. When Pushkin's Salieri calls Mozart a God, the latter crushes

the excessive adulation of his worshipper by replying: 'Maybe, but my divinity is famished with hunger.' Pushkin himself was quite capable of referring dismissively to his own work: 'The other day I shat about a thousand lines of a story' – letter to Vyazemsky of 3 September 1831.

131 Stepan, or Stenka, Razin: seventeenth-century Don Cossack chieftain who in 1670 led a rebellion later joined by serfs and peasants against the tsar and the boyars. After his forces were finally defeated at Simbirsk, he retreated to his homeland on the Don River, where he was betrayed by rival chiefs loyal to the government, brought to Moscow, and executed, to be for ever mythologized as a sort of Russian Robin Hood. (Translator's Note)

132 See chapter 4, note 116 to the letter dated 7 July 1963.

133 Shostakovich strongly objected to the savagery of lines like this:

> My sin, good people, was not to hang
> The boyars from the towers.
> The sin I see in my own eyes
> Was not to hang enough of them.

But Yevtushenko was resistant to Shostakovich's arguments.

134 A critical commonplace of the time, here employed ironically.

135 Heavy coats of rough cloth worn by peasants. (Translator's Note)

136 On 20 September, as soon as Shostakovich arrived in Leningrad, he telephoned to ask me round to his sister's apartment so that he could play the piece through to me, and then have dinner. Venyamin Basner was there as well. I sat next to the piano and turned pages as Shostakovich played; when he reached certain passages, abundant tears flowed down his cheeks. I could not help thinking of how Tchaikovsky wept at the fate of his own creation, Hermann. It was almost as though Shostakovich was hearing, not his own, but another's intensely moving music. The whole work, words and music, affected me strongly with its vividness, power and beauty, and by the representation of the multicoloured, kaleidoscopic background of Moscow against which Stepan Razin moved inexorably to his death. The fate of the hero was deeply dramatic and moving.

Razin's theme is contrasted musically with the themes of the Crowd and the State. Not only the essence of the whole work but its contemporary relevance is encapsulated in this internal and external conflict. Especially evocative is the role of the Crowd: at the start of the piece it surges exultantly into the square, intent on the entertainment that Stepan Razin's execution will provide, but then an amazing transformation takes place in its mood as spiritual truth begins to dawn.

There is a gap at the end of the letter – several lines have been cut out.

137 After Shostakovich had played through *The Execution of Stepan Razin* to us on 20 September in Leningrad, I sat down and wrote him a detailed letter setting out my opinion of this wonderful work, of his music and the text.

138 Shostakovich is referring to the unexpected twists and turns of thought that zigzag through Yevtushenko's verse, sometimes apparently running counter to the beliefs he expresses in his best work. This earned him in some quarters

the reputation of being an opportunist and a conformist, but Shostakovich was sure that at heart he was not.

139 Anatoly Kankarovich, composer, conductor and critic.

140 Shostakovich often expressed to me his indignation with such literary fusspots and pedants, whom he considered soulless, prim and insensitive to the essential content of the works they were judging. To him, Kankarovich was one of them, having completely missed the profoundly dramatic point of the a capella *Ten Poems on Texts by Revolutionary Poets*, written with the heart's blood in 1951 – a time of harsh Stalinist repression – to poems which stripped away the masks from aggressors not only of the past but of the present time.

141 Shostakovich had no time for literary purists who failed to appreciate the artistic power of Leskov's remarkable novella.

142 Literally, 'terrible'; 'pupils (of the eye)'. (Translator's Note)

143 Literally, 'whose life'; 'of Dzerzhinsky', the genitive form. Names, like other nouns, decline in Russian. (Translator's Note)

144 Shostakovich doggedly and consistently upheld Yevtushenko against the attacks of the nitpicking critics he so detested. Needless to say, there were also many poets of an entirely different style and persuasion whom he loved, and whose verses he sensitively absorbed and embodied in his music: the poetry of Alexander Blok, Marina Tsvetayeva, Guillaume Apollinaire, Rainer Maria Rilke, Robert Burns, not to mention Pushkin and Shakespeare.

145 Shostakovich invited my wife and me to attend the première of *The Execution of Stepan Razin*. We travelled to Moscow on 27 December, and on the morning of the 28th I accompanied Dmitry Dmitriyevich to the general rehearsal, where something quite extraordinary occurred. The veteran Bolshoy Theatre soloist Ivan Petrov, who had been rehearsing the role of Stepan Razin, simply failed to turn up at the general rehearsal without a word of warning. He had evidently made a prudent calculation that Shostakovich's symphonic poem would fail to earn the approval of the authorities, and therefore judged it worthwhile to offend Shostakovich and the conductor Kirill Kondrashin.

A replacement for Petrov was urgently sought and found in Vitaly Gromadsky, and the concert went ahead. But Petrov's shabby behaviour meant that the morning of 28 December was an alarming and upsetting time.

The work was received with colossal enthusiasm. After the ovation that greeted Shostakovich's arrival on the platform, a second wave carried Yevtushenko on its crest.

The Moscow press devoted not a single line to the première of *The Execution of Stepan Razin*, so Petrov's premonition had in that sense proved correct. Nevertheless, the work had its second performance as planned on 5 January 1965.

146 The poet Aleksandr Prokofiev had served for many years as First Secretary of the Leningrad Writers' Organization, but had been voted out of office in January 1965. The venerable poet, accustomed to the respect of his peers, had taken this vote of no confidence by his colleagues very hard.

Shostakovich had been an admirer of the younger Prokofiev's poetry, distinguished as it was by the colour and freshness of its intonation. He had had great sympathy for him when the irrational fury of Stalin had been unleashed on his head for his translation from Ukrainian of the 'pernicious versifying' of Vladimir Sosyury's 'Love for the Ukraine'. Later, however, there had been a rift between the two men over an insulting speech Prokofiev delivered at Zoshchenko's funeral. Hence the veiled irony of 'the truth will prevail'.

147 Mikhail Dudin, the poet who took Aleksandr Prokofiev's place as First Secretary of the Leningrad Writers' Organization.

148 This score was finished in June 1965.

149 This long poem, one chapter of which is *The Execution of Stepan Razin*, was the subject of a ban and was removed from the January issue of the journal *Youth*. Shostakovich was deeply upset by this evidence that Stalin's legacy was still, twelve years after his death, affecting the world of literature. In the event, the poem was rehabilitated and was printed in the May issue of the journal. Shostakovich was delighted, and sent me a copy of the magazine.

150 As I have noted in other letters, Shostakovich not infrequently experienced an apparent crisis of failing powers that seemed to him at the time not only real but irreversible.

151 The director of the film, Grigory Roshal.

152 Sergey Slonimsky, composer and musicologist.

153 Shostakovich was upset by this attack on Yevtushenko, particularly on 'Baby Yar'.

154 This refers to a film scenario for a film to be entitled *Dmitry Shostakovich* which I had created for Lennaúchfilm [Leningrad Educational Film Studio – Translator's Note] in collaboration with the composer Aleksandr Chernov and the screenwriter Yury Nepomnyashchy. The film was to mark the sixtieth birthday of the composer. The studio had sent the scenario for comment also to Khachaturian and to the composer Mikhail Chulaki.

155 'Decree of the Central Committee of the Communist Party (Bolshevik) of 10 February 1948 concerning Muradeli's opera *The Great Friendship*.'

156 Khachaturian's approach coincided precisely with my own, and there were also dramatic episodes in the scenario relating to the notorious 'Muddle Instead of Music' article in *Pravda*. But Goskino RSFSR, the umbrella cinema organization of the Russian Federation which embraced Lennaúchfilm, demanded the removal of all material which might be seen as having had a damaging effect on the composer's life. This was the Brezhnev era, when all references to the arbitrary effects of Stalin's regime on the arts and literature (and other areas as well) were forbidden. I categorically rejected Goskino RSFSR's demands and declined to be involved with a misleading representation of Shostakovich's artistic life as an uninterrupted idyll of creativity. In consequence, the film was never made.

157 Naturally, Shostakovich felt entitled to be proud of the fact that he had ignored the Decree's ineptly dogmatic directions as to how music should be

composed, but continued on his own path, writing music according to the stronger imperatives of his soul and his intellect.

158 I did get a letter to this effect from Khachaturian.

159 A nature reserve in Belorussia. (Translator's Note)

160 Although I was as usual spending the summer at Sestroretsk, which was only about ten kilometres from Repino, Shostakovich kept up his ingrained habit of writing letters.

161 Shostakovich liked dogs, albeit in a quiet way and without fussing or sentimentalizing over them. He loved the beauty of horses, but this excitement over bison and wild boar was somewhat of a surprise to me.

162 To the end of his days, Shostakovich remained open to new experiences, whether in art and music or in the secrets and wonders of nature.

163 For a long time the Thirteenth Symphony had been the subject of an unofficial ban, so its return to the [Moscow] Philharmonic's platform was a matter for rejoicing. Throughout its years of proscription, Shostakovich had always maintained to me that it was one of his best works. He did not necessarily, however, always hold this opinion: Shostakovich did not alter his convictions, but he did sometimes change his opinions about his own works. The time that the Thirteenth Symphony was most dear to him was while it was under attack. On 21 June the composer invited me to Repino so that we could together mark the third anniversary of the symphony's completion, which we did with considerable ceremony. Thirteen candles were lighted in the cottage; we reminisced about the work's composition, and drank a toast to its future life on the concert platform. Shostakovich loved and valued ritual.

On 20 September 1965, the Thirteenth Symphony was performed as scheduled in the Great Hall of the Moscow Conservatoire. I attended the concert at the composer's invitation and witnessed its enormous success. Like a living organism, the symphony had grown in stature and beauty.

164 A popular humorous magazine. (Translator's Note)

165 After the dramatic poem *The Execution of Stepan Razin*, Shostakovich clearly felt the need to relax in a more lighthearted vein. Much the same thing had happened in the spring of 1942, when, immediately after finishing the magnificent Seventh Symphony, he embarked on the comic opera *The Gamblers*, based on Gogol's play.

The Five Romances to Texts from Krokodil were written in what amounted to a single sitting. Shostakovich read the paper on the day it came out, 30 August, and by 2 or 3 September the songs were already composed. He had a phenomenal ability to pick out from any text what others missed and see its potential for musical setting. Other examples are the verses of Sasha Chorny and of Captain Lebyadkin from Dostoyevsky's novel *The Possessed*, from which he created wonderful musical lampoons.

166 Shostakovich enclosed five separate typewritten sheets, each bearing one of the five extracts from the magazine, having carefully corrected all the misprints.

167 Adapted quotation from a famous lyric poem by Tyuchev, 'I love the thunderstorm in early May'. (Translator's Note)

168   The hope was soon realized. On 16 September Shostakovich came to Leningrad and showed me the songs, full of sparkling wit and parody, the music seamlessly following the inflections of the spoken word and the comic characters sketched in vivid colours.

169   The writer Anna Karavayeva.

170   The forthcoming filming of *Katerina Izmailova* filled Shostakovich with a sense of vague unease. On 15 October the previous year, he and I had both attended a meeting of the artistic committee of Group Three of the Lenfilm conglomerate, at which the script for the opera film of *Katerina Izmailova* had been discussed. The film director Mikhail Shapiro and I (in my capacity as editorial consultant) invited Shostakovich to collaborate on the development of the screenplay; he has an additional credit in the titles as author of the screenplay. The picture, in which Galina Vishnevskaya took the title role, both singing and acting, was finished in September 1966 and was generally considered to be a successful, interesting and vivid representation. Shostakovich liked it.

171   Maksim Shostakovich was about to make his conducting debut with his father's Tenth Symphony. Paternal feelings in no way inhibited Shostakovich from applying strictly objective standards to his son's artistic and professional attainments.

172   I had arranged a small reception honouring Shostakovich, but I considered it had been a rather unsuccessful event.

173   Ivan Sollertinsky's widow had damaged her spine in a fall, and as a result had been forced to give up her work as a pianist.

174   A cheap and chauvinistic novel by Ivan Shevtsov which had created a stir at the time.

175   By Stepan himself. (Translator's Note)

176   Shostakovich does not do himself justice. Everything he conceived is perfectly realized; the misunderstanding arose from my not having expressed myself clearly. I was referring to the very beginning of the piece, where the vast crowd is jostling and mocking: 'Today's a holiday! They're bringing Stenka Razin!'

177   Shostakovich was undoubtedly correct in his fear that attending the Plenum would involve him in listening to a whole series of feeble or mediocre works. This would have been a particular trial to him at a time when he was immersed in the tragic Fourteenth Symphony, a work to which he attached immense importance, as became clear in a later letter to me, written after the composition had been completed.

178   On 13 March I had moved into an apartment at No. 44 Bolshaya Pushkarskaya Street. By a strange combination of circumstances, the building I had moved to was diagonally opposite No. 37 in the same street, in which Shostakovich had had his last Leningrad apartment – the same in which he had played through to me the introduction and invasion theme of the Seventh Symphony in August 1941. I regarded this as fate. On the innumerable occasions when I subsequently passed this building, now shorn of its former occupant, it always struck me with a feeling of sadness. It seemed to have a

melancholy, frowning air, as if brooding on its former resident who had now abandoned it for ever. These are not just fine words: I am expressing my feelings in all sincerity, and if they strike the reader as not true to life, they are still true for me.

179 Until this move, my wife and I had been living in a communal apartment. In his large-hearted way, Dmitry Dmitriyevich was even more pleased about the move than I was. Something similar had occurred when, before the war, Ivan Sollertinsky had succeeding in getting himself a separate apartment.

180 Shostakovich's airy dismissal of what was after all a serious matter may have had something to do with the fact that he was, creatively speaking, astride winged Pegasus at the time, inspiration at full flood in a whole series of works, as detailed in the letter.

181 The text is a paraphrase of Pushkin's epigram 'History of a Versifier'. Assuming the mask of the ill-starred poet, Shostakovich created a wildly funny and original musical humoresque in the spirit of romantic irony, wherein the author contemplates his own persona and subjects himself to mocking self-criticism. In the wonderfully extended signature to the Complete Collection of his Works, Shostakovich lists to comically pompous effect his honours, positions and duties.

182 Shostakovich came to my new apartment with Irina Antonovna as arranged, at 4 p.m. on 9 April. He brought housewarming presents: an enormous radiogram and records of his First, Fifth, Eighth and Ninth Symphonies, the Suite from *Hamlet* and Britten's *War Requiem*, all inscribed with personal messages.

These were his choices from his own extensive record collection. He was in the best of spirits, and everything about our extremely modest flat delighted him. Before sitting down to table, he suddenly asked Vera Vasiliyevna for a hammer and a nail, then, taking from his pocket a ten-rouble note, attached it to the wall. 'There,' he said with a smile, 'that is to make sure that you will always have plenty of money.' Shostakovich had great respect for rituals, traditions and symbols, although he was not superstitious like Pushkin. After the meal, he told us that he had composed three movements of the Second Cello Concerto, but the third movement was, in his words, 'very bad' and he proposed to start it again from the beginning.

183 Shostakovich, having been initially dissatisfied with the third movement, had completely rewritten it.

184 *Bubliki* are thick, ring-shaped rolls, a bit like bagels. (Translator's Note)

185 Shostakovich calls them *Humoresques* here, but they are usually known as *Romances*. (Translator's Note)

186 After such a long absence from the concert platform as a pianist – and what a pianist he had been! – now, in 1966, he is seized with fear. It is painful to read these lines. It could well be that the long years of nervous strain had exacerbated the condition in his right hand.

187 The brand name of the radiogram Shostakovich had given us as a housewarming present.

188 Distinguished Kirghiz writer born 1928, writing in both Russian and Kirghiz. (Translator's Note)

189 The Second Cello Concerto

190 Shostakovich had had some bad experiences with the mail. He was always concerned over the fate of his manuscripts, but unlike, for instance, Sergey Prokofiev, he was incapable of keeping them safely.

191 The Fourth Symphony of Nikolai Peyko and the First Symphony of Galina Ustvolskaya.

192 *Poem In Memory of the Fallen in the Blockade of Leningrad*, for four trumpets, two pianos, organ, strings and percussion by Andrey Petrov.

193 This paradoxical statement should be understood as Shostakovich's reluctance to complain about his health, which was actually far from good.

194 The speech was N. G. Yegorïchev's address to the congress held in honour of the ninety-sixth anniversary of Lenin's birth, published in *Literaturnaya Gazeta* on 23 April. Both Shostakovich and I detected in it hints of a movement to rehabilitate Stalin's regime, which spelt out to us the same message: the 'thaw' was coming to an end.

195 Shostakovich was an unusually attentive reader of anything that he liked, whether literature or a letter. I do not know whether Chingiz Aitmatov was aware that Shostakovich had read his excellent short novel right through three times, or whether the merciless power of the castration scene had all but reduced him to hysterics.

For myself, I remember that I also balked at reading these pages, although I realized that they contained much that was profound as well as painful. In the novella the hero's wife says something like 'Gulsary is not the first, neither will he be the last', by which she means that stallions even when even they are gelded are the backbone, the strength and the flower of the horse tribe. If Gulsary had not been gelded, it would have been difficult for his new rider – one of the chiefs – to ride him, as he was used to more docile mounts. At all events, this was my interpretation, as I set it out for Shostakovich in a letter. He agreed with it.

196 Jokes are never very successful if they have to be explained, but this one depends on the fact that in Russian the masculine (shepherd) and neuter (egg) pronoun is the same when it is the object of a verb, thus Irinka's inclination is ambiguous. The word for an egg is also a vulgar term for the testicle. (Translator's Note)

197 The signature was in Shostakovich's own hand. On 16 June I went to the hospital and, greatly apprehensive, entered Ward 11. Shostakovich greeted me with his favourite phrase: 'I'm feeling fine.' This catch-all phrase, rich in nuances for the initiated, was most confusing to those who were not fully seized of the composer's enigmatic character.

We talked of this and that, and for some reason the talk turned to Mozart. Shostakovich said that of all Mozart's operas he preferred *The Marriage of Figaro*. He then added: 'If I compare Mozart's *Requiem* with Britten's *War Requiem*, I think I must award the palm to Britten.' Shostakovich's ideas about music owed nothing to conventional wisdom. My first visit lasted

[293]

over an hour, despite having been allotted no more than fifteen to twenty minutes by Irina Antonovna.

On 21 June, a festival opened in the Leningrad Philharmonia dedicated to Shostakovich's music. Mravinsky directed the orchestra in magnificent performances of the Sixth and Tenth Symphonies, but the absence of the composer caused me an almost physical sensation of loss.

Two days later, I visited the hospital once more. Shostakovich was much exercised about the forthcoming performance of the Thirteenth Symphony in the festival. He said, sadly: 'It is such a shame I can't be present, after all it has been four years since it was played in Leningrad.'

The programme in the Philharmonia on 25 June included the Thirteenth Symphony and the First Cello Concerto. The packed hall gave a tremendous ovation to Yevgeny Yevtushenko, who had come from Moscow for the occasion. The poet addressed the audience from the stage, saying: 'The guilty party mainly responsible for this evening's success, Dmitry Dmitriyevich, is not in the hall. He is in hospital, but if you applaud him now, he will hear you.' After these words the applause redoubled. When I told Shostakovich about this touching tribute, he was deeply moved.

On 4 July I again went to the hospital. Shostakovich, speaking of the peculiarities of musical taste, said: 'When I was young, I had a friend, a very good musician, who placed Meyerbeer above any other operatic composer.' I replied that I myself considered the fourth act of *Les Huguenots* beyond praise, and no whit inferior to the best pages of Verdi. Shostakovich responded: 'That may be so, but look at the quantity of rubbish Meyerbeer wrote besides. The point is, the true genius knows exactly how much really good music to write, and how much second-rate.' I found this an extremely interesting and original idea, and thought I detected an undercurrent of autobiography in it.

Shostakovich was reading *The Diary of Anne Frank* in hospital. It took fifteen years from its appearance in the West for it to be published in our country. 'An admirably leisurely progress' was Shostakovich's ironic comment.

I regularly went to see him while he lay in hospital, right up to the beginning of August, when he went to Melnichy Ruchey to convalesce.

198　Maya Dubyanskaya – Shostakovich had the surname slightly wrong – was a director of music programmes for television. On 28 February 1966 Leningrad TV had aired a programme in memory of Ivan Sollertinsky, and the following had taken part: Dmitry Shostakovich, Irakli Andronikov, Yulian Vainkop, Isaak Glikman, Mikhail Druskin, and Pavel Serebryakov. A group photograph of all those taking part had, evidently, been sent to Dmitry Dmitriyevich in hospital.

199　At the time I was in Repino, staying in the Cinematographers' Rest House.

200　Shostakovich stayed at the Composers' Rest House in Repino until 16th September. On the 25th he celebrated his sixtieth birthday in Moscow, an event my wife and I attended.

201　I am sure that Shostakovich, reading this story in *Prostor*, was reminded of the even greater horror we experienced together eighteen years previously. I had come to visit him at the Government dacha in Komarovo, the one from which he was later evicted. This was in August 1948, at the time when the sessions of the Lenin All-Union Agricultural Academy were in full swing, and we read with horrified revulsion the reports in *Pravda* of the papers submitted by Lysenko, and the ensuing discussions. It seemed to us as though the pages of the newspaper ran red with the blood of the geneticists who had been gleefully crushed and destroyed by Lysenko and his cohorts. We were appalled.

I recall that one Lysenkoite asked his chief the obviously stage-managed question: had Trofim Denisovich's paper met with the approval of Comrade Stalin? And when the answer was given in the affirmative, all those present (according to the newspaper) erupted in a storm of applause. Such approval from the highest power in the land could presage nothing but the total triumph of the Lysenkoites over the followers of their boss's rival, Weisman.

A short while earlier, in February of the same year, Shostakovich, Prokofiev and other composers had been vilified as a consequence of the Decree on Vano Muradeli's opera *The Great Friendship*. The wounds inflicted on Shostakovich had by no means healed, and as he heard the triumphant howling of Stalin's butchers in the Lysenko camp, they reopened as wide as ever.

Reading *Pravda* that August of 1948 inevitably made us think of Zoshchenko and Akhmatova, who had been crucified two years earlier in the pages of the country's principal newspaper . . . Shostakovich aligned himself with writers, doctors, biologists, whenever they became victims of the Terror. In his eyes, those who indifferently turned their backs on the sufferings of others were themselves accomplices to the crimes, and this was a principle to which he remained true until the end of his life.

202 Shostakovich loved and admired Britten not only as a composer but as a person. Dedicating his Fourteenth Symphony to Britten was a deeply considered gesture.

203 The little present was a rubber stamp with Shostakovich's full name and address. Such things gave him much innocent pleasure, and he used it instead of filling in by hand the space for the sender's name and address.

204 The Second Cello Concerto, scheduled for performance at the Leningrad Conservatoire at the end of November 1966. It was I who had organized this concert, and it came about at a banquet arranged by Mstislav Rostropovich to celebrate Shostakovich's sixtieth birthday (the composer himself was physically too weak to attend). I knew that Rostropovich had fallen out with the Leningrad Philharmonia because of their refusal to programme the Second Cello Concerto (sadly, the blame for this must be attributed to Yevgeny Mravinsky). I suggested to Rostropovich that he should perform it with the student orchestra of the Conservatoire, conducted by Nikolai Rabinovich. The proposal was accepted with alacrity by all those present, not least by Rostropovich himself. As a result, two months later the tremendously successful Leningrad première of the Second Cello Concerto took place not in the Philharmonia, but in the Conservatoire. This was highly irregular and the

cause of great bewilderment to music lovers, not to mention the musicians of the Philharmonia.

205 At this stage Shostakovich did not know that the concert was due to take place not in the Great Hall but the Small Hall of the Conservatoire.

206 Happily, this gloomy prediction was not fulfilled, and once Shostakovich recovered sufficiently he made many more visits to Leningrad.

207 A song cycle by Revol Bunin, one of Shostakovich's students at the Moscow Conservatoire. I had written enthusiastically to Shostakovich about these songs.

208 This letter is in response to mine in which I had described the ecstatic reception accorded to the performance of the Second Cello Concerto in the Small Hall of the Leningrad Conservatoire.

209 After the war, it was Mravinsky's practice each year to spend the whole summer in the depths of the forest on the Karelian isthmus, enjoying the unspoilt countryside. His favourite writer was Mikhail Prishvin, in whose wonderful books he was at that time totally engrossed.

210 Shostakovich had been worried about the performance of the Thirteenth Symphony, due to be conducted by Igor Blazhkov in the middle of December. On 9 December Shostakovich telephoned me and asked me to go to the rehearsal and report back on my impressions. He himself was unable to come to Leningrad, owing to the condition of his leg, an absence he was naturally fretting over. The concert was an enormous success. It is practically impossible to ruin this symphony; its effect on listeners is irresistible. I wrote as much to Shostakovich.

211 Shostakovich loved Schumann's music. I remember an occasion before the war when he happened to be at a morning rehearsal in the Glinka Capella. When he saw me, he said: 'I have just heard Schumann's *Träumerei*. What ravishing music from a composer with such an unhappy fate.' (His exact words.)

212 This work may have provided the creative impulse for Shostakovich's own wonderful *Suite on Verses of Michelangelo Buonarotti*, for bass and symphony orchestra, composed eight years later, in 1974.

Chapter V Failing Health, 1967–1969

1 By my reckoning, we had not met for about four months. This seemed too long to Shostakovich, who felt that he needed more frequent and regular encounters.

2 I honestly do not know whether this appellation was a witty invention of Shostakovich's or whether it was a genuine title awarded to Sibelius representing 'the creative art of the nation'.

3 The heart attack Shostakovich suffered in the summer of 1966.

4 The thoughts on life and death that so preoccupied Shostakovich at this time were, in my opinion, the genesis of the Fourteenth Symphony, although the writer states elsewhere that the catalyst was Musorgsky's *Songs and Dances of Death*. [See the first letter dated 19 March 1969 – Translator's Note]

5 A reference to his own article 'Thoughts on the path travelled' ('*Dumï o proydyonnom puti*', *Sovetskaya muzïka* 9, 1956, 9–15. (Translator's Note)

6 In this bout of black melancholy, Shostakovich plumbs the depths of self-abnegation, downgrading his genuine fame to mere 'publicity' and in so doing echoing the malicious fabrications of evil-minded detractors who throughout the 1930s never stopped their enviously parroted complaints about the 'publicity' surrounding his name.

7 A despairing rejection of two of his greatest works, and those dearest to his heart. '*Fuk*' is an expostulation employed by Gogol's character Sobakevich in *Dead Souls*, signifying nonsense, rubbish. Shostakovich borrowed it for the libretto of his Gogol opera *The Nose*.

8 A miscalculation of two years.

9 The last three songs are usually known by the titles 'The Storm', 'Secret Signs' and 'Music'. (Translator's Note)

10 Shostakovich had asked me to find out the address of a friend of his youth, S. M. Gershov.

11 Shostakovich had at one time the intention to write an opera on *The Life of Galileo*, but after seeing this production at the Taganka Theatre he abandoned it.

12 My brother, the sculptor, had just had an operation.

13 Superstitiously, I had tried hard to dissuade Shostakovich from setting Pushkin's poem 'The Monument' ('A monument not made by hands I raised up to myself'), reminding him that Pushkin had summed up his own life and work in this poem, losing his life within a year and a half of its composition.

14 I.e. carriages with upholstered seats. (Translator's Note)

15 In his youth, Shostakovich never paid any attention to what sort of carriage he travelled in, or any other aspect of comfort. It was not his character that had altered, merely the effects of his many illnesses that caused him to be thus 'spoilt'.

16 In Shostakovich's capacity as a Deputy of the Supreme Soviet of the USSR.

17 A petition for an honour to be conferred on the conductor Nikolai Rabinovich, whom Shostakovich esteemed highly as a man and as a musician.

18 The film of *Katerina Izmailova* was to be shown at the Cannes Film Festival, and both the composer and the director of the film, Mikhail Shapiro, had been invited.

19 The Second Violin Concerto, which was completed five weeks later, in the middle of May, during a stay in Repino.

20 The opera and film director.

21 *Life in the Lyric Theatre* was the title of the book by the well-known opera director E. I. Kaplan.

22 The pianist Aleksandr Geronimus.

23 On 19 May 1967 Shostakovich, accompanied by Irina Antonovna and his sister Mariya, came to supper with us at home. Shostakovich was in excellent spirits, and drank a glass of vodka with me to celebrate the completion of the

Second Violin Concerto. He wanted to play it through to us, but was prevented by a desperately out-of-tune upright piano and by the copiousness of the meal we had eaten. I was delighted by Shostakovich's cheerfulness and his much-improved physical state. After supper, he departed for Moscow, carrying in his briefcase a magnificent work destined for a great future both in our country and abroad.

24 In my opinion, the Blok cycle reveals the anguish of Shostakovich's soul with unique clarity and poignancy. The tragic songs – 'Gamayun, Bird of Prophecy' and 'Oh What Rage Beyond the Window' – form a contrast with the glorious lyricism of the other songs, while the last one, 'At Night When Agitation Stills' has an overwhelmingly radiant beauty.

Dmitry Dmitriyevich invited me to come to Moscow at the beginning of February 1967 to get to know the cycle. On 10 February, at Zhukovka, in the twilight of the dying day, he played me the songs, leaving me with an unforgettable impression. In them, it seemed to me, Shostakovich had written his confession, maintaining hope and belief in the future despite his sufferings. I could well understand the joy of which he writes at hearing the true sound of the songs as he had envisaged them. The wonderful music and the words of the young poet had released him from the burden of everyday anxieties.

25 Whenever Shostakovich set himself a compositional task, he generally completed it, come what may, within the time limits he had set for himself, notwithstanding any fatigue he might – as in this case – have been experiencing.

26 Shostakovich found most animals attractive. He loved dogs and liked having them in the house, but never slobbered over them, adopting an attitude of restrained tenderness.

27 Premières of the symphonic poem *October* and the Second Violin Concerto with David Oistrakh were scheduled in Moscow for the end of September.

28 A volume of Shostakovich's *Collected Vocal Works* was published in 1967.

29 Shostakovich's attitude to Sergey Eisenstein and Mikhail Dovzhenko was anything but straightforward. He was, needless to say, full of fellow feeling for them when they became victims of persecution. There were many scenes from *The Battleship Potyomkin* that he admired, including the famous Odessa Steps. And he took pleasure in writing the music for *Michurin*, Dovzhenko's film about the tragic events of 1949. I recall Shostakovich's admiration for the great mastery and poetic feeling with which Dovzhenko created his screen images of spring awakening, and he said to me that he felt his music had been successful in its response to the magnificent landscapes which played such an important part in the film.

However, there were several aesthetic principles underlying Eisenstein's and Dovzhenko's work which Shostakovich rejected. For example, he found the super-refinement characteristic of their metaphorical language overdone. He felt that it inhibited identification with the heroes of the action and empathy with their fate, and generally speaking constituted an approach to cinema inimical to the full achievement of the art form's high ideals.

Shostakovich found Eisenstein's film of *Ivan The Terrible* distasteful, especially the second sequence which bore the typically Stalinist-era title of 'The Boyars' Plot'. He could appreciate that the film had been masterfully executed, but was still nauseated by the content because of the pervasive spirit of Stalinism hovering above the tendentious treatment of historical fact and the character of Ivan himself. Dmitry Dmitriyevich detested Tsar Ivan, so much so that he was always surprised at Rimsky-Korsakov's willingness in *Pskovityanka* to glamorize the monster's image.

As for cinematographic geniuses, in Shostakovich's opinion there was only one person who could legitimately lay claim to the title, and that was Charlie Chaplin. His delight in Chaplin's films never waned.

30 I detect in the final phrase a slight modification of the starry-eyed initial reaction to Rada Volshaninova's gypsy singing, which may have ended up seeming to Shostakovich a little overstated. [*Zakusky* are the savoury snacks without which no Russian would contemplate drinking vodka – Translator's Note]

31 In my letter thanking Shostakovich for the gift of his *Collected Vocal Works*, I had made a joke of the comic misprint which had crept in to the dedication to me of 'Macpherson Before his Execution'. As printed, my first name and patronymic appeared as 'Issak Dovïdovich'. But Shostakovich was not amused at all, scourging himself mercilessly for the oversight. Assuming quite wrongly that I would be affronted by the mistake, he suggests in a fit of temper that I 'throw it out with the rubbish'.

In my next letter I continued the joke by explaining to Shostakovich that the misprint was entirely reasonable in that names like Isaak and Davïd are not normally encountered in our newspapers, and that proofreaders are not in the habit of reading the Bible. Shostakovich agreed, but continued to be angry, typically not with the proofreaders, but with himself. In the second edition of the *Collected Vocal Works*, the matter was, as Mayakovsky might have said, 'properly seasoned', and my name appeared correctly: Shostakovich saw to it personally.

32 *Satires (Pictures of the Past)*, Op. 109. 'Kreutzer Sonata' is the last song in the set.

33 Shostakovich was recovering in the Kuntsevo hospital. At the beginning of September, soon after his last letter to me, he had fallen and broken his leg. Misfortune after misfortune was raining down on him. I could hardly keep back the tears at the courage and gallows humour of this letter.

34 In the midst of yet another distressful stay in hospital, Shostakovich still remembered my wife's traditional observance of 30 September as the name day of Faith, Hope and Charity. [In Russian, Vera, Nadezhda, Lyubov – Translator's Note]

35 The annual celebration of the October Revolution. (Translator's Note)

36 The Second Violin Concerto.

37 I travelled to Moscow to see Shostakovich and to attend the performance of the concert on 23 October in the Great Hall of the Conservatoire. Galina Vishnevskaya sang the *Seven Romances on Poems of Aleksandr Blok*,

accompanied by a trio consisting of David Oistrakh, Mstislav Rostropovich and Moysey Vainberg. The performance of these beautiful songs was outstanding, but it was heartrending to think that Shostakovich was unable be with them on the platform playing the piano part, especially conceived, as he said, to take account of his limited physical capabilities, but was reduced to listening on the radio at home in Zhukovka. The concert was received with tremendous appreciation, and afterwards Irina Antonovna, who had a driving licence, took me out to Zhukovka, where she had arranged a candlelit supper in the romantic spirit of the young Blok. Dmitry Dmitriyevich was helped downstairs to the dining-room and took part in the meal in high spirits. He had enjoyed the performance, and raised his glass in a toast to 'a work I composed apparently not in vain'. The following day we talked long about many things, many of them melancholy but relieved by those flashes of humour that never completely left him.

38 As already mentioned, (see preface, pp. xxvii–xxviii), Vladimir Lebedev was not only a gifted artist but an inveterate sports fan. Before the war, he, Shostakovich and I regularly went to football matches together, and we also often enjoyed his generous hospitality. We would go to his apartment, a spacious studio on the top floor of a tall building on Belinsky Street, near the Fontanka, feast our eyes on his pictures, and have supper. He was an enchanting person.

39 Nadezhda Yureneva spent several months studying the Blok songs, and sang them in the presence of the composer in the Small Hall of the Leningrad Philharmonia on 17 April 1968.

40 I was an admirer of Nadezhda Yureneva's musicianship and her technical mastery, but I thought that in some respects Dmitry Dmitriyevich was somewhat overstating her merits, and had written to him to that effect.

41 Shostakovich attached enormous importance to the words, which he considered should be not only audible but clearly understood in the auditorium. It was for that reason that always wanted *Katerina Izmailova* to be performed not in the original Russian but in the language of the country where it was being performed, even if the translation did not meet the most exacting standards.

42 This sarcastic rejoinder was in answer to my facetious revelation of the singer's having broken off her engagement after a betrothal ceremony at which I was present.

43 *The Quiet Don* (Part Two) was produced in November 1967 at the Kirov Theatre, conducted by Konstantin Simeonov and produced by Roman Tikhomirov. I sent Shostakovich a detailed account of my impressions of the production.

44 A make of short-wave radio produced in Latvia, widely used for listening to the BBC World Service. (Translator's Note)

45 Shostakovich naturally understood Liszt's importance in the history of music, but in his maturity he had little enthusiasm for his music. I recall his liking the songs 'Die Loreley' and 'Laura'.

46 When we talked of times gone by, it always struck me how dispassionately Shostakovich would speak of those who had done him harm. He used the stock phrase: 'they knew not what they did'. But he was always merciless towards informers whose lies had destroyed the innocent, and towards the arch-destroyer of them all – Stalin.

47 The customary ironic refrain, reflecting the fact that 1967 was full of misfortunes and physical suffering for Shostakovich.

48 Usually known as *Colas Breugnon*. (Translator's Note)

49 In the pre-war years, Bragin persistently tried to enlist Shostakovich's collaboration on one or another of his projects. The perennial state of over-excitement in which Bragin lived, forever building castles in the air and suggesting unfeasible plans and projects to composers, accounts for the sarcastic tone of Shostakovich's letter and its melancholy postscript. I knew personally this artless dreamer who, incidentally, was by no means devoid of literary talent.

50 Shostakovich said to me on several occasions that every time he listened to *Das Lied* it was an overwhelming experience for him, and the last movement – 'Der Abschied' – reduced him to tears.

51 Shostakovich's passion for *The Stone Guest* was long-lived and immutable. It never failed to astonish him that this opera was ignored on the stages of the Moscow and Leningrad theatres.

52 Shostakovich's material circumstances were volatile. At times he was seriously in want, but this could and did change with income from publication and performances of his works.

53 Either francs or roubles would have been extremely useful to Shostakovich at this time.

54 In his younger days, Shostakovich did not mind hot weather, but as he got older it exhausted and frightened him. In many letters he complains of the heat as a torment with which it is impossible to come to terms.

55 Shostakovich means Repino, which marches with Komarovo.

56 Despite his eminence, Shostakovich was quite unable to make demands in the matter of his own comfort and service. He was too modest and reticent to do so, and generally put up with whatever he was given.

57 See note 3 to the letter dated 17 February 1960.

58 Not in the Philharmonia or the Conservatoire, but a separate concert hall near the Finland Station. (Translator's Note)

59 In this concert devoted to Shostakovich's works, the student choir of the Conservatoire sang his choral cycle *Ten Poems on Texts by Revolutionary Poets*.

60 Shostakovich, great artist and rare human being that he was, gives vent to his deep dissatisfaction with himself. Something akin to this occurred with Lev Tolstoy and with Pushkin, who likewise set themselves impossibly high standards. Reading this stark final reply, garnished with the exclamation mark that Shostakovich so rarely employed, I could not help calling to mind Pushkin's *Memories*, which I take the liberty of quoting here:

As silent memory before my very eyes
Unveils the scroll on which my life is writ,
Then I, recoiling from the sight of so much shame,
Shudder and curse and shed the bitter tears
Of anguish, that for all they flow so free
These piteous lines can never wash away.

Shostakovich too could not wash away the piteous lines, but bitterly recalled them on the eve of his birthday.

61 Shostakovich was continually bombarded with requests for help in getting jobs, titles and positions from all sorts of musicians, well known and not so well known. It was a burden to him, but he yielded to the most persistent – and their name was legion.

62 Shostakovich's memory never failed to astound me. He had remembered something I told him over twenty years before, about being at a birthday party for Simkin at which the guests gulped down toast after toast to 'the great leader and teacher Comrade Stalin'. I had relayed my appalled fascination to Shostakovich, but he merely shrugged his shoulders and replied, smiling morosely: 'I have never understood what comes over people. Even when they're at home they will drink to any leader set over them.' Simkin himself was a good violinist and a decent man, and refrained from joining in his guests' eulogy of Stalin.

63 The sonata was composed under my eyes during August, but I did not hear it until David Oistrakh and Sviatoslav Richter played it magnificently in the Small and Great Halls of the Leningrad Philharmonia on 23 and 25 September. The timing of the première was designed to coincide with Shostakovich's birthday.

64 Rather unexpectedly, Shostakovich changed his mind, overcoming his physical weakness sufficiently to come to Leningrad and attend all three performances of the Twelfth Quartet. Full of dramatic power, it was enthusiastically received. It was painful to see how difficult it was for Shostakovich, leaning on a stick, to struggle on to the stage of the Small Hall to acknowledge the storm of applause. He was reluctant even to make the attempt, but felt that it would be impolite to ignore the audience's manifest delight in the work. I could not help thinking back to the easy grace with which he had mounted the same stage but a short time before.

On 3 November, following the performance in the Composers' House, Shostakovich and I together celebrated in modest style the première of the Twelfth Quartet in his room at the Yevropeyskaya Hotel.

65 Yevgeny Chukovsky, a film cameraman, the husband of Shostakovich's daughter Galina.

66 Shostakovich obviously did not wish to expand into lyrical reminiscences about his extraordinarily high-profile début into the world of opera in Leningrad nearly forty years previously. Why was this? My own view is that it was because Shostakovich never liked to gild or sentimentalize his own youth, considering himself at every stage of his life to be a fully formed adult. I never

heard him use phrases like 'when I was young and green'. Although he had recently written to me about memories crowding in on him, this did not mean that he necessarily wanted to share them.

Did this most modest of composers, painstakingly correcting the mistakes in the piano score of his forty-year-old opera, have any inkling that in a very few years' time this work, for so long spat on and reviled as a misbegotten child of formalism, would be revived with such triumphant success in Moscow and abroad?

67 This film was directed by Gleb Panfilov to a screenplay by Yevgeny Gavrilovich. The composer, Vadim Bibergan, was a former postgraduate student of Shostakovich.

68 Describing Natalya Gutman as a 'competition prizewinner', Shostakovich indicates that for the present she was on a lower level than Rostropovich. This may have been the case in 1968, but later she became a truly outstanding cellist and incidentally a brilliant exponent of Shostakovich's works.

69 Shostakovich did not, of course, think it interesting to inform me that he received an ovation from the delegates when he appeared on the platform.

70 The musicologist wife of the conductor Igor Blazhkov had committed suicide.

71 A slang phrase from Odessa, popularized by Isaak Babel's *Odessa Tales* of Jewish life in the port and their hero, the archetypal rogue Benya Krik. (Translator's Note)

72 Dr. Gavriil Ilizarov.

73 Shostakovich was tormented by impossible dreams of having strong and healthy legs once again, and this did on occasion depress his ordinarily powerful spirit.

74 The work in question was the Fourteenth Symphony. Shostakovich had not yet himself realized the gigantic scale of the creative forces to which he was playing host. I found his mocking, deprecatory attitude to the work he was creating simply astounding. That hospital ward was witnessing the birth of great music which he describes as 'senile graphomania' – an addiction to scribbling. Used as I was to Shostakovich, I had never experienced anything quite like this before. Was he perhaps teasing me? I well knew how contemptuous he could be about some of the so-called music that he was obliged to compose, but in the present case he was talking about the incarnation of some of his deepest thoughts that had been gestating in him for many years. Surely it must have been a tease for him to write, as he does, that he found writing the oratorio (as he first calls it) 'a fascinating entertainment' – words hardly appropriate to music burning with such elemental energy.

The enigma was eventually solved in an unexpectedly direct manner: the moment he had finished the Fourteenth Symphony, Shostakovich acknowledged it as his finest work, outstripping anything that had preceded it.

75 The Moscow Chamber Orchestra, founded and directed by Rudolf Barshai.

76 Ivan Ivanovich Sollertinsky died during the night of 10–11 February 1944.

77 Although Shostakovich admired Irakli Andronikov's gifts, he considered that his portrayal of Sollertinsky exaggerated his subject's eccentricity to such an

extent that he made him appear a grotesque figure to those who had not known him. Andronikov's account of Sollertinsky was none the less imbued with a genuine love for him.

78 These were indeed the qualities on which I laid stress in my address at the Composers' House. I had not cared much for the series of amusing anecdotes which made up the bulk of the speeches, however entertaining they were to the audience. I said that Sollertinsky's life had been far from easy, often indeed a torment to him, that he suffered all kinds of abuse from officials and journalists in positions of power, and that he was as capable of tears as he was of laughter. My somewhat low-key remarks, in contrast to the jokes and puns of most of the other speakers, produced quite an effect.

79 To have completed the piano score of the Fourteenth Symphony, which was done on 16 February 1969, was an extraordinary feat, for this stunningly original work was written with great rapidity – and moreover, in the unsympathetic surroundings of a hospital ward. As usual, there is no trace of pride in this achievement; his report confines itself to the bare fact.

80 Presumably the facts that the symphony had as many as eleven movements and apparently lacked the usual symphonic structural integration, together with the outwardly heterogeneous nature of the textual sources, were the cause of Shostakovich's uncertainty as to what precise genre his new composition should be ascribed. However, in time he became persuaded that the work as a whole was both distinguished by a dramatic unity and pervaded by a symphonic ethos, and so the Fourteenth Symphony was born.

81 Shostakovich was attracted by Küchelbecker's freedom-loving and anti-despotic verse, taking it as the text for the ninth movement of the symphony.

82 The completion of the Fourteenth Symphony had boosted Shostakovich's morale, as several clues in this letter testify. He wanted to wet the head of his new composition with vodka, naturally not in hospital but in Repino with me, touchingly and naïvely offering to pay for the treat. This Bacchic project was finally achieved in Repino on 12 April.

Here I should add that that on this happy occasion Dmitry Dmitriyevich got slightly tipsy and at the supper table was the most enchanting, graceful and happy company imaginable. In circumstances like this (and there were many during our life) I looked happily at Shostakovich and thought of Chekhov's description of his grandfather and grandmother: 'The wine made them good-humoured and witty, it gladdened their hearts and stimulated their minds.' (Letter to A. S. Suvorin of 10 October 1888.)

83 An unexpected but characteristic modulation to humour in the midst of a deeply serious discussion about the essential meaning of the Fourteenth Symphony. 'Kreutzer Sonata' is a grotesquely satirical scene between an over-educated lodger and the fat laundress Fyokla – a representative of 'the people'.

84 It may have been at the beginning of 1969 that the notion of addressing the question of death finally came to fruition for Shostakovich, but it had in fact been preoccupying him for a long time before that. It was no accident, it seems

to me, that he should have made an orchestral version of Musorgsky's *Songs and Dances of Death* as long ago as 1962.

85 The poems chosen by Shostakovich, all by different poets, vary greatly in language and style, but come together in a magical unity through the power of the music, such that they seemed to me to have been foreordained to belong together even without the intervention of the composer. The heroes and heroines of the symphony, bound together by the power of fate, stretch out their hands to one another and form a ring of blazing fire. From that ring the eighth and ninth movements – 'The Zaporozhian Cossack's Answer to the Sultan of Constantinople' and 'O Delvig, Delvig!' – emerge and grow to unique, resonant and substantial life.

86 Thoughts like these regularly troubled Shostakovich while he was engaged in composition.

87 An extraordinarily revealing observation both from the professional and the personal perspective. Shostakovich was so struck by his own composition that he elevated it above all that he had written before. It is a paradoxical view, and not one to which he was subsequently to return. It must have arisen spontaneously, while the composer was still in thrall to the fierce heat of an inspired eruption that had temporarily eclipsed the true nature of the great symphonies, operas, quartets and song cycles he had already created.

88 The composer Nikolai Peyko had pedantically criticized the poems of the Thirteenth Symphony. Despite this, Shostakovich had a high regard for Peyko's compositions.

89 This complaint is not a joke: it reflects Shostakovich's real unhappiness that his health increasingly obliged him to renounce aspects of daily life that he used to take for granted.

90 Lorca's *De Profundis*, in the translation by I. Tïnyanova.

91 I did as Shostakovich asked, and provided another version avoiding the problematical word.

92 Aware of my veneration for the text, Shostakovich worried that I might be upset at the cuts he had made in Apollinaire's poem. His fears were, however, groundless: 'In the Santé Jail' is one of the most dramatic movements of the symphony. The music of this seventh movement conveys with incredible mastery the dread, unrelieved darkness of prison and the terrible silence of the cell, a theme which had long oppressed Shostakovich through all the years of Stalin's terror.

93 Since the letter of 19 March 1969 Shostakovich had changed 'burning blood' to 'black blood'. (Translator's Note)

94 On 12 April, Shostakovich, who was in Repino at the time, invited me to come to Moscow for the première of the Violin Sonata which was scheduled for 3 and 4 May. It soon became clear that I would not be able to come and I had let Shostakovich know this. His thought process is interesting: fear that his own anxiety over the première would affect my own peace of mind.

95 This did not in fact happen. Richter's touring plans changed, and he was able to play the Violin Sonata with David Oistrakh on 23 and 24 September in the Small and Great Halls of the Philharmonia.

96 Shostakovich could have quoted his beloved Aleksandr Blok here: 'We rest only when we dream'.

97 Shostakovich never allowed paternal feelings to get in the way of a strictly objective assessment of his son's achievements as a conductor.

98 Shostakovich dreamed of a bass soloist for his Thirteenth and Fourteenth Symphonies who would be endowed with not only musicianship and a good voice, but also brains. He often said: 'These are not works for idiots.'

99 Shostakovich had intended to play me some of the movements of the Fourteenth on 12 April 1969, after the dinner in Cottage No. 20 at Repino celebrating the completion of the work, but he felt so tired after the meal that unfortunately he had not been up to carrying out his plan.

100 In fact, the concerts took place on 23 and 24 September 1969.

101 The wife of the composer Venyamin Basner ended her life by suicide in a state of depression.

102 Recalling the life of Yefim Galanter, Shostakovich was no doubt thinking of a favourite phrase from Gogol that he was fond of repeating: 'This is a tedious world, gentlemen!'

103 I had invited Shostakovich to the première of *Benvenuto Cellini*, produced by Roman Tikhomirov in collaboration with me at the Maly Opera, but he was not able to attend. This confession of worship was something of a surprise to me, since Berlioz was not, so far as I was aware, among those composers Shostakovich loved most. I knew that he admired the freshness and brilliance of the orchestration, the extraordinary originality and splendour of such works as the *Symphonie Fantastique*, *Harold in Italy*, *Romeo and Juliet*, the Requiem, but I would not have said that he 'worshipped' Berlioz. Berlioz was, however, idolized by Ivan Sollertinsky, who was responsible for including many of his works in Philharmonia programmes during the 1930s, and I clearly remember that Shostakovich never missed a concert in which a work of his was to be performed.

104 Shostakovich was acquainted with Arnold in Leningrad and, being interested in such things during the thirties, played cards with him from time to time. Arnold was by way of being an expert, and Shostakovich generally lost. It was said that even Mayakovsky, who certainly knew his way around a pack of cards, could not prevail against him. Arnold, as he was universally known, owing to his first name and surname being the same, was a colourful figure in the Leningrad landscape. Tall, slender, even thin, he affected a wide-brimmed black hat rather like a sombrero, and was never without a cane in his hand. Seen every day strolling down Nevsky Prospect, he always looked to me exactly like an Argentinian who had stepped straight out of a cinema poster. To stroll down Nevsky had become something of a cult among the city's artistic community, and the young Shostakovich also adopted a custom which seemed to have its roots in a bygone age, perhaps that of Pushkin.

105 Pavel Apostolov, who for a time was a functionary of the Central Committee of the Party, was for many years an implacable opponent of formalism in music. Since one of the leading lights of this 'pernicious tendency' was Shostakovich, their relationship was no warmer than might be expected. So

when, having heard four movements of the symphony, Apostolov was struck down during the fifth, whose title is 'On Watch', one could be forgiven for detecting the finger of fate. Poor Apostolov was perpetually 'On Watch'. Relating this dramatic occurrence, Dmitry Dmitriyevich sees no need for superfluous or tasteless commentary, counting on my knowledge of the deceased's activities.

106 In fact, Apostolov died on 19 July, almost a month later. See Fay, L. E., *Shostakovich: A Life*, Oxford, 2000, 262. (Translator's Note)

107 The Lenfilm Studio conceived (and later realized) a project to make a film version of Shostakovich's ballet *The Young Girl and the Hooligan*. On my active intervention, the Director of Lenfilm, Ilya Kiselyov, had approached the composer, seeking his agreement to the idea.

108 Heroically overcoming his physical disabilities, Shostakovich never lost his love for travel or his thirst for knowledge, hence his predilection for working out complicated routes for journeys. This unquenchable curiosity was a mark of the evergreen youthfulness of his spirit.

109 Shostakovich's interest in the work of his composer colleagues showed no sign of flagging, wherever in the world he came across them.

110 A remedy for heart conditions common in Russia. (Translator's Note)

111 Shostakovich's continuing ill health only sharpened his love for nature, which gradually ripened into an intense worship. The natural world inspired him with inner peace and a joyful attitude to the world at large.

112 A continual refrain in Shostakovich's biography. Hot weather invariably induced in him ennui, melancholy and a feeling of hopelessness. When hot weather gave place to cold his energy would return and with it his desire to create.

113 I.e. when the composer was seven years old. This fact is stated without irony or even an exclamation mark, and the reason may be the one I have already mentioned, that Shostakovich always considered himself to be grown up at any age, even at seven. I have the impression that the meeting with his cousin, a historian by profession, slightly depressed Shostakovich; I observed several times that he had little fellow feeling for distant kin whom he did not know particularly well, and that he went to some lengths to protect himself from importunate connections with relations to whom he felt no emotional ties.

114 Shostakovich came to Leningrad as arranged, and the next day saw the outset of a triumphant week of his music. David Oistrakh and Sviatoslav Richter played his wonderful Violin Sonata in the Small Hall of the Philharmonia on 23 September and in the Great Hall on the 24th. There is no need to describe the phenomenal success of these concerts or my intense pleasure at the great artistry of the composer and his interpreters. On the 25th there was an intermezzo, a scene-change, when Shostakovich organized a birthday celebration dinner at the Composers' House in Repino. Vera Vasiliyevna and I were among the small number of guests, all of whom were devoted admirers of the host. At the beginning of the evening, Shostakovich was lively and in good spirits, but towards the end he became rather melancholy, doubtless

[307]

from fatigue and from the nervous tension of the concerts that had taken place.

Still to come was the long-awaited première of the Fourteenth Symphony. This took place on 29 September in the Capella Concert Hall, where there was a tremendous hullabaloo from the crush of people who had not managed to get hold of tickets but were desperate to hear the concert at whatever cost. Inside were not only the entire Leningrad musical world, but as a result of the rumours of the unusual new symphony that had been flying about the town, many people who did not normally attend symphony concerts, such as Arkady Raikin and Grigory Kozintsev. [Arkady Raikin, noted actor and comedian; Grigory Kozintsev, film director, for many of whose films including the *Maksim Trilogy*, *New Babylon*, *Hamlet* and *King Lear*, Shostakovich wrote the music – Translator's Note] Expectations were in no way disappointed: the orchestra under Rudolf Barshai played magnificently; Galina Vishnevskaya demonstrated her outstanding abilities as singer and actress – both are needed for full artistic realization of the symphony – and the bass Yevgeny Vladimirov coped well with his most demanding part. 'Overwhelming' is the only word adequate to describe the effect produced on the audience by the indissoluble unity between words and music. Speaking personally, I was literally entranced, so much so that I remained under its spell for long afterwards. I seemed to see, as if in a dream, the heroes and heroines of the symphony, to hear their voices and see their pain-twisted faces. As the final notes of the conclusion died away, a silence of grief mixed with celebration reigned in the hall. Something made me turn towards the box in which Yevgeny Mravinsky was sitting, and I saw him rise to his full great height. Astonishingly, he seemed to be moving his hand as if conducting – but this was an illusion: he was merely applauding with all his might. Following his lead, the entire audience rose to its feet and the ovation began. Shostakovich himself was stunned by what he had heard, although it was the work of his own hands. The weakness of his legs made it difficult for him to go on stage and acknowledge the clamour of the audience, which seemed as though it would never end.

After the concert, Dmitry Dmitriyevich gave a banquet for fifty people in the Sadko restaurant, to which he invited the whole orchestra and its conductor. I recall making a short, simply-phrased but emotional toast which must have gone to Shostakovich's heart, for he got up from his place and came over to me, glass in hand, and we kissed. The symphony was repeated on 1 October with the same gigantic success. Since Vishnevskaya had had to leave urgently for a concert tour to Berlin, the soprano soloist's part was excellently taken by Margarita Miroshnikova. That same unforgettable evening (1 October), Shostakovich and Irina Antonovna left for Moscow, and so ended a triumphant week which had a profound effect on musical Leningrad.

115 The only reason I can think of why Shostakovich should have written to me a few hours before the Moscow première of the Fourteenth Symphony would

be to allay the nerves that invariably accompanied any première of his works, and to draw on my reserves of moral support for him. This may seem fanciful to some readers, but I knew Dmitry Dmitriyevich too well not to recognize even the smallest details of his moods and the intricate patterns of his thoughts.

116 In Leningrad, Shostakovich had been an amazingly faithful attender of concerts at the Philharmonia, seldom missing any of them. In Moscow he continued the practice and was regularly to be seen at performances in the Small and Great Halls of the Conservatoire.

In our own day, Leningrad composers very rarely go to concerts, on the grounds that they claim to know the works being performed. Shostakovich also 'knew' Prokofiev's Classical and Beethoven's Ninth Symphonies, but still found it worthwhile to hear another (not the first, nor the last) performance of works he knew well.

117 Shostakovich always hated errors in performance, even those the audience did not notice. Probably Vishnevskaya and Barshai had an attack of nerves during this concert, since their performance had been irreproachable in Leningrad.

118 Shostakovich had respect for Sergey Slonimsky as an excellent musician and an interesting composer. I recall him praising to me Slonimsky's article on *The Execution of Stepan Razin*, even though he generally did not care how his works were reviewed (see the letter dated 23 April 1965). Shostakovich often told me verbally and in writing how much pleasure he derived from discovering good music in works by his fellow composers. Taken as a whole, Slonimsky's opera *Virineya* was one such work.

119 I was horrified by the diagnosis, and immediately had visions of Franklin D. Roosevelt in his wheelchair. I found it incredible that Shostakovich could react so calmly to the information he had been given. Perhaps he did not altogether believe his doctors?

120 Shostakovich had already shown that he was capable of writing great music in the dispiriting environment of hospital, but he also managed to keep abreast of various aspects of contemporary literature – good and bad. Firmly among the latter, in his opinion, was Vsevolod Kochetov's novel *What Do You Want?* published in volumes 9, 10 and 11 of the magazine *October* in 1969. Shostakovich's reference to this book is sardonic in the extreme, pointing to the author's derivative use of motifs from the famously dreadful *The Aphis*, while as a pendant to Kochetov's novel Shostakovich mentions two other repulsively vulgar examples.

121 I had proposed that theatre directors, even the most gifted, could not produce work that could properly be described as 'classic' or 'genius', since the truly classic, as distinct from the talented, maintains its validity in any age. It always remains contemporary, while no production even by such as Stanislavsky or Meyerhold can sustain its artistic power beyond its original staging. Shostakovich agreed with this thesis, and even though the production he mentions by Zavadsky had made a powerful impression on him, he still considered theatrical production as a whole an ephemeral art.

[309]

122 Shostakovich knew his Dostoyevsky very well indeed and had a deep understanding of his work. He used to say to me that for any director, provided he was not completely untalented, to engage with the great writer would inevitably bring artistic dividends. As an example, he would quote the film of *The Brothers Karamazov*, by which the director, I. A. Pïrev, had elevated himself several rungs up the artistic ladder.

It is worth noting that problems of stage production had occupied Shostakovich for many years, dating from his contact with Meyerhold, whose work he had known well in his early years. Several productions of *Katerina Izmailova*, both at home and abroad, had been painful experiences for him.

123 I find a strong echo of Zoshchenko's style and manner in this account of the medical luminary and his suite. Reading this caustic description would have been funny if the subject had not been so sad.

I visited Shostakovich in hospital on 3 December, and found him in a small ward on his own, which he counted a blessing. He greeted me joyfully, said not a word about his ailments, but wanted to talk about general matters. One of the topics we discussed was the sad fate of Aleksandr Solzhenitsïn, whose talent Shostakovich greatly admired. Irina Antonovna had installed a miniature television set in the ward, which helped to relieve the sick man's isolation.

Dmitry Dmitriyevich was clad in grotesquely ill-fitting pyjamas supplied by the VIP hospital, the jacket far too long and the trousers too short. Catching my puzzled look, Shostakovich stammered: 'No one to dress up for here; good thing too.' Usually he was rather particular about his appearance. We talked for about two hours, and then Shostakovich walked me to the landing and managed to squeeze out a parting smile. I felt very downcast.

124 The Fourteenth Symphony continued to arouse the keenest interest among a wide circle of music audiences, and received many performances. Shostakovich, in whom the fire of its creation had not yet died down, tried to hear as many of these performances as he could.

125 Shostakovich was probably finding it hard to get out of his mind the mistakes Vishnevskaya had made on one occasion, although in general he considered her a complete mistress of the singer's art.

126 The film by Grigory Kozintsev. Shostakovich kept to his plan and came to Leningrad for one day on 15 January 1970. The Lenfilm administrators booked a room for him, not in the Yevropeyskaya Hotel where he usually stayed, but in the Astoria. On arrival, Shostakovich telephoned me and we agreed to meet at the Lenfilm Studios at 12 o'clock to view the cuts. Needless to say, the director was on tenterhooks. Shostakovich, as was his wont, praised everything that he saw, and indeed there was plenty to praise. However, the actor playing the title role, Z. Gerdt, delivered his storm speech in a lacklustre, prosaic style that I thought would have been suited to the weather forecast. Shostakovich shared my opinion and said: 'In defiance of the actor, and probably the director, I propose to write a real storm. The storm is one of the best passages in the whole of Shakespeare.' Later, I persuaded Kozintsev to reshoot the entire scene on the heath.

When we returned to the Astoria and sat down to dinner, I recalled the lovely song sung by the Fool in the film, and remarked that it resembled the *Three Lilies* of the Fourteenth Symphony. Shostakovich smiled and responded: 'You noticed the resemblance, as did I, but tell me, which is more important, the symphony or the film?'

During the dinner, Shostakovich told me that he had decided to go to Kurgan to see Ilizarov, who was promising to cure his hands and legs. Not wishing to pursue this melancholy subject, he launched without a pause into an account of the projected recording of the Fourteenth Symphony in Moscow.

Our dinner lasted three hours, and the three of us, Dmitry Dmitriyevich, Irina Antonovna and I, were completely undisturbed. Outside the frost-decked windows, dusk fell. Several times Shostakovich rose from the table, walked to the window, and feasted his eyes upon St Isaac's Square. Late that evening, he left for Moscow.

Chapter VI Intimations of Mortality, 1970–1975

1 I visited Shostakovich on 29 January and was generally happy both with the way he was looking and the way he was evidently feeling. We drank a glass of vodka to celebrate our meeting; I thought this a good augury of his physical well-being. In a burst of youthful enthusiasm he described his concept of a 'home theatre'. This consisted of a small group of friends gathering in his apartment to listen to the recording from Berlin of his opera *The Nose*, with an interval after each act just as in the theatre, during which the guests would repair to the dining-room for drinks and refreshments. The *mise-en-scène* had apparently worked well, and Dmitry Dmitriyevich invited me to a future performance in his 'home theatre'. It was wonderful to listen to his excited account, and I thought to myself: whatever gives him pleasure. For however much there was in his life to grieve over, yet, thank God, the youthfulness of his inner self never deserted him.

2 In the summer of 1966, when Shostakovich suffered his heart attack.

3 I did telephone Shostakovich on 24 March. He told me that the three weeks of treatment he had undergone thus far seemed to have helped him, and he reposed great hopes in Dr Ilizarov.

4 The poem was 'The Old Woman Came By Commuter Train'.

5 Shostakovich's discovery of Aitmatov came from reading his novel *Farewell Gulsar!*, after which he developed a passion for this superb writer which I soon grew to share.

6 The music for Kozintsev's film.

7 May 1970 saw a distinct remission in the mysterious illness that afflicted Shostakovich. Thanks to the talent and dedication of Dr Ilizarov, Shostakovich experienced a real resurgence of his strength, and this filled him with such joy that he was anxious not to waste a drop of it. I was much moved by this artless account of his 'achievements', but alas the happiness was not to last long. The illness, whatever its cause, was by no means vanquished and returned after a brief respite to wreak havoc once again on Shostakovich's hands and legs.

8 Vladimir Nikolayevich Orlov was a great expert on the art of Aleksandr Blok,

and the author of a wonderful book on him called *Gamayun*. As Irina Antonovna was aware, I knew him quite well, and she had prevailed on Dmitry Dmitriyevich to ask me to intercede on her friend's behalf. Naturally I did so, although I knew perfectly well that Shostakovich himself would be quite indifferent to the fate of any article written about his compositions.

9 In the event, Shostakovich altered his plans and stayed in Repino until the end of July. I saw him on 18 June, after an interval of three months, and was overjoyed at the good the treatment had evidently done him: he was walking quite differently and could move his hands freely; he looked well. I envisaged Ilizarov as a cross between a doctor and a miracle-worker.

Shostakovich and I saw one another regularly during his stay in Repino, and there were a good many lunches and dinners at the familiar Cottage No. 20. On 10 July we spent the whole day in the documentary–film studios on the Kryukov Canal. On 26 July, the day before he left Repino, Shostakovich showed me the splendid choral vocalise he planned for the grand finale of the film of *King Lear*. He expressed regret at the likelihood that this music, to which he was very attached, would, as so often happens, fail to make its mark and would be lost in the cinematography.

10 Maksim Krastin and Onik Sarkisov, administrative and artistic directors respectively of the Leningrad Philharmonia.

11 Afanasy Ponomaryov was the former director of the Leningrad Philharmonia and I could not understand why Shostakovich wanted to link his name with those of Sollertinsky and Mravinsky. In fact, I objected to it, and Shostakovich agreed.

12 I naturally wrote a little article as requested. Shostakovich's strictures on himself for his lack of literary skills are disingenuous: the many articles, letters and speeches that came from his pen are filled with a direct, expressive language a world away from the contrivance and artificiality of 'elegant constructions'.

13 My brother, the sculptor and artist, had made Shostakovich a present of several of his works.

14 This brief piece of unvarnished information announces a work full of tragic power. Such was certainly my impression when I heard it on 13 December in the Small Hall of the Leningrad Conservatoire. The combination of two unlucky thirteens in no way inhibited the great success with which the quartet was received.

15 Shostakovich refers to his projected visit to Leningrad in December for the première of the Thirteenth Quartet. On 10 December he spoke to me on the telephone to tell me that he would be coming to Leningrad two days later, and asking me to keep Saturday evening free for a rendezvous. That evening I went to visit him in the Yevropeyskaya Hotel, and on my arrival found the table in his room laid for supper. Shostakovich greeted me joyfully, but my own pleasure in the meeting was mixed with dismay at the deterioration in his walking and the weakness in his right hand. By unspoken agreement, nothing was said, but during supper Shostakovich told me, with evident regret, that he was experiencing, in his words, 'an epistolary crisis' – in other words that he

had lost much of his former enthusiasm for writing letters. He begged me not to take offence if, in consequence of this, he wrote to me less frequently: 'Instead I shall telephone you more often.' And this indeed happened.

I did feel myself deprived, going for long periods without letters from Shostakovich in the last years of his life; after all, I had spent decades training myself to decipher his scrawl which had become dear to my heart and mind.

When Irina Antonovna and I started discussing arrangements for the following day's concert, it emerged that the Small Hall of the Philharmonia was completely sold out and there was not a single spare ticket to be had. At this, Dmitry Dmitriyevich came up with a solution worthy of Solomon. Turning to me, he said: 'You sit in my seat and I'll stay backstage. After all, I've already heard the Thirteenth Quartet.' The incredible innocence of this made me burst out laughing, but Shostakovich saw nothing amusing in his perfectly sincere proposal.

Next day, the ticket problem was sorted out. The programme for the concert consisted of the First, Twelfth and Thirteenth Quartets, and graphically illustrated the long and difficult road travelled by the composer: the bright beginnings of the First Quartet, through the bleak landscape of the Twelfth, to the tragic paragraphs of the Thirteenth, which I saw as a younger sibling of the Fourteenth Symphony. The whole audience rose to its feet at the conclusion of the new quartet, and would not be satisfied until it had been repeated in its entirety.

When a hall full of people stands in obedience to the power of authority, the only effect is one of knee-jerking banality. The sight of the same thing happening at the wave of a wand by a man with no power whatsoever except his genius is by contrast extraordinarily moving.

After the concert I called in to the Yevropeyskaya Hotel to bid Shostakovich farewell before he left to return to Moscow. On 11 January I received a telegram from him, congratulating me on my birthday.

16   On 1 February I received a telephone call from Shostakovich asking me to come to visit him for several days to discuss some important matters. I could not do this at the time, so instead I sent him a long and detailed letter. It was not until 10 May that we met again, in Moscow, and naturally I was a prey to anxious feelings about seeing him after an interval of as long as five months. However, happily I did not discern any worsening of his condition, although the stay in Kurgan had not produced any real benefits either. He came to life somewhat at mealtimes, otherwise he was morose and taciturn.

In the course of a walk we took together at Zhukovka, Shostakovich told me that he had set to music a poem by Yevtushenko devoted to the suicide of Marina Tsvetayeva, and he wanted me to hear both words and music. [This is evidently Yevtushenko's poem 'Yelabuga Nail'; Shostakovich's setting has as yet not been published. See Fay, L. E., *Shostakovich: A Life*, Oxford, 2000, 270 – Translator's Note]

He then recounted to me with some irritation a shameful story about the publication of the Thirteenth Symphony. Of course, the very last thing our own music publishing firms would want to do was bring out this seditious work, but suddenly it became known that a firm in West Germany was printing it. In response to this, the authorities hastily ordered the score to be published at home. 'And so,' said Shostakovich, 'the net result is that a publisher in West Germany succeeded in getting one up on our Soviet music press.' We laughed about this, but the laughter was somewhat hollow.

Sitting of an evening in Shostakovich's study, embellished with a wonderful photographic portrait of Meyerhold, we listened on the radio to a whole range of music that was being showcased at the Congress of Soviet Composers, most of it drab and uninteresting. Shostakovich, deep in thought, said: 'You know, when I hear this kind of music, I do wonder if my music also sounds like this?' The question hung in the air, but I forbore to assure him that no, his music was of quite another kind.

On 13 May, the day I left to return to Leningrad, we went in together from Zhukovka to Moscow, and that evening attended a concert in the Great Hall of the Conservatoire devoted to the above-mentioned Composers' Congress. Shostakovich's attitude to his colleagues' work was generally one of respect, even of praise, but he found this concert a depressing affair. During the performance of one piece, listed in the programme as *Merry Scherzo*, Dmitry Dmitriyevich, with an absolutely straight face, whispered to me: 'Please tickle me to make me laugh.' He never lost his sense of humour, even with the fox gnawing at his vitals. I do remember that he reacted very positively to Yury Falik's *Concerto for Orchestra (Till Eulenspiegel)*, marvellously conducted by Dmitry Kitayenko.

After the concert, we had supper in the Shostakoviches' Moscow apartment, and Irina Antonovna drove me to the station. Dmitry Dmitriyevich had wanted to see me off as well, but his strength suddenly gave out on what was a very stuffy and airless evening – Moscow can be very hot in May.

17 On this occasion, Shostakovich's stay in Kurgan was not a long one (less than a month) but it was fruitful not only medically but musically. While in the hospital he managed to write the admirable first movement of the Fifteenth Symphony, after which he could hardly wait to get to Repino, partly to recover from the treatment and partly to get on with the new work.

On 1 July Shostakovich called me from Repino and asked me to come over to see him as soon as I could. We met regularly over the ensuing month, and in those July days there took place between us several conversations of more than passing interest. (In the passages that follow, I have faithfully transcribed Shostakovich's remarks from notes I made at the time.)

3 July

Shostakovich spoke of the Second Cello Concerto, which had never been performed at the Leningrad Philharmonia (as mentioned before, Rostropovich played it once in the Small Hall of the Conservatoire). Dmitry Dmitriyevich said: 'I realise Leningrad audiences can very well get on without hearing the Second Cello Concerto, but all the same it would be no bad thing for it to be played there.' The irony masked a clear if nostalgic desire to hear the work in the Philharmonia, which had seen the premières of nearly all Shostakovich's compositions.

Shostakovich asked me to find out more about the young cellist Boris Pergamenshchikov, who was said to be a fine player, and to do something about organizing a performance (at the time there had been a serious falling-out between Rostropovich and the Philharmonia). Listening to him, I reflected on the strange psychological twist that would make a man who had been present at first performances of his works, not just in Leningrad and Moscow but all over the world, still feel a thorn in his side from the Leningrad Philharmonia's (which meant in effect Mravinsky's) cold-shouldering of the Second Cello Concerto. Shostakovich did not labour the point – it was made in passing – but it went straight to my heart. And his wish to have the work performed in Leningrad never was granted during his lifetime.

13 July

Irina Antonovna served up shashlik and drinks. Shostakovich was in high spirits and working flat out on the Fifteenth Symphony. A period of intense creativity such as this always charged up both his morale and his physical capacities, and during this time he completed the second movement and almost all of the third movement of the symphony. [Venyamin Basner states that the first three movements had all been composed before the composer arrived in Repino. See Wilson, E., *Shostakovich: A Life Remembered*, London, 1994, 436 – Translator's Note]

'I still have to cobble together the finale,' Shostakovich said in the ironic tone he often used when speaking of his compositions, 'but, you know, rather like my Ninth, the symphony lacks a basic idea.'

18 July

We spoke again of the Fifteenth Symphony, which Shostakovich was hoping to finish by the end of the month while he was at Repino. Interestingly, we touched on the theme of whether quotations represent a justifiable device. There are many woven into the fabric of this symphony: Rossini's *William Tell* overture; Beethoven's Sixth Symphony; Wagner's *Ring of the Nibelungen*. Shostakovich said to me, with an enigmatic and, it seemed to me, slightly guilty smile: 'I don't myself quite know why the quotations are there, but I could *not*, could *not*, *not* include them.' The thrice-repeated negative was pronounced with great force. I offered the thought that since the creative process was not always accompanied by logic, it was possible that he had been guided by pure intuition. Dmitry Dmitriyevich ruminated and said: 'Maybe, maybe.'

29 July

Shostakovich had completed the Fifteenth Symphony in a remarkably short space of time. It was to be, alas, the final one of his great cycle. As if looking back to mark the event, he reflected: 'I think that of the fifteen, two are quite unworthy: the Second and Third.' Trying to avoid overstatement or seem to be showing off, his face nevertheless shone with contentment and he concluded that the occasion called for a modest celebration.

He said that he needed to get on quickly with a four-hand piano version of the symphony, which he had asked Moysey Vainberg and Boris Tchaikovsky to play. The next day he left with Irina Antonovna for Moscow. His parting comment was a characteristic one: 'The new symphony is still warm, and I like it. But perhaps after some time has gone by I shall think quite differently about it.'

18 In a recent letter I had told Shostakovich how listening to the sparkling gaiety of the Sixth Symphony's finale lifted my spirits from fits of depression.

19 Stravinsky's *Dialogues* were published in the USSR in 1971, in a translation by Mikhail Druskin. It so happened that Shostakovich and I were simultaneously reading this fascinating book, stuffed with erudition, wit, toxic sarcasm and biliously misanthropic utterances.

From his earliest years, Shostakovich admired and frequently referred to many of Stravinsky's works, marvelling at their imaginative power. Something of his feelings for the composer of *Petrushka* and *The Rite of Spring* can be gauged from the fact that he kept a photograph of Stravinsky under the glass covering his work-table in the Moscow apartment, so that every time he sat down to work the gnarled, ill-favoured, clever and austere face of the great master would be looking up at him. But Shostakovich detested Stravinsky's hideous egocentricity, his icy indifference to the fate of defenceless composers, poets and writers who were hunted down, morally destroyed, tortured and dragged through the mud in the years of Stalin's terror. He thought of Prokofiev, Akhmatova, Zoshchenko, himself and many, many others. But Stravinsky looked on with Olympian detachment while all these heartrending tragedies were being played out, and this was why Shostakovich had contempt for him while idolizing him as a musician. In sharp contrast to Stravinsky, those who suffered at the hands of evil men aroused in him the keenest sympathy, and I well remember how moved he was whenever he spoke of prisoners in the camps – whether they were people he knew well, not so well, or not at all, things he knew of from letters and from foreign radio broadcasts.

20 I had relayed to Shostakovich various unpleasant details of the systemically defective plumbing in my apartment.

21 Needless to say, Shostakovich never took care of his own health at all, having a fatalistic attitude towards it, but during the years of terror his nervous system was so subjected to merciless attacks that he never to the end of his days fully recovered from them.

22 The naïve simplicity of regarding, in all seriousness, the effects on the organism of a glass of vodka – which he savoured alike in times of happiness and distress – as a sort of litmus test for heart disease or health, is both touching and striking.

23 The film director who made the cinema version of *Katerina Izmailova*.

24 In calling V. M. Kirshon a 'proletarian playwright', Shostakovich refers to the widespread but wholly undeserved fame he enjoyed in the late twenties and

early thirties. At that time he was considered a popular hero, but in 1937 he became an 'enemy of the people'.

25 On 4 January Shostakovich telephoned me and repeated his invitation to come to the première of the Fifteenth Symphony. His voice was buoyant; evidently his nerves were not leading him their usual pre-première dance and of course this pleased and relieved me. I arrived in Moscow on 8 January. Irina Antonovna met me at the station in the car, and took me to the apartment, where Dmitry Dmitriyevich was waiting for us. He did not look bad that morning, saying as usual that he felt fine, but behind that 'fine' I thought I detected a hint of 'you can believe me or not, as you choose'.

After breakfast, all three of us went to the Great Hall of the Conservatoire for the general rehearsal of the Fifteenth Symphony. There were problems: the first bassoon was ill and the deputy had not turned up. This caused a delay of almost an hour, during which Shostakovich, although he was clearly fretting, did not complain or blame anyone; he sat patiently in the foyer, waiting for the player to arrive, repeating in a monotone: 'You know, in all my life as a musician, such a thing has never happened. I don't remember such a thing ever happening.'

Eventually the musician arrived and the symphony was heard in all its beauty, drama and charm. It seemed for all the world as though the quotations from Rossini and Wagner on which Shostakovich had put his stamp had somehow become his own.

The concert took place in the evening. The Moscow musical élite were there in force, the atmosphere one of celebration. Outwardly, Shostakovich was calm. I sat next to him in the sixth row: he had gone to some trouble to arrange this, presumably because he did not want to have an unknown or uncongenial neighbour on this occasion. Several times between movements, he whispered to me: 'Maksim is doing fine.' The ovation at the end of the symphony brought the entire audience to its feet, clapping as if they would never cease. Shostakovich managed with some difficulty to make repeated appearances on stage, but when Maksim and the orchestra made as if to encore the finale, the composer led the musicians off the stage.

As I left the Great Hall, I was jostled in the crowd and fell over, hurting my leg. However, I made it to the car and we went out to Zhukovka. Shostakovich observed that he hoped it was the first and last trick that St Cassian would play on me. [The feast day of St John Cassian is celebrated on 29 February. 1972 was a leap year – Translator's Note] In honour of the occasion, Irina Antonovna had laid on a supper just for intimate friends. Contrary to his recent practice of going to bed early, Shostakovich stayed late at the party. When we talked of the concert that had taken place, he said: 'I think I've written a smashing symphony.' 'Smashing' was not a word normally in his vocabulary.

The following morning, Irina Antonovna and I set out for the Moscow apartment, Shostakovich offering me one of his walking sticks and bidding me take care of my injured leg. That evening I had a visit from Yury Grigorovich

[Chief Choreographer of the Bolshoy Ballet – Translator's Note], who expertly bandaged my leg for me. It was during our conversation on this occasion that he first mentioned to me his desire to mount a new production of *The Golden Age*; however, it was to be ten years before this plan came to fruition.

26 Shostakovich had not reproached the conductor Gennady Provatorov for the shortcomings of the singers when *Katerina Izmailova* was in rehearsal in December 1962. In fact, in conversation with me, I recall him praising the performance of E. Andreyeva in the title role; moreover, the recording of the production with the same conductor won the Grand Prix du Disque in Paris. But now, ten years later, Shostakovich's phenomenal ear and memory could recall the singers and their 'shameless inaccuracy' when Provatorov was on the podium. He was, of course, perfectly justified in his strictures, but had not thought it tactful to say anything before the première.

27 It is hard to explain the failure of the gifted Dmitry Kitayenko to measure up. Probably, still young and professionally relatively inexperienced, he had not fully mastered the extraordinary complexities of the score nor succeeded in working out a convincing portrayal of its meaning. However, in time to come Kitayenko would conduct the symphonies of Shostakovich with great success.

28 Before the Revolution the Maly Opera and Ballet Theatre of Leningrad was known as the Mikhailovsky Theatre. *Katerina Izmailova* had been revived there in 1965, conducted by Eduard Grikurov.

29 Gavriil Popov, whose talent as a composer Shostakovich much admired.

30 A line from Pushkin's poem 'I Wander Through the Noisy Streets'.

31 Shostakovich knew that I was an intimate friend of Yevgeny Mravinsky, and asked me to find out the proposed performance dates for the Fifteenth Symphony, but to do so 'tactfully' (underlining the word) in such a way that the celebrated conductor would not feel that I was trying to put pressure on him to perform the symphony. Shostakovich's own self-esteem prevented him from approaching Mravinsky directly, seeing that the latter had evidently not thought it worthwhile to let the composer know of his intentions. Shostakovich found this unusual behaviour offensive and upsetting.

32 I am sure that Shostakovich would not have called to mind the delicate and rather disagreeable history of the premières of the Thirteenth Symphony and the Second Cello Concerto if Mravinsky had not given him cause with his odd behaviour over the Fifteenth Symphony.

   Mravinsky idolized Shostakovich as a composer and loved him very much as a man. He was overjoyed when Shostakovich dedicated the Eighth Symphony to him and was forever grateful for this mark of appreciation of his exceptional gifts as a conductor. Mravinsky was three years, three months and three days older than Shostakovich – not much of a difference in age, but enough to make him seem to want to take care of his younger friend, and to colour his attitude to him with a kind of suppressed tenderness. On the surface their relationship was anything but demonstrative, and despite what some memoir writers assert, they always addressed one another in the formal manner. Mravinsky and I often went together to see Shostakovich off on the train. When we had said our goodbyes, we would stand on the platform and look through the closed window of the train at the figure of Shostakovich standing in the corridor. On one occasion he had a rather gloomy and frowning expression on his face, with that unruly lock of hair falling down over his forehead, and Yevgeny Aleksandrovich, moved to tenderness and rolling his 'r's' in a slightly French way, said: 'Oh, how I do love you, my little sparrow!'

It was raining hard, and Shostakovich, gesticulating energetically through the window, motioned us to go home, but we just went on standing there while Mravinsky repeated several times his 'Oh, how I do love you, my little sparrow!' There was so much tenderness in this avian metaphor, which Shostakovich, while of course he could not actually hear it, with his preternaturally acute antennae no doubt felt in his soul.

Throughout the persecution of Shostakovich which followed the 1948 Central Committee Decree, Mravinsky behaved with exemplary courage and nobility, speaking out eloquently in public to defend the victim. During the storm of applause at the conclusion of one performance of the Fifth Symphony, at which the composer was not present, Yevgeny Aleksandrovich raised the score of the great work he had just conducted high above his head. Zealous hirelings of the regime were quick to relay news of the conductor's 'impermissibly demonstrative' act to Moscow, as a result of which he was severely mauled in the national press.

When, towards the end of 1953 storm clouds gathered over the Tenth Symphony and a question mark hung over its performance in Leningrad, Mravinsky, after consultation with me, went personally to Moscow to do battle with the 'Fighters against Formalism', and he performed the symphony in triumph in December of that year.

Nevertheless, mixed in with Mravinsky's generally irreproachable attitude to Shostakovich were occasional inexplicable moments of crisis. One such was when he was impelled by a sudden caprice (there is no other word for it) to avoid conducting the premières of the Thirteenth Symphony and the Second Cello Concerto – which incidentally brought about a complete rupture of the relationship between Mstislav Rostropovich and the Leningrad Philharmonia. Mravinsky's extraordinary decision simply does not square with his admiration of both these works. Shostakovich was, naturally, deeply distressed by this action, but mastered his feelings and behaved with great correctness, refusing to utter a word against Mravinsky. Their relationship not only survived, but survived in all essentials unchanged. Mravinsky continued to conduct the symphonies of Shostakovich; he celebrated the arrival of the Fourteenth and prepared the Leningrad première of the Fifteenth with exemplary care.

33 Shostakovich often spoke of such feelings of nostalgia. Every now and again he experienced vague but strong desires to become a Leningrader once again.

34 Shostakovich spent about a month in the GDR and in West Berlin. On 30 June he arrived in Leningrad, to leave with Irina Antonovna that same evening on board the steamer *Baltika* for London, thence on to Ireland where he was to receive an honorary doctorate from Dublin University.

One evening in Leningrad, Shostakovich invited me to dine in his room at the Yevropeyskaya Hotel. The room was very stuffy, and Shostakovich was exhausted by the appalling heat – the temperature was up to 32 degrees. He hoped that it would be cooler in their cabin. He had had the idea to travel by sea, he said, because 'at least for four days nobody will be able to ring me up, and nobody will ask me anything about anything. That's already a bonus.'

Shostakovich told of having heard a performance of Stockhausen's *Hymnen*. He said: 'It is a very strange piece, and puzzling in many respects, but it does contain certain individual combinations of sounds that struck me as interesting. They could, for example, be used to produce a mysterious kind of effect.' After a long pause, he continued: 'For instance, the ghost's appearance in Oscar Wilde's story "The Canterville Ghost". I've been thinking of writing an opera on this subject, and you could write the libretto for me. But it must have a comic finale. There are some delightful Americans, and it is generally a very nice story.' I said that the young Leningrad composer Aleksandr Knaifel had already written an opera based on Wilde's story, but this disconcerted Shostakovich not a whit. He merely repled: 'Well, that doesn't matter. Why shouldn't there be two operas on "The Canterville Ghost", and mine will have a libretto by you.'

Alas, this project, like the idea of writing an opera on Chekhov's 'The Black Monk', came to nothing. Shostakovich told me that he had recently heard Rodion Shchedrin's opera *Not Love Alone*, and he found Shchedrin to be very talented.

On 21 July, on his return from the trip to England, Shostakovich telephoned me and invited me once again to dine at the Yevropeyskaya Hotel. He told me that he had been a guest of Benjamin Britten at Aldeburgh, which he described as an enchanting seaside town in the depths of the country. Britten had shown him his still-unfinished opera, *Death in Venice*, based on Thomas Mann's novella, which Shostakovich had liked very much.

He had been awarded his honorary doctorate from the University of Dublin, and had been received by the country's aged President Éamon de Valéra, who, having outlived his contemporaries, now lived in an august isolation that provoked feelings of elegiac melancholy. In London he had been the guest of Prime Minister Edward Heath, a passionate lover of music. Heath, in Shostakovich's perception, was not lacking in a British sense of humour.

35 Shostakovich had made me a present of an expensive Braun electric shaver from West Germany, and had given it to his daughter to pass on to me.

36 The outstanding conductor, Nikolai Rabinovich, one of my dearest friends, died on 26 June 1972.

37 A postscript to the article Shostakovich had written in 1944 about Ivan Sollertinsky.

38 Lyudmila Mikheyeva-Sollertinskaya, compiler and author of commentaries in the book *Memories of I. I. Sollertinsky*, which was at the time being prepared for publication by the publishers Sovetsky Kompozitor (Soviet Composer). It was eventually published by them in 1974, under the joint editorship of I. D. Glikman, M. S. Druskin and D. D. Shostakovich.

39 In Stalin's time, functionaries of the so-called 'High Command' used to order
Shostakovich about as unceremoniously as if he were just a piece of property,
despatching him on various errands, including foreign trips. They, after all,
could see 'more clearly' to which places he should and should not go. The same
attitude towards him persisted for two decades after Stalin's death.

40 Baku had hosted the Decade of Literature and the Arts celebrations.
Shostakovich's enforced attendance did his health no good at all.

41 After the Fifteenth Symphony, more than a year went by before Shostakovich
took up his pen once more, a pause which seemed to him inordinately long.
Composing was his lifeblood, and in many of his letters he agonizes about an
interruption in the flow of works. These expressions of concern were usually
followed by yet more great works, and so it was in this case, although the grim
reaper was not to allow him much more time for creative work.

42 In fact, two years before this, Dmitry Dmitriyevich had told me that he found
it a burden to read letters, and replying to them was a form of torture –
although in this conversation he made an exception for our correspondence. In
former times he relished correspondence with congenial people, but his
attitude must have changed as the gravity of his illnesses progressed. And he
may well have found it upsetting when correspondents in perfect health failed
to show interest in or genuine concern for his own unenviable fate in this
respect.

43 Shostakovich did sometimes share his wretchedness with me, and seeing the
tears in his eyes made them start in my own. At such times Heine's poetic but
far from comforting words would come to me: 'The artist is like the child in
the fairy-tale, whose tears become as pearls. Oh! And then the universal
wicked stepmother goes on beating the poor child unmercifully, so that it
should shed yet more tear-pearls.' It seems to me that many of Shostakovich's
scores are pearls that once were tears.

44 I found it hard to offer any consolation to my friend. All I can remember is
citing the example of Verdi, who wrote nothing after the Requiem for ten
years, so Shostakovich was quite wrong to think that 'a spring had broken in
his brain'.

45 See Preface, pp. xxvii–xxviii.

46 I did not need to have recourse to the telephone, as this was not to be a long
stay in hospital. By 24 March he was already in Repino, from where he
telephoned and asked me to go to see him as soon as possible. I did so the
following day, when I found him in very high spirits. As he said, smiling
brightly, 'his ability to write music had come back to him'. This was reason
enough for us to clink glasses of whisky during the meal.

I stayed for about three hours. A week later, Shostakovich and his wife came
to dinner with us, an occasion which passed off very happily. Shostakovich
regaled us with amusing stories of the ineptitude of the productions of *Katerina
Izmailova* and *The Nose* that he had recently seen in Berlin. They had been,
it seems, full of pointless contrasts: bleak joylessness one minute followed
by radiant optimism, none of it bearing any relationship to Shostakovich's
music.

On 4 April, at Irina Antonovna's suggestion, all three of us went to the Bolshoy Drama Theatre [not the Bolshoy Opera and Ballet Theatre in Moscow – Translator's Note] to see Mikhail Bulgakov's play *Molière*. Unfortunately, in this play the eponymous hero is a nonentity instead of the giant he really was. We could not understand why Bulgakov felt he needed to perpetuate the lie about Molière's incestuous marriage. Shostakovich summed up his feelings: 'No, there's no point in going to the theatre. We should only go to concerts.'

On 11 April I spent the evening at Repino right up to the time that the Shostakoviches left to go to the station. Shostakovich was in reasonably good spirits. In Repino he had managed to compose all one movement and half of another of a new quartet, which was to be No. 14. The conversation turned to the strange and mysterious power of music. Shostakovich said: 'All music is good music, so long as it is in the right place. I remember finding myself at a performance in Moscow of *Three Sisters*, and the production included a really hackneyed song from Chekhov's own time. Imagine – this music, in itself completely worthless, had a great effect on me, because it was where it belonged.'

He went on to say that for a long time he had been thinking about Braga's *Serenade*, which plays an important role in Chekhov's story 'The Black Monk'. He said: 'Not long ago I decided I wanted to write an opera on "The Black Monk". And so I was asking where I could get hold of the music of the *Serenade*. And you know, under the influence of Chekhov, I found the music rather exciting. I even began to think that I might have the germ of my opera. But it would not be easy to write an opera on "The Black Monk": the story has so little in the way of action.'

47 Seaside resort in Estonia. (Translator's Note)

48 In May and June 1973, Shostakovich heroically summoned up the strength to travel to Copenhagen, for the Danish premières of *Katerina Izmailova* and the Fifteenth Symphony, and then via Le Havre to take the steamer *Mikhail Lermontov* to America. He did not think it worthwhile to mention that an American university [Northwestern University in Evanston, Illinois – Translator's Note] had made him an honorary Doctor of Fine Arts, for he was perfectly indifferent to all such honorific titles with the exception – aware that this was an honour that had also been given to Tchaikovsky – of Oxford University.

49 The sheet in question measures 14 cm by 20 cm, and is written on on both sides. The bottom edge is very uneven, with great gashes in it. The relish with which he advertises the appalling workmanship perpetrated by the town of Chernigov testifies to his good humour, certainly the result of creative satisfaction – in less than two weeks, he had written six songs to Marina Tsvetayeva's poems, although in the letter he offers no description or comment about them. I heard them for the first time on 30 October 1973 in the Great Hall of the Leningrad Conservatoire, beautifully sung by Irina Bogachova, accompanied by Sofya Vakman. Shostakovich was still in hospital and could not attend, but the audience warmly applauded him in his absence. The

Tsvetayeva Songs are a wonderful, exciting cycle, full of spiritual depth and lyrical inspiration, drama and (in 'The Poet and the Tsar') anger.

50 Irina Bogachova, soloist of the Kirov Opera.

51 This visit did not take place. Shostakovich telephoned me on 6 October and told me that he did not feel well enough to make the journey.

52 When Irina Bogachova eventually received the invitation to sing the Tsvetayeva songs, she was delighted and flattered, but until he had heard from her, Shostakovich could not but be unsure of her reaction. No doubt he remembered how Boris Gmïrya had turned down the solo part in the Thirteenth Symphony, although of course he had done so not for artistic reasons but from fear of incurring the wrath of the authorities in Kiev over the 'Baby Yar' poem.

53 Kondraty Rïleyev (1795–1826), poet and one of the leaders of the 1825 Decembrist Uprising by liberal noblemen. He was hanged in 1826 with four other leaders of the rebellion. Küchelbecker, author of one of the poems Shostakovich set in his Fourteenth Symphony, was another Decembrist poet who, although escaping execution, spent the remainder of his life in prison and exile. (Translator's Note)

54 This has also been translated into English as *We Never Make Mistakes*. (Translator's Note)

55 Also known as 'A Pure Soul'. (Translator's Note)

56 It was the grotesque in the figure of the Captain that had initially attracted Shostakovich, but when I heard Yevgeny Nesterenko sing the cycle, I became aware of the penetrating sarcasm of the composer's artistic conception.

It is perfectly obvious that as poetry Michelangelo's Sonnets and Captain Lebyadkin could hardly be further apart from one another, and it called for all Shostakovich's inexhaustible powers of invention to compose two such utterly different cycles one after the other. Yet only a short while before this he had been bitterly complaining that he had not a single musical thought in his head.

Appendix II

1 A phrase beloved by Pushkin.

2 Following the publication of the article there was a single further performance of *Lady Macbeth* in Leningrad. [The last contemporary performance in the Soviet Union took place in the Nemirovich-Danchenko Musical Theatre in Moscow on 7 March 1936. See Fay, L.E., *Shostakovich: A Life*, Oxford, 2000, 306, n. 11 – Translator's Note] The Leningrad conductor was Samuil Samosud, who in the meantime had, however, made frantic attempts to introduce cuts in the score. Needless to say, I was present, along with many friends of Shostakovich in the audience, all ardent admirers of the newly disgraced opera. The audience was numb with shock, many of them who were apprised of the content of the article no doubt trying their hardest to discern the 'muddle' buried in the wonderful music. I was in an agony of nerves, as was my friend and companion in the stalls, the conductor Nikolai Rabinovich. The

final chorus sounded like the death knell of a great opera. Shostakovich was not present at the performance.

3 Kerzhentsev published his advice to Shostakovich, particularly the recommendation that he should immerse himself in the folk music of the peoples of the Soviet Union, in a speech to the Third Plenum of the Central Committee of Workers in the Arts (RABIS). The speech was later published in *Sovetskoye Isskustvo* on 17 February 1936. See Fay, L. E., *Shostakovich: A Life*, Oxford, 2000, 89, n. 10. (Translator's Note)

4 The polite form of address in Russian to all except intimate friends and family, or children or servants. (Translator's Note)

5 The article 'Ballet Falsity' appeared in *Pravda* on 6 February 1936.

6 Later research has shown that the Sollertinsky/Don Quixote project dates from 1935, so its abandonment may well have been a consequence of the press campaign of 1936. (Translator's Note)

7 Shostakovich also told me that he did not in any case regard ballet as an appropriate medium for a work of such monumental stature as Cervantes's *Don Quixote*.

8 The orchestra on this occasion was conducted by Isai Sherman, and he must have been unwell at the time; he had a thick scarf around his neck and his voice was hoarse and almost inaudible.

9 Now called the Primorsky Restaurant.

10 Headquarters of the Leningrad Communist Party. (Translator's Note)

11 I thank my lucky stars that, not being a member of the Union of Composers, I was able to avoid the unwelcome necessity of choosing between the frying pan and the fire.

12 Kabalevsky's children vigorously contest this version of their father's conduct in this matter. See M. Kabalevskaya and Yu. Kabalevsky, '*Kazn' Ledi Makbet: vozvrashchayus' k napechatennomu*', *Sovetskaya kul' tura*, 16 November 1989, 3, quoted in Fay, L.E., *Shostakovich: A Life*, Oxford, 2000. (Translator's Note)

Index

[325]